D1047222

BEHAVIOR MODIFICATION AND THE CHILD

CONTEMPORARY PROBLEMS OF CHILDHOOD: A Bibliographic Series
Series Editor: Carol Ann Winchell

THE GIFTED STUDENT: An Annotated Bibliography
Jean Laubenfels

CHILD ABUSE AND NEGLECT: An Annotated Bibliography
Beatrice J. Kalisch

BEHAVIOR MODIFICATION AND THE CHILD

AN ANNOTATED BIBLIOGRAPHY

Hazel B. Benson

Contemporary Problems of Childhood, Number 3

GREENWOOD PRESS
Westport, Connecticut • London, England

Library of Congress Cataloging in Publication Data

Benson, Hazel B
Behavior modification and the child.

(Contemporary problems of childhood; no. 3 ISSN 0147-1082)
Includes indexes.
1. Behavior modification--Bibliography.
2. Mentally ill children--Bibliography. 3. Handicapped children--Bibliography. I. Title.
II. Series.
Z7204.B45B45 [BF637.B4] 618.9'28'914 79-7358
ISBN 0-313-21489-1

Library of Congress Catalog Card Number: 79-7358
ISBN: 0-313-21489-1
ISSN: 0147-1082

First published in 1979

Greenwood Press, Inc.
51 Riverside Avenue, Westport, Connecticut 06880

Printed in the United States of America

10 9 8 7 6 5 4 3 2 1

To Ben,
Stephen,
and Barbara

CONTENTS

SERIES FOREWORD

The attention focused on children's problems has become increasingly pronounced in the United States during the last two decades. Particular interest and involvement have been directed toward certain problems: pathological conditions, the handicapped child, the educationally and culturally deprived child, and various behavior disorders. This interest has produced a voluminous body of knowledge. One needs only a cursory perusal through the literature to realize that it has now proliferated into an extensive, but unorganized, number of publications. Through modern technology, masses of material have been flowing from the presses; given this plethora of publication, it is frequently difficult to locate specific materials. A Tower of Babel situation has developed in that some of this valuable information is unknown to the researcher who might wish to be aware of its existence.

The purpose of *Contemporary Problems of Childhood* is to identify, collect, classify, abstract, and index relevant material on the following topics in need of systematic control: the gifted child, child abuse, behavior modification techniques with children, the autistic child, the child with dyslexia, and the hyperkinetic syndrome. Not only have these topics been the subject of academe, but the mass media—magazines, newspapers, and commercial and educational television specials—have recently devoted considerable attention to these problems. To bring some order to this discipline, it was decided to issue a series of volumes, each considering one of these topics and following the format of an earlier volume by this editor, *The Hyperkinetic Child: A Bibliography of Medical, Educational, and Psychological Studies* (Greenwood Press, 1975). Volumes are intended to aid the retrieval of information for educators, psychologists, physicians, researchers, parents, and others interested in etiology, diagnosis, and management.

The volumes in the series are broad in scope, interdisciplinary, comprehensive in coverage, and contain retrospective and current citations. The titles cited mainly reflect developments over the last decade, but some earlier titles of relevance are included. Selection of citations is based on the quality and direct applicability to the topic under consideration. For these publications only English-language sources are selected.

The entries are culled from extensive searches of manual and computerized information sources. Basic indexing and abstracting services, as well as many diverse and widely scattered sources, have been searched. Books, chapters in books, journal articles, conference reports, pamphlets, government documents, dissertations, and proceedings of symposiums are included. Since a bewildering variety of terminology exists for each subject, compilers have attempted to weed out unexplicitly defined topics.

Front matter contains appropriate introductory material: preface, contents, and a "state-of-the-art" message by a specialist in the area. Entries are classified and arranged alphabetically by author under the correct subject heading and appear only once in the bibliography.

Citations include complete and verified bibliographic information: author, title, source, volume, issue number, publisher, place, date, number of pages, and references. An attempt is made to annotate all citations that can be located, giving context, scope, and possible findings and results of the book or article.

Appendixes, author and key-word subject indexes, and journal abbreviations complete each volume.

It is hoped that the documentation provided by *Contemporary Problems of Childhood* will facilitate access to retrospective and current sources of information and help bring bibliographic control to this rapidly expanding body of literature.

Carol A. Winchell
General Editor

PREFACE

PURPOSE

The past twenty-five to thirty years have seen the application of behavioral principles move from the confines of the laboratory into clinical, classroom, home, and rehabilitation settings. Few therapeutic techniques have gained such wide acceptance in such short time. By the mid-1960s behavioral techniques were being applied to an almost limitless variety of disabilities and conduct problems. This rapid movement has been accompanied by a vast outpouring of literature on the subject. At least five new scholarly journals, with a major emphasis on behavior modification, have appeared within the last ten years.

This annotated bibliography brings together representative references on the use of behavior modification with children. It aims to provide access to the literature for researchers, educators, clinicians, students, parents, and others engaged in providing direct care to children.

COVERAGE

Primarily, the bibliography covers the years 1956 to 1977— a time span that saw the rapid development, dissemination, and utilization of behavioral techniques with children in the United States and elsewhere. A smaller number of citations from the early 1950s are included, as well as one or two "classic" studies from earlier years that dealt with the systematic desensitization of fear. An unannotated addendum contains citations primarily from late 1977 and 1978.

SCOPE

Over 250 popular and professional journals in the fields of medicine, allied health, education, psychology, social work, and rehabilitation are covered, as well as both manual and computerized abstracting and indexing sources. Also included are books, chapters in books, conference reports, government documents, pamphlets, and doctoral dissertations.

Excluded from this bibliography are animal studies, studies conducted with adults (unless considerable emphasis is also given to children), foreign language references, newspaper articles, personal correspondence, speeches, and unpublished papers.

In view of the vast amount of material on this topic it was necessary to be selective. For example, most of the school-based studies focus on non-academic behaviors that interfere with academic functioning in the classroom. However, a few citations have been included on the use of reinforcement techniques in relation to specific academic subjects.

ARRANGEMENT

Entries are grouped according to the major categories in the contents: for example, general introductory material, behavioral techniques for specific behaviors and handicapping conditions, the use of behavior modification techniques in specific settings such as the classroom, and training in behavioral techniques. A large-scale comparative study by Turner, Young, and Rachman (Item No. 442) might have been placed in the section on Research, but was included in the section on Enuresis since that was the primary focus of the study. An article by Doherty (Item No. 2104) on the evaluation of a token economy system was placed in the section on Research instead of the section on Token Economies since the major emphasis in the article was on the method of evaluation. In general, citations will be found within the category of the predominant focus of the item. The Selective Key Word Index (see under Indexes) provides an alternative method of subject access.

One section is devoted to books containing reprinted articles. In these days of lost and mutilated volumes and copyright restrictions, it is often difficult to obtain the originals. Wherever possible, alternative sources are suggested at the end of the citation, for example (Reprinted in Item No. 21). By turning to Item No. 21 in the bibliography the reader will be able to locate an alternative source for the article.

Within each section, arrangement is alphabetical by author. Entry numbers preceding the author's name run consecutively throughout the text. ED numbers (ERIC Document Numbers) have been included where available, for example (ED 118 245). ERIC Documents are available in microfiche at many research libraries or may be ordered from the ERIC Document Reproduction Service, P.O. Box 190, Arlington, Virginia 22210. Refer to the most recent issue of *Resources in Education* for current ordering information.

THE ENTRIES

For books and monographs the complete citation includes author(s), title, edition, place, publisher, date, pages, inclusive pages of sections appearing as parts of larger works, and presence of bibliography.

Journal citations contain author (three are given; et al. is used to indicate additional names), title of the article, journal abbreviation, volume number, issue number (in parentheses), inclusive pages, month, year, the number of references, and reprint and Eric Document information where appropriate. (See sample book and journal entries immediately preceding the text.)

For dissertations the user is referred to *Dissertations Abstracts Internatinal* with author, title, volume number, section, pages, and date given.

Books and conference proceedings have been verified and entered in the bibliography under the United States Library of Congress *National Union Catalog: Author List* entry to facilitate retrieval for the user.

Annotations are given for all entries except dissertations and items in the addendum.

APPENDIXES

Appendix A identifies the basic bibliographic tools that were used in identifying and verifying the citations in this bibliography.

Appendix B lists audiovisual materials alphabetically by title. Wherever possible the intended audience for the audiovisual materials is indicated.

Appendix C provides a glossary of the terms most commonly encountered in the field of behavior modification. It is not intended to be an exhaustive listing. For a more complete listing and explanation of terms, the reader is referred to Owen R. White's *Glossary of Behavioral Terminology*, Champaign, Illinois: Research Press, 1971.

INDEXES

The Author Index includes the names of all individuals cited as author, joint author, editor, or compiler, including up to three names per citation. Numbers following the names refer to item numbers in the text.

The Selective Key Word Index alphabetically lists important words in entry titles. The user may find it convenient to use the broader subject arrangement under the categories in the contents, or this index may be consulted for more specific aspects of the topic. In general only unique terms are given; phrases are used to put certain words in more meaningful contexts; and "see also" references are used to refer the reader to similar concepts. Numbers following the words refer to item numbers in the text.

The List of Journal Abbreviations lists alphabetically all journals cited in the text. Journal title abbreviations have been formulated according to the rules of the *American National Standard for the Abbreviation of Titles of Periodicals*, and the individual words of the title are abbreviated according to the forms given in the *International List of Periodical Title Word Abbreviations.*

ACKNOWLEDGMENTS

Many people have assisted in the completion of this project. Special thanks are due to Dr. William A. Bricker of the Department of Special Education, Kent State University, who generously wrote the Introduction; Beverly I. McDonald, Head, Authority Files Section, Cataloguing Services, The Ohio State University Libraries, for her assistance with the finer points of filing and alphabetizing; Noelle Van Pulis, Information Specialist, Mechanized Information Center, The Ohio State University Libraries, who helped develop the Key Word Index; my colleagues at the Health Sciences Library, The Ohio State University, who smoothed my path and my fevered brow; the staff of the Interlibrary Loan Department at the Health Sciences Library, who retrieved much elusive material; Anne Warmington, Librarian, Children's Hospital, Columbus, Ohio, who brought to my attention many important references; Jean Stouder, who meticulously typed the final manuscript; and Carol A. Winchell, Series Editor, whose assistance, experience, and attention to detail were invaluable. Finally, the support and encouragement of my family is gratefully acknowledged.

INTRODUCTION

The modification of human behavior has a long history with many notable examples. Plato's discussion with a servant which was used to demonstrate inherent knowledge of complex principles by an untutored person is a clear example of shaping through successive approximations. Itard's work with Victor included many of the processes used today in the application of behavioral principles including task analysis, positive reinforcement, time out from reinforcement, discrimination training, imitation, and training in generalization. Guthrie used many examples in extending behavior theory into practice as did Thorndike, Watson, and Mowrer.

The examples mentioned above can be combined with a multitude of instances from daily living to suggest valid principles of behavior modification that are being supplied in every sphere of human existence. The problem is to bring these principles into daily use as formal principles of human behavior that are taught in elementary and secondary schools as well as in college classrooms. In this way, the application of the principles can be made available to all rather than restricted to use by therapists, counselors, and teachers. Formal knowledge of the principles would entail the ability to operationalize ambiguous terms that confuse and frighten people. This knowledge would allow people to define interactional processes in functional terms so that the frequency of misunderstanding would be reduced dramatically. To define processes functionally is a means for also differentiating the effects of interaction from the intent of the interaction. This latter outgrowth of knowledge of behavioral principles is probably the most important in coming to grips and effectively solving human problems.

This bibliography offers dramatic evidence of how far we have come in the utilization of principles for solving a wide range of human problems. From toilet training to camping, from anorexia to obesity, and from severe behavioral problems to the elimination of shyness and test anxiety, the evidence demonstrates the pervasive nature of behavioral management and behavior modification.

The wealth of documented evidence concerning application should not be equated with a ready reference source of prescriptions to solve human problems. In actual practice, the basis for success lies not in the application of previously successful techniques but in the experimental or applied analyses of the behavior that preceded the successes. Each person responds to contingencies of reinforcement in about the same manner, but the specifics of the contingencies in terms of motivation and the aspects of the antecedent environment to which one is responsive are exceedingly ideosyncratic. Some children respond to verbal praise—as evidenced by rapid change in a socially approving environment—while others have learned to avoid the praise of teachers to experience instead the consequences provided by peers for disrupting classroom activities: peer recognition is extremely reinforcing to some children. In terms of controlling environments, the specifics of stimulation cannot be prescribed and, therefore, must be analyzed on a child by child basis. In reading, the errors that children make are generally not random; the words they read that are errors are probably controlled by some aspect of the printed page, as, for example, when a child calls all words beginning with /th/ "the." Finding the components of the situation that control the error production is a first step in providing remediation.

There are many erroneous beliefs about behavioral approaches to education, therapy, or management. One is the often-stated dictum that behaviorism is only one theory of many that can be used. B. F. Skinner, and those who have followed his leadership in the field of behavioral technology, have been careful to note that the analysis of behavior is a means for establishing factual relationships between ongoing forms of behavior and the antecedent and consequent events that surround it. Changes of behavior that occur as a function of changes in antecedents and consequences are similarly analyzed as factual relationships which can be agreed upon by two or more people. Such facts are the basis out of which theory can be derived, but are not themselves theoretical propositions.

If we wish to change the rate or the probability of behavior, we must seek among a tremendous number of alternatives before we may find one or more that have the desired effects. Existing literature may provide some useful leads, but, in the end, the events that finally function to alter rate or probability will have to be discovered rather than predicted. All forms of human behavior are subject to such analyses and all forms of behavioral change can, if the situations surrounding the change are reasonably controlled, be attributed to change in the surrounding environmental events.

Equating the use of the system with bribery is another belief that stands in the way of full utilization of behavioral principles. There is something about the use of extrinsic reinforcement that offends many professionals. However, an examination of the literature has revealed no example of the application of behavioral principles to produce illegal or immoral behavior.

We pay teachers to teach and therapists to improve the conditions of our lives and we do not equate the payment with bribery. If we use extrinsic reinforcement to motivate a student through the early difficult days of learning to read, there is nothing illegal or immoral if the final outcome is a student who has learned to read with sufficient proficiency that he does so often in the absence of extrinsic rewards.

Children can receive tremendous benefit from the application of behavioral principles. Yet finding arrangements that successfully motivate behavior or result in the acquisition of a generalized repertoire in a particular domain seems sterile to some and offensive to others. However, because of the work done in the field of behavioral analysis, we now believe that all human beings can learn, regardless of the type or severity of their handicap.

The new law, P.L. 94-142 Education for all Handicapped Children, mandates the education of all children regardless of type or severity of handicap; and behavioral analysis will be a major contributory factor to the successful implementation of this law. If behavioral principles are taught to parents, physicians, teachers, and therapists, large numbers of children can be kept at home, treated in the community, and educated in the public schools, rather than being isolated in large and costly state institutions.

The successful application of behavioral analysis is well documented in this book. However, there are areas where the behavioral analysis literature is meager. It cannot be said that the analysis of behavior has yet covered the complete range and complexity of human behavior. For instance, one finds little documentation on how to teach a child to produce a truly creative product. Despite extensive behavioral literature on speech and language problems, the expectation for success in terms of moving a mute handicapped adolescent to the point of conversational language is relatively low.

There is much left to learn, many facts yet to be gathered before behavioral approaches will be universally applicable. A great deal has been done over the past twenty years, and the efforts of numerous clinicians and educators are well represented and organized in this book.

William A. Bricker, Ph.D.
Department of Special Education
Kent State University

SAMPLE BOOK ENTRY

① ② ③

58 Bellack, Alan S., and Hersen, Michel. *Behavior modification: an introductory textbook.* Baltimore, Maryland: Williams & Wilkins, 1977. 374 p. (Bibliography).

④ ⑤ ⑥ ⑦ ⑧

⑨ This undergraduate or graduate level text is organized around intervention strategies rather than around specific disorders, and offers the theoretical, empirical, ethical, and legal issues pertinent to each of the techniques. Some prior knowledge of abnormal psychology and learning theory is assumed. One chapter is devoted to operant applications with children and covers the alleviation of behavioral deficits, the reduction of behavioral excesses, token economies, the use of behavior modification in the home, and ethical considerations.

1. Item number
2. Author(s)
3. Title of book
4. Place of publication
5. Publisher
6. Date of publication
7. Number of pages
8. Presence of bibliography
9. Annotation

SAMPLE JOURNAL ENTRY

① ② ③

282 Phillips, Elery L. "Achievement Place: token reinforcement procedures in a home-style rehabilitation setting for 'pre-delinquent' boys." *J Appl Behav Anal* 1(3): 213-23, Fall, 1968. (18 references).

④ ⑤ ⑥ ⑦

⑧

(Reprinted in Item Nos. 38, 40, 43, 47, 210).

⑨

⑩ Reports the successful use of token reinforcement procedures in modifying the behavior of three pre-delinquent adolescent boys in a residential setting. Tokens were awarded by the house parents for specific appropriate behaviors and were taken away for specific inappropriate behaviors. Back-up reinforcers were naturally available in the setting.

1. Item number
2. Author(s)
3. Title of article
4. Name of journal (abbreviation)
5. Volume and issue number
6. Inclusive pagination
7. Month and year of publication
8. Number of biblographical references
9. Reprint information (See Section II)
10. Annotation

BEHAVIOR MODIFICATION AND THE CHILD

I.

Bibliographies

1 Barnard, James W., and Orlando, Robert. "Behavior modification: a bibliography." *IMRID Papers Rep* 4(3): 1-65, 1967.

This bibliography, consisting of 866 items primarily from the early 1960's, emphasizes specific methods of behavior modification with both children and adults. Items are drawn from journals, monographs, theses, and unpublished papers.

2 *Behavior modification: a selective bibliography.* Arlington, Virginia: Council for Exceptional Children, Information Center on Exceptional Children, 1972. 23p. (ED 065 957).

Consists of approximately eighty abstracts drawn from the holdings of the C.E.C. Information Center. Publication dates of documents range from 1964 to 1971.

3 *Behavior modification--emotionally disturbed and behavior problems: a selective bibliography*. Reston, Virginia: Council for Exceptional Children, Information Center on Exceptional Children, 1976. 24p. (Exceptional Child Bibliography Series No. 608). (ED 129 008).

Enumerates approximately eighty documents and journal articles covering the years 1965 to 1975.

4 *Behavior modification: exceptional child bibliography series.* Arlington, Virginia: Council for Exceptional Children, Information Center on Exceptional Children, 1971. 20p. (ED 050 528).

Contains eighty-one references selected from *Exceptional Child Education Abstracts* and includes research reports, conference papers, journal articles, texts, and program guides. Author and subject indexes are also provided.

5 *Behavior modification in the classroom: an abstract bibliography*. U. S. Department of Health, Education, and Welfare, National Institute of Education. Washington, D.C.: U.S. Government Printing Office, 1975. (ED 118 245).

Lists forty annotated citations to documents in the ERIC microfiche collection and to journal articles. The references include samples of programs, examples of implementation and evaluation, and discussions of critical issues.

6 Bernstein, Gail S. *Training, modifying, and maintaining behavior managers: a comprehensive bibliography*. New York: Microfiche Publications, 1976. (Document NAPS-02966).

Contains citations to nearly 300 published and unpublished articles and is divided into seven areas: general interest, apparatus, ethical issues, evaluation, programmed texts, reviews, and training. The articles included deal with the training of college students, teachers, counselors, institutional staff, therapists, and parents.

7 Blampied, Neville M., and Black, William A. M. "Training in behavior therapy and behavior modification in colleges and universities: a bibliography." Teach Psychol 3(2): 90-91, April, 1976.
This bibliography of forty-three published papers is intended for those who teach or intend to teach courses in behavior therapy or behavior modification. Excluded are those papers addressed specifically to teaching para- and non-professionals.

8 Botterbusch, Karl F., and Esser, Thomas J. A selected, annotated bibliography of books on behavior modification. Menomonie, Wisconsin: University of Wisconsin - Stout, Department of Rehabilitation and Manpower Services, 1974. 40p. (ED 114 568).
A selection of books for the use of vocational evaluation and work adjustment professionals is presented. The citations are divided into three levels: (1) basic books, for those with little or no background in psychology; (2) intermediate, for those with a limited background; and (3) advanced, for those who have had academic training in psychology.

9 Brown, Daniel G. Behavior modification in child and school mental health: an annotated bibliography on applications with parents and teachers. Rockville, Maryland: National Institute of Mental Health, for sale by the Superintendent of Documents. Washington, D.C.: U.S. Government Printing Office, 1971. 41p. (DHEW Publication, No. HSM 71-9043).
Contains 118 annotated citations covering the period from 1959 to 1971. The references are divided into three sections: (1) applications with parents; (2) applications with teachers; and (3) applications with parents and teachers. Many references will be useful to others working with children. A wide variety of behavioral problems is covered.

10 ————. Behavior modification in child, school, and family mental health: an annotated bibliography on applications with parents and teachers and in marriage and family counseling. Champaign, Illinois: Research Press, 1972. 105p.
This annotated bibliography of 209 books, articles, unpublished papers, and films gives the address of the author of each paper and the publishers and prices of books and films.

11 Conditioned learning in the brain-damaged child. Bethesda, Maryland: National Library of Medicine, 1970. 5p. (Literature Search No. 70-17).
This computer-generated bibliography, produced by the National Library of Medicine's Medical Literature Analysis and Retrieval System (MEDLARS), lists seventy-five citations from journals covering the period from January, 1967 through March, 1970.

12 Howard, Norma K. Discipline and behavior: an abstract bibliography. Urbana, Illinois: ERIC Clearinghouse on Early Childhood Education, 1974. 58p. (ED 092 243).
Includes references to 202 ERIC documents on discipline and behavior modification with young children.

13 Insalaco, Carl, and Shea, Richard J. Behavior modification: an annotated bibliography, 1965-1969. Columbia, South Carolina: University of South Carolina, Psychology Department, 1970. 171p.
This collection of 1308 annotated references to books, journal articles, and some unpublished papers includes 245 references concerning children and adolescents, and 160 dealing with mental retardation.

14 Litow, Leon. Classroom interdependent group-oriented contingencies: an annotated bibliography. 1975. 19p. Available from ERIC Document Reproduction Service, P.O. Box 190, Arlington, Virginia 22210. (ED 134 886).
Twenty-six studies from 1968-1972 cover the empirical evaluation of the relative effectiveness of interdependent group-oriented contingencies within the classroom setting.

15 Morrow, William R. Behavior therapy bibliography, 1950-1969. Columbia, Missouri: University of Missouri Press, 1971. 165p.
Nine hundred English language items, arranged alphabetically, are annotated with reference to the type of experimental design, setting variables, subject variables, target behaviors, and type of modification procedure. Tables are included that group references by these annotation categories.

16 Rutherford, Robert B., Jr. Behavior modification and therapy with juvenile delinquents: a comprehensive bibliography. 1976. 16p. Available from ERIC Document Reproduction Service, P.O. Box 190, Arlington, Virginia 22210. (ED 120 627).
Presents 177 citations which include journal articles, books, and papers from 1960 to 1975 with a few "in press" items from 1976.

17 ————. "Bibliography of books in behavior modification and behavior therapy." Am Assoc Educ Sev Profoundly Handicap Rev 1(4): 78-106, March, 1976.
Lists approximately 300 books arranged alphabetically by author. Each entry is coded according to one or more categories such as behavioral counseling, behavioral research, and the severely and profoundly retarded.

18 Severely and multiply handicapped--program descriptions/operant conditioning: a selective bibliography. Reston, Virginia: Council for Exceptional Children, 1976. 30p. (Exceptional Child Bibliography Series No. 614). (ED 129 020).
This annotated bibliography, citing approximately 140 documents and journal articles, covers the years 1967 to 1975.

19 Theiss, Frances Case. "Behavior modification, 1971: a selected, annotated bibliography." Libr J 97: 1866-70, May 15, 1972.
Included in seventy-six citations to articles, most of which deal with children, are studies of behavior modifying drugs.

20 York, Robert. Selected bibliography related to parents as behavior modifiers. Seattle, Washington: Washington University, Child Development and Mental Retardation Center, 1975. 7p. (ED 108 418).
Sets forth approximately seventy citations which cover the years 1958 to 1972.

II.

Books of Reprinted Articles

21 Ashem, Beatrice A., and Poser, Ernest G., eds. Adaptive learning: behavior modification with children. New York: Pergamon, 1973. 439p. (Pergamon General Psychology Series, No. 29).
Contains a collection of forty-one of the best articles on the use of behavior modification with: (1) the normal child; (2) the emotionally disturbed child; and (3) the autistic, schizophrenic, organically dysfunctional, and the retarded child. A fourth section considers the training of professional and non-professional workers in the techniques of behavioral change.

22 Becker, Wesley C., ed. An empirical basis for change in education: selections on behavioral psychology for teachers. Chicago: Science Research Associates, 1971. 522p.
Thirty-seven readings, intended to be used as a supplemental text in courses for teachers on behavior modification procedures, include papers on techniques for handling behavior problems, pupil motivation, token systems, and one section on programming educational sequences.

23 Bijou, Sidney W., and Baer, Donald M., eds. Child development: readings in experimental analysis. New York: Appleton-Century-Crofts, 1967. 408p.
This collection of readings covers basic principles and concepts and their applications to social behavior, deviant behavior, and education.

24 Bradfield, Robert H., ed. Behavioral modification of learning disabilities. San Rafael, California: Academic Therapy, 1971. 172p.
Consists of a compilation of articles, some reprinted from other sources, on the use of behavior modification in the handling of various learning disabilities. The volume is divided into three sections: (1) general applications, including precision teaching and parent training; (2) methods, in particular with reading and language disabilities, and short attention span; and (3) programs in operation, with emphasis on the classroom setting. A bibliography is included with each chapter.

25 Brown, Alan R., and Avery, Connie, eds. Modifying children's behavior: a book of readings. Springfield, Illinois: Thomas, 1974. 277p.
Twenty-one reprinted articles, intended for special education and regular teachers, includes many articles which are directly applicable to the classroom setting.

26 Cohen, Leo, ed. Behavior modification: a sourcebook for psychology and education. New York: MSS Information Corporation, 1971. 185p.

This volume of articles, primarily reprinted from other sources, is intended as a supplementary text for students in introductory courses in education and psychology. Emphasis is placed on the modification of classroom behavior.

27 Daniels, Lloyd Keith, ed. The management of childhood behavior problems in school and at home. Springfield, Illinois: Thomas, 1974. 456p.
Eighty-one reprinted articles, dealing with the most common behavior problems, are arranged in three sections: (1) avoidance problems, or behavior that should be increased; (2) behavior that should be decreased; and (3) using the parents as therapists.

28 Erickson, Marilyn T., and Nelson, Rosemery O., eds. Readings in behavior modification. New York: MSS Information Corporation, 1973. 296p.
Many of the thirty reprinted articles are concerned with modifying the behavior of the child.

29 Erickson, Marilyn T., and Williams, Ben, eds. Readings in behavior modification research with children. New York: MSS Information Corporation, 1973. 333p.
Thirty-one reprinted papers deal with the modification of various childhood problems, including child psychoses, learning disabilities, neuroses, juvenile delinquency, school problems, behavior problems, and cultural deprivation.

30 Eysenck, Hans J., ed. Experiments in behaviour therapy: readings in modern methods of treatment of mental disorders derived from learning therapy. New York: Pergamon, 1964. 558p.
Assembles reprinted and original articles on the application of learning theories and conditioning to behavior disorders. Most papers are concerned with adults, but one section of nine articles deals with children.

31 Franks, Cyril M., ed. Conditioning techniques in clinical practice and research. New York: Springer, 1964. 328p.
Brings together a selection of reprinted papers which cover the use of conditioning techniques in the clinical setting. Some articles are relative to children.

32 Gelfand, Donna M., ed. Social learning in childhood: readings in theory and application. Belmont, California: Brooks/Cole, 1969. 415p.
Forty readings, many of which deal with the practical application of learning principles and techniques, are divided into six chapters presented in chronological order according to the age of the child. Papers are selected on the basis of research prominence and scientific importance (several classic studies are included), intelligibility (although familiarity with the techniques is advisable), and helpfulness and interest.

33 Gibson, David, and Brown, Roy I., eds. Managing the severely retarded: a sampler. Springfield, Illinois: Thomas, 1976. 482p.
These reprinted articles emphasize behavioral enhancement approaches to the development of self-care skills, self-abuse abatement, and contact skills training. Included are articles on the general strategies of training and the problems of implementation in the institutional setting.

34 Graziano, Anthony M., ed. Behavior therapy with children. Chicago: Aldine, 1971. 458p.
A volume of reprints divided into six sections. The first section deals with the background and principles of behavior modification. Sections two through five deal with the applications in shaping behaviors with the mentally retarded, the psychotic, the school child, and the child with mild conduct problems. Section six considers the implications of behavior modification concepts and the training of both professional therapists, teachers, and parents in the new techniques.

35 ———. Behavior therapy with children: II. Chicago: Aldine, 1975. 640p.
Emphasizes the behavioral treatment of children's problems in the clinical setting. The introduction provides an historical perspective, placing behavior therapy in its relationship to other forms of therapy, and indicating possible future developments. The thirty-nine reprinted articles, which were selected from journals published between 1968 and early 1975, provide an overall view of the current state of the art. Volume II is organized into ten sections, each with its own introduction: (1) social and political issues; (2) mental retardation; (3) psychotic behavior; (4) self-stimulatory behavior; (5) somatic systems; (6) children's fears; (7) aggressive and anti-social behavior; (8) schools; (9) family systems; and (10) self-control. An extensive bibliography follows.

36 Guerney, Bernard G., Jr., ed. Psychotherapeutic agents: new roles for non-professionals, parents, and teachers. New York: Holt, Rinehart & Winston, 1969. 595p.
A collection of readings on the methods by which mental health non-professionals (peers, teachers, parents, students) may be utilized to meet mental health needs. Emphasis is placed on the presentation of remedial methods and strategies. Many of the readings deal with the use of behavior modification techniques.

37 Klein, Roger D.; Hapkiewicz, Walter G.; Roden, Aubrey H., eds. Behavior modification in educational settings. Springfield, Illinois: Thomas, 1973. 552p.
This selection of thirty-three reprinted articles is grouped according to the population being treated (preschool, school age, socially and emotionally maladjusted, brain-injured, and retarded) and by the broad area of behavior being treated (e.g., academic, social behavior).

38 Lovaas, Ole I., and Bucher, Bradley D., eds. Perspectives in behavior modification with deviant children. Englewood Cliffs, New Jersey: Prentice-Hall, 1974. 562p. (Prentice-Hall Series in Developmental Psychology).
Thirty-two reprinted articles on the use of behavior modification in the treatment of childhood maladaptive behavior are included in this collection. The first three articles cover research design; sections two through seven group articles according to treatment settings and behavioral characteristics; the last three articles indicate avenues of future research. A familiarity with basic concepts before using the book is advisable.

39 O'Leary, K. Daniel, and O'Leary, Susan G., eds. Classroom management: the successful use of behavior modification. New York: Pergamon, 1972. 664p. (Pergamon General Psychology Series, No. 27).

Brings together thirty-seven articles intended for students in education and psychology, practicing teachers, and for clinical, educational, and school psychologists. Comments are made on each article, and a concluding chapter discusses the implementation of the procedures.

40 Pitts, Carl E., ed. Operant conditioning in the classroom: introductory readings in educational psychology. New York: Crowell, 1971. 386p.
This book of readings is intended as an accompaniment to the author's text Introduction to educational psychology: an operant conditioning approach. Part I contains readings on the theory; Part II covers the techniques; Part III reports on research conducted in schools.

41 Ruskin, Robert S., ed. Selected readings in behavior modification. New York: MSS Information Corporation, 1972. 142p.
The fourteen papers included in this volume (most of them reprinted from other sources) are designed for use in a course on behavior modification. Several of the papers deal with children in the school setting.

42 Staats, Arthur W., ed. Human learning: studies extending conditioning principles to complex behavior. New York: Holt, Rinehart & Winston, 1964. 520p.
This volume of reprinted articles, intended for the psychology student, assumes an understanding of the basic principles of operant and respondent conditioning. Approximately half of the articles deal with children. The volume is divided into nine sections which cover such general areas as child learning, verbal behavior, social interaction, and behavioral treatment.

43 Stedman, James M.; Patton, William F.; Walton, Kay F., eds. Clinical studies in behavior therapy with children, adolescents and their families. Springfield, Illinois: Thomas, 1973. 399p.
Presents a collection of readings chosen for their ability to demonstrate the principles of applied learning within the format of a practical case history. The readings are divided into seven chapters: (1) concepts and issues (including an original article on terminology and major concepts); (2) common and less common presenting problems; (3) classroom management; (4) child groups; (5) delinquents; (6) families; and (7) the severely disturbed child. An annotated bibliography of thirty-six additional articles is also included.

44 Thomas, Edwin J., ed. Behavior modification procedure: a sourcebook. Chicago: Aldine, 1974. 323p.
A sourcebook which assumes a knowledge of the principles involved, and includes reprinted papers on procedures in various settings, such as school and family groups.

45 Ullmann, Leonard P., and Krasner, Leonard, eds. Case studies in behavior modification. New York: Holt, Rinehart & Winston, 1965. 401p.
This collection of fifty papers is intended for students and professional workers. A lengthy introduction by the editors provides a comprehensive background for the readings which deal with both adults and children. One section of thirteen papers is devoted to deviant behaviors in children.

46 Ulrich, Roger; Stachnik, Thomas; Mabry, John, eds. Control of human behavior: Vol. I. Expanding the behavioral laboratory. Glenview, Illinois: Scott, Foresman, 1966. 349p.
Forty-eight reprinted articles are included. They cover: (1) the scientific analysis of behavior; (2) applications of behavior control; (3) fallacies in the interpretation and control of behavior; and (4) implications of behavior control. The section on applications contains several articles relating to children.

47 ———. Control of human behavior: Vol. II. From cure to prevention. Glenview, Illinois: Scott, Foresman, 1970. 378p.
Included in this collection are fifty reprinted articles devoted to the application of behavioral principles with both children and adults in a wide variety of settings.

48 Williams, Phillip, ed. Behaviour problems in school: a source book of readings. London: University of London Press, 1974. 250p.
Consists of a compilation of fifteen reprinted papers relative to the nature, identification, causes, and methods of treatment of behavior problems in school. Only two of the papers is concerned with the use of behavior modification techniques.

49 Willis, Jerry W., and Giles, Donna, eds. Great experiments in behavior modification. Indianapolis, Indiana: Hackett, 1976. 288p. (Great Experiments in Psychology Series).
Contains abstracts of 116 research articles, many of which apply to children. Designed for use as a supplementary text in psychology and education courses, the volume is arranged in nine different interest areas, including preschool studies, educational applications, institutional programs, juvenile delinquency, community and organizational applications, and training of behavioral engineers. Indices include subject, target behavior, and treatment and research design listings.

III.

General Introductory Material

A. LEARNING THEORY AND THE PRINCIPLES OF BEHAVIOR MODIFICATION

50 Agras, W. Stewart, ed. Behavior modification, principles and clinical applications. Boston: Little, Brown, 1972. 227p. (Bibliography).
Provides an overview of research having application to clinical problems and descriptions of such techniques as token economies, aversive procedures, systematic desensitization, and flooding. Most of the studies are concerned with adults, but there is an annotated therapeutic index which enables the reader to locate those studies dealing with childhood problems.

51 Annual review of behavior therapy: theory and practice: Vol. 1. 1973. Edited by Cyril M. Franks and G. Terence Wilson. New York: Brunner/Mazel, 1973. 817p.
Presents a collection of forty-seven papers, some of which deal with children, and representing a survey of the literature to mid-1972. The volume is divided into chapters covering such topics as various techniques, assessment and measurement, clinical studies, new applications, and apparatus. Each chapter is introduced by a commentary which gives a state-of-the-art appraisal.

52 Annual review of behavior therapy: theory and practice: Vol. 4. 1976. Edited by Cyril M. Franks and G. Terence Wilson. New York: Brunner/Mazel, 1976. 914p.
Six articles in this collection deal specifically with behavior modification in the home and the classroom. Topics covered are hyperactivity, learning disabilities, seizure disorders, language training with nonverbal children, generalization and maintenance of classroom treatment effects, and intervention in families of delinquent and pre-delinquent children.

53 Baer, Donald M. "Some remedial uses of the reinforcement contingency." In: Shlien, John M., ed. Research in psychotherapy, 3rd, Chicago, 1966. Proceedings. Washington, D.C.: American Psychological Association, 1968. 3-20. (10 References).
Advocates the systematic and constructive use of reinforcement techniques, since the principles of reinforcement are in effect in all situations encountered by the child.

54 Bandura, Albert. "Behavioral psychotherapy." Sci Am 216(3): 78-86, March, 1967.
This state-of-the-art report on the uses of behavioral therapy cites examples from current research.

55 ————. Principles of behavior modification. New York: Holt, Rinehart & Winston, 1969. 677p. (Bibliography).
Deals with the basic psychological principles of learning and reviews theoretical and experimental advances in social learning. Chapters are included on the mechanisms regulating behavior, selection of goals, modeling procedures, positive and aversive control, and extinction. Included are extensive bibliographic references at the end of every chapter.

56 Banff International Conference on Behavior Modification, 2nd, 1970. Behavior modification for exceptional children and youth. Edited by Leo A. Hamerlynck and Frank C. Clark. Calgary, Alberta, Canada: University of Calgary Press, 1971. 148p.
Contains nine conference papers covering both basic principles and applied programs with the emphasis on exceptional children and youth. Topics includ: (1) the teaching of speech and self-help skills to the retarded; (2) the development of appropriate classroom behavior in the disturbed child; (3) the modification of deviant sexual behavior in the adolescent; and (4) behavior modification in the juvenile delinquent.

57 Banff International Conference on Behavior Modification, 3rd, 1971. Implementing behavioral programs for schools and clinics. Edited by F. W. Clark; D. R. Evans; and L. A. Hamerlynck. Champaign, Illinois: Research Press, 1972. 201p.
These seven conference papers are divided into two sections: (1) preparing consultants for clinical settings; and (2) agents of change for the classroom. The papers elaborate on the triadic model of consultant, mediator, and target in a variety of clinical and educational settings, and include articles on the training of psychiatric nurses, aides and attendants, and special education, consulting, and classroom teachers.

58 Bellack, Alan S., and Hersen, Michel. Behavior modification: an introductory textbook. Baltimore, Maryland: Williams & Wilkins, 1977. 374p. (Bibliography).
This undergraduate or graduate level text is organized around intervention strategies rather than around specific disorders, and offers the theoretical, empirical, ethical, and legal issues pertinent to each of the techniques. Some prior knowledge of abnormal psychology and learning theory is assumed. One chapter is devoted to operant applications with children and covers the alleviation of behavioral deficits, the reduction of behavioral excesses, token economies, the use of behavior modification in the home, and ethical considerations.

59 Bergin, Alan, and Garfield, Sol, eds. Handbook of psychotherapy and behavior change: an empirical analysis. New York: Wiley, 1971. 956p. (Bibliography).
Comprehensively reviews and evaluates current psychotherapeutic practices. A chapter is included on the use of behavioral intervention procedures in the classroom and in the home.

60 Bijou, Sidney W. "An empirical concept of reinforcement and a functional analysis of child behavior." J Genet Psychol 104: 215-23, June, 1964. (35 References).
Discusses the concept that the data of psychological development are progressive changes in behavior that evolve from interactions with the environment of development.

61 ————. "Experimental studies of child behavior, normal and deviant." In: Krasner, Leonard, and Ullmann, Leonard P., eds. Research in behavior modification. New York: Holt, Rinehart & Winston, 1965. 56-81.

Presents a review of research on various aspects of child behavior. Included are studies on "problem" parent-child relationships, mild emotional and behavioral problems in nursery school children, institutionalized severely disturbed children, and retarded children with academic deficits. The clinical implications of each study are discussed.

62 Bijou, Sidney W., and Baer, Donald M. "Operant methods in child behavior and development." In: Honig, W., ed. Operant behavior: areas of research and application. New York: Appleton-Century-Crofts, 1966. 718-89. (93 References). (Reprinted in Item No. 23).

This state-of-the-art review offers a basis for a positivistic approach and a theory of behavior development, but deals primarily with the techniques of measurement and experimentation.

63 Bijou, Sidney W., and Redd, William H. "Child behavior therapy." In: Arieti, Silvano, ed. American handbook of psychiatry: Vol. 5. 2nd ed. New York: Basic Books, 1975. 319-44. (120 References).

Presents an overview of child behavior therapy divided into six sections: (1) historical background; (2) theoretical models; (3) behavioral diagnosis; (4) treatment procedures; (5) evaluation of therapy; and (6) implications and future trends. Areas requiring further research are indicated.

64 Bijou, Sidney W., and Ribes-Inesta, Emilio, eds. Behavior modification: issues and extensions. New York: Academic Press, 1972. 157p. (Bibliography).

These papers, delivered at a conference in Mexico in 1971, contain both theoretical and practical aspects. Only a few papers are relative to the treatment of children.

65 Birnbrauer, J. S.; Burchard, John D.; Burchard, Sara N. "Wanted: behavior analysts." In: Bradfield, Robert H., ed. Behavior modification: the human effort. San Rafael, California: Dimensions, 1970. 19-76. (59 References).

Presents the concepts, methods, and possible applications of behavior analysis. Particularly useful are references, arranged in chart form, to studies selected on the basis of the target behavior. The article warns against over-simplification and gives examples of difficulties frequently encountered with methods of dealing with them. Some advice is given on the selection and training of non-professional analysts.

66 Blackham, Garth J., and Silberman, Adolph. Modification of child and adolescent behavior. 2nd ed. Belmont, California: Wadsworth, 1975. 318p. (235 References).

The first six chapters of this volume cover basic theory of management, methods, and the observation and recording of behavior. Chapters seven through nine deal with the specifics of changing behavior in the classroom, in the therapeutic situation, and in the home. Many examples are given, and specific problems can be located easily through the glossary/index. Each chapter contains a summary, and two appendices aid in the selection of appropriate reinforcers.

67 Blackman, Derek. Operant conditioning: an experimental analysis of behaviour. London: Methuen, 1974. 247p. (Bibliography). (Methuen's Manuals of Psychology).
This basic text on operant conditioning includes a chapter on the applications to education and another on operant conditioning and clinical psychology. The latter contains a number of references to studies conducted with children.

68 Blackwood, Ralph O. Operant control of behavior: elimination of misbehavior and motivation of children. Akron, Ohio: Exordium Press, 1971. 248p. (Bibliography).
Provides a non-technical explanation of behavioral principles and methods of applying them. Included are instructions on identifying and charting the target behaviors.

69 Bootzin, Richard R. Behavior modification and therapy: an introduction. Cambridge, Massachusetts: Winthrop, 1975. 180p. (Bibliography).
Serves as a broad introduction to the principles and techniques of behavior modification. Examples are used which range from everyday problems to the more severe behavioral disorders.

70 Bradfield, Robert H., ed. Behavior modification: the human effort. San Rafael, California: Dimensions, 1970. 218p. (Bibliography).
Ten articles, originally presented as conference papers, deal with the principles and applications of behavior modification. Topics include details of procedures involved in the engineered classroom, in the acquisition of language, and in special settings, e.g., the disadvantaged and childhood schizophrenics. A final section deals with ethical and moral issues.

71 Brown, Bertram S. "Behavior modification: what it is--and isn't." Todays Educ 65: 67-69, January-February, 1976. (5 References).
Discusses the techniques that have proven successful in the classroom and examines the most often voiced criticisms.

72 ————. Behavior modification: what it is--and isn't. Rockville, Maryland: National Institute of Mental Health; for sale by the Superintendent of Documents. Washington, D.C.: U.S. Government Printing Office, 1976. 9p. (DHEW Publication, No. (ADM) 76-408).
A short pamphlet, reprinted from an article in Today's Education, outlines the basic principles and applications in the education field.

73 Brown, Bertram S.; Wienckowski, Louis A.; Stolz, Stephanie B. Behavior modification: perspective on a current issue. Washington, D.C.: U.S. Department of Health, Education, and Welfare, 1975. 26p. (53 References). (DHEW Publication, No. (ADM) 75-202).
Comprehensively reviews the history, definitions, possible applications, methodology, and ethical problems of the subject.

74 Brown, Daniel G. "Behavior modification with children." Ment Hyg 56(1): 22-30, Winter, 1972. (35 References).
Summarizes principles, reviews literature, and discusses criticisms.

75 Bucher, Bradley, and Lovaas, O. Ivar. "Operant procedures in behavior modification with children." In: Levis, Donald J., ed. Learning approaches to therapeutic behavior change. Chicago: Aldine, 1970. 36-64. (30 References).

Reviews and evaluates studies on the use of operant procedures in childhood. The article criticizes the failure to take advantage of the analytic power of the single-subject design, the lack of basic background information generally given on the subject, and the lack of unfavorable reports.

76 Burkhard, Barbara Jean. "Contingent behavior in children: an economic approach to Premack's theory of reinforcement." For a summary see: Diss Abstr Int 37B(11): 5852, May, 1977.

Clark, F. W.; Evans, D. R.; Hamerlynck, L. A., eds. see Banff International Conference on Behavior Modification, 3rd, 1971. Implementing behavioral programs for schools and clinics. (Item No. 57).

77 Craighead, W. Edward; Kazdin, Alan E.; Mahoney, Michael J. Behavior modification: principles, issues, and applications. Boston: Houghton Mifflin, 1976. 556p. (Bibliography).
Although this basic text is intended primarily for undergraduates, it is useful also to professionals in applied settings. The book covers principles of behavior modification and includes fifteen original contributions on the employment of those principles across a wide variety of settings, populations, and behaviors. Most applications are with adults, but there is a chapter by Ronald S. Drabman on behavior modification in the classroom.

78 Cullen, Chris; Hattersley, John; Tennant, Laurence. "Behavior modification--some implications of a radical behaviorist view." Bull Br Psychol Soc 30: 65-69, 1977. (28 References).
Emphasizes the relationships between behavior and the environment and argues for a recognition of these relationships when instituting some form of behavioral intervention. Three relevant issues are considered in this context: (1) token economies and institutional populations; (2) language training; and (3) the concept of reinforcement.

79 Evans, Ian M., and Nelson, Rosemery O. "Assessment of child behavior problems." In: Ciminero, Anthony R.; Calhoun, Karen S.; and Adams, Henry E., eds. Handbook of behavioral assessment. New York: Wiley, 1977. 603-18. (Wiley Series on Personality Processes).
Reviews general issues in assessment of the child and examines the instruments and procedures available to the clinician. These include behavioral interviews with parent and child, behavioral checklists, behavioral observation in the simulated situation, observation in the natural situation, and the utilization of certain aspects of psychometric tests. The authors finally examine the problems encountered in the assessment of specific behavioral difficulities, such as social withdrawal and brain damage.

80 Favell, Judith Elbert. The power of positive reinforcement: a handbook of behavior modification. Springfield, Illinois: Thomas, 1977. 266p. (Bibliography).
Describes measurement, experimental design, and treatment methods. Although primarily intended as a training and resource book for college students and health and educational professionals, portions of the text could be used in training programs for the paraprofessional.

81 Ferster, Charles B.; Boren, Mary Carol Perrott; Culbertson, Stuart. Behavior principles. 2nd ed. Englewood Cliffs, New Jersey: Prentice-Hall, 1975. 702p. (Bibliography).
This psychology text focuses on the principles of operant and reflex behavior. It does not assume any previous knowledge of psychology.

Franks, Cyril M., and Wilson, G. Terence, eds.
see Annual review of behavior therapy: theory and practice: Vol. 1. 1973. (Item No. 51).

Franks, Cyril M., and Wilson, G. Terence, eds.
see Annual review of behavior therapy: theory and practice: Vol. 4. 1976. (Item No. 52).

82 Gambrill, Eileen D. Behavior modification: handbook of assessment, intervention, and evaluation. San Francisco: Jossey-Bass, 1977. 1231p. (Bibliography). (Jossey-Bass Behavioral Science Series).
Presents a comprehensive view--intended for the practicing professional or the graduate student--of the history, concepts, methodologies, and applications of behavior modification. Chapters of particular interest are those on behavioral intervention with children, adolescents, and their families, behavioral intervention in educational settings, and the chapter on severe behavior disturbance which contains material on autism and mental retardation. Several of the other chapters also contain material relevant to the management of children and adolescents and their problems.

83 Gelfand, Donna M., and Hartmann, Donald P. Child behavior analysis and therapy. New York: Pergamon, 1975. 332p. (Bibliography). (Pergamon General Psychology Series, No. 50).
This text contains comprehensive descriptions of each step of child behavior analysis from the selection of the subject, the target behavior, and treatment methods through collection of data and program evaluation. Directed toward the advanced undergraduate and graduate student and practicing professionals, the volume contains useful tables, checklists, and appendices.

84 Gentry, William Doyle, ed. Applied behavior modification. St. Louis, Missouri: Mosby, 1975. 164p. (Bibliography).
Presents an overview of the applicability of behavior modification in various settings. Chapter II concentrates on parents as behavior modifiers, describes the two basic approaches to parent-training (single-family and group training), and draws attention to the problems encountered in utilizing parents. Chapter III is devoted to the use of behavior modification techniques in the school, not only for dealing with behavioral problems, but as a tool for academic advancement.

85 Goetz, Elizabeth. "A guide to behavior modification." Day Care Early Educ 3(4): 21-23, 46, 1976. (0 References).
Briefly reviews principles and techniques.

86 Graham, Philip. "Management in child psychiatry: recent trends." Br J Psychiatry 129: 97-108, 1976. (57 References).
Reports on behavior modification as one of several new techniques in child psychiatry and criticizes the tendency toward single-case reports.

87 Hall, John Preston. "Attitudes towards behavioral techniques and behavior modification and differences in personality, locus of control, and dogmatism." For a summary see: Diss Abstr Int 37A(7): 4132, January, 1976.

88 Halpern, Werner I., and Kissel, Stanley. Human resources for troubled children. New York: Wiley, 1976. 263p. (Bibliography). (Wiley Series on Personality Processes).
Examines various treatment strategies. One chapter is devoted to behavior modification in which examples are given of possible applications of techniques.

Hamerlynck, Leo A., and Clark, Frank C., eds.
see Banff International Conference on Behavior Modification, 2nd., 1970. Behavior modification for exceptional children and youth. (Item No. 56).

89 Harshbarger, Dwight, and Maley, Roger F., eds. Behavior analysis and systems analysis: an integrative approach to mental health programs. Kalamazoo, Michigan: Behaviordelia, 1974. 403p. (Bibliography).
Addresses the problems of behavior analysis and systems analysis and suggests an integration of the two fields. Intervention on the community level and the use of non-professionals as change agents are emphasized. A review of token economy systems is included.

90 Ince, Laurence P. Behavior modification in rehabilitation medicine. Springfield, Illinois: Thomas, 1976. 302p. (Bibliography).
This volume is intended primarily for the paramedical professions, but is of use to anyone working in the rehabilitation field. Section I gives a general orientation, and succeeding chapters are devoted to the use of behavior modification techniques by the physical therapist, the occupational therapist, and the speech therapist in the handling of behavioral and management problems.

International Symposium on Behavior Modification, 1st, Minneapolis, 1972.
see Thompson, Travis, and Dockens, William S., III. Applications of behavior modification. (Item No. 127).

91 Kanfer, Frederick H., and Phillips, Jeanne S. "Behavior therapy: a panacea for all ills or a passing fancy?" Arch Gen Psychiatry 15(2): 114-28, August, 1966.
Reviews attempts to provide an organizational outline of apparently divergent behavior therapy techniques and compares techniques of instigation, replication, and intervention therapies. The integration of these methods with other phases of clinical enterprise and stronger research evidence is advocated.

92 Katz, Roger C., and Zlutnick, Steven, eds. Behavior therapy and health care: principles and applications. New York: Pergamon, 1975. 624p. (Bibliography). (Pergamon General Psychology Series, No. 43).
Consists of a collection of reprinted and original articles with chapters grouped by organ system, e.g., the genitourinary system, the gastrointestinal system, etc. Not all the articles deal with children, but a number of articles are included on some of the more common childhood problems--enuresis, encopresis, asthma, and vomiting. The collection is intended for students and health professionals.

93 Kazdin, Alan E. Behavior modification in applied settings. Homewood, Illinois: Dorsey, 1975. 292p. (Bibliography). (Dorsey Series in Psychology).
Intended as a bridge between scholarly reviews and "how-to-do-it" manuals, this volume discusses broad concepts, methodology, techniques, maintenance, and ethical issues. It provides illustrations from a variety of settings, including day-care centers, schools, and the home.

94 ————. The token economy: a review and evaluation. New York: Plenum, 1977. 342p. (Bibliography). (Plenum Behavior Therapy Series).
Contains introductory chapters on the principles of operant conditioning and the development and implementation of token economies. The use of the technique across a variety of populations, including the mentally retarded, the delinquent, the school child, and the emotionally disturbed, are reviewed. Later chapters cover such topics as training, generalization, and ethical issues.

95 Kazdin, Alan E., and Bootzin, Richard R. "The token economy: an evaluative review." J Appl Behav Anal 5(3): 343-72, 1972. (153 References).
Provides a state-of-the-art review of the extensive literature on token economies. The authors indicate particular problem areas, such as staff training and client resistance, and three areas having insufficient investigation: (1) generalization of behavioral gains; (2) the modification of complex behaviors, such as language and social behavior; and (3) individual-difference variables. An extensive bibliography is included.

96 Kazdin, Alan E., and Pulaski, Joan L. "Joseph Lancaster and behavior modification in education." J Hist Behav Sci 13(3): 261-66, July, 1977. (28 References).
Compares behavior modification and Lancaster's monitorial system of education devised and practiced in England in the early 1800's.

97 Leitenberg, Harold, ed. Handbook of behavior modification and behavior therapy. Englewood Cliffs, New Jersey: Prentice-Hall, 1976. 671p. (Bibliography). (Century Psychology Series).
Provides a detailed examination of research on the use of behavioral strategies for the treatment of specific behavior disorders in a variety of clinical settings. The second of three sections deals with children and youth and contains six chapters covering psychotic children, mental retardation, juvenile delinquency, and intervention in the preschool, school, and home. Each chapter is written by a leading authority in the field and gives a state-of-the-art review, accompanied by an extensive bibliography.

98 Liberman, Robert P. A guide to behavioral analysis and therapy. New York: Pergamon, 1972. 343p. (Bibliography). (Pergamon General Psychology Series, No. 19).
This programmed text introduces the basic principles and the techniques of applying those principles. Many of the examples given are of cases involving children.

99 McCarroll, Leslie. "The relationship of perceptual organization to success or failure of behavior modification programs." For a summary see: Diss Abstr Int 36A(4): 2081, October, 1976.

100 Macht, Joel. Teaching our children. New York: Wiley, 1975. 143p. (Bibliography).
Intended for teachers and parents, this text explains in non-technical terms the principles of behavior modification and how these techniques can be applied to encourage desired behavior. Many examples are included from commonly occurring situations in the home.

101 MacNamara, Roger. "Compleat behavior modifier: confessions of an over-zealous operant conditioner." Ment Retard 15(1): 34-37, February, 1977. (1 Reference).
Argues humorously for the placement of behavior modification in proper perspective. The author deplores the unobjective reports of success, but expresses the view that it is a useful technique which should be a controlled element in programs for the developmentally disabled.

102 Madsen, Clifford K., and Madsen, Charles H., Jr. Parents/children/discipline: a positive approach. Boston: Allyn and Bacon, 1972. 213p.
This book is divided into three parts: Part I covers the major issues in child rearing; Part II contains specific examples of research that are applicable to the home situation; and Part III contains a list of possible reinforcers. Included are examples of record-keeping charts and forms.

103 Marholin, David, II, and Bijou, Sidney W. "A behavioral approach to assessment of children's behavioral disorders." Child Welfare 56(2): 93-106, February, 1977. (30 References).
Describes a behavioral model which emphasizes precise, detailed definition of the problem, and careful monitoring of behavior before, during, and after treatment.

104 Martin, Reed. Legal challenges to behavior modification: trends in schools, corrections and mental health. Champaign, Illinois: Research Press, 1975. 179p. (Bibliography).
Intended for an audience of practitioners and administrators of behavior change programs, the organization of this volume reflects the step-by-step planning and implementation of such a program. Each chapter contains a valuable review checklist, and the final chapter is devoted to an annotated table of relevant legal cases, some of which are still being appealed.

105 Mayer, Doris Y. "A psychotherapist's note on behaviour therapy." Br J Psychiatry 115(521): 429-33, April, 1969. (11 References).
Critically examines recent reports of successes using behavior therapy. Parallels between aversive therapy and traditional methods of child discipline, which may have adverse effects in later life, are suggested.

106 Mikulas, William L. Behavior modification: an overview. New York: Harper & Row, 1972. 179p. (Bibliography).
Provides a brief review of principles and applications across a wide variety of settings.

107 Miller, L. Keith. Everyday behavior analysis. Monterey, California: Brooks/Cole, 1976. 310p. (Bibliography).
This programmed text introduces the student to the basic principles of behavior modification and uses examples from everyday situations. Not particularly related to children.

108 Miller, Lovick C.; Barrett, Curtis L.; Hampe, I. Edward. "Impact of application of principles of learning." In: Rie, Herbert E., ed. Perspectives in child psychopathology. New York: Aldine/Atherton, 1971. 351-86. (89 References).
Reviews the history, principle developments, and therapeutic applications and contains a short section on ethical problems.

National Society for the Study of Education, Yearbook, 75th, pt. 1. see Thoresen, Carl E., ed. Behavior modification in education. (Item No. 128).

109 Nay, W. Robert. Behavioral intervention: contemporary strategies. New York: Halsted, 1976. 384p. (Bibliography).
This professional level text affords a comprehensive coverage of behavioral methods for both children and adult populations. Contemporary legal and ethical questions are discussed.

110 O'Leary, K. Daniel, and Wilson, G. Terence. Behavior therapy: application and outcome. Englewood Cliffs, New Jersey: Prentice-Hall, 1975. 496p. (Bibliography). (Prentice-Hall Series on Social Learning Theory).
Intended for upper-level undergraduate, graduate, and medical students, this text: (1) covers the development of behavior therapy and its basic principles; (2) presents various problems of both children and adults, with discussions of etiology and treatment; (3) examines issues such as ethics, symptom substitution, generalization, and long-term effectiveness; and (4) suggests directions for future emphasis and research.

111 Patterson, G. R. "Behavior intervention procedures in the classroom and in the home." In: Bergin, A. E., and Garfield, S. L., eds. Handbook of psychotherapy and behavior change. New York: Wiley, 1971. 751-75.
Reviews procedures, developed prior to 1971, for altering the behavior of family members, teachers, and members of peer groups of children displaying deviant behaviors. Areas in need of further research are indicated.

112 ———. "Responsiveness to social stimuli." In: Krasner, Leonard, and Ullmann, Leonard P., eds. Research in behavior modification. New York: Holt, Rinehart & Winston, 1965. 157-78.
Reports on research in which a stimulus-response theory of learning was used to investigate the development of personality behaviors in children. It is emphasized that the greater the "value" attached to a behavior by peers or parents, the more likely that behavior is to elicit reinforcing responses.

113 Phillips, Debora, and Mordock, John B. "Behavior therapy with children: some general guidelines and specific suggestions." In: Daniels, Lloyd Keith, ed. The management of childhood behavior problems in school and at home. Springfield, Illinois: Thomas, 1974. 349-60. (24 References).
Examines the principles of behavior therapy and procedures for use with children and their families. A case history is included.

114 Powers, Richard B., and Osborne, James Grayson. Fundamentals of behavior. St. Paul, Minnesota: West, 1976. 405p. (Bibliography).

Introduces beginning students in psychology to conditioning principles. Each chapter contains assignments and examination questions.

115 Redd, William H., and Sleator, William. Take charge: a personal guide to behavior modification. New York: Random House, 1976. 183p.
This simple text explains the techniques and various applications of behavior modification and includes a chapter on classroom use.

116 Rickard, Henry C., ed. Behavioral intervention in human problems. New York: Pergamon, 1971. 422p. (Bibliography). (Pergamon General Psychology Series, No. 10).
Presents a collection of papers describing programs in which the emphasis is on the modification of behavior through the control of the consequences of behavior. Six of the sixteen programs deal with children.

117 Risley, Todd R., and Baer, Donald M. "Operant behavior modification: the development of behavior." In: Caldwell, Bettye M., and Ricciuti, Henry N., eds. Review of child development research: Vol. 3. Chicago: University of Chicago Press, 1973. 283-329. (86 References).
Reviews principles, methods, and research. The ethical implications of the topic are also considered.

118 Rose, Sheldon D. Treating children in groups: a behavioral approach. San Francisco: Jossey-Bass, 1972. 223p. (Bibliography). (Jossey-Bass Behavioral Science Series).
Intended for the professional or paraprofessional working with children, this text assumes a knowledge of behavioral principles. It describes the application of such techniques as individual and group contingencies, contracting, modeling, rehearsal, and desensitization, in a variety of group situations.

119 Ross, Alan O. Psychological disorders of children: a behavioral approach to theory, research, and therapy. New York: McGraw-Hill, 1974. 360p. (Bibliography). (McGraw-Hill Series in Psychology).
Intended for students in psychology, social work, special education, and child psychiatry, the text assumes a familiarity with the basic principles of learning theory. A behavioral interpretation is presented and a rationale for behavioral treatment of such childhood disorders as autism, learning difficulties, mental subnormality, juvenile delinquency, psychophysiological disorders, and aggressive, withdrawn, and psychotic behavior.

120 Saunders, Jon Terry. "The social identity of behavior modification." For a summary see: Diss Abstr Int 36B(12): 6397, June, 1976.

121 Schaefer, Halmuth H., and Martin, Patrick L. Behavioral therapy. 2nd ed. New York: McGraw-Hill, 1975. 378p. (Bibliography).
This text is intended for use in the education of psychiatric personnel. All new terms are explained, and each chapter is preceded by questions that will be answered in the text, and followed by exercises to be completed. The book deals primarily with the adult psychiatric patient, although a small section on childhood problems is included.

122 Semb, George, ed. Behavior analysis and education. Lawrence, Kansas: University of Kansas, Department of Human Development, 1972. 442p. (ED 080 416).

Brings together papers covering current concepts, research, programs for handicapped children, the use of students as behavioral engineers, teacher training programs, and current techniques and procedures.

123 Sherman, A. Robert. Behavior modification: theory and practice. Monterey, California: Brooks/Cole, 1973. 183p. (Bibliography).
This introduction to the principles and techniques of behavior modification emphasizes the wide relevance of the concepts. Case histories are used to illustrate the varied applications.

124 Staats, Arthur W. Child learning, intelligence, and personality: principles of a behavioral interaction approach. New York: Harper & Row, 1971. 358p. (Bibliography).
Presents an overall concept of personality and intellectual development from the behavioral standpoint and describes types of determining conditions involved.

125 Stevenson, Harold W. Children's learning. New York: Appleton-Century-Crofts, 1972. 388p. (Bibliography). (Century Psychology Series).
Contains five chapters which review major studies on reinforcement and learning.

126 Sulzer-Azároff, Beth, and Mayer, G. Roy. Applying behavior-analysis procedures with children and youth. New York: Holt, Rinehart & Winston, 1977. 541p. (Bibliography).
This text is intended primarily for use in courses in school counseling, education, and psychology, and is arranged in units to facilitate incorporation into such courses. Chapters cover such topics as ethics, principles, program implementation, and specific techniques. Each chapter contains study guide questions and a summary.

Symposium on Behavior Modification, 1st, University of Veracruz, 1971. see Bijou, Sidney W., and Ribes-Inesta, Emilio, eds. Behavior modification: issues and extensions. (Item No. 64).

127 Thompson, Travis, and Dockens, William S., III, eds. Applications of behavior modification. New York: Academic Press, 1975. 540p. (Bibliography).
Assembles a collection of twenty-seven research papers presented at an International Symposium on Behavior Modification held in Minneapolis, Minnesota in 1972. Many of the papers are reports of research conducted with adults, but there are seven papers on the modification of preacademic and academic skills in children, three papers on behavior modification with disturbed children, one paper on the use of behavior modification with retarded children, and two papers on the training of behavior therapists.

128 Thoresen, Carl E., ed. Behavior modification in education. National Society for the Study of Education, Yearbook, 72, pt. 1. Chicago: University of Chicago Press, 1973. 474p. (Bibliography).
Fourteen review articles on theory and application deal with teaching in the classroom, specific problem areas (such as autism, mental retardation, and blindness), behavioral systems, and the philosophy and ethics of behavior modification.

129 Vance, Barbara J. "Social learning theory and guidance in early childhood." Young Child 21(1): 30-42, October, 1965. (35 References). (Reprinted in Item No. 32).
Briefly reviews behavioral techniques and advocates consistency in the application of these techniques by the parents and teachers of young children.

130 Whaley, Donald L., and Malott, Richard W. Elementary principles of behavior. New York: Appleton-Century-Crofts, 1971. 454p. (Bibliography).
Covers the basic principles of learning theory and operant conditioning for the college level audience.

131 Winters, Stanley A., and Cox, Eunice, eds. Behavior modification techniques for the special educator. New York: MSS Information Corporation, 1972. 309p. (Bibliography).
Presents a collection of articles, some original and some reprinted, which report on the application of behavioral techniques in a variety of settings and across a wide range of problems. Intended for the special educator, it assumes a familiarity with the basic behavioral concepts and techniques.

B. ETHICAL CONSIDERATIONS

132 Alexander, Ronald G. "Toward a moral criterion for use by behavior modifiers." Paper presented at the 2nd Annual meeting of the Midwestern Association of Behavior Analysis, Chicago, May 1-4, 1976. 25p. (ED 140 118).
Seeks to determine which set of moral criteria psychologists use for moral guidance in a morally pluralistic society. It is suggested that a moral principle can be extracted from Skinner's operant conditioning.

133 Bufford, Rodger, K. "God and behavior mod: some thoughts concerning relationships between biblical principles and behavior modification." J Psychol Theol 5(1): 13-22, 1977. (14 References).
Compares and contrasts various biblical principles and behavioral approaches to establishing positive behavior. Behavioral technology is concluded to be broadly consistent with the biblical view of man.

134 Carrera, Frank, III, and Adams, Paul L. "An ethical perspective on operant conditioning." J Am Acad Child Psychiatry 9(4): 607-23, October, 1970. (18 References).
Examines the major disadvantages of operant techniques and advocates a non-doctrinaire approach to the psychotherapeutic treatment of children.

135 Carrison, Muriel Paskin. "Behavior modification: education's Watergate." Paper presented at the 81st Annual meeting of the American Psychological Association, Montreal, Canada, August 27-31, 1973. 15p. (ED 082 826).
Examines and criticizes theory and experimental assumptions. The philosophy of behavior modification is presented as a direct contradiction to the principles of a free democratic society.

136 Cooke, Thomas P., and Cooke, Sharon. "Behavior modification: answers to some ethical issues." Psychol Sch 11(1): 5-10, 1974. (27 References).

Attempts to answer some of the most often heard criticisms, including "the treatment of symptom rather than the cause," "symptom substitution," "use of aversive techniques," "bribery," and "curtailment of freedom."

137 Cote, Robert William. "Behavior modification: some questions." Elem Sch J 74(1): 44-47, 1973. (0 References).
Advocates careful assessment of a behavior modification program before it is undertaken.

138 Holland, James. "Ethical considerations in behavior modification." J Humanistic Psychol 16(3): 71-78, Summer, 1976. (13 References).
Examines ethical issues and, while not devoted exclusively to the use of behavior modification with children, the article raises such questions as the ethics of controlling the behavior of one person for the benefit of some other person or group.

139 Hyldahl, Thomas R. "An analysis of the value assumptions and conflicts in behavior modification." For a summary see: Diss Abstr Int 37A(12): 7606, June, 1976.

140 O'Donnell, Patrick A., and Ohlson, Glenn A. "Aversive stimulation--criteria for application." Paper presented at the 54th Annual International Convention of the Council for Exceptional Children, Chicago, April 4-9, 1976. 6p. (ED 122 553).
Considers criteria and ethical issues and suggests research in the comparison of negative and positive reinforcement of similar behaviors.

141 O'Leary, K. Daniel; Poulos, Rita W.; Devine, Vernon T. "Tangible reinforcers: bonuses or bribes?" J Consult Clin Psychol 38(1): 1-8, 1972. (29 References). (Reprinted in Item No. 35).
Discusses the issue of bribery--often raised by parents and teachers--and advocates the use of tangible reinforcers only after other procedures of prompting and reinforcing with natural reinforcers have been tried.

142 Peterson, Robert F. "Power, programming, and punishment: could we be overcontrolling our children?" In: Mash, Eric J.; Hamerlynck, Leo A.; and Handy, Lee C., eds. Behavior modification and families. Banff International Conference on Behavior Modification, 6th, 1974. New York: Brunner/Mazel, 1976. 338-52. (20 References).
Explores the ethical issues involved in the use of control in the endeavor to develop independent, well-functioning adults.

143 Roos, Philip. "Human rights and behavior modification." Ment Retard 12(3): 3-6, June, 1974. (21 References).
Examines the nature of criticisms and presents suggestions for minimizing them while preserving the viability of behavior modification.

144 Smith, Anne B. "Humanism and behavior modification: is there a conflict?" Elem Sch J 74(2): 59-67, 1973. (14 References).
Discusses some common fallacies about behavior modification, especially as they relate to the classroom.

145 Stolz, Stephanie B. "Why no guidelines for behavior modification?" J Appl Behav Anal 10(3): 541-47, Fall, 1977. (28 References).
Reviews the guidelines for behavioral programs published by the National Association for Retarded Children and suggests that such guidelines carry many disadvantages. The author advocates a strict adherence to the ethical codes of the therapists' professions.

IV.

Behavioral Techniques for Specific Behaviors

A. AGGRESSION

146 Allison, Tom S., and Allison, Sharon L. "Time-out from reinforcement: effect on sibling aggression." Psychol Rec 21(1): 81-86, Winter, 1971. (11 References).
Time-out from social reinforcement was effective in reducing aggressive behavior of a twenty-six-month-old girl toward her eleven-month-old brother.

147 Arnesen, Richard B.; Libby, Roy; Miller, Paul H. "Altering the behavior of an aggressive institutionalized boy through paradoxical communication." J Nerv Ment Dis 157(1): 63-65, July, 1973. (5 References).
The chronically aggressive behavior of an adolescent boy was effectively modulated by removing the reinforcement of staff attention.

148 Bostow, Darrel E., and Bailey, J. B. "Modification of severe disruptive and aggressive behavior using brief time-out and reinforcement procedures." J Appl Behav Anal 2(1): 31-37, 1969. (13 References). (Reprinted in Item No. 28).
Describes the successful modification of two retarded patients, one an adult and the other a seven-year-old boy, with aggressive behavior of at least eighteen months duration. Methods included time-out in a specially constructed plywood booth and edible reinforcers for non-aggressive behavior.

149 Brown, Arthur Henry, III. "Modifying aggressive behaviors in families with pre-adolescent girls." For a summary see: Diss Abstr Int 37B(11): 5808, May, 1977.

150 Engeln, Richard; Knutson, John; Laughy, Linwood; et al. "Behavior modification techniques applied to a family unit--a case study." J Child Psychol Psychiatry 9(3/4): 245-52, 1968. (8 References). (Reprinted in Item No. 43).
Describes a program of systematic reinforcement, involving the whole family, which dealt with the extremely aggressive behavior of a six-year-old boy.

151 Gittelman, Martin. "Behavior rehearsal as a technique in child treatment." J Child Psychol Psychiatry 6(3/4): 251-55, 1965. (10 References). (Reprinted in Item No. 36).
Provides a description of a technique used in the treatment of aggressive children in an out-patient group setting. Included is a case history of a thirteen-year-old boy treated over a period of two-and-one-half months.

152 Harder, Diane Marie. "A comparison of the effects of timeout, punishment and extinction on an aggressive behavior in children." For a summary see: Diss Abstr Int 38B(1): 360, July, 1977.

153 Kauffman, James M., and Hallahan, Daniel P. "Control of rough physical behavior using novel contingencies and directive teaching." Percept Mot Skills 36(3): 1225-26, June, 1973. (2 References).
The aggressive play of a six-year-old boy was controlled by the use of a contingency involving playing cards in a free-play setting.

154 McNamara, John Regis. "The broad based application of social learning theory to treat aggression in a preschool child." J Clin Psychol 26(2): 245-47, April, 1970. (10 References).
Differential reinforcement of prosocial peer model and subject responses, coupled with sociological intervention at home, were used to modify the hyper-aggressive behavior of a six-year-old boy.

155 Ollendick, Thomas H., and Matson, Johnny L. "An initial investigation into the parameters of overcorrection." Psychol Rep 39(3, pt. 2): 1139-42, December, 1976. (6 References).
Aggressive-disruptive behaviors of hitting and crying were eliminated in two young children by overcorrection. Components of the procedures are discussed.

156 Patterson, Gerald R. "The aggressive child: victim and architect of a coersive system." In: Mash, Eric J.; Hamerlynck, Leo A.; and Handy, Lee C., eds. Behavior modification and families. Banff International Conference on Behavior Modification, 6th, 1974. New York: Brunner/Mazel, 1976. 267-316. (101 References).
Describes a functional analysis of family interactions in the homes of aggressive and non-aggressive children. Reactions to parental punishment are noted, together with the responses of the parents and siblings to the behavior of the target child. The changes among family members during and following the institution of a social learning-based parent-training program are examined. Emphasis is on the spiraling effect of aversive behavior.

157 ————. "Reprogramming the families of aggressive boys." In: Thoreson, Carl E., ed. Behavior modification in education. National Society for the Study of Education, Yearbook, 72nd, pt. 1. Chicago: University of Chicago Press, 1973. 154-92. (87 References).
Summarizes the evolution of family intervention programs, primarily with the families of aggressive boys.

158 Patterson, Gerald R.; Cobb, J. A.; Ray, Roberta S. "A social engineering technology for retraining the families of aggressive boys." In: Adams, Henry E., and Unikel, Irving P., eds. Issues and trends in behavior therapy. Springfield, Illinois: Thomas, 1973. 139-210. (117 References).
Presents the underlying principles, intervention strategies, and data for a set of standardized social engineering procedures designed to alter the behavior of highly aggressive children. Emphasis is placed on training the parents to apply social learning principles.

159 Patterson, Gerald R., and Guttman, Herta M. "Retraining of aggressive boys by their parents: review of recent literature and follow-up evaluation." Can Psychiatr Assoc J 19(2): 142-61, April, 1974. (47 References).
Reviews literature and reports on a five-year program conducted with twenty-seven families. Areas needing further research are indicated.

160 Patterson, Gerald R., and Reid, J. B. "Intervention for families of aggressive boys: a replication study." Behav Res Ther 11(4): 383-94, November, 1973. (32 References).
Replicates an earlier study (see Item No. 158) in which parents were trained to alter the behaviors of their aggressive children. The training program was based on social learning principles.

161 Sloane, Howard N.; Johnston, Margaret K.; Bijou, Sidney W. "Successive modification of aggressive behavior and aggressive fantasy play by management of contingencies." J Child Psychol Psychiatry 8(3/4): 217-26, 1967. (14 References). (Reprinted in Item No. 37).
Aggressive acts and excessive fantasy play were reduced in a four-and-one-half-year-old boy by the withdrawal of positive reinforcement and time-out procedures. Social reinforcement was presented for appropriate behavior.

162 Stedman, James M.; Peterson, Travis L.; Cardarelle, James. "Application of a token system in a pre-adolescent boys' group." J Behav Ther Exp Psychiatry 2(1): 23-29, 1971. (3 References). (Reprinted in Item No. 43).
Contingent reinforcement was successfully employed to modify aggressive behavior in a group of eight boys, ten to twelve-and-one-half years in age. Tokens were exchangeable for attendance at the next session, attendance at a party, and field trips.

B. ANOREXIA NERVOSA

163 Agras, W. Stewart; Barlow, David H.; Chapin, Harvey N.; et al. "Behavior modification of anorexia nervosa." Arch Gen Psychiatry 30(3): 279-86, March, 1974.
Presents the case histories of five patients, two adults and three children or adolescents, who were treated with a combination of positive and negative reinforcement and informational feedback. Feedback of information appeared to be the most important variable.

164 Agras, W. Stewart, and Werne, Joellen. "Behavior modification in anorexia nervosa: research foundations." In: Vigersky, Robert A., ed. Anorexia nervosa. New York: Raven, 1977. 291-303. (18 References).
Reviews the research--which began with case reports and proceeded to controlled experiments--and describes a typical therapeutic program. Much more research needs to be done before an effective therapy becomes a reality.

165 Azerrad, Jacob, and Stafford, Richard L. "Restoration of eating behavior in anorexia nervosa through operant conditioning and environmental manipulation." Behav Res Ther 7(2): 165-71, May, 1969. (3 References). (Reprinted in Item No. 21).

Describes the successful treatment of a thirteen-year-old anorexic girl by a token system of positive reinforcement. Reward points (redeemable for material items and home visits) were contingent upon the amount of food eaten each day.

166 Bhanji, S. "Operant conditioning in anorexia nervosa." Curr Psychiatr Ther 15: 59-64, 1975. (11 References).
Reviews the literature and describes an operant conditioning program conducted with eleven girls between the ages of thirteen and twenty-one years.

167 Bhanji, S., and Thompson, J. "Operant conditioning in the treatment of anorexia nervosa: a review and retrospective study of eleven cases." Br J Psychiatry 124(579): 166-72, February, 1974. (11 References).
Surveys the literature and describes the treatment of eleven girls from thirteen to twenty-one years of age, with an operant conditioning technique using rewards of the patient's own choosing.

168 Garfinkel, Paul E.; Kline, Stephen A.; Stancer, Harvey C. "Treatment of anorexia nervosa using operant conditioning techniques." J Nerv Ment Dis 157(6): 428-33, 1973. (16 References).
Describes the successful treatment of five anorexic teenage girls with operant conditioning methods. A system of rewards was tailored for each of the patients and included physical activity, social rewards, and progressive ward privileges.

169 Garfinkel, Paul E.; Moldofsky, Harvey; Garner, David M. "Prognosis in anorexia nervosa as influenced by clinical features, treatment and self-perception." Can Med Assoc J 117(9): 1041-45, November, 1977. (35 References).
Reports on a follow-up study conducted with forty-two patients. The results indicate that although many patients gained weight rapidly with a behavior modification regimen, there was little evidence to suggest that this technique is superior to other, more conventional types of therapy.

170 Hallsten, Edwin A., Jr. "Adolescent anorexia nervosa treated by desensitization." Behav Res Ther 3(2): 87-91, May, 1965. (11 References).
A twelve-year-old girl was successfully treated for anorexia nervosa in a hospital setting. Visits from relatives were made contingent upon weight gains (although this program was not strictly adhered to by the parents), and imagery was used to reduce fears of obesity.

171 Halmi, Katherine A.; Powers, Pauline; Cunningham, Sheila. "Treatment of anorexia nervosa with behavior modification: effectiveness of formula feeding and isolation." Arch Gen Psychiatry 32(1): 93-96, January, 1975.
Eight anorectic patients--four of whom were adolescents--were treated by means of a behavior modification program in which rewards were contingent upon weight gain. All the patients had substantial weight gain while hospitalized and were maintaining or continuing to gain at a short-term follow-up.

172 Jacob, R. G.; Nordlund, O.; Schwieler, G. H. "Treatment of anorexia in early infancy--some behavioral approaches." In: Brengelmann,

J. C., ed. Progress in behavior therapy. New York: Springer-Verlag, 1975. 35-38. (7 References).
Describes three cases of chronic anorexia in which improvement was seen only after a deprivational state.

173 Leitenberg, Harold; Agras, W. Stewart; Thomson, Laurence E. "A sequential analysis of the effect of selective positive reinforcement in modifying anorexia nervosa." Behav Res Ther 6(2): 211-18, May, 1968. (17 References).
Two hospitalized adolescent girls were successfully treated by means of ignoring all physical complaints and reinforcing progressive weight gains by praise and pleasurable activities, such as watching TV, knitting, and playing games.

174 Liebman, Ronald; Minuchin, Salvador; Baker, Lester. "An integrated treatment program for anorexia nervosa." Am J Psychiatry 131(4): 432-36, April, 1974. (17 References).
Advocates the use of behavioral conditioning within the context of structural family therapy. Studies of four patients are included.

175 Liebman, Ronald; Minuchin, Salvador; Baker, Lester; et al. "The treatment of anorexia nervosa." Curr Psychiatr Ther 15: 51-57, 1975. (15 References).
Reports on the treatment of ten girls, between the ages of nine and eighteen years, with a combination of operant conditioning and structural family therapy.

176 Perlman, Lawrence M., and Bender, Sheila S. "Operant reinforcement with structural family therapy in treating anorexia nervosa." J Fam Couns 3(2): 38-46, 1975. (14 References).
Involvement in menu planning and free activity days contingent upon weight gain were used in a therapy plan involving the whole family.

177 Pertschuk, Michael J. "Behavior therapy: extended follow-up." In: Vigersky, Robert A., ed. Anorexia nervosa. New York: Raven, 1977. 305-13. (19 References).
Assesses the immediate and long-term impact of behavioral therapy conducted during a period of hospitalization. The subjects were twenty-seven patients, thirteen of whom were under the age of twenty. Most of the patients showed improvement at follow-up.

178 Schmidt, Mary P. W., and Duncan, Beverly A. B. "Modifying eating behavior in anorexia nervosa." Am J Nurs 74(9): 1646-48, September, 1974. (4 References).
Outlines a treatment plan based on behavioral techniques for the adolescent anorexic. Included is a daily schedule of activities that is rigidly enforced by all staff members.

179 Scrignar, C. B. "Food as the reinforcer in the outpatient treatment of anorexia nervosa." J Behav Ther Exp Psychiatry 2(1): 31-36, 1971. (12 References). (Reprinted in Item No. 43).
Describes the use of highly preferred foods as reinforcers i. the treatment of a fourteen-year-old anorexic who had developed a pattern of vomiting after eating.

180 Werry, J. S., and Bull, D. "Anorexia nervosa: a case study using behavior therapy." J Am Acad Child Psychiatry 14(4): 646-51, Autumn, 1975. (3 References).

A fifteen-year-old anorexic girl was successfully treated by making attention and pleasurable activities contingent upon weight gain.

181 Williams, Warwick. "A comprehensive behavior modification programme for the treatment of anorexia nervosa: results in six cases." Aust NZ J Psychiatry 10(4): 321-24, 1976. (4 References).
Describes a program that was judged to be a failure, although specific reasons for the failure are not pinpointed.

C. ASTHMA

182 Creer, Thomas L. "The use of time-out from positive reinforcement procedure with asthmatic children." J Psychosom Res 14(2): 117-20, 1970. (1 Reference).
The use of time-out from the positive reinforcement of hospitalization was effective in curtailing the frequency and duration of hospitalizations in two ten-year-old boys with chronic asthma.

183 Creer, Thomas L., and Miklich, Donald R. "The application of a self-modeling procedure to modify inappropriate behavior: a preliminary report." Behav Res Ther 8(1): 91-92, February, 1970. (1 Reference).
Offers a brief preliminary report on the use of a self-monitoring technique with a ten-year-old asthmatic boy. Videotapes of both his appropriate and inappropriate behaviors were viewed by the boy with a resultant lessening of immature behavior.

184 Creer, Thomas L., and Yoches, Carol. "The modification of an inappropriate behavioral pattern in asthmatic children." J Chronic Dis 24(7): 507-13, September, 1971. (13 References).
Non-attending behaviors in the classroom were reduced in two asthmatic boys (aged seven and nine years) by punishing such behaviors in an experimental setting.

185 Gardner, James E. "A blending of behavior therapy techniques in an approach to an asthmatic child." Psychotherapy 5(1): 46-49, Winter, 1968. (6 References).
Describes the treatment of a six-year-old boy by withdrawing attention for inappropriate behavior, reinforcing appropriate behaviors, developing alternative responses to stress, and using a conditioned placebo.

186 Lukeman, Diane. "Conditioning methods of treating childhood asthma." J Child Psychol Psychiatry 16(2): 165-68, April, 1975. (14 References).
This review of the literature indicates some successes in conditioning methods of treatment.

187 Miklich, Donald R.; Renne, Charles M.; Creer, Thomas L.; et al. "The clinical utility of behavior therapy as an adjunctive treatment for asthma." J Allergy Clin Immunol 60(5): 285-94, November, 1977. (30 References).
Systematic desensitization by reciprocal inhibition was used to reduce anxiety reported by nineteen children before and during asthmatic symptoms. A few patients appeared to show a clinically useful response but, on the average, the effect was small.

188 Moore, Norah. "Behaviour therapy in bronchial asthma: a controlled study." J Psychosom Res 9(3): 257-76, December, 1965. (33 References).
Results of a study conducted with six adults and six children indicate that reciprocal inhibition is the crucial factor in effecting improvement in respiratory function.

189 Neisworth, John T., and Moore, Florese. "Operant treatment of asthmatic responding with the parent as therapist." Behav Ther 3(1): 95-99, 1972. (9 References). (Reprinted in Item Nos. 43, 49).
Reports on the successful modification of chronic asthma in a seven-year-old boy. Therapy was conducted by the parents who withheld attention during the boy's coughing and sneezing, and reinforced non-asthmatic behavior.

190 Renne, Charles M., and Creer, Thomas L. "Training children with asthma to use inhalation therapy equipment." J Appl Behav Anal 9(1): 1-11, Spring, 1976. (15 References).
Documents the use of token reinforcement with four children in order to promote the use of bronchodilator medication apparatus.

191 White, Margaret L. "Children's perceptions of contingency relationships in asthma." For a summary see: Diss Abstr Int 36B(3): 1465, September, 1975.

192 Wohl, Theodore H. "Behavior modification: its application to the study and treatment of childhood asthma." J Asthma Res 9(1): 41-45, September, 1971. (13 References).
Briefly reviews the rationale of a behavioral approach. Current research is surveyed.

D. CONSTIPATION

193 Daniels, Lloyd Keith. "The treatment of childhood colitis by training the parents in reinforcement procedures: a case study." In: Daniels, Lloyd Keith, ed. The management of childhood behavior problems in school and at home. Springfield, Illinois: Thomas, 1974. 361-64. (16 References).
Describes the procedures used over a twelve-week period with a six-year-old hyperactive boy. At a thirteen month follow-up, the hyperactivity remained controlled, and bowel movements occurred regularly.

194 Lal, H., and Lindsley, O. R. "Therapy of chronic constipation in a young child by rearranging social contingencies." Behav Res Ther 6(4): 484-85, November, 1968. (0 References).
Gives a short case history of a three-year-old boy suffering from chronic constipation who was conditioned to defecate by making play in the bathtub contingent upon his elimination.

195 Tomlinson, J. R. "The treatment of bowel retention by operant procedures: a case study." J Behav Ther Exp Psychiatry 1(1): 83-85, March, 1970. (3 References).
Describes the use of bubble gum reinforcers which were used to establish successful bowel elimination in a three-year-old boy.

E. CRYING

196 Etzel, Barbara C., and Gewirtz, Jacob L. "Experimental modification of caretaker-maintained high-rate operant crying in a six- and a twenty-week-old infant (infans tyrannotearus): extinction of crying with reinforcement of eye contact and smiling." J Exp Child Psychol 5(3): 303-17, September, 1967. (12 References). (Reprinted in Item No. 32).
The excessive crying of two infants (which was being reinforced by attention given them by attendants) was modified in the experimental situation by giving social reinforcement for non-crying behavior and removing it for crying behavior.

197 Hart, Betty M.; Allen, K. Eileen; Buell, Joan S.; et al. "Effects of social reinforcement on operant crying." J Exp Child Psychol 1(2): 145-53, 1964. (6 References). (Reprinted in Item No. 45).
Presents two studies of systematic use of positive social reinforcement to lessen frequent crying in two four-year-old boys.

198 Patterson, Roger L. "Time-out and assertive training for a dependent child." Behav Ther 3(3): 466-68, 1972. (1 Reference).
Summarizes the successful treatment of a frequently crying nine-year-old boy.

199 Yawkey, Thomas D., and Griffith, Diane Le Penna. "The effects of the Premack Principle on affective behaviors of young children." Child Study J 4(2): 59-70, 1974. (55 References).
Reports on an investigation of the applicability of behavior modification techniques to operant crying in a regular kindergarten classroom.

F. DELINQUENCY

1. Behavioral Handling of the Delinquent

200 Alexander, James F. "Behavior modification and delinquent youth." In: Cull, John G., and Hardy, Richard E. Behavior modification in rehabilitation settings: applied principles. Springfield, Illinois: Thomas, 1974. 158-77. (30 References).
Describes concepts and techniques. Behavior modification is advocated as the most powerful and efficient method of treating juvenile delinquents.

201 Braukmann, Curtis J., and Fixsen, Dean L. "Behavior modification with delinquents." In: Hersen, Michel; Eisler, Richard M.; and Miller, Peter M., eds. Progress in behavior modification: Vol. 1. New York: Academic Press, 1975. 191-231. (160 References).
Reviews the programs and experiments, reported over a ten-year period, which use behavior modification techniques with juvenile delinquents. Emphasis is on the evaluation of both the programs and the procedures employed.

202 Burchard, John D., and Harig, Paul T. "Behavior modification and juvenile delinquency." In: Leitenberg, Harold, ed. Handbook of behavior modification and behavior therapy. Englewood Cliffs, New Jersey: Prentice-Hall, 1976. 405-52. (67 References).
Reviews the literature on the use of behavior modification with juvenile delinquents, with a detailed analysis of a few programs in three dif-

ferent areas: institutional programs, community-based residential programs, and community-based prevention programs. The authors advocate the directing of attention to the delinquent youth's environment which may be maintaining the problem behavior, and the teaching of behavior modification techniques to the youths themselves.

203 Cohen, Harold L. "Behavior modification and socially deviant youth." In: Thoresen, Carl E., ed. Behavior modification in education. National Society for the Study of Education, Yearbook, 72nd, pt. 1. Chicago: University of Chicago Press, 1973. 291-314. (16 References).
Surveys the use of behavior modification with delinquent youth. Examples are drawn from programs conducted within a correctional institution and from within a public school.

204 Davidson, William S., II. "The diversion of juvenile delinquents: an examination of the processes and relative efficacy of child advocacy and behavioral contracting." For a summary see: Diss Abstr Int 37B(1): 456, July, 1976.

205 Davidson, William S., II, and Seidman, Edward. "Studies of behavior modification and juvenile delinquency: a review, methodological critique, and social perspective." Psychol Bull 81(12): 998-1011, December, 1974. (64 References). (Reprinted in Item No. 35).
Reviews the published literature, from 1960 through June, 1973, concerned with the use of behavioral techniques in the modification of delinquent behavior. The article is organized according to the type of behavior, e.g., educational behaviors, program behaviors, and delinquent behaviors. Criticism is offered of the research designs generally adopted.

206 Eitzen, D. Stanley. "The effects of behavior modification on the attitudes of delinquents." Behav Res Ther 13(4): 295-99, October, 1975. (14 References).
Compares thirteen-year-old delinquent boys in an institution using behavior modification techniques with a control group of eighth-grade boys from the same community. Marked improvement was seen in the self-esteem and attitudes of the delinquent boys, and no support was seen for a behavior modification milieu making the subjects more manipulative.

207 Johnston, Marie. "Responsiveness of delinquents and non-delinquents to social reinforcement." Br J Soc Clin Psychol 15(1): 41-49, February, 1976. (31 References).
Results of this study tended to support the hypothesis that delinquents are less responsive to social reinforcement and punishment than non-delinquents.

208 Klein, Helen Altman. "Behaviorally oriented treatment for juvenile offenders." Correct Soc Psychiatry J Appl Behav Ther 21(2): 17-21, 1975. (28 References).
Examines a number of programs and evaluates their effectiveness.

209 Stephens, Thomas M. "Using reinforcement and social modeling with delinquent youth." Rev Educ Res 43(3): 323-40, Summer, 1973. (48 References).
Examines recent research literature, including studies on responses in social situations, interpersonal interactions, and performances on jobs and in school.

210 Stumphauzer, Jerome S., ed. Behavior therapy with delinquents. Springfield, Illinois: Thomas, 1973. 358p. (Bibliography).
This text is intended for those charged with the responsibility of changing the behavior of the young offender (probation officers, psychologists, psychiatrists, social workers, teachers, and police officers) but could also be used as a supplementary text in courses on juvenile delinquency and criminology. The collection of papers, some of which are reprinted from other sources, are divided into four sections: (1) basic scientific, ethical, and practical issues; (2) basic research; (3) institutional applications; and (4) applications in the community.

211 ————. "Modifying delinquent behavior: beginnings and current practices." Adolescence 11(41): 13-28, Spring, 1976. (46 References).
Reviews behavior therapy techniques in use in institutions and clinical settings, and advocates direct community intervention as the most parsimonious method of modifying and preventing delinquent behavior. Several model programs are described.

2. Techniques with the Delinquent

a. Specific Techniques

212 Brown G. Duane, and Tyler, Vernon O., Jr. "Time-out from reinforcement: a technique for dethroning the 'duke' of an institutionalized delinquent group." J Child Psychol Psychiatry 9(3/4): 203-11, 1968. (15 References).
Isolation from the peer group, contingent upon aggressive or "duke-like" behavior of a delinquent, resulted in a rapid decline in disruptive behavior.

213 Burchard, John, and Tyler, Vernon O., Jr. "The modification of delinquent behavior through operant conditioning." Behav Res Ther 2(4): 245-50, November, 1965. (13 References). (Reprinted in Item Nos. 28, 29, 43).
Reports on the use of operant conditioning to modify the delinquent behavior of a thirteen-year-old boy who had been unsuccessfully treated by other methods for four-and-one-half years. It was discerned that his anti-social behavior was being reinforced by increased attention. Systematic use of time-out, differential reinforcement, and discrimination training over a five-month period resulted in a declining rate of antisocial behavior and a decrease in seriousness of offenses.

214 Dietrich, Coralie. "Differential effects of task and reinforcement variables on performance of three groups of behavior problem children." J Abnorm Child Psychol 4(2): 155-71, 1976. (76 References).
Results of a study with thirty-six delinquent boys indicate that subjects classified as Conduct Disorder, and Inadequate-Immature, performed optimally under conditions of simple emotional task structure and material reward, and subjects in the Personality Disorder groups responded best to verbal reinforcement.

215 Ganzer, Victor J. "The use of modeling techniques in rehabilitation of the juvenile offender." In: Cull, John G., and Hardy, Richard E., eds. Behavior modification in rehabilitation settings: applied

principles. Springfield, Illinois: Thomas, 1974. 130-57. (22 References).
Reviews research, describes the development and application of modeling principles with male juvenile delinquents, and discusses potential uses of modeling in other rehabilitation programs.

216 Graubard, Paul S. "Utilizing the group in teaching disturbed delinquents to learn." Except Child 36(4): 267-72, 1969. (15 References).
Group reinforcers for appropriate classroom behavior, plus individual reinforcers, were effective in developing improved learning in eight delinquent boys.

217 Hanson, Gary White. "Behavior modification of appointment attendance among youthful delinquents." For a summary see: Diss Abstr Int 32B(11): 6648, May, 1972.

218 Jesness, Carl F. "Comparative effectiveness of behavior modification and transactional analysis programs for delinquents." J Consult Clin Psychol 43(6): 758-79, 1975. (40 References).
In this comparison study conducted with 983 delinquents, both forms of treatment resulted in improved behavior.

219 Kanofsky, David Franklin. "The effects of changes in response cost on the deviant behaviors of female adolescent delinquents." For a summary see: Diss Abstr Int 34B(11): 5682, May, 1974.

220 Kreuger, Doris El-Tawil. "Operant group therapy with delinquent boys using therapist's versus peer's reinforcement." For a summary see: Diss Abstr Int 31B(11): 6877, May, 1971.

221 Madsen, C. K., and Madsen, C. H., Jr. "Music as a behavior modification technique with a juvenile delinquent." J Music Ther 5: 72-76, 1968.
This case report describes the successful use of music and participant music activities (such as guitar lessons, guitar withdrawal, and recorded music) as reinforcement for a fifteen-year-old delinquent.

222 Pappachriston, James. "The effectiveness of modeling a socially approved and a socially disapproved behavior with a group of delinquent and non-delinquent boys." For a summary see: Diss Abstr Int 35B(2): 1059, August, 1974.

223 Schwitzgebel, Robert L. "Short-term operant conditioning of adolescent offenders on socially relevant variables." J Abnorm Psychol 72(2): 134-42, April, 1967. (25 References).
A significant increase was seen in the frequency of behaviors followed by positive consequences, but no significant decrease was seen in hostile statements when followed by mild aversive consequences.

224 Schwitzgebel, Robert L., and Kolb, D. A. "Inducing behavior change in adolescent delinquents." Behav Res Ther 1(4): 297-304, November, 1964. (13 References). (Reprinted in Item No. 32).
Describes the use of positive reinforcement to induce a group of delinquent adolescents to attend at "work." The "work" consisted of talking into a tape recorder about anything they wished. This technique was used to establish a positive relationship between the therapist and the subject.

225 Stuart, Richard B.; Jayaratne, Sirinika; Tripodi, Tony. "Changing adolescent deviant behavior through reprogramming behavior of parents and teachers: experimental evaluation." Can J Behav Sci 8(2): 132-44, 1976. (16 References).
Behavioral contracts, designed to modify both parent-child and teacher-student interactions, were used with a group of pre-delinquent youths. The results indicate statistically significant differences in four areas, with small but positive changes in the nine areas.

226 Stuart, Richard B., and Tripodi, Tony. "Experimental evaluation of three time-constrained behavioral treatments for predelinquents and delinquents." In: Rubin, Richard D.; Brady, J. Paul; and Henderson, John D., eds. Advances in behavior therapy: Vol. 4. New York: Academic Press, 1973. 1-12. (14 References).
Results of a comparison study of the effects of treatment prescribed to terminate in fifteen, forty-five, or ninety days, indicated no significant differences.

227 Switzer, E. Beth; Deal, Terrence E.; Bailey, Jon S. "The reduction of stealing in second graders using a group contingency." J Appl Behav Anal 10(2): 267-72, Summer, 1977. (10 References).
A multiple-baseline design across classes of second graders showed the use of a group contingency resulting in a significant reduction in stealing behavior. The anti-stealing lecture method was found to be totally ineffective.

228 Wahler, Robert G. "Some structural aspects of deviant child behavior." J Appl Behav Anal 8(1): 27-42, Spring, 1975. (12 References).
Examines a three-year study of covariation within behavior repertoires in two pre-delinquent boys. The effects of contingency procedures are investigated.

229 Watson, Lois Jeanne. "The effects of covert modeling and covert reinforcement on acquisition of job interview skills by youth offenders." For a summary see: Diss Abstr Int 37B(8): 4229, February, 1977.

230 Wetzel, Ralph. "Use of behavioral techniques in a case of compulsive stealing." J Consult Psychol 30(5): 367-74, October, 1966. (13 References). (Reprinted in Item No. 32).
Compulsive stealing was eliminated in a ten-year-old boy using non-professionals in a field situation.

b. Token Economies

231 Aitchison, R. A., and Green, Donald R. "A token reinforcement system for large wards of institutionalized adolescents." Behav Res Ther 12(3): 181-90, September, 1974. (11 References).
Describes the use of a token economy system in a ward of fifty to sixty male and female juvenile offenders using a staff of only five psychiatric aides. Two target behaviors were selected: room maintenance and ward maintenance. The reinforcers used were already available in the hospital setting. There is some discussion of the importance and methods of obtaining the cooperation of the staff who are to administer such a program.

232 Ardoff, David G., and Weaver, Jerome F. Token economy at the classroom level. 1975. 49p. Available from ERIC Document Reproduction Service, P. O. Box 190, Arlington, Virginia 22210. (ED 113 917).
Evaluates a pilot study conducted with 116 delinquent boys. Improvements were noted in academic and social skills. A handbook is included that was produced as a result of the program.

233 Bednar, Richard L.; Zelhart, Paul F.; Greathouse, Larry; et al. "Operant conditioning principles in the treatment of learning and behavior problems with delinquent boys." J Couns Psychol 17(6): 492-97, 1970. (10 References).
In a test conducted with thirty-two delinquent adolescent boys, the subjects reinforced with monetary tokens showed significantly more improvement in reading skills than the subjects in the unreinforced group.

234 Carpenter, Patricia, and Caron, Robert. "Green stamp therapy: modification of delinquent behavior through food trading stamps." In: American Psychological Association, San Francisco, 76th, 1968. Proceedings. 531-32. (8 References).
Consists of preliminary report of a program in which green stamps were awarded to members of a boys' activity therapy group for such behaviors as attendance, promptness, and helpfulness.

235 Holt, Michael M.; Hobbs, Tom R.; Hankins, Ron. "Effects of token reinforcement on delinquent's classroom behavior." Psychol Sch 13(3): 341-47, 1976. (9 References).
Reports on a study conducted with nineteen delinquent boys in a correctional institution in which token reinforcement exerted noticeable control over total appropriate classroom behavior, but there were indications that the use of global, composite measures may have masked the program's effects on important component behaviors.

236 Karachi, Loren, and Levinson, Robert B. "A token economy in a correctional institution for youthful offenders." Howard J Penology Crime Prev 13: 20-30, 1970. (19 References). (Reprinted in Item No. 210).
Describes the operation of a token economy system, indicates the advantages, and provides a preliminary assessment of the results.

237 Staats, Arthur W., and Butterfield, William H. "Treatment of nonreading in a culturally deprived juvenile delinquent: an application of reinforcement principles." Child Dev 36(4): 925-42, 1965. (16 References). (Reprinted in Item No. 22).
Demonstrates the use of a token reinforcement system to develop reading skills in a culturally deprived delinquent fourteen-year-old boy. The materials used were adaptations of standard reading materials.

238 Tyler, Vernon O., Jr. "Application of operant token reinforcement to academic performance of an institutionalized delinquent." Psychol Rep 21(1): 249-60, August, 1967. (19 References).
Tokens earned with daily and weekly school grades were exchangeable for various items. Over a thirty-week period the boy's weekly grades improved slightly, but the teachers reported that the boy still disliked school.

239 Tyler, Vernon O., Jr., and Brown, G. Duane. "Token reinforcement of academic performance with institutionalized delinquent boys." J

Educ Psychol 59(3): 164-68, 1968. (15 References). (Reprinted in Item No. 37).
Furnishes the results of a study of fifteen institutionalized delinquent boys (ages thirteen to fifteen), which compared retention of material with a contingent and with a non-contingent reinforcement program. The study confirmed the hypothesis that test scores would be higher with contingency reinforcement.

240 Wilkinson, Leland, and Reppucci, N. Dickon. "Perceptions of social climate among participants in token economy and non-token economy cottages in a juvenile correctional institution." Am J Community Psychol 1(1): 36-43, 1973. (16 References).
Significant differences for both staff and residents were found between the two populations on most social climate variables.

3. Program Implementation with the Delinquent

a. General Aspects of Program Development

241 Burchard, John D. "Behavior modification with delinquents: some unforseen contingencies." Paper presented to the American Orthopsychiatric Association Convention, Washington, D.C., March 21-24, 1971. (ED 054 491).
Discusses several issues which hinder the success of programs. In particular are noted: (1) the need to relate programs on an empirical or analytical basis; (2) the need to focus on possible side effects which are incompatible with long-range goals; and (3) the need to focus on generalization.

242 Davidson, William S., and Robinson, Michael J. "Community psychology and behavior modification: a community-based program for the prevention of delinquency." Correct Soc Psychiatry J Behav Technol 21(1): 1-12, 1975. (28 References).
Describes a successful community-based non-residential program for predelinquents in which privileges were earned by a points system.

243 Fo, Walter S., and O'Donnell, Clifford R. "The buddy system: relationship and contingency conditions in a community intervention program for youth with nonprofessionals as behavior change agents." J Consult Clin Psychol 42(2): 163-69, April, 1974. (15 References). (Reprinted in Item No. 35).
Reports on the investigation of the efficacy of various treatment techniques employed in a community-based project which employed non-professionals in a buddy system for the modification of deviant behavior in youth. Buddies received initial and on-going training and supervision from behavior analysts. Systematic application of contingent rewards resulted in an increase in socially desirable behavior.

244 James, Ralph. "Behavior modification in court and community treatment programs for juvenile offenders." Paper presented at the American Psychological Association, 79th, September 3-7, 1971. Washington, D.C., 1971. 14p. (0 References).
Relates the details on a community-based program which utilized contingency contracting with written behavorial agreements entered into by both the boys and their parents.

245 McGovern, Kevin. "A behavioral approach to intervention." In: Browning, Philip L., ed. Rehabilitation and the retarded offender. Springfield, Illinois: Thomas, 1976. 179-93. (43 References).
Advocates treatment of adolescent offenders by the use of behavioral assessment and training in the community rather than in institutions.

246 Martin, Marian; Burkholder, Rachel; Rosenthal, Ted L. "Programming behavior change and reintegration into school milieux of extreme adolescent deviates." Behav Res Ther 6(3): 371-83, August, 1968. (17 References).
Addresses the problem of reintegrating the adolescent with deviant behavior into the regular classroom. Nine students, ranging in age from thirteen to eighteen years, were admitted to a special classroom where behavior modification, employing a token reinforcement system, was used. A carefully phased sequential system was developed to enable the students to re-enter the regular classroom. Follow-up indicates that four of the five students had made marked progress.

247 Rice, Ruth Dianne. "Educo-therapy: a new approach to delinquent behavior." J Learn Disabil 3(1): 16-23, 1970. (28 References).
Describes a program combining aspects of several different educational and psychological theories (including behavior modification) in the treatment of ten delinquent girls, ages eleven to sixteen.

248 Rose, Sheldon D.; Sundel, Martin; Delange, Janice; et al. "The Hartwig project: a behavioral approach to the treatment of juvenile offenders." In: Ulrich, Roger; Stachnik, Thomas; and Mabry, John, eds. Control of human behavior: Vol. 2. From cure to prevention. Glenview, Illinois: Scott, Foresman, 1970. 220-30.
Focuses on the results of a demonstration project in which behavioral techniques of several different kinds were used with a group of juvenile offenders, ranging in age from eight to sixteen years, over a period of two-and-one-half years.

b. Family Intervention Programs

249 Alexander, James F., and Parsons, Bruce V. "Short-term behavioral intervention with delinquent families: impact on family process and recidivism." J Abnorm Psychol 81(3): 219-25, June, 1973. (22 References). (Reprinted in Item No. 35).
Describes an intervention program conducted with forty-six families which was designed to: (1) assess family behaviors that maintain delinquent behavior; (2) modify communication patterns in the directions of greater clarity and precision, increased reciprocity, and presentation of alternative solutions; and (3) institute a pattern of contingency contracting within the family. Reduction in recidivism was demonstrated.

250 Bailey, Jon S. "Home-based reinforcement and the modification of pre-delinquents' classroom behavior." For a summary see: Diss Abstr Int 31B(6): 3720, December, 1970.

251 Bailey, Jon S.; Wolf, Montrose M.; Phillips, Elery L. "Home-based reinforcement and the modification of pre-delinquents' classroom behavior." J Appl Behav Anal 3(3): 223-33, Fall, 1970. (16 References).
Reports on three studies which demonstrated the effectiveness of reinforcers delivered at home for classroom study behavior and compliance with class rules.

252 Douds, Alexander F.; Engelsgjerd, Michael; Collingwood, Thomas R. "Behavior contracting with youthful offenders and their parents." Child Welfare 56(6): 409-17, June, 1977. (6 References).
Contains a detailed description of the use of behavior contracting in the Youth Services Program of the Dallas Police Department. This method has been effective in improving family relations and in reducing recidivism in juvenile offenders. An example of the "family management contract" is included.

253 Gant, Bobby Lee. "Assessment and modification of delinquent family interaction." For a summary see: Diss Abstr Int 38B(7): 3393, January, 1978.

254 Jayaratne, Srinika Devapriya. "The effect of contract-based behavioral intervention on some decision-making characteristics in delinquent families." For a summary see: Diss Abstr Int 36A(10): 6964, April, 1976.

255 Lipinski, Judith M., and Lawrence, P. Scott. "Reciprocal contracting with families of adolescents." Paper presented at the meeting of the Association for the Advancement of Behavior Therapy, Miami Beach, December, 1973. 29p. (15 References). (ED 101 222).
Presents the theoretical framework of exchange contracts and three pilot case studies. Possible problems are discussed and suggestions made on implementation procedures.

256 Parsons, Bruce V., Jr., and Alexander, James F. "Short-term family intervention: a therapy outcome study." J Consult Clin Psychol 41(2): 195-201, 1973. (35 References).
Documents an attempt to increase reciprocity, activity, and clarity in communication patterns of delinquent families.

257 Reid, John B. "A family intervention approach to delinquent behavior." In: Browning, Philip L., ed. Rehabilitation and the retarded offender. Springfield, Illinois: Thomas, 1976. 194-206. (24 References).
Outlines a program for pre-adolescents referred for aggressive out-of-control behavior, in which the parents were instructed in behavioral methods.

258 Shostak, David Arthur. "Family versus individual oriented behavior therapy as treatment approaches to juvenile delinquency." For a summary see: Diss Abstr Int 38B(7): 3474, January, 1978.

259 Stuart, Richard B. "Assessment and change of the communicational patterns of juvenile delinquents and their parents." In: Rubin, Richard D.; Fensterheim, Herbert; Lazarus, Arnold A.; et al., eds. Advances in behavior therapy: Vol. III. New York: Academic Press, 1971. 183-96. (47 References).
Presents three studies indicating that parent-adolescent interactions in families which have produced delinquents are significantly less positive than interactions in the families of non-delinquents, but that these aversive patterns can be systematically modified.

260 ————. "Behavioral contracting within the families of delinquents." J Behav Ther Exp Psychiatry 2(1): 1-11, 1971. (25 References). (Reprinted in Item Nos. 38, 43, 210).

Advocates the technique of behavioral contracting to strengthen family and school control over the behavior of delinquents. A detailed case history of a sixteen-year-old girl is included with examples of privileges, responsibilities, and monitoring forms.

261 Stuart, Richard B., and Lott, Leroy A., Jr. "Behavioral contracting with delinquents: a cautionary note." J Behav Ther Exp Psychiatry 3(3): 161-69, September, 1972. (17 References).
Sets forth details of a program conducted with seventy-nine pre-delinquent and delinquent youths and their families. Results indicate a need to structure treatment so as to reduce the impact of individual therapist characteristics, and for close attention to be paid to the tactics of service delivery.

262 Stuart, Richard B.; Tripodi, Tony; Jayaratne, Sirinika; *et al.* "An experiment in social engineering in serving the families of predelinquents." J Abnorm Child Psychol 4(3): 243-61, 1976. (34 References).
Behavioral contracting resulted in significant improvement on five measures: rating of school behavior by the person who had made the original referral, by the teachers, by the mother, and by the father, and the rating of parent-child interactions by the mother.

263 Stumphauzer, Jerome S. "Elimination of stealing by self-reinforcement of alternative behavior and family contracting." J Behav Ther Exp Psychiatry 7(3): 265-68, 1976. (12 References).
Long-standing stealing behavior was eliminated in a twelve-year-old girl by a combination of self-reinforcement of alternative behavior and family contracting.

264 Weathers, Lawrence, and Liberman, Robert Paul. "Contingency contracting with families of delinquent adolescents." Behav Ther 6(3): 356-66, 1975. (12 References).
Reports on a program of contingency contracting conducted with twenty-eight recidivistic delinquent adolescents and their parents. Results indicate that it was not an effective intervention strategy.

c. Residential Programs

265 Achievement Place: a model for delinquency treatment. Bethesda, Maryland: National Institute for Mental Health, Center for Studies of Crime and Delinquency. For sale by the Superintendent of Documents. Washington, D.C.: U.S. Government Printing Office, 1974. 7p. (DHEW Publication No. (ADM) 74-83).
Briefly describes an alternative approach to delinquency treatment based on a token reinforcement system.

266 Buehler, Roy E.; Patterson, Gerald R.; Furniss, Jean M. "The reinforcement of behavior in institutional settings." Behav Res Ther 4(3): 157-67, August, 1966. (13 References). (Reprinted in Item Nos. 32, 36, 210).
Analyzes the social reinforcers occurring among the inmates and the staff in institutions for delinquent children. Three studies indicate that the social living system tends to reinforce delinquent behavior.

267 Davidson, William S., II, and Wolfred, Timothy R. "Evaluation of a community-based behavior modification program for prevention of

delinquency: the failure of success." Community Ment Health J 13(4): 296-306, Winter, 1977. (30 References).
Examines the techniques used in a residential program for fifty-three pre-delinquent youth and evaluates the generalization of the effects from the treatment setting to natural settings. Doubts are raised concerning the long-term effectiveness of such a program and suggestions are made for further research.

268 Dickson, Andrew L.; Gonzalez, Jose M.; Shatus, Erwin L. "Using badges and tokens in a therapeutic society for adolescent boys." Hosp Community Psychiatry 26(6): 343-44, June, 1975. (0 References).
Details briefly the highly structured system of visible rewards given for appropriate behavior in a hospital setting.

269 Eitzen, D. Stanley. "Impact of behavior modification techniques on locus of control of delinquent boys." Psychol Rep 35(3): 1317-18, December, 1974. (8 References).
Relates the results of a study conducted with twenty-one juvenile delinquent boys in a residential treatment setting. The scores at post-test were significantly more internal than those at pre-test.

270 ————. "Self-concept of delinquents in a behavior modification treatment program." J Soc Psychol 99(2): 203-6, 1976. (4 References).
In a study using a questionnaire, the self-concept of sixteen delinquent boys was found to have improved at the completion of their stay in a residential behavior modification program.

271 Fineman, Kenneth R. "An operant conditioning program in a juvenile detention facility." Psychol Rep 22(3): 1119-20, June, 1968. (1 Reference).
Reports on a six-month exploratory study which demonstrated the effectiveness of a program based on a behavior contingent point system. Immediacy of reinforcement was believed to be a decisive factor in its success.

272 Fixsen, Dean L.; Phillips, Elery L.; Wolf, Montrose M. "Achievement Place: experiments in self-government with pre-delinquents." J Appl Behav Anal 6(1): 31-47, 1973. (18 References).
Seeks to analyze some of the variables that affect the youth's participation in establishing consequences for rule violations, and also to determine the role of the youths in reporting rule violations.

273 ————. "Achievement Place: the reliability of self-reporting and peer-reporting and their effects on behavior." J Appl Behav Anal 5(1): 19-30, 1972. (7 References).
Indicates that at least some boys are not naturally reliable observers and that the reliability of self-reporting and peer-reporting can be improved with appropriate contingencies.

274 Fixsen, Dean L.; Wolf, Montrose M.; Phillips, Elery L. "Achievement Place: a teaching family model of community-based group homes for youth in trouble." In: Hamerlynck, Leo A.; Handy, Lee C.; and Mash, Eric J., eds. Behavior change: methodology, concepts, and practice. Banff International Conference on Behavior Modification, 4th, 1972. Champaign, Illinois: Research Press, 1974. 241-68. (10 References).

Describes in detail an effective community-based treatment program for anti-social youths which consists of three basic parts: (1) a token economy; (2) the social behavior of the teacher/parents; and (3) a semi-self-government system.

275 Fodor, Iris E. "The use of behavior-modification techniques with female delinquents." Child Welfare 51(2): 93-101, February, 1972. (6 References).
Outlines an approach used in a training school for delinquent girls which focused on the establishment of self-control rates, rather than on changing environmental contingencies.

276 Hendrix, Clinton Eugene, Jr. "The effects of two behavioral approaches on modifying social behavior in incarcerated male delinquents." For a summary see: Diss Abstr Int 37B(1): 493, July, 1976.

277 Hobbs, Tom R., and Holt, Michael M. "The effects of token reinforcement on the behavior of delinquents in cottage settings." J Appl Behav Anal 9(2): 189-98, 1976. (36 References).
Presents data collected over a fourteen-month period on 125 adolescent males. Emphasis is placed on social behavior, rule following, and task completion.

278 Jones, Richard R. "Achievement Place: the independent evaluator's perspective." Paper presented at the Annual Convention of the American Psychological Association, 84th, Washington, D.C., September 3-7, 1976. 23p. (ED 136 104).
Describes the methodology used in the evaluation of relative effectiveness. Included are seven graphs and charts summarizing the criteria.

279 Liberman, Robert Paul; Ferris, Chris; Salgado, Paul; et al. "Replication of the Achievement Place model in California." J Appl Behav Anal 8(3): 287-99, Fall, 1975. (18 References).
Replicates successfully the study reported by Phillips, Elery L. (1968). (Item No. 282).

280 Meichenbaum, Donald H.; Bowers, Kenneth S.; Ross, Robert R. "Modification of classroom behavior of institutionalized female adolescent offenders." Behav Res Ther 6(3): 343-53, August, 1968. (8 References). (Reprinted in Item Nos. 21, 29, 210).
Demonstrates that high frequency inappropriate classroom behavior is susceptible to modification by operant procedures. The subjects were ten institutionalized female offenders. A highly reliable time-sampling assessment technique, which dichotomized classroom behavior into appropriate and inappropriate categories, was used. An operant procedure, using money as a reinforcer, was implemented over a three-week period, at the end of which time the subjects' classroom behavior was comparable to the behavior of the control group of non-institutionalized peers.

281 Meyer, Margrit; Odom, E. E.; Wax, Bernard S. "Birth and life of an incentive system in a residential institution for adolescents." Child Welfare 52(8): 503-9, October, 1973. (4 References).
Describes the implementation and results of a program conducted with disturbed and misbehaving adolescents.

282 Phillips, Elery L. "Achievement Place: token reinforcement procedures in a home-style rehabilitation setting for 'pre-delinquent' boys." J Appl Behav Anal 1(3): 213-23, 1968. (18 References). (Reprinted in Item Nos. 38, 40, 43, 47, 210).
Reports the successful use of token reinforcement procedures in modifying the behavior of three pre-delinquent adolescent boys in a residential setting. Tokens were awarded by the house parents for specific appropriate behaviors and were taken away for specific inappropriate behaviors. Back-up reinforcers were naturally available in the setting.

283 Phillips, Elery L.; Phillips, Elaine A.; Fixsen, Dean L.; et al. "Achievement Place: modification of the behaviors of pre-delinquent boys within a token economy." J Appl Behav Anal 4(1): 45-59, 1971. (8 References). (Reprinted in Item Nos. 28, 29).
Describes four experiments conducted with six pre-delinquent boys in a community-based center. Target behaviors were promptness at evening meals, room-cleaning, saving of money, and watching a television news program.

284 Phillips, Elery L.; Phillips, Elaine A.; Wolf, Montrose M.; et al. "Achievement Place: development of the elected manager system." J Appl Behav Anal 6(4): 541-61, 1973. (19 References). (Reprinted in Item No. 35).
Evaluates several different administrative systems. The system that best met the criteria of effectiveness and preference involved a democratically elected peer manager who had the authority both to give and take away points for his peers' performances.

285 Reppucci, N. Dickon. "Social psychology of institutional change: general principles for intervention." Am J Community Psychol 1(4): 330-41, October-December, 1973. (26 References).
Discusses principles for achieving total institutional change. Particular attention is paid to a state training school for male delinquents in which a rehabilitative program, based on social-learning principles, was implemented.

286 Seymour, Frederick W., and Stokes, Trevor F. "Self-recording in training girls to increase work and evoke praise in an institution for offenders." J Appl Behav Anal 9(1): 41-54, Spring, 1976. (11 References).
Reports on a study conducted with four adolescent girls using self-recording with back-up reinforcers.

287 Shatus, Erwin Lamar. "Treatment of disruptive classroom behavior in male, hospitalized delinquents using two covert procedures." For a summary see: Diss Abstr Int 34B(8): 4057, February, 1974.

288 Stumphauzer, Jerome S. "Modification of delay choices in institutionalized youthful offenders through social reinforcement." Psychon Sci 18(4): 222-23, February 24, 1970. (6 References). (Reprinted in Item No. 210).
The selection of long-term--as opposed to short-term--rewards by four nineteen-year-old inmates of a correctional institution was enhanced by the use of verbal approval.

289 Timbers, Gary Dean. "Achievement Place for girls: token reinforcement, social reinforcement and instructional procedures in a family-

style treatment setting for 'pre-delinquent' girls." For a summary see: Diss Abstr Int 35B(9): 4636, March, 1975.

290 Tyler, Vernon O., Jr., and Brown, G. Duane. "The use of swift, brief isolation as a group control device for institutionalized delinquents." Behav Res Ther 5(1): 1-9, February, 1967. (29 References). (Reprinted in Item No. 210).
Describes the use of a swift, fifteen-minute isolation in controlling the undesirable behavior of fifteen institutionalized delinquent boys, ages thirteen to fifteen. There was no "reward" for desirable behavior, and behavior deteriorated rapidly when sanctions were removed.

G. Drug Abuse

291 Coghlan, Alban J.; Gold, Steven R.; Dohrenwend, Edward F.; et al. "A psychobehavioral residential drug abuse program: a new adventure in adolescent psychiatry." Int J Addict 8(5): 767-77, 1973. (12 References).
Describes a residential program which integrates psychodynamic understanding and the principles of behavior modification in the treatment of drug-addicted adolescents. A case-history is included of a sixteen-year-old boy. A discussion of the implications for services to drug abusers completes the article.

292 Matefy, Robert E. "Behavior therapy to extinguish spontaneous recurrences of LSD effects: a case study." J Nerv Ment Dis 156(4): 226-31, April, 1973. (16 References).
Systematic desensitization was used in conjunction with other behavioral techniques in the treatment of a seventeen-year-old boy experiencing LSD flashbacks.

H. Eating

1. Development of Good Eating Habits

293 Hall, Jane S., and Holmberg, Margaret C. "The effect of teacher behaviors and food serving arrangements on young children's eating in a day care center." Child Care Q 3(2): 97-108, 1974. (4 References).
Instructions, teacher praise, and other contingencies were used to encourage eating of different kinds of food in two children (aged two years, eight months, and two years, seven months.).

294 Lovaas, O. Ivar. "Control of food intake in children by reinforcement of relevant verbal behavior." J Abnorm Soc Psychiatry 68(6): 672-78, 1964. (6 References).
A study conducted with sixteen nursery school children indicated that when positive reinforcement was associated with the verbal response denoting a food, then the consumption of that food increased.

295 Madsen, Charles H., Jr.; Madsen, Clifford K.; Thompson, Faith. "Increasing rural Head Start children's consumption of middle-class meals." J Appl Behav Anal 7(2): 257-62, Summer, 1974.
Demonstrates the use of edible rewards in the form of small candies and sugar-coated cereal, to increase the consumption of nutritional breakfasts by rural, black, economically impoverished Head Start children.

2. Eating Problems

296 Bernal, Martha E. "Behavioral treatment of a child's eating problem." J Behav Ther Exp Psychiatry 3(1): 43-50, 1972. (9 References).
Cites the use, over a period of twenty months, of successive approximation in the modification of a four-year-old girl's feeding behaviors which included a refusal to feed herself, and a refusal of certain foods. Reinforcers included social attention, preferred foods, and favorite television programs.

297 Palmer, Sushma; Thompson, Robert J., Jr.; Linscheid, Thomas R. "Applied behavior analysis in the treatment of childhood feeding problems." Dev Med Child Neurol 17(3): 333-39, June, 1975. (20 References).
Examines behavioral mismanagement as a cause of feeding problems. A case report of a six-year-old handicapped boy is documented.

298 Thompson, Robert J., Jr., and Palmer, Sushma. "Treatment of feeding problems -- a behavioral approach." J Nutr Educ 6(2): 63-66, April-June, 1974. (15 References).
Reports on the utilization of behavior modification to treat feeding problems in a preschool boy.

299 White, John Graham. "The use of learning theory in the psychological treatment of children." J Clin Psychol 15(2): 226-29, 1959. (14 References). (Reprinted in Item Nos. 30, 31).
Relates the case history of a five-and-one-half-year-old girl who had refused solid foods for three months, and in whom normal eating habits were re-established by means of the application of learning principles.

300 Wright, Logan. "Conditioning of consummatory responses in young children." J Clin Psychol 27(3): 416-19, July, 1971. (2 References).
Three female patients, between two and six years of age who refused to accept either fluids or solid foods, were subjected to conditioning programs involving operant techniques and shaping.

I. EMOTIONAL DISTURBANCE

1. Behavioral Handling of the Emotionally Disturbed Child

301 Arora, M., and Srinivasa, Murthy R. "Behavior therapy with children." Child Psychiatry Q 9(1): 1-13, 1976.
Reviews the principles and techniques of behavior therapy with psychologically disturbed children. Although recognition is given to the value of the methods, more research is advocated.

302 Auxter, David. "Operant conditioning of motor skills for the emotionally disturbed." Am Correct Ther J 23(1): 28-31, January-February, 1969. (4 References).
Documents the use of tokens and charts to enhance the development of physical and motor skills in a group of ten boys (ages nine to twelve years). Each of the boys exhibited some degree of emotional disturbance and there was a high degree of motor variability within the group.

303 Ayllon, Teodoro; Garber, Stephen W.; Allison, Mary G. "Behavioral treatment of childhood neurosis." Psychiatry 40(4): 315-22, November, 1977. (13 References).
Presents a case study of a four-year-old boy exhibiting neurotic symptoms. Therapy focused on changing the symptom-environment relationships experienced by the child by changing parental reaction to his behavior. Follow-ups at two months and two years indicated that the child was symptom-free.

304 Browning, Robert M., and Stover, Donald O. Behavior modification in child treatment: an experimental and clinical approach. Chicago: Aldine/Atherton, 1971. 422p. (Modern Applications in Psychology Series).
Advocates the use of a scientific approach to clinical practice. This volume offers considerable detail on methods of measurement, treatment designs, techniques, and the values of social reinforcers. Detailed case histories of five disturbed children are included, together with the form of treatment used with them at a treatment center.

305 Delfini, Leo F.; Bernal, Martha E.; Rosen, Paul M. "Comparison of deviant and normal boys in home settings." In: Mash, Eric J.; Hamerlynck, Leo A.; and Handy, Lee C., eds. Behavior modification and families. Banff International Conference on Behavior Modification, 6th, 1974. New York: Brunner/Mazel, 1976. 228-48. (12 References).
Compares the behavior of twenty-one deviant and twenty-one normal kindergarten and first-grade boys in the home setting using naturalistic observation methods. The deviant group was found to exhibit a significantly higher rate of disruptive behavior.

306 Ferster, Charles B. "Clinical reinforcement." Semin Psychiatry 4(2): 101-11, May, 1972. (15 References).
Analyzes the dynamics of positive reinforcement with examples from child therapy. The conclusion is drawn that its use should be instrumental in achieving client-oriented, non-arbitrary, and uncoercive clinical practice.

307 Forness, Steven R., and MacMillan, Donald L. "The origins of behavior modification with exceptional children." Except Child 37(2): 93-100, October, 1970. (44 References). (Reprinted in Item No. 25).
Traces the history of behavior modification from the early twenties through the sixties. Emphasis is placed on the modification of deviant behavior in children.

308 Garner, Howard G. "A truce in the 'war for the child.'" Except Child 42(6): 315-20, March, 1976. (22 References).
Advocates a combination of behavior modification techniques and the more traditional psychodynamic interventions.

309 Jodrell, Ruth D., and Sanson-Fisher, Robert. "Basic concepts of behavior therapy: an experiment involving disturbed adolescent girls." Am J Occup Ther 29(10): 620-24, 1975. (10 References).
Summarizes the basic principles and approaches of behavior therapy and describes their use in teaching social skills to disturbed adolescent girls.

310 Johansson, Mary Ann Latvala. "Evaluation of group therapy with children: a behavioral approach." For a summary see: Diss Abstr Int 34B(7): 3499, January, 1974.

311 Lehrer, Paul M., and Kris, Anton O. "Combined use of behavioral and psychoanalytic approaches in the treatment of severely disturbed adolescents." Semin Psychiatry 4(2): 165-70, May, 1972. (41 References).
Argues that behavior therapy provides a direct and systematic approach in the non-verbal and verbal control of behavior that can facilitate the patient's emotional growth.

312 Lewis, Wilbert W. "From Project Re-ed to ecological planning." Phi Delta Kappan 55(8): 538-40, April, 1974. (0 References).
Describes a program that combined features of therapy and behavior modification and centered on the social consequences of a disturbed child's behavior.

313 Lillesand, Diane B. "A behavioral-psychodynamic approach to day treatment for emotionally disturbed children." Child Welfare 56(9): 613-19, November, 1977. (4 References).
Details are given on a low-cost, short-term day treatment program for emotionally disturbed children that combined behavioral and psychodynamic techniques. The program proved successful in returning children to public school classes.

314 Rachman, S. "Learning theory and child psychology: therapeutic possibilities." J Child Psychol Psychiatry 3(3/4): 149-63, 1962. (79 References).
Reviews the applications of learning theory to child psychology prior to 1962. Most of the articles deal with the elimination of unadaptive behavior.

315 Ross, Alan O. "Learning theory and therapy with children." Psychotherapy 1(3): 102-8, May, 1964. (27 References).
Examines theoretical and practical implications and indicates the amount of research still required.

316 Sherman, James A., and Baer, Donald M. "Appraisal of operant therapy techniques with children and adults." In: Franks, C. M., ed. Behavior therapy: appraisal and status. New York: McGraw-Hill, 1969. 192-219.
Surveys behavior therapy literature dealing with the use of operant conditioning procedures to modify deviant, disruptive, or maladaptive human behavior.

317 Werry, John S., and Wollersheim, Janet P. "Behavior therapy with children: a broad overview." J Am Acad Child Psychiatry 6(2): 346-70, April, 1967. (96 References).
Reviews the concepts and techniques of behavior therapy, as well as the types of maladaptive behavior in children with which the techniques may be effective.

2. Techniques with the Emotionally Disturbed Child

a. Specific Techniques

318 Campbell, Lowell M., III. "A variation of thought-stopping in a twelve-year-old boy: a case report." J Behav Ther Exp Psychiatry 4(1): 69-70, 1974. (5 References). (Reprinted in Item No. 35).
A twelve-year-old boy was taught a thought-stopping technique in order to eliminate morbid rumination on the death of his sister. Treatment was successfully concluded within a four-week period.

319 Carlin, Albert S., and Armstrong, Hubert E. "Rewarding social responsibility in disturbed children: a group play technique." Psychotherapy 5(3): 169-74, Fall, 1968. (6 References).
Provides details of the treatment program for a group of severely disturbed preadolescent boys. The program involved teaching the children that the behavior of other group members is partially their own responsibility. A token reinforcement of social participation was utilized.

320 Clement, Paul W. "Operant conditioning in group psychotherapy with children." J Sch Health 38(5): 271-78, May, 1968. (Reprinted in Item No. 47).
Describes the use made of operant conditioning techniques in several group situations and in one case of individualized therapy. Positive behaviors were generally reinforced with candy.

321 ————. "Training children to be their own behavior therapists." J Sch Health 43(10): 615-20, December, 1973. (16 References).
Reviews articles dealing with behavioral self-regulation in children. Included is a case history of a fourth-grade boy with multiple behavior problems.

322 Coon, Robert C.; Escandell, Vincent A.; Coon, Kathryn B.; et al. "Using an academic peer interaction contingency with emotionally disturbed children." J Exp Educ 44(3): 17-20, Spring, 1976. (9 References).
The addition of peer-oriented contingencies to an on-going token economy resulted in positive changes in interpersonal interactions within the classroom.

323 Drabman, Ronald; Spitalnik, Robert; Hagamen, Mary B.; et al. "The Five-Two Program: an integrated approach to treating severely disturbed children." Hosp Community Psychiatry 24(1): 33-36, January, 1973.
Describes a program which relies heavily on operant conditioning techniques. Following short-term hospitalization, the child is gradually returned to living with the family. The parents are instructed in operant conditioning methods, and the child may also attend a school which employs the same techniques.

324 Geibink, John; Stover, Donald; Fahl, Mary Ann. "Teaching adaptive responses to frustration to emotionally disturbed boys." J Consult Clin Psychol 32(3): 366-68, 1968. (1 Reference).
Six boys, ages ten to twelve, in a residential treatment center, were taught alternative responses to frustration by means of a game which simulated frustrating situations.

325 Hauserman, Norma; Zweback, Stanley; Plotkin, Alan. "Use of concrete reinforcement to facilitate verbal initiations in adolescent group therapy." J Consult Clin Psychol 38(1): 90-96, 1972. (19 References).
Token reinforcement was successfully used with six hospitalized adolescents. Social peer pressure resulted in "relevant-irrelevant" verbal discrimination.

326 Hobbs, Steven Alan. "Effects of duration of timeout on targeted and non-targeted deviant child behaviors." For a summary see: Diss Abstr Int 37B(12): 6328, June, 1977.

327 Kubany, Edward S., and Sloggett, Barbara. "Behavior therapy approach to office diagnosis and treatment of children." Prof Psychol 7(4): 525-32, November, 1976. (18 References).
Outlines techniques used by the authors in dealing with child patients exhibiting various maladaptive behaviors.

328 Laws, D. Richard; Brown, Richard A.; Epstein, Jordan; et al. "Reduction of inappropriate social behavior in disturbed children by an untrained paraprofessional therapist." Behav Ther 2(4): 519-33, 1971. (28 References).
Stereotyped mannerisms, inattention, and inappropriate verbalizations were reduced and appropriate social and verbal responses were increased by a paraprofessional working under minimal but highly directive supervision.

329 Lazarus, Arnold A. "Learning principles in the treatment of disturbed children." In: Lazarus, Arnold A., ed. Behavior therapy and beyond. New York: McGraw-Hill, 1971. 201-15.
Outlines specific modes of intervention in the treatment of childhood problems such as autism, anxiety, and low self-esteem.

330 Liston, Walter. "Mobius strips, Perquackey, and the Dutch Chocolate Apple." Paper presented at the meeting of the American Personnel and Guidance Association, San Diego, February 9-12, 1973. 39p. (37 References). (ED 080 921).
Advocates the use of behavior therapy with adolescents. The use of behavioral contracts is seen to be especially effective.

331 McKenzie, Thomas L., and Rushall, Brent S. "Effects of self-recording on attendance and performance in a competitive swimming training environment." J Appl Behav Anal 7(2): 199-206, Summer, 1974. (13 References).
Demonstrates the effectiveness of reinforcement contingencies in controlling problem behaviors in a sporting environment. Attendance was improved and work output was increased by the use of a publicly displayed program board.

332 Monkman, Marjorie McQueen. A milieu therapy program for behaviorally disturbed children. Springfield, Illinois: Thomas, 1972. 293p. (Bibliography).
Traces the development and implementation of an experimental, residential treatment program employing behavior modification methods for mentally retarded and/or emotionally disturbed children. Appendices include descriptions of staff roles, examples of report forms, and detailed treatment programs.

333 Murray, Vincent D'Arcy. "Behavior modification: a comparison of a fixed-ratio with a variable-ratio schedule of reinforcement on adolescents in a residential setting." For a summary see: Diss Abstr Int 36A(4): 2137, October, 1975.

334 Nelson, C. Michael; Worell, Judith; Polsgrove, Lewis. "Behaviorally disordered peers as contingency managers." Behav Ther 4(2): 270-76, 1973. (16 References).
Reports on a study conducted in a summer camp in which peer management was successful in changing the target behavior of the protege in eight out of nine cases.

335 Patterson, G. R. "A basis for identifying stimuli which control behaviors in natural settings." Child Dev 45(4): 900-911, 1974. (23 References).
Offers procedures for identifying stimuli in the natural environment, the presence of which were associated with altered probabilities for both the initiation and persistence of noxious responses.

336 ————. "Interventions for boys with conduct problems: multiple settings, treatments, and criteria." J Consult Clin Psychol 42(4): 471-81, August, 1974. (49 References).
Summarizes the outcome of procedures for intervention and data collection in the home for twenty-seven boys referred for conduct problems. At termination and follow-up, the data showed significant reductions in problem behaviors.

337 Piturro, Marlene Cohen. "The modification of behavior and self-report as a function of group contingencies in institutionalized dependent and neglected children." For a summary see: Diss Abstr Int 35B(5): 2442, November, 1974.

338 Reichle, Joe; Brubakker, David; Tetreault, George. "Eliminating perserverative speech by positive reinforcement and time-out in a psychotic child." J Behav Ther Exp Psychiatry 7(2): 179-83, 1976. (24 References).
Reinforcement, time-out, and combined reinforcement-time-out contingencies were used to extinguish perseverative verbal behavior in a five-year, nine-month-old psychotic boy in a short-term residential center.

339 Rosenberg, Harry E., and Graubard, Paul. "Peer use of behavior modification." Focus Except Child 7(6): 1-10, 1975. (6 References).
Children exhibiting deviant behavior were trained in behavior modification techniques. The children were then able to use the techniques on "normal" children and on adults in order to improve their relationships with them.

340 Ross, Andrew L. "Combining behavior modification and group work techniques in a day treatment center." Child Welfare 53(7): 435-44, July, 1974. (6 References).
Documents the effective combination of techniques in the treatment of emotionally disturbed children.

341 Rossman, Paul G., and Knesper, David J. "The early phase of hospital treatment for disruptive adolescents: the integration of behavioral and dynamic techniques." J Am Acad Clin Psychiatry 15(4): 693-708, Autumn, 1976. (18 References).

Presents two case histories in which socially appropriate behavior was reinforced. Emphasis is placed on the complementarity between the initial use of behavioral treatment strategies and the subsequent psychotherapy.

342 Sachs, David A. "The efficacy of time-out procedures in a variety of behavior problems." J Behav Ther Exp Psychiatry 4(3): 237-42, 1973. (4 References).
Variations of time-out from reinforcement were used with three emotionally disturbed children, in the contexts of self-stimulative and inappropriate behaviors. These were visibly efficient methods of controlling undesirable behavior.

343 Scarboro, Millard Eugene. "An investigation of the effects of response-contingent ignoring and isolation on the compliance and oppositional behavior in children." For a summary see: Diss Abstr Int 35B(8): 4195, February, 1975.

344 Simkins, Lawrence D. "Modification of duration of peer interactions in emotionally disturbed children." J Soc Psychol 84(2): 287-99, August, 1971. (9 References).
Investigates the variables that may be associated with the acquisition and maintenance of social interactions in a group of emotionally disturbed children. The subjects were eight girls, ages nine to twelve years, in a residential school.

345 Stabler, Brian, and Warren, Ann B. "Behavioral contracting in treating trichotillomania: case report." Psychol Rep 34(2): 401-2, April, 1974. (8 References).
Hair-pulling was markedly reduced, within a period of seven days, in a fourteen-year-old girl with a two-year history of trichotillomania.

346 Turner, Ruby. "A method of working with disturbed children." Am J Nurs 70(10): 2146-51, October, 1970. (7 References).
Reports on the use of behavior modification techniques in the team treatment of five psychotic children. Two case histories are documented.

347 Wagner, Mervyn K. "A case of public masturbation treated by operant conditioning." J Child Psychol Psychiatry 9(1): 61-65, 1968. (8 References).
Compulsive masturbation in an eleven-year-old girl was treated by her teacher's use of positive reinforcement for an incompatible response.

348 Wahler, Robert G. "Some ecological problems in child behavior modification." In: Bijou, Sidney W., and Ribes-Inesta, Emilio, eds. Behavior modification: issues and extensions. New York: Academic Press, 1972. 7-18. (32 References).
Outlines the procedures involved in the assessment and treatment of deviant child behavior as it occurs in natural settings. Emphasis is placed on the importance of and the difficulties surrounding generalization.

349 Wahler, Robert G., and Cormier, William H. "The ecological interview: a first step in out-patient child behavior therapy." J Behav Ther Exp Psychiatry 1(4): 279-89, 1970. (16 References). (Reprinted in Item No. 44).
Describes the ecological interview in detail, with particular reference to its mapping function. Emphasis is placed on the educational aspects of the interview for the client.

350 Weeks, Philip. "Abnormal emotional reaction in an adolescent." Nurs Times 69(45): 1485-87, November 8, 1973. (0 References).
Presents a case history in which a reward system was used to improve the behavior of a disturbed fifteen-year-old girl.

351 Wilhelm, Kurt. "The effects of peer reinforcement on conforming behaviors of normal and emotionally disturbed children." For a summary see: Diss Abstr Int 37A(8): 5008, February, 1976.

352 Zide, Barry, and Pardoe, Russel. "Use of behavior modification therapy in a recalcitrant burned child." Plast Reconstr Surg 57(3): 378-81, 1976. (12 References).
Presents the case report of a thirteen-year-old boy for whom a weekly point system was devised to deal with his manipulative behavior.

b. Aversion

353 Alderton, Harvey R. "The role of punishment in the inpatient treatment of psychiatrically disturbed children." Can Psychiatr Assoc J 12(1): 17-24, February, 1967. (18 References).
Reviews the reported effects of punishment on behavior and considers the psychological functions necessary before punishment can have the intended effects. It is concluded that punishment is an ineffective treatment technique for seriously disturbed children.

354 Kolvin, Israel. "'Aversive imagery' treatment in adolescents." Behav Res Ther 5(3): 245-48, August, 1967. (9 References). (Reprinted in Item No. 21).
Describes the use of aversive imagery in the treatment of intellectually dull and verbally unforthcoming adolescents. Details of two cases are given, one involving fetishism and the other an addiction to sniffing gasoline.

355 MacCulloch, M. J.; Williams, C.; Birtles, C. J. "The successful application of aversion therapy to an adolescent exhibitionist." J Behav Ther Exp Psychiatry 2(1): 61-66, March, 1971. (17 References). (Reprinted in Item Nos. 43, 210).
Describes the use of anticipatory avoidance aversion therapy in the treatment of a twelve-year-old exhibitionist.

356 Simmons, James Q., III, and Reed, Barbara Jean. "Therapeutic punishment in severely disturbed children." Curr Psychiatr Ther 9: 11-18, 1969. (18 References).
Reviews the literature on therapeutic punishment. Emphasis is placed on the importance of the clear definition of the unacceptable behaviors, the immediacy with which the aversive stimulation is applied, and the provision of an alternative acceptable behavior which earns a positive reward. A case history is included.

c. Token Economies

357 Ayllon, Teodoro, and Azrin, Nathan H. The token economy: a motivational system for therapy and rehabilitation. New York: Appleton-Century-Crofts, 1968. 288p. (Bibliography). (Century Psychology Series).
Contains detailed procedures for establishing and maintaining a token economy system in an institutional setting. The volume is addressed

primarily to practitioners in such a setting and assumes no background in psychology. Although dealing primarily with adults, some of the procedures are applicable to children.

358 Birnbrauer, J. S., and Lawler, Julia. "Token reinforcement for learning." Ment Retard 2(5): 275-79, October, 1964. (13 References).
Describes a token economy system employed with fifty-four behaviorally and/or academically disabled children in two special classrooms. Tokens are preferred to other reinforcers such as trinkets and edibles. A plan for "weaning" pupils from tokens is outlined.

359 Dettweiler, Lawrence E.; Acker, Margaret A.; Guthrie, Barnaby F.; et al. "Toward a community approach to behavior modification with emotionally disturbed children." In: Thompson, Travis, and Dockens, Williams S., III, eds. Applications of behavior modification. New York: Academic Press, 1975. 265-84. (5 References).
Deals with the use of a token economy system in a residential setting for disturbed children in which it was found necessary to change the behavior of the staff and parents. An outline history of six children is presented together with a detailed case history of a six-year-old boy.

360 Marks, Isaac M.; Cameron, Paul M.; Silberfeld, Michel. "Operant therapy for an abnormal personality." Br Med J 1(750): 647-48, March 20, 1971.
Presents a case report of a girl exhibiting severely abnormal behavior who was successfully treated by a token system. Tokens were earned initially by attempts at social interactions and later by the performance of tasks involving more responsibility.

361 Pitta, Patricia Joyce. "Effects of token reinforcement on modifying instruction-following behaviors in emotionally disturbed children." For a summary see: Diss Abstr Int 36A(3): 1400, September, 1975.

362 Santogrossi, David A.; O'Leary, K. Daniel; Romanczyk, Raymond G.; et al. "Self-evaluation by adolescents in a psychiatric hospital school token program." J Appl Behav Anal 6(2): 277-87, Summer, 1973. (17 References).
Reports on the use of token reinforcement program, administered by a teacher, which resulted in the reduction of disruptive behavior in nine adolescent psychiatric patients. Rewarded self-evaluation resulted in a return to former rates of disruptive behavior.

363 Schwarz, Michael L., and Hawkins, Robert P. "Application of delayed reinforcement procedures to the behavior of an elementary school child." J Appl Behav Anal 3(2): 85-96, Summer, 1970. (12 References).
Documents the use of tokens exchangeable for gifts to modify three specific behaviors (face-touching, posture, and voice-loudness) in a mildly maladjusted sixth-grade girl.

364 Wagner, Bernard R., and Breitmeyer, Rudolf G. "PACE: a residential community oriented behavior modification program for adolescents." Adolescence 10(38): 277-86, Summer, 1975. (20 References).
Reviews token systems for adolescents and describes a residential behavior modification program for emotionally disturbed predelinquent, and mentally retarded adolescents. Follow-up results are included.

365 Willis, Jerry. "Contingent token reinforcement in an educational program for emotionally disturbed children." In: Rickard, Henry C., and Dinoff, Michael, eds. Behavior modification in children. Tuscaloosa, Alabama: University of Alabama Press, 1974. 157-70.
Evaluates a token reinforcement system that was utilized with thirty-six children in a camp for emotionally disturbed children. The group receiving contingent token reinforcement performed better than the other groups throughout the twenty-six days of the experiment.

3. Program Implementation with the Emotionally Disturbed Child

a. Family Intervention Programs

366 Ayllon, Teodoro, and Skuban, William. "Accountability in psychotherapy: a test case." J Behav Ther Exp Psychiatry 4(1): 19-30, 1973. (33 References). (Reprinted in Item No. 35).
Documents a case history of an emotionally disturbed eight-year-old boy with whose parents a contractual agreement for treatment was made. The use of such therapeutic contracts is advocated in order to foster confidence on the part of the parents and the patient, and accountability on the part of the therapist.

367 Barten, Harvey H., and Barten, Sybil S., eds. Children and their parents in brief therapy. New York: Behavioral Publications, 1973. 323p. (Bibliography).
Consists of a collection of papers reporting a variety of innovative experiments with short-term treatment of children and their parents. Two papers deal specifically with behavior modification techniques.

368 Fine, Stuart. "Family therapy and a behavioral approach to childhood obsessive-compulsive neurosis." Arch Gen Psychiatry 28(5): 695-97, May, 1973.
Describes two cases of childhood obsessive-compulsive neurosis treated by a combined approach of extinguishing the rituals by interrupting them and by brief family psychotherapy. Families seemed to obtain mutual support from being interviewed together.

369 Herbert, Emily W.; Pinkston, Elsie M.; Hayden, M. Loeman; et al. "Adverse effects of differential parental attention." J Appl Behav Anal 6(1): 15-30, Spring, 1973. (21 References). (Reprinted in Item No. 35).
Traces the apparent increase in undesirable behaviors in four out of five deviant children treated with differential parental attention. A careful evaluation of operant techniques is recommended for all service programs.

370 Mealiea, Wallace L., Jr. "Conjoint-behavior therapy: the modification of family constellations." In: Mash, Eric J.; Handy, Lee C.; and Hamerlynck, Leo A., eds. Behavior modification approaches to parenting. Banff International Conference on Behavior Modification, 6th, 1974. New York: Brunner/Mazel, 1976. 152-66. (29 References).
Assesses an attempt to combine marital therapy for parents and behavior therapy for the children in the family. Five case histories are included.

371 O'Leary, K. Daniel, and Kent, Ronald N. "A behavioral consultation program for parents and teachers of children with conduct problems." In: Spitzer, Robert L., and Klein, Donald F., eds. Evaluation of psychological therapies. Baltimore, Maryland: Johns Hopkins University Press, 1976. 89-95.
Evaluates a behavioral treatment program conducted on an outpatient basis.

372 O'Leary, K. Daniel; Turkewitz, Hillary; Taffel, Suzanne J. "Parent and therapist evaluation of behavior therapy in a child psychological clinic." J Consult Clin Psychol 41(2): 279-83, October, 1973. (8 References). (Reprinted in Item No. 35).
Focuses on the description of their child's problems by the parents, who were required to indicate improvements on a seven-point scale rather than by giving a narrative rating. There was a high rate of agreement between parents and therapists.

373 Swenson, Carl R. "Intervention strategies and procedures for helping parents of severely emotionally disturbed children in home settings." Paper presented at the 55th Annual International Convention, The Council for Exceptional Children, Atlanta, April 11-15, 1977. 27p. (ED 139 149).
Describes the parent training component of an adjustment program for severely emotionally disturbed school-aged children. Three case studies are presented illustrating the application of plan sheets, token reinforcement procedures, and a multipurpose reporting system.

374 Wahler, Robert G. "Deviant child behavior within the family: developmental speculations and behavior change strategies." In: Leitenberg, Harold, ed. Handbook of behavior modification and behavior therapy. Englewood Cliffs, New Jersey: Prentice-Hall, 1976. 516-43. (100 References).
Summarizes the research dealing with the family within which a child displays deviant behavior. The reports are grouped by deviance categories, e.g., oppositional behavior, age-inappropriate behavior, cross-gender behavior, etc., and by assessment and intervention strategies. Attention is drawn to the problems of maintenance of behavior change encountered by many researchers.

375 Wiltz, N. A. "Behavioral therapy techniques in treatment of emotionally disturbed children and their families." Child Welfare 52(8): 483-92, October, 1973. (6 References).
Describes a program for the assessment of and the planning of treatment for emotionally disturbed children in a natural setting. It is emphasized that a division of interactions into fine components is a basic element of the behavioral approach to child and family therapy.

b. Residential Programs

376 Bardill, Donald R. "A behavior-contracting program of group treatment for early adolescents in a residential treatment setting." Int J Group Psychother 27(3): 389-400, July, 1977. (7 References).
Considers the behavior-contracting procedures initiated as part of a larger group therapy program. The subjects were boys ranging in age from nine to fourteen years, most of whom had experienced severe emotional and economic deprivation. Points earned were converted into money and off-campus outings.

377 Case, Paul S. "A systems approach to modifying behavior in a children's residential center." Child Care Q 5(1): 35-41, 1976.
Reports on the use of behavioral techniques in a residential treatment center for boys between the ages of six and fifteen, presenting a variety of emotional, behavioral, and educational problems. The use of the Daily Behavior Rating System is advocated.

378 Davids, Anthony, and Berenson, Jon K. "Integration of a behavior modification program into a traditionally oriented residential treatment center for children." J Autism Child Schizo 7(3): 269-85, September, 1977. (7 References).
Discusses the positive and negative aspects of introducing a behavior modification program into a traditional setting. Case studies are included, together with a description of the current status of a program which incorporates psychodynamic and behavioral approaches, medication, special education, and parental training.

379 Dinwiddie, F. William. "Humanistic behaviorism: a model for rapprochement in residential treatment milieus." Child Psychiatry Hum Dev 5(4): 254-59, Summer, 1975. (2 References).
Advocates a blending of medical and applied behavior analysis models to achieve the most effective treatment in residential centers.

380 Gold, Margaret Rona. "Cottage Seven: intended and unintended consequences of a behavior modification program." For a summary see: Diss Abstr Int 37B(4): 1969, October, 1976.

381 Heiner, Hans. "Self-control in individual and group behavior modification programs for emotionally disturbed children." In: Thompson, Travis, and Dockens, William S., III, eds. Applications of behavior modification. New York: Academic Press, 1975. 285-98. (23 References).
Describes a behavior modification program at a residential treatment center for emotionally disturbed children. Active participation of the child in the planning of a program is advocated in order to foster the development of self-control.

382 Jansma, Paul. "Behavior modification principles applied to male adolescents by a physical educator in a mental hospital." For a summary see: Diss Abstr Int 33A(6): 2751, December, 1972.

383 Laufer, Charles Davis. "Behavior modification as a psychotherapeutic treatment modality in a residential school for emotionally disturbed children: a field study of the process of program implementation." For a summary see: Diss Abstr Int 37B(2): 976, August, 1976.

384 Lehrer, Paul; Schiff, Lawrence; Kris, Anton. "Operant conditioning in a comprehensive treatment program for adolescents." Arch Gen Psychiatry 25(6): 515-21, December, 1971.
Describes the use of a twenty-four-hour a day operant conditioning program--including a token economy system--with adolescent mental patients. The techniques were used in the classroom, on the wards, and at home following parental instruction, and in conjunction with psychotherapy. Five case histories are cited.

385 Millman, Howard L., and Schaefer, Charles E. "Behavioral change: program evaluation and staff feedback." Child Welfare 54(10): 692-702, December, 1975. (8 References).
Offers a program for the systematic evaluation of a residential treatment system for boys with behavioral and learning problems. The subjects were rated every six months, and the data were analyzed and summarized for the staff members who were then able to study the subjects' behavior in relation to that of their peers.

386 Pizzat, Frank J. Behavior modification in residential treatment for children: a model of a program. New York: Behavioral Publications, 1973. 98p.
Sets forth a program for the establishment of behavior modification procedures in a residential center providing treatment for children with emotional and/or behavioral problems. Descriptions are included of organization, implementation, staff training, and evaluation.

387 Scallon, Richard J.; Vitale, James; Eschenauer, Robert. "Behavior modification in a residence and school for adolescent boys: a team approach." Child Welfare 55(8): 561-71, September-October, 1976. (1 Reference).
Emphasizes the necessity for close communication and cooperation between educators and child care workers in the implementation of a program for boys with learning and behavior problems.

388 Shafer, John, Jr., and Hansen, Steven V. "Using behavior therapy with selected adolescent patients." Hosp Community Psychiatry 24(1): 30-32, January, 1973. (1 Reference).
Describes the establishment of a behavior modification program in a maximum security unit of a psychiatric hospital. Nurses and aides were reported to be enthusiastic about the rapid behavior changes of the patients.

389 Tansey, David Arthur. "Prediction of degree of success in an adolescent modified token economy from WISC, HSPQ, and demographic data." For a summary see: Diss Abstr Int 35B(10): 5141, April, 1975.

J. ENCOPRESIS

390 Bach, Roger, and Moylan, Joseph J. "Parents administer behavior therapy for inappropriate urination and encopresis: a case study." J Behav Ther Exp Psychiatry 6(3): 239-41, October, 1975. (7 References).
The parents of a six-year-old boy administered money rewards for appropriate toilet behavior and ignored soiling.

391 Balson, Paul M. "Case study: encopresis: a case with symptom substitution?" Behav Ther 4(1): 134-36, January, 1973. (8 References).
Examines the case of an eight-year-old boy in whom the appearance of temper tantrums following behavioral treatment for encopresis might be labeled symptom substitution.

392 Cashmore, G. R. "The reduction of soiling behaviour in an eleven-year-old boy with the parent as therapist." NZ Med J 84(572): 238-39, September 22, 1976. (4 References).
Daily soiling behavior of six years' duration was effectively reduced by the use of a chart with contingent rewards for non-soiling behavior.

393 Conger, Judy Cohen. "The treatment of encopresis by the management of social consequences." Behav Ther 1(3): 386-90, August, 1970. (7 References).

Encopresis was eliminated in a nine-year-old boy by means of withdrawal of maternal attention and physical contact, contingent upon soiling behavior.

394 Davis, Hilton; Mitchell, William S.; Marks, Frances. "A behavioral programme for the modification of encopresis." Child Care Health Dev 2(5): 273-82, September-October, 1976.

Describes a program implemented by the parents in the home setting. The success of the methods with seven of eleven subjects is reported, together with the possible reasons for the lack of success with the other four children.

395 Davis, H. M.; Marks, F. M.; Mitchell, W. S. "Pilot study of encopretic children treated by behavior modification." Practitioner 219 (1310): 228-30, August, 1977. (4 References).

Characterizes eleven encopretic children and reports the results of a program administered by the parents. Treatment was successful in seven of the eleven children. Behavioral techniques for this disorder are advocated provided the parents are well motivated and have sufficient control of the child.

396 Edelman, Robert I. "Operant conditioning of encopresis." J Behav Ther Exp Psychiatry 2(1): 71-73, March, 1971. (6 References).

A twelve-year-old encopretic girl was treated by a combination of punishment for soiling behavior and reward for non-soiling behavior.

397 Ferinden, William, Jr., and Van Handel, Donald. "Elimination of soiling behavior in an elementary school child through the application of aversive techniques." J Sch Psychol 8(4): 267-69, 1970. (2 References).

Presents a case study illustrating the use of aversive techniques in a school setting. The soiling behavior of a seven-year-old boy was corrected by requiring him to clean himself and make up lost school time.

398 Gelber, H., and Meyer, V. "Behavior therapy and encopresis: the complexities involved in treatment." Behav Res Ther 2(3): 227-31, August, 1965. (7 References).

Reports on the successful in-patient treatment of encopresis in a thirteen-year-old boy of normal intelligence. The therapy was completed in sixty-two days and consisted primarily of rewarding appropriate defecation with free-time.

399 Harvey, D. H. P. "Re-instatement of regular defecation routines in a four-year-old boy." NZ Med J 84(572): 236-38, September 22, 1976. (5 References).

A program of positive reinforcement contingent upon being placed on the toilet and immediate positive reinforcement for bowel movements was successful in re-establishing regular defecation.

400 Johnson, James H., and Van Bourgondien, Mary E. "Behavior-therapy and encopresis: a selective review of the literature." J Clin Child Psychol 6(1): 15-19, Spring, 1977. (26 References).

Considers the general nature of childhood encopresis and reviews the literature. Few controlled studies were found, but a number of published case reports indicate that behavioral approaches may be of value in treating the encopretic child. Suggestions are made for future research.

401 Kohlenberg, Robert J. "Operant conditioning of human anal sphincter pressure." J Appl Behav Anal 6(2): 201-8, Summer, 1973. (6 References).
Reports on the use of monetary reinforcement to aid in the development of anal sphincter pressure in a thirteen-year-old encopretic boy.

402 Logan, Daniel L., and Garner, Diane. "Effective behavior modification for reducing chronic soiling." Am Ann Deaf 116(3): 382-84, June, 1971. (3 References).
Documents the successful treatment of a seven-year-old boy by the use of a portable buzzer alarm system, together with praise and other reinforcers.

403 Neale, D. H. "Behavior therapy and encopresis in children." Behav Res Ther 1(2): 139-49, May, 1963. (13 References). (Reprinted in Item Nos. 21, 43).
Presents the case histories of four boys with longstanding psychogenic encopresis who were treated with behavioral therapy techniques.

404 Pedrini, Bonnie C., and Pedrini, D. T. "Reinforcement procedures in the control of encopresis: a case study." Psychol Rep 28(3): 937-38, June, 1971. (4 References).
Offers a case report of an eleven-year-old boy whose encopresis was successfully treated by the use of reinforcement with coupons exchangeable for books. At a seven-month check-up the boy was not receiving specific reinforcers and had apparently internalized the control.

405 Peterson, Donald R., and London, Perry. "A role for cognition in the behavioral treatment of a child's eliminative disturbance." In: Ullmann, Leonard P., and Krasner, Leonard, eds. Case studies in behavior modification. New York: Holt, Rinehart & Winston, 1965. 289-95. (17 References).
Advocates the use of behavioral techniques in the establishment of normal eliminative patterns. A case history of a three-year-old boy is used to illustrate this strategy.

406 Rickard, Henry C., and Griffin, John L. "Reducing soiling behavior in a therapeutic summer camp." In: Krumboltz, John D., and Thoresen, Carl E., eds. Behavioral counseling: cases and techniques. New York: Holt, Rinehart & Winston, 1969. 36-41.
Describes the use of social and candy reinforcers to bring about bowel control in a seven-year-old boy. The program was administered by camp counselors.

407 Seymour, Frederick W. "The treatment of encopresis using behaviour modification." Aust Paediatric J 12(4): 326-29, 1976. (7 References).
Tokens with tangible back-up rewards were used in developing appropriate defecatory behavior in twelve children.

K. ENURESIS

408 Baker, Bruce L. "Symptom treatment and symptom substitution in enuresis." J Abnorm Psychol 74(1): 42-49, February, 1969. (24 References). (Reprinted in Items Nos. 21, 28, 29, 38).
Explores aspects of the therapist-patient relationship and the possibility of symptom substitution in a study conducted with thirty enuretic children.

409 Bindelglas, Paul M. "The enuretic child." J Fam Pract 2(5): 375-80, October, 1975.
Outlines five major approaches to therapy, including conditioning techniques. Emphasis is placed on the need to tailor the therapy to the individual.

410 Blumberg, Louis Michael. "A self-monitored, non-mechanical conditioning treatment for nocturnal enuresis." For a summary see: Diss Abstr Int 37B(3): 1476, September, 1976.

411 Browning, Robert M. "Operantly strengthening UCR (Awakening) as a prerequisite to treatment of persistent enuresis." Behav Res Ther 5(4): 371-72, November, 1967. (2 References).
A severely psychoneurotic ten-year-old boy was conditioned to awaken in response to the bell in the "bell and pad" technique for enuresis. A reward system, initially employing toys, trinkets, and candy, was later converted to a points system.

412 Catalina, Don Albert. "Enuresis: the effect of parent contingent wake-up." For a summary see: Diss Abstr Int 37B(6): 3065, December, 1976.

413 Collins, Robert W. "The effect of delaying the unconditioned stimulus in the conditioning treatment of enuresis." For a summary see: Diss Abstr Int 30B(11): 5234, May, 1970.

414 De Leon, George, and Mandell, Wallace. "A comparison of conditioning and psychotherapy in the treatment of functional enuresis." J Clin Psychol 22(3): 326-30, July, 1966. (2 References).
Shows a higher success rate with conditioning methods than with psychotherapeutic methods in treating eighty-seven enuretic children.

415 Doleys, Daniel M. "Behavioral treatments for nocturnal enuresis in children: a review of the recent literature." Psychol Bull 84(1): 30-54, January, 1977. (112 References).
This comprehensive review of the literature divides remedial procedures into three categories: (1) those that used the standard urine alarm or bell and pad; (2) those that employed retention control training; and (3) those that modified existing stimuli or consequent events but did not use the urine alarm or retention control as the primary mode of treatment. Results are presented and evaluated under each of the categories, and guidelines for future research are given.

416 Finley, W. W.; Besserman, R. L.; Bennett, Lois Francine; et al. "The effect of continuous, intermittent, and 'placebo' reinforcement on the effectiveness of the conditioning treatment for enuresis nocturna." Behav Res Ther 11(3): 289-97, August, 1973. (8 References).

Indicates that continuous and intermittent reinforcement were equally successful in establishing control with thirty enuretic boys, but that the relapse rate was significantly greater with continuous reinforcement. The placebo group showed no improvement over the six weeks of treatment.

417 Finley, William W.; Wansley, Richard A.; Blenkarn, Mary Margaret. "Conditioning treatment of enuresis using a seventy per cent intermittent reinforcement schedule." Behav Res Ther 15(5): 419-27, 1977. (26 References).
Reports on a large-scale investigation of the use of automated equipment with eighty enuretic children. For all ages combined, the observed relapse rate of 25 percent was found to be significantly lower than reported in the literature over the past ten years.

418 Forrester, R. M.; Stein, Zena; Susser, M. W. "A trial of conditioning therapy in nocturnal enuresis." Dev Med Child Neurol 6(2): 158-66, April, 1964. (13 References).
Compares a conditioning alarm system and amphetamine therapy. The alarm system was found to give significantly better results.

419 Forsythe, W. I., and Redmond, A. "Enuresis and the electric alarm: study of two hundred cases." Br Med J 1(690): 211-13, January 24, 1970. (12 References).
Of 200 children with persistent enuresis, 66 percent were cured after treatment with an electric alarm over a thirty-week period.

420 Freyman, Richard. "A follow-up study of enuresis treated with a bell apparatus." J Child Psychol Psychiatry 4(3/4): 199-206, December, 1963. (18 References).
Describes the treatment of seventy-one nocturnal enuretics. Follow-up indicated that 38 percent of the children remained dry or almost completely dry after ten months.

421 Geppert, Thomas V. "Management of nocturnal enuresis by conditioned response." JAMA 152: 381-83, May 30, 1953. (4 References). (Reprinted in Item No. 31).
Describes the treatment of a group of forty-two nocturnal enuretics by means of a "pad and buzzer" system. Enuresis was arrested in thirty-eight of the patients.

422 Gorman, Shepard Benjamin. "Intermittent punishment schedules in the conditioning treatment of enuresis." For a summary see: Diss Abstr Int 37B(8): 4138, February, 1977.

423 James, Leonard E. "The efficacy of behavior therapy and therapist A-B status, expectancy, conscientiousness and reinforcement style: an experiment in the parental treatment of enuresis." For a summary see: Diss Abstr Int 32B(7): 4218, January, 1972.

424 James, Leonard E., and Foreman, Milton E. "A-B status of behavior therapy technicians as related to success of Mowrer's conditioning treatment for enuresis." J Consult Clin Psychol 41(2): 224-28, October, 1973. (26 References).
Documents a study conducted with thirty-six enuretic children treated by their mothers who received a one-hour consultation/training session.

425 Kimmel, H. D., and Kimmel, Ellen. "An instrumental conditioning method for the treatment of enuresis." J Behav Ther Exp Psychiatry 1(2): 121-23, June, 1970. (1 Reference). (Reprinted in Item No. 43).
Cites three enuretic children in whom nocturnal control was rapidly achieved by means of training designed to delay urination during the day. Edible reinforcers were used.

426 Lovibond, S. H. Conditioning and enuresis. New York: Macmillan, 1964. 219p. (Bibliography). (Pergamon Press Books).
Reviews major theories of enuresis and methods of treatment, and reports on a survey conducted with 120 enuretics and 121 non-enuretics. Therapy by conditioning methods is advocated, and detailed instructions are given.

427 Lynch, N. Timothy. "A comparison of avoidance and classical conditioning in the treatment of nocturnal enuresis." For a summary see: Diss Abstr Int 34B(10): 5200, April, 1974.

428 McDonagh, Mary Jo. "Is operant conditioning effective in reducing enuresis and encopresis in children?" Perspect Psychiatr Care 9(1): 17-23, 1971. (9 References).
Presents the case histories of one encopretic and two enuretic boys treated with a combination of candy and social reinforcers.

429 Marshall, Sumner; Marshall, Hermine; Lyon, Richards P. "Enuresis: an analysis of various therapeutic approaches." Pediatrics 52(6): 813-17, December, 1973. (23 References).
Compares various techniques used with 300 enuretic children. The data indicate that a "responsibility-reinforcement" technique was the most successful.

430 Martin, Barclay, and Kubly, Delores. "Results of treatment of enuresis by a conditioned response method." J Consult Psychol 19(1): 71-73, February, 1955. (4 References).
Reports on the results of a questionnaire administered to the parents of 118 enuretic children. Seventy-four percent of the cases indicated successful outcome.

431 Morgan, R. T. T. "Problems in the conditioning treatment of enuresis." In: Brengelmann, J. C., ed. Progress in behavior therapy. New York: Springer-Verlag, 1975. 39-42. (8 References).
Studies the problems of nonattendance, termination, slow response, and relapse.

432 Mowrer, O. H., and Mowrer, Willie Mae. "Enuresis: a method for its study and treatment." Am J Orthopsychiatry 8(3): 436-59, July, 1938. (55 References).
Thirty enuretic children, aged between three and thirteen years, were successfully treated by means of a "pad and bell" apparatus. The treatments were successfully concluded within two months.

433 Nordquist, Vey Michael. "The modification of a child's enuresis: some response-response relationships." J Appl Behav Anal 4(3): 241-47, Fall, 1971. (7 References).
Gives the details of the treatment of a five-and-one-half-year-old boy's tantrum behavior by means of time-out and differential reinforcement. There was a lessening of both his tantrum behavior and his enuresis.

434 Popler, Kenneth. "Token reinforcement in treatment of nocturnal enuresis: a case study and six month follow-up." J Behav Ther Exp Psychiatry 7(1): 83-84, March, 1976. (10 References).
The nocturnal enuresis of a fourteen-year-old male was successfully eliminated in twenty-eight weeks by the use of token awards.

435 Rosenberg, Jerome. "An investigation into the effects of prompting-attention in an operant conditioning control of nocturnal enuresis." For a summary see: Diss Abstr Int 30B(2): 854, August, 1969.

436 Ross, Joel. "Behavioral treatment of enuresis: case study." Psychol Rep 35(1): 286, August, 1974. (0 References).
Indicates that a contingency management procedure might be more effective with enuretics who do not wet their beds every night, since keeping dry is in their behavior repertoire.

437 Sacks, Stanley; De Leon, George; Blackman, Sheldon. "Psychological changes associated with conditioning functional enuresis." J Clin Psychol 30(3): 271-76, July, 1974. (9 References).
Presents data that indicate that successfully conditioned enuretic children manifested no increase in reported symptoms, school or personality maladjustment for one year after treatment.

438 Schlipmann, Peter Joseph. "A study of functional bladder capacity and fluid retention training combined with classical conditioning of enuresis." For a summary see: Diss Abstr Int 34B(12): 6224, June, 1974.

439 Taylor, P. D., and Turner, R. K. "A clinical trial of continuous, intermittent and overlearning 'bell and pad' treatments for nocturnal enuresis." Behav Res Ther 13(4): 281-93, October, 1975. (54 References).
Investigates the relative effectiveness of intermittent reinforcement and overlearning procedures in reducing the relapse rate for "bell and pad" treatment of six enuretic children. The results indicate that overlearning was the more successful method. Some discussion is included on the present status of this treatment, and implications for further research are noted.

440 Tough, J. H.; Hawkins, Robert P.; McArthur, Moira; et al. "Modification of enuretic behavior by punishment: a new use for an old device." Behav Ther 2(4): 567-74, October, 1971. (15 References).
Documents the use of cold baths as an aversive consequence for nocturnal enuresis in two subjects.

441 Turner, R. K., and Young, G. C. "CNS stimulant drugs and conditioning treatment of nocturnal enuresis: a long term follow-up study." Behav Res Ther 4(3): 225-28, August, 1966. (5 References).
Documents the results of a long-term follow-up study of enuretics treated by conditioning techniques. Those patients treated with a combination of "bell and pad" and stimulant drugs had the highest relapse rate. Suggestions are made for further research.

442 Turner, R. K.; Young, G. C.; Rachman, S. "Treatment of nocturnal enuresis by conditioning techniques." Behav Res Ther 8(4): 367-81, November, 1970. (62 References).

Examines the results of a large-scale comparative study of 115 enuretic children who were divided into five groups. Three groups received forms of conditioning treatments, two groups received "placebo" or "arousal" control treatments. The investigation confirmed the success of conditioning treatment in bringing about the initial arrest of enuresis, but the relapse rate was high. There was tentative evidence that intermittent conditioning offers a way of reducing the frequency of relapse. A comprehensive bibliography accompanies the article.

443 Werry, John S. "The conditioning treatment of enuresis." Am J Psychiatry 123(2): 226-29, August, 1966. (16 References).
Reviews the literature and reports on the operant procedures used at a special clinic for enuretic children.

444 Wickes, Ian G. "Treatment of persistent enuresis with the electric buzzer." Arch Dis Child 33: 160-64, April, 1958. (0 References). (Reprinted in Item No. 46).
A favorable response was obtained in sixty-five out of 100 severe enuretics using a "pad and buzzer" system.

445 Wright, Logan, and Craig, Shelley C. "A comparative study of amphetamine, ephedrine-atropine mixture, placebo, and behavioral conditioning in the treatment of nocturnal enuresis." J Okla State Med Assoc 67(10): 430-33, October, 1974. (8 References).
Describes the results of a study conducted with twenty-one enuretic children between the ages of four and ten. The conditioned group maintained a significant decrease in enuretic behavior; the drug group showed an initial decrease which could not be maintained.

446 Young, G. C., and Morgan, R. T. T. "Analysis of factors associated with the extinction of a conditioned response." Behav Res Ther 11(2): 219-22, May, 1973. (19 References).
Investigates the reasons for relapse of enuretics previously brought under control by conditioning therapy. Forty factors of possible relevance are tabulated, and overlearning is suggested as a possible counteraction.

447 ———. "Conditioning techniques and enuresis." Med J Aust 2(7): 329-32, August 18, 1973. (39 References).
Discusses the various treatment methods available and advocates the use of conditioning techniques.

448 ———. "Overlearning in the conditioning treatment of enuresis." Behav Res Ther 10(2): 147-51, May, 1972. (6 References).
Investigates the causes of the high relapse rate following conditioning of childhood enuresis. Overlearning is suggested as the best tool in the reduction of the relapse rate, and it is recommended that overlearning be combined with the treatment process.

449 Young, G. C., and Turner, R. K. "CNS stimulant drugs and conditioning treatment of nocturnal enuresis." Behav Res Ther 3(2): 93-101, May, 1965. (11 References).
Compares the effects of the use of conditioning used alone and in combination with two different drugs, Dexedrine and Methedrine. The results indicated that treatment was facilitated by the use of these drugs, particularly Methedrine. The relapse rate was slightly higher with Dexedrine.

L. FIRE-SETTING

450 Denholtz, Myron S. "'At home' aversion treatment of compulsive fire-setting behavior: case report." In: Rubin, Richard D.; Fensterheim, Herbert; Henderson, John D.; et al., eds. Advances in behavior therapy. Proceedings of the Fourth Conference of the Association for Advancement of Behavior Therapy. New York: Academic Press, 1972. 81-84. (4 References).
Describes the successful home treatment of a seventeen-year-old boy, employing slides and a portable electric shocker.

451 Holland, Cornelius J. "Elimination by the parents of fire-setting behavior in a seven-year-old boy." Behav Res Ther 7(1): 135-37, February, 1969. (2 References). (Reprinted in Item Nos. 21, 43).
Presents a case report which demonstrates the elimination of fire-setting behavior by parents who had been instructed by a therapist. The boy was never seen by the therapist. A combination of positive reinforcement and threat of punishment-by-loss was used.

452 Stawar, Terry L. "Fable mod: operantly structured fantasies as an adjunct in modification of fire-setting behavior." J Behav Ther Exp Psychiatry 7(3): 285-87, 1976. (9 References).
Fire-setting behavior of a seven-year-old boy was eliminated by the use of operantly constructed fantasies. After two fantasy sessions, the incompatible response was well established, and no further episodes of fire-setting were noted. The therapeutic implications of operantly structured fantasies are discussed.

M. INFANT BEHAVIORS: HEAD-TURNING, SMILING, SUCKING, VOCALIZING

453 Apolloni, Tony, and Cooke, Thomas P. "Peer behavior conceptualized as a variable influencing infant and toddler development." Am J Orthopsychiatry 45(1): 4-17, January, 1975. (61 References).
Reviews the developmental literature and hypothesizes that interaction between infants may facilitate behavioral development. The enhancement of such interaction is advocated, and further avenues of research are indicated.

454 Brackbill, Yvonne. "Extinction of the smiling response in infants as a function of reinforcement schedule." Child Dev 29(1): 115-24, March, 1958. (8 References). (Reprinted in Item No. 32).
Demonstrates the cessation of the smiling response with eight normal infants between the ages of three-and-one-half and four-and-one-half months when smiling was no longer reinforced by adults.

455 Caron, Rose F. "Visual reinforcement of head-turning in young infants." J Exp Child Psychol 5(4): 489-511, December, 1967. (35 References).
Examines the effects of contingent visual stimulation on the acquisition and maintenance of a unilateral head-rotation response in three-and-one-half-month-old infants.

456 Gekoski, Marcy J. "Visual attention and operant conditioning in infancy: a second look." For a summary see: Diss Abstr Int 38B(2): 875, August, 1977.

457 Haugan, Gertrude Marion. "The effects of various types of reinforcement on conditioning of infant vocalizations." For a summary see: Diss Abstr Int 32B(3): 1875, September, 1971.

458 Hulsebus, Robert C. "Operant conditioning of infant behavior: a review." Adv Child Dev Behav 8: 111-58, 1973. (115 References).
Reviews the published investigations in which infant behaviors were followed by positive reinforcement.

459 Levison, Cathryn A., and Levison, Peter K. "Operant conditioning of head-turning for visual reinforcement in three-month infants." Psychon Sci 8(12): 529-30, August 25, 1967. (5 References).
Uses twenty-six infants to demonstrate that rapid conditioning of a directional head-turning, extinction, and conditioning of a response reversal can be obtained using visual stimulus patterns as reinforcement.

460 Lipsitt, Lewis P.; Kaye, Herbert; Bosack, Theodore N. "Enhancement of neonatal sucking through reinforcement." J Exp Child Psychol 4(2): 163-68, October, 1966. (8 References). (Reprinted in Item No. 32).
Reinforcement with a dextrose solution of a tube-sucking response in twenty infants enhanced tube-sucking behavior. Cessation of reinforcement had the opposite effect.

461 Moore, John M.; Wilson, Wesley R.; Thompson, Gary. "Visual reinforcement of head-turn responses in infants under twelve months of age." J Speech Hear Disord 42(3): 328-34, August, 1977. (18 References).
Investigates the use of visual reinforcement (with an animated toy animal) of auditory localization responses in infants. The study indicated that infants as young as five months were susceptible to this form of operant conditioning.

462 Pumroy, Donald K., and Pumroy, Shirley S. "A case study in discrimination learning." J Genet Psychol 110(1): 87-89, March, 1967.
A twenty-one-month-old boy was conditioned by the use of a light not to awaken his parents before 8:00 a.m.

463 Rheingold, Harriet L.; Gewirtz, Jacob L.; Ross, Helen W. "Social conditioning of vocalizations in the infant." J Comp Physiol Psychol 52(1): 68-73, February, 1959. (12 References). (Reprinted in Item Nos. 23, 32, 42).
Reports on a study conducted with twenty-one infants (median age 3.0 months) in which vocalizations were enhanced by social reinforcement.

464 Siqueland, Elnar R. "Operant conditioning of head turning in four-month infants." Psychon Sci 1(8): 223-24, August, 1964. (6 References). (Reprinted in Item No. 32).
Head rotations to the right or to the left of a central position were selectively strengthened by the experimental presentation of milk in thirty four-month-old infants.

465 Todd, Gibson A., and Palmer, Bruce. "Social reinforcement of infant babbling." Child Dev 39(2): 591-96, June, 1968. (5 References).
Indicates that the presence of an adult was not a necessary component in the social reinforcement of infant vocalization, but that adult presence did enhance the results.

466 Tomlinson-Keasey C. "Conditioning of infant vocalizations in the home environment." J Genet Psychol 120(1): 75-82, March, 1972. (8 References).
Three-month-old infants were used to study operant conditioning of vocalizations with the use of nonsocial reinforcement.

467 Trehub, Sandra E., and Chang, Hsing-wu. "Speech as reinforcing stimulation for infants." Dev Psychol 13(2): 170-71, March, 1977. (4 References).
Reports briefly on an experiment conducted with thirty-two infants (five to fifteen weeks of age) in which the presentation of speech stimulation contingent on the infants' non-nutritive sucking resulted in a significant change in the rate of sucking compared to infants receiving no sound stimulation.

468 Weisberg, Paul. "Social and nonsocial conditioning of infant vocalization." Child Dev 34(2): 377-88, June, 1963. (10 References).
Investigates the effects of a series of short-term experimental manipulations on the vocal behavior of infants.

N. LANGUAGE

469 Appelman, Karen; Allen, K. Eileen; Turner, Keith D. "The conditioning of language in a nonverbal child conducted in a special education classroom." J Speech Hear Disord 40(1): 3-12, February, 1975. (15 References).
Speech therapy, using behavior modification methods, was conducted in a classroom setting with a nonverbal, four-and-one-half-year-old boy who showed a measurable increase in spontaneous vocalizations. It was demonstrated that the classroom can provide a suitable setting for speech conditioning.

470 Bricker, William A., and Bricker, Diane D. "A program of language training for the severely language handicapped child." Except Child 37(2): 101-11, October, 1970. (38 References).
Describes sequential procedures utilizing behavior modification techniques. Language components dealt with include operant audiometry, receptive vocabulary, imitation, naming, and sentence production.

471 Cook, Charlotte, and Adams, Henry E. "Modification of verbal behavior in speech deficient children." Behav Res Ther 4(4): 265-71, November, 1966. (7 References).
Describes the operant techniques used to modify the verbal behavior of three children. Varied reinforcers were used, including candy, praise, and puppets. Results included increased vocalizations and an increase in the number of words used.

472 Fygetakis, L., and Gray, B. B. "Programmed conditioning of linguistic competence." Behav Res Ther 8(2): 153-63, May, 1970. (11 References).
Presents the details of two programmed conditioning techniques which increased the syntactic competence of three language deficient preschool children. The procedures enabled the children to formulate the underlying grammatical rules utilizing only surface structure language as input.

473 Fygetakis, L. Juana, and Ingram, David. "Language rehabilitation and programmed conditioning: a case study." J Learn Disabil 6(2): 60-64, February, 1973. (15 References).
Documents the clinical findings on a five-year-old girl with a very reduced language system. The girl was trained for five months by a system combining recent knowledge about the acquisition of English with techniques of behavior modification.

474 Garcia, Eugene E., and De Haven, Everett D. "Use of operant techniques in the establishment and generalization of language: a review and analysis." Am J Ment Defic 79(2): 169-78, September, 1974. (50 References).
Reviews the literature on operant techniques used in speech and language remediation. Suggestions are made for further research, especially in the areas of generative speech training and generalized speech usage.

475 Goren, Elizabeth R.; Romanczyk, Raymond G.; Harris, Sandra L. "A functional analysis of echolalic speech: the effects of antecedent and consequent events." Behav Modif 1(4): 481-98, October, 1977. (10 References).
Examines the effects of antecedents and consequences on the echolalic behavior of four atypical children. Results showed marked individual differences as well as some inconsistencies in responding. It is suggested that echolalia varies as a function of the subject, the environmental antecedents, and contingencies, and should not be treated as a one dimensional response pattern.

476 Gray, Burl B. "Language acquisition through programmed conditioning." In: Bradfield, Robert H., ed. Behavior modification: the human effort. Belmont, California: Dimensions, 1970. 99-122. (24 References).
Outlines the procedures used to enhance language acquisition in a preschool population. Emphasis is placed on rewarding desired verbal behavior using redeemable tokens, rather than on punishment for incorrect responses.

477 Gray, B. B., and Fygetakis, L. "The development of language as a function of programmed conditioning." Behav Res Ther 6(4): 455-60, November, 1968. (4 References).
A follow-up study of Item No. 478 which dealt with the acquisition of language by dysphasic children. This study deals with the response generalization at the syntactical level and uses the same methods of reinforcement as the earlier study.

478 ———. "Mediated language acquisition for dysphasic children." Behav Res Ther 6(3): 263-80, August, 1968. (20 References).
Presents a detailed report of a method of language acquisition based upon conditioning procedures and programming methods. The subjects were six children between the ages of four and six years who were enrolled in a special preschool program for dysphasic children. Behavioral control was established first by means of a token-toy method of reinforcement which was then transferred to the language learning situation. Volunteers were successfully used in carrying out this program. See Item No. 477 for a follow-up study.

479 Gray, Burl B., and Ryan, Bruce P. A language program for the nonlanguage child. Champaign, Illinois: Research Press, 1973. 181p. (Bibliography).

Presents a behavioral interpretation of language development and training with a detailed description of specific programs. Also contained is a report on the authors' work with a cross-section of language disorders and suggestions for further research.

480 Harris, Sandra L. "Teaching language to non-verbal children--with emphasis on problems of generalization." Psychol Bull 82(4): 565-80, July, 1975. (125 References).
This literature review is arranged in four sections: (1) attention; (2) nonverbal imitation; (3) verbal imitation; and (4) functional language. The focus is on the problems of generalization, and it is advocated that increased attention be given to generalization under wide-ranging conditions.

481 Hart, Betty M., and Risley, Todd R. "Establishing the use of descriptive adjectives in the spontaneous speech of disadvantaged preschool children." J Appl Behav Anal 1(2): 109-20, Spring, 1968. (18 References). (Reprinted in Item Nos. 29, 38, 40).
Describes the use of reinforcement techniques to increase the verbal skills (specifically the use of noun-adjective combinations) in fifteen disadvantaged preschool children. Traditional teaching procedures were effective in increasing skills in the teaching situation, but it was only through the application of environmental contingencies that color names as descriptive adjectives were established in spontaneous vocabularies.

482 Hatten, John T., and Hatten Pequetti A. "A foster home approach to speech therapy." J Speech Hear Disord 36(2): 257-63, May, 1971. (8 References).
Describes a language development program for a six-year-old boy who was placed in a foster home in which both parents were speech clinicians.

483 Lahey, Benjamin B., ed. The modification of language behavior. Springfield, Illinois: Thomas, 1973. 322p. (Bibliography).
Summarizes recent advances in the application of behavior modification techniques to linguistic problems. Chapters are included on language development in retarded and autistic children.

484 McReynolds, Leija V. "Application of timeout from positive reinforcement for increasing the efficiency of speech training." J Appl Behav Anal 2(3): 199-205, Fall, 1969. (5 References). (Reprinted in Item No. 21).
Outlines the use of positive reinforcement to increase the appropriate verbal behavior of an almost nonverbal, brain damaged, five-year-old boy. The use of time-out from positive reinforcement to decrease his use of jargon is explained.

485 ————. "Verbal sequence discrimination training for language impaired children." J Speech Hear Disord 32(3): 249-56, August, 1967. (6 References).
Discusses the principle of positive reinforcement and its use in the discrimination training of children diagnosed as having auditory discrimination and auditory memory problems.

486 Nelson, Rosemary O., and Evans, Ian M. "The combination of learning principles and speech therapy techniques in the treatment of noncommunicating children." J Child Psychol Psychiatry 9(2): 111-24, November, 1968. (19 References). (Reprinted in Item No. 29).

Sets forth a program of visual-tactile cues which was incorporated into an operant speech training program. The techniques were used with four non-communicating children--two autistic, one educationally subnormal, and one with executive aphasia. The implications of the resultant successes and failures are that there should be a greater interaction between traditional speech therapy techniques and the principles of operant conditioning.

487 Peirce, Henry Brown. "Operant conditioning: its efficacy in affecting the verbal behavior of young children with severe language disability." For a summary see: Diss Abstr Int 31B(9): 5692, March, 1971.

488 Picaizen, Ganea; Berger, Anita A.; Baronofsky, Dorothy; et al. "Application of operant techniques to speech therapy with non-verbal children." J Commun Disord 2(3): 203-11, August, 1969. (21 References).
Offers two case histories of three-year-old nonverbal girls for whom successive approximation and differential reinforcement were successful in producing vocalizations followed by speech.

489 Reynolds, Nancy J., and Risley, Todd R. "The role of social and material reinforcers in increasing talking of a disadvantaged preschool child." J Appl Behav Anal 1(3): 253-62, 1968. (10 References). (Reprinted in Item No. 40).
Demonstrates the use of teacher attention and access to preschool materials as the reinforcers in increasing the verbal output of a disadvantaged four-year-old girl.

490 Risley, Todd R., and Hart, Betty M. "Developing correspondence between the non-verbal and verbal behavior of preschool children." J Appl Behav Anal 1(4): 267-81, 1968. (4 References). (Reprinted in Item No. 38).
Correspondence between nonverbal and verbal behavior was developed in twelve preschool children by the use of edible reinforcers, so that their nonverbal behavior could be altered simply by reinforcing their verbal behavior.

491 Rosen, Marvin; Wesner, Chester; Richardson, Paul; et al. "A preschool program for promoting language acquisition." Hosp Community Psychiatry 22(9): 280-82, September, 1971.
Describes a program of language training which focuses on operant conditioning techniques. Parents are urged to continue the procedures at home.

492 Salzinger, Kurt; Feldman, Richard S.; Cowan, Judith E.; et al. "Operant conditioning of verbal behavior of two young speech-deficient boys." In: Krasner, Leonard, and Ullmann, Leonard P., eds. Research in behavior modification. New York: Holt, Rinehart & Winston, 1965. 82-105.
Documents the use of operant conditioning techniques (primarily using candy and social reinforcers) to shape the vocal and verbal behaviors in two hospitalized boys, aged three to four years.

493 Salzinger, Suzanne; Salzinger, K.; Portnoy, S.; et al. "Operant conditioning of continuous speech in young children." Child Dev 33: 683-95, 1962. (12 References). (Reprinted in Item No. 42).

The spontaneous continuous speech of children (ranging in age from five to seven years) was reinforced under various experimental conditions. The speech rate increased when reinforcement was administered and decreased or stabilized when reinforcement was withheld.

494 Sloane, Howard N., Jr., and MacAulay, Barbara D., eds. Operant procedures in remedial speech and language training. Boston: Houghton-Mifflin, 1968. 444p.
This collection of nineteen papers by various authors covers the use of behavioral techniques across a wide range of speech and language problems. Included are background papers on the environmental control of verbal behavior and the basic behavioral mechanism of imitation.

495 Stark, Joel. "Language habilitation in children." In: Bradfield, Robert H., ed. Behavioral modification of learning disabilities. San Rafael, California: Academic Therapy, 1971. 91-102. (17 References).
Sets forth the procedures for a language development program which employs immediate reinforcement for observable verbal response.

496 Stremel, Kathleen, and Waryas, Carol. "A behavioral-psycholinguistic approach to language training." ASHA Monogr 18: 96-130, August, 1974. (14 References).
Presents a series of sequential language training programs and assessment procedures for the child with delayed or deficient language structures. Behavior modification methods are incorporated into each step of the procedures.

497 Weiss, Henry H., and Born, Barbara. "Speech training or language acquisition? A distinction when speech training is taught by operant conditioning procedures." Am J Orthopsychiatry 37(1): 49-55, January, 1967. (6 References).
Behavior modification procedures were employed to teach speech to a seven-and-one-half-year-old boy. Failure to generalize outside the experimental setting was noted.

O. MUTISM

498 Bauermeister, Jose J., and Jemail, Jay Ann. "Modification of 'elective mutism' in the classroom setting: a case study." Behav Ther 6(2): 246-50, March, 1975. (14 References).
Social and tangible reinforcers were made contingent upon the verbal class participation of an eight-year-old, third grade boy, who had been observed to communicate freely outside the classroom. Follow-up one year later indicated that the treatment gains had been maintained.

499 Beissel, G. F. "Increasing verbalization by a disadvantaged pre-school child." Psychol Rep 30(3): 931-34, June, 1972. (7 References).
Contingent social reinforcement resulted in an increased level of verbalizations in a five-year-old girl classified as a "non-talker."

500 Blake, Phillip, and Moss, Thelma. "The development of socialization skills in an electively mute child." Behav Res Ther 5(4): 349-56, November, 1967. (15 References).
Describes the modification of an electively mute four-year-old child. An especially designed booth in which lighting and rewards could be regu-

lated was used. The child's disruptive behavior was extinguished initially, thereby making it possible to establish eye contact and to teach her both nonverbal and verbal imitative behavior.

501 Brison, David W. "Case studies in school psychology. A non-talking child in kindergarten: an application of behavior therapy." J Sch Psychol 4(4): 65-69, 1966. (3 References).
Traces the progress of a kindergarten child who did not talk in the school setting and whose behavior was modified by the teacher's gradually ceasing to reinforce nonverbal behavior. A three year follow-up indicated no further speech problems.

502 Colligan, Ross W.; Colligan, Robert C.; Dilliard, Maxine K. "Contingency management in the classroom treatment of long-term elective mutism: a case report." J Sch Psychol 15(1): 9-17, Spring, 1977. (16 References).
Presents the case of an eleven-year-old boy with a six-year history of elective mutism in school. The program consisted of three stages: (1) relationship-building to develop teacher-pupil interaction into a reinforcing event; (2) audible response eliciting; and (3) generalization throughout the school.

503 Griffith, Earl E.; Schnelle, John F.; McNees, M. Patrick; et al. "Elective mutism in a first grader: the remediation of a complex behavioral problem." J Abnorm Child Psychol 3(2): 127-34, 1975. (7 References).
Spontaneous and prompted speech were produced in a six-year-old mute by a reinforcement system employed by the teacher and her aide. Three separate school classes participated in the study and speech was seen to develop in each of the three. Follow-up in the next school year showed evidence of a continued improvement.

504 Kerr, Nancy; Meyerson, Lee; Michael, Jack. "A procedure for shaping vocalizations in a mute child." In: Ullmann, Leonard P., and Krasner, Leonard, eds. Case studies in behavior modification. New York: Holt, Rinehart & Winston, 1965. 366-70. (2 References).
Documents a case in which vocalizing was developed in a previously mute three-year-old girl by means of positive reinforcement with close body contact.

505 Munford, Paul R.; Reardon, Diane; Liberman, Robert P.; et al. "Behavioral treatment of hysterical coughing and mutism: a case study." J Consult Clin Psychol 44(6): 1008-14, December, 1976. (10 References).
After the failure of a course of electrical aversive conditioning with a seventeen-year-old patient, extinction and shaping were found to be effective in reducing coughing and mutism.

506 Nolan, J. Dennis, and Pence, Connie. "Operant conditioning principles in the treatment of a selectively mute child." J Consult Clin Psychol 35(2): 265-68, October, 1970. (5 References).
Describes the procedures--used over a period of eight months--which established relatively normal speaking patterns in a mute child. At a one-year follow-up the child's speech was indistinguishable from her classmates.

507 Norman, Arthur, and Broman, Harvey J. "Volume feedback and generalization techniques in shaping speech of an electively mute boy: a case study." Percept Mot Skills 31(2): 463-70, October, 1970. (9 References).
Reports on the successful treatment of an electively mute twelve-year-old boy using visual feedback from the volume-level meter of a tape recorder and various other methods.

508 Reid, John B.; Hawkins, Nancy; Keutzer, Carolin; et al. "A marathon behavior modification of a selectively mute child." J Child Psychol Psychiatry 8(1): 27-30, May, 1967. (5 References). (Reprinted in Item No. 21).
Sets forth the details of a technique for using reinforcement and stimulus fading for generalization of speech in a selectively mute six-year-old girl. The procedure was successfully completed in one day.

509 Robertshaw, C. Stuart; Kelly, Thomas J.; Hiebert, Harold D. "Contingent time off to increase verbal behavior: a case report." J Consult Clin Psychol 41(3): 459-61, December, 1973. (10 References).
A withdrawn sixteen-year-old boy earned his way out of a mental health clinic by increasing his verbal behavior to an established criterion performance.

510 Stark, Joel; Rosenbaum, Robert L.; Schwartz, Dorothea; et al. "The non-verbal child: some clinical guidelines." J Speech Hear Disord 38(1): 59-72, February, 1973. (22 References).
Discusses reinforcement theory and presents illustrative cases. Emphasis is placed on the application of an experimental approach to the modification of language behavior.

511 Wulbert, Margaret; Nyman, Barry A.; Snow, David; et al. "The efficacy of stimulus fading and contingency management in the treatment of elective mutism: a case study." J Appl Behav Anal 6(3): 435-41, Fall, 1973. (5 References).
Reports on a study, conducted with a six-year-old elective mute girl, that indicates that the most effective treatment is a combined use of stimulus fading and contingency management. The fading procedure was ineffective unless combined with the use of time-out for non-response.

P. OBESITY

512 Aragona, Jon; Cassady, John; Drabman, Ronald S. "Treating overweight children through parental training and contingency contracting." J Appl Behav Anal 8(3): 269-78, Fall, 1975. (27 References).
Compares the effects of three treatment regimes, response-cost plus reinforcement, response-cost alone, and no treatment with fifteen overweight girls ranging in age from five to fifteen years. Both experimental groups lost more weight than the control group.

513 Barnes, H. Verdain, and Berger, Ruth. "An approach to the obese adolescent." Med Clin North Am 59(6): 1507-16, November, 1975. (20 References).
Contrasts several methods of handling obesity in adolescents. Behavior modification is recommended utilizing paramedical personnel to oversee the treatment.

514 Dinoff, Michael; Rickard, Henry C.; Colwick, John. "Weight reduction through successive contracts." Am J Orthopsychiatry 42(1): 110-13, January, 1972. (13 References).
Contractual agreements made with an overweight, bright, emotionally disturbed ten-year-old boy resulted in a loss of thirty pounds over a seven-week period.

515 Epstein, Leonard H.; Parker, Lynn; McCoy, James F.; et al. "Descriptive analysis of eating regulation in obese and nonobese children." J Appl Behav Anal 9(4): 407-15, Winter, 1976. (15 References).
Depicts the eating behaviors of several obese and nonobese children over a six-month period. Placing eating utensils on the table between bites and contingent praise resulted in decreased food intake.

516 Foxx, Richard W. "Social reinforcement of weight reduction: a case report on an obese retarded adolescent." Ment Retard 10(4): 21-23, August, 1972. (20 References). (Reprinted in Item No. 35).
Rapid weight loss of seventy-nine pounds over a period of forty-two weeks by an obese, mildly retarded fourteen-year-old girl was attributed to attention and praise delivered by the experimenter for weight loss per week at or below a specified level.

517 Gillick, Susan Lee. "Training parents as therapists in the treatment of juvenile obesity." For a summary see: Diss Abstr Int 35B(10): 5111, April, 1975.

518 Grace, Dixie Lee. "Self monitoring in the modification of obesity in childhood." For a summary see: Diss Abstr Int 37B(5): 2505, November, 1976.

519 Gross, Ina; Wheeler, Mary; Hess, Karl. "The treatment of obesity in adolescents using behavioral self-control." Clin Pediatr 15(10): 920-24, October, 1976. (11 References).
Describes a study conducted with eleven girls (thirteen to seventeen years of age) from lower middle-class socioeconomic levels, using positive reinforcement. The subjects planned a specific self-reward for attainment of short-term alternative activity to eating.

520 Jordan, Henry A., and Levitz, Leonard S. "Behavior modification in the treatment of childhood obesity." Curr Concepts Nutr 3: 141-50, 1975. (8 References).
Outlines the steps necessary to implement a program with children on an out-patient basis.

521 Morgavan, Cheryl Buser. "Effects of the degree of children's obesity and compliant vs. non-compliant behavior on adults' evaluations and reinforcement of the children." For a summary see: Diss Abstr Int 37B(4): 1919, October, 1976.

522 Rivinus, T. M.; Drummond, T.; Combrinck-Graham, L. "A group-behavior treatment program for overweight children: results of a pilot study." In: Laron, Z., and Dickerson, Z., eds. The adipose child. Basel, Switzerland: Karger, 1975. 212-23. (33 References).
Relates the details of a group modification plan employed with ten obese children ranging in age from eight to thirteen years. Methods included modeling of appropriate eating habits, contracts, and rewards for desired behavior change. A panel discussion is included.

523 Shapiro, Joan R. "A comparison of various reward and monitoring procedures in the behavioral treatment of overweight children." For a summary see: Diss Abstr Int 36B(11): 5816, May, 1976.

524 Simkins, Lynda Katherine Stone. "An exploratory study of the effectiveness of two behavioral programs for weight reduction in parents and children." For a summary see: Diss Abstr Int 38A(5): 2567, November, 1977.

525 Werner, Russell T. "Weight reduction and weight control strategies for obese individuals: a case for behavior modification." J Sch Health 46(10): 602-6, December, 1976. (19 References).
Compares the results achieved by the four strategies commonly used to remediate obesity (diet restriction, drugs, surgery, and behavior modification). It is concluded that behavior modification is the most effective treatment on a long-term basis.

Q. PAIN

526 Sank, Lawrence I., and Biglan, Anthony. "Operant treatment of a case of recurrent abdominal pain in a ten-year-old boy." Behav Ther 5(5): 677-81, October, 1974. (3 References).
A token system was instituted which decreased the reported level of abdominal pain, increased school attendance, and ended the occurrence of severe pain attacks in the patient.

527 Yen, Sherman, and McIntire, Roger W. "Operant therapy for constant headache complaints: a simple response-cost approach." Psychol Rep 28(1): 267-70, February, 1971. (8 References).
Headache complaints of nine months duration were eliminated in a fourteen-year-old girl within eight weeks by requesting her to complete a written report on each headache.

R. PHOBIAS

1. Miscellaneous

528 Bentler, Peter M. "An infant's phobia treated with reciprocal inhibition therapy." J Child Psychol Psychiatry 3(3/4): 185-89, July-December, 1962. (6 References). (Reprinted in Item No. 45).
Presents a case report in which fear of water was eliminated in an eleven-month-old girl by the use of toys floating in water and by body contact with the mother.

529 Cavior, Norman, and Deutsch, Anne-Marie. "Systematic desensitization to reduce dream-induced anxiety." J Nerv Ment Dis 161(6): 433-35, December, 1975. (4 References).
A modified program of systematic desensitization was employed, together with instruction in a standard relaxation procedure, in the treatment of a sixteen-year-old inmate in an institution for juvenile offenders.

530 Freeman, Betty Jo; Roy, R. Ronald; Hemmick, Sally. "Extinction of a phobia of physical examination in a seven-year-old mentally retarded boy: a case study." Behav Res Ther 14(1): 63-64, 1976. (6 References).
Briefly reports on the reduction of a phobic condition by the pairing of the anxiety-producing situation with an anxiety-free situation, i.e., a

comfortable relationship between the patient and a nurse. The phobia was reduced in eleven sessions.

531 Hersen, Michel. "Treatment of a compulsive and phobic disorder through a total behavior therapy program: a case study." Psychotherapy 5(4): 220-25, December, 1968. (7 References). (Reprinted in Item No. 29).
Describes the successful treatment of a twelve-year-old phobic boy by means of a type of stimulus-response implosive therapy. The boy had previously undergone a six-month period of psychoanalytic therapy with little improvement.

532 Jersild, Arthur T., and Holmes, Frances B. "Methods of overcoming children's fears." J Psychol 1(1): 75-104, 1935. (4 References).
Reports on a study conducted by interviewing the parents of forty-seven children. Several techniques of treatment are discussed, including a form of "positive reconditioning" and approximation.

533 Kanfer, Frederick H.; Karoly, Paul; Newman, Alexander. "Reduction of children's fear of the dark by competence-related and situational threat-related verbal cues." J Consult Clin Psychol 43(2): 251-58, April, 1975. (20 References). (Reprinted in Item No. 35).
Presents a report on a study conducted with forty-five five- and six-year-old children who demonstrated marked fear of the dark. Two types of verbal controlling responses were used to reduce their fears.

534 Kelley, Crystal Anne Knight. "Play desensitization of fear of darkness in preschool children." For a summary see: Diss Abstr Int 35B(1): 510, July, 1974.

535 ————. "Play desensitization of fear of darkness in preschool children." Behav Res Ther 14(1): 79-81, 1976. (12 References).
Briefly reports on the use of systematic desensitization involving gradual exposure to the feared stimulus through symbolic play. The results obtained with forty preschool children indicated no significant reduction in fear of darkness.

536 Kushner, Malcolm. "Desensitization of post traumatic phobia." In: Ullmann, Leonard P., and Krasner, Leonard, eds. Case studies in behavior modification. New York: Holt, Rinehart & Winston, 1965. 193-95. (4 References).
Relaxation techniques and systematic desensitization were used to treat a seventeen-year-old boy traumatized by a minor traffic accident.

537 Lazarus, Arnold A. "The elimination of children's phobias by deconditioning." Med Proc (South Africa) 5(12): 261-65, June 13, 1959. (30 References).
Documents the elimination of phobias in eighteen children by a variety of conditioning techniques.

538 ————. "The elimination of children's fears by deconditioning." In: Eysenck, H. J., ed. Behavior therapy and the neuroses. New York: MacMillan, 1960. 114-22. (30 References).
Reports on the use of reciprocal inhibition with a group of eighteen phobic children ranging in age from three-and-one-half to twelve years. Four case histories are included.

539 Lazarus, Arnold A., and Abramovitz, Arnold. "The use of 'emotive imagery' in the treatment of children's phobias." J Ment Sci 108: 191-95, March, 1962. (6 References). (Reprinted in Item Nos. 21, 25, 30, 45).
Reports on the use of reciprocal inhibition technique for the treatment of nine phobic children whose symptoms were relieved in a very short time. No signs of recurrence over a twelve-month period were observed.

540 McCarthy, Barbara Powell. "How to help troubled children cope with fears and problems." Parents Mag 46(8): 44-45, 76, 82, August, 1971.
Advocates the use of behavior therapy for problems such as fear of loud noises, school phobia, and enuresis.

541 McNamara, J. Regis. "Behavior therapy in the classroom." J Sch Psychol 7(1): 48-51, 1968-69. (11 References). (Reprinted in Item No. 37).
Traces the development, procedures, and results of a program used to treat a five-year-old girl's bathroom phobia. The techniques included reciprocal inhibition, shaping, and the sequential presentation of fear-associated cues in the presence of preferred toys. A three-month follow-up showed no remission.

542 Miller, Lovick C.; Barrett, Curtis L.; Hampe, Edward; et al. "Comparison of reciprocal inhibition, psychotherapy, and waiting list control for phobic children." J Abnorm Psychol 79(3): 269-79, June, 1972. (48 References).
Compares three alternative types of therapy used with sixty-seven phobic children, ages six to fifteen. All therapies were found to be equally effective and all treatment effects were achieved with the children aged six to ten.

543 Montenegro, Herman. "Severe separation anxiety in two preschool children: successfully treated by reciprocal inhibition." J Child Psychol Psychiatry 9(2): 93-103, November, 1968. (21 References). (Reprinted in Item No. 21).
Details the day-by-day procedures employed in the treatment of separation anxiety in two preschool children. Real-life systematic desensitization was based on reciprocal inhibition.

544 Obler, Martin, and Terwilliger, Robert F. "Pilot study on the effectiveness of systematic desensitization with neurologically impaired children with phobic disorders." J Consult Clin Psychol 34(3): 314-18, June, 1970. (23 References). (Reprinted in Item No. 38).
Documents the successful use of systematic desensitization with thirty emotionally disturbed, neurologically impaired children who demonstrated phobic reactions either to the use of a public bus or to the sight of a live dog.

545 Ollendick, Thomas H., and Gruen, Gerald E. "Treatment of a bodily injury phobia with implosive therapy." J Consult Clin Psychol 38(3): 389-93, June, 1972. (14 References).
Presents a case report on the use of implosive therapy in two sessions with an eight-year-old phobic boy. Although both sessions elicited severe anxiety in the boy, a marked reduction in sleepless nights ensued.

546 O'Reilly, Patricia P. "Densensitization of fire bell phobia." J Sch Psychol 9(1): 55-57, 1971. (1 Reference). (Reprinted in Item No. 27).
Depicts the elimination of fire bell phobia in a six-year-old first-grade child by means of reciprocal inhibition. The school psychologist was instrumental in helping the child and the entire class to overcome the problem.

547 Tasto, Donald L. "Systematic desensitization, muscle relaxation and visual imagery in the counterconditioning of a four-year-old phobic child." Behav Res Ther 7(4): 409-11, November, 1969. (5 References). (Reprinted in Item Nos. 21, 35).
Reports on the successful elimination of severe phobia for loud, sudden noises in a four-year-old boy by means of muscle relaxation and in vivo conditioning. The treatment was completed in six sessions.

548 Wish, Peter A.; Hasazi, Joseph E.; Jurgela, Albert R. "Automated direct deconditioning of a childhood phobia." J Behav Ther Exp Psychiatry 4(3): 279-83, 1973. (9 References). (Reprinted in Item No. 35).
Presents a case history of an eleven-year-old boy with a chronic fear of loud noises. Treatment was completed within eight days and involved direct deconditioning at home using tape recordings of the feared sounds.

2. Animal Phobia

549 Bandura, Albert. "Modelling approaches to the modification of phobic disorders." Int Psychiatry Clin 6(1): 201-23, 1969. (25 References).
Summarizes two studies on dog phobias conducted with children and one study on snake phobia conducted with adolescents and adults.

550 Bandura, Albert; Grusec, Joan E.; Menlove, Frances L. "Vicarious extinction of avoidance behavior." J Pers Soc Psychol 5(1): 16-23, January, 1967. (12 References). (Reprinted in Item Nos. 21, 28, 38, 39).
Reports on an experiment conducted with forty-eight nursery school children in which the vicarious extinction of their fearful and avoidant responses toward dogs was explored.

551 Greer, John G.; Rainey, Theodore H.; Anderson, Robert M. "Modified systematic desensitization with a severely retarded child." In: Anderson, Robert M., Greer, John G. eds. Educating the severely and profoundly retarded. Baltimore, Maryland: University Park Press, 1976. 227-32. (11 References).
Traces the systematic desensitization of a severely retarded six-year-old boy's phobic reaction to dogs and cats.

552 Hill, Jae H.; Liebert, Robert M.; Mott, David E. W. "Vicarious extinction of avoidance behavior through films: an initial test." Psychol Rep 22(1): 192, February, 1968. (1 Reference).
Watching a film of a boy playing with a dog was successfully used to reduce fear of dogs in eight out of nine preschool boys.

553 Jones, Mary Cover. "The elimination of children's fears." J Exp Psychol 7(5): 382-90, October, 1924. (Reprinted in Item No. 26).

Compares different methods of removing fear responses of young children. The two most successful methods were direct conditioning and social imitation.

554 ———. "A laboratory study of fear: the case of Peter." Pedagog Semin 31: 308-15, 1924. (1 Reference). (Reprinted in Item No. 32).
Describes in detail the elimination of a fear response to animals in a three-year-old boy.

555 Kornhaber, Robert C., and Schroeder, Harold E. "Importance of model similarity on extinction of avoidance behavior in children." J Consult Clin Psychol 43(5): 601-7, October, 1975. (24 References).
Demonstrates that more similar models produce the greatest change regardless of the dimension on which similarity occurred. The subjects were forty second- and third-grade snake-phobic children.

556 MacDonald, Marian L. "Multiple impact behavior therapy in a child's dog phobia." J Behav Ther Exp Psychiatry 6(4): 317-22, December, 1975. (21 References).
An eleven-year-old boy's fear of dogs was eliminated by a variety of coordinated, learning-based procedures.

557 Murphy, Cynthia M., and Bootzin, Richard R. "Active and passive participation in the contact desensitization of snake fear in children." Behav Ther 4(2): 203-11, March, 1973. (9 References).
Compares active and passive desensitization procedures, both of which were found to be highly effective in reducing snake fear in children.

558 Ney, Philip G. "Combined psychotherapy and deconditioning of a child's phobia." Can Psychiatr Assoc J 13(4): 293-94, August, 1968. (3 References).
Presents a case report of a four-and-one-half-year-old boy whose fear of bees was brought under control by the use of reciprocal inhibition.

559 Ritter, Brunhilde. "The group desensitization of children's snake phobias using vicarious and contact desensitization procedures." Behav Res Ther 6(1): 1-6, February, 1968. (14 References). (Reprinted in Item No. 21).
Contrasts vicarious desensitization and contact desensitization using forty-four snake-phobic preadolescent children.

3. School Phobia

560 Ayllon, Teodoro; Smith, D.; Rogers, M. "Behavioral management of school phobia." J Behav Ther Exp Psychiatry 1(2): 125-38, June, 1970. (18 References). (Reprinted in Item Nos. 37, 38, 43).
Behavioral procedures were applied to the analysis and modification of school phobia in an eight-year-old girl. Following a redefinition of the problem as zero or low probability of school attendance, the rewards for staying home were removed, and refusal to attend resulted in punishment. Regular school attendance was established in forty-five days.

561 Brown, Ronald E.; Copeland, Rodney E.; Hall, R. Vance. "School phobia: effects of behavior modification treatment applied by an elementary school principal." Child Study J 4(3): 125-34, 1974. (11 References).

Systematic reinforcing and shaping procedures were used by a school principal to modify an eleven-year-old boy's school phobia. Tickets to a football game were used as a reward.

562 Chapel, James L. "Treatment of a case of school phobia by reciprocal inhibition." Can Psychiatr Assoc J 12(1): 25-28, February, 1967. (6 References).
Presents a case history of an eleven-year-old boy whose school phobia was brought under control in six weeks. Conventional therapy had failed to bring about the desired results. Attention is drawn to the need for tolerance in such situations.

563 Edlund, Calvin A. "A reinforcement approach to the elimination of a child's school phobia." Ment Hyg 55(4): 433-36, October, 1971. (5 References).
Describes the successful treatment of a seven-year-old girl's school phobia using reinforcers available at home.

564 Garvey, W. P., and Hegrenes, J. R. "Desensitization techniques in the treatment of school phobia." Am J Orthopsychiatry 36(1): 147-52, January, 1966.
Traces the series of graded steps of anxiety-producing situations that were worked through in the treatment of a ten-year-old boy's school phobia. Treatment was completed in twenty days.

565 Hersen, Michel. "Behavior modification approach to a school-phobia case." J Clin Psychol 26(1): 128-32, January, 1970. (6 References).
A program involving the mother, the school guidance counselor, and the boy himself resulted in the elimination of school avoidant reactions within a period of fifteen weeks.

566 ————. "The behavioral treatment of school phobia: current techniques." J Nerv Ment Dis 153(2): 99-107, August, 1971. (33 References).
Reviews case histories and indicates that a variety of behavioral approaches appear effective in extinguishing school phobic behavior. Further research is advocated--particularly that which involves more detailed long-term follow-up procedures.

567 Kelly, Eugene W., Jr. "School phobia: a review of theory and treatment." Psychol Sch 10(1): 33-42, January, 1973. (45 References).
Discusses various approaches, including behavior modification, in eliminating school phobia. Desensitization and positive reinforcement for school attendance are the most commonly used techniques. Quick recognition of the problem is deemed essential to the development of a successful remedial program.

568 Kennedy, Wallace A. "A behavioristic, community-oriented approach to school phobia and other disorders." In: Rickard, Henry C., ed. Behavioral intervention in human problems. New York: Pergamon, 1971. 37-60. (24 References).
Reviews methods of treating school phobia and describes in detail a behavior modification method conducted with fifty children in a university-based clinic.

569 Lazarus, Arnold A.; Davison, Gerald C.; Polefka, David A. "Classical and operant factors in the treatment of a school phobia." J Abnorm Psychol 70(3): 225-29, June, 1965. (Reprinted in Item Nos. 21, 25, 27, 28, 29).
A case history of a nine-year-old boy is used to demonstrate the advantages of employing both classical and operant conditioning procedures. Therapists were interchanged without impeding therapeutic progress.

570 Patterson, G. R. "A learning theory approach to the treatment of the school phobic child." In: Ullmann, Leonard P., and Krasner, Leonard, eds. Case studies in behavior modification. New York: Holt, Rinehart & Winston, 1965. 279-85. (14 References). (Reprinted in Item Nos. 22, 27).
Describes the use of interference and reinforcement in the treatment of a seven-year-old school-phobic boy. Twenty-minute conditioning sessions were followed by highly structured ten-minute parent interviews. A marked improvement was noted after a series of twenty-three such sessions.

571 Perkin, G. J.; Rowe, G. P.; Farmer, R. G. "Operant conditioning of emotional responsiveness as a prerequisite for behavioural analysis: a case study of an adolescent school phobic." Aust NZ J Psychiatry 7(3): 180-84, September, 1973. (12 References).
Documents the increase of the patient's emotional responsiveness to a level at which a behavioral analysis could be undertaken. The additional behavioral techniques used are also described.

572 Tahmisian, James A., and McReynolds, William T. "Use of parents as behavioral engineers in the treatment of a school-phobic girl." J Couns Psychol 18(3): 225-28, May, 1971. (11 References).
Describes the treatment of a thirteen-year-old school-phobic girl by the parents' removal of the reinforcing aspects of non-attendance. Treatment was completed within a three-week period.

S. RUMINATION

573 Cunningham, Charles E., and Linscheid, Thomas R. "Elimination of chronic infant ruminating by electric shock." Behav Ther 7(2): 231-34, March, 1976. (10 References).
Mild electric shock was effective in eliminating ruminative vomiting in a nine-month-old infant. There was an immediate suppression of ruminating, an increase in weight, and an improvement in social responsiveness. Follow-up at six months showed a continued improvement with no recurrence of rumination.

574 Lang, Peter J., and Melamed, Barbara G. "Avoidance conditioning therapy of an infant with chronic ruminative vomiting." J Abnorm Psychol 74(1): 1-8, February, 1969. (13 References).
Reports on the use of electric shock to reduce life-threatening vomiting and ruminative behavior in a nine-month-old boy. EMG records were used to assess response characteristics and to determine shock contingencies. Cessation of the vomiting was followed by weight gain.

575 Luckey, Robert E.; Watson, Carrie M.; Musick, James K. "Aversive conditioning as a means of inhibiting vomiting and rumination." Am J Ment Defic 73(1): 139-42, July, 1968. (14 References). (Reprinted in Item No. 33).

Presents a case report on the successful use of mild electric shock to reduce vomiting and chronic rumination in a six-year-old severely retarded boy. Marked improvement was evident by the fifth day of conditioning with no significant recurrence during the follow-up period of ninety-three days. A general improvement in overall behavior was also found, and the child appeared to become increasingly amenable to self-care training.

576 Murray, Michael E.; Keele, Doman K.; McCarver, James W. "Behavioral treatment of rumination: a case study." Clin Pediatr 15(7): 591-93, 596, July, 1976. (8 References).
Documents the quick and effective control of rumination in a six-month-old boy by a combination of behavioral procedures, including stimulus control, reinforcement, and punishment.

577 Sajwaj, Thomas; Libet, Julian; Agras, Stewart. "Lemon-juice therapy: the control of life-threatening rumination in a six-month-old infant." J Appl Behav Anal 7(4): 557-63, Winter, 1974. (14 References).
Cites the successful use of lemon juice as a punisher in the treatment of chronic rumination. The use of lemon juice is advocated in preference to electric shock or massive noncontingent attention.

578 Sheinbein, Marc. "Treatment for the hospitalized infantile ruminator: programmed brief social behavior reinforcers." Clin Pediatr 14(8): 719-24, August, 1975. (4 References).
Presents a case study of a nineteen-month-old boy whose regurgitation was controlled by the use of social reinforcers when he did not regurgitate and the use of restraints when he did.

579 White, James C., Jr., and Taylor, Donna J. "Noxious conditioning as a treatment for rumination." Ment Retard 5(1): 30-33, February, 1967. (9 References).
Electric shock was successfully used to reduce rumination in two retarded patients, one of whom was a fourteen-year-old male.

T. SELF-CONCEPT

580 Danzig, Lawrence. "Teacher use of behavior modification techniques to improve the self-concept of educable mentally retarded pupils." For a summary see: Diss Abstr Int 38A(7): 4089, January, 1978.

581 Hauserman, Norma; Miller, Jay S.; Bond, Frances T. "A behavioral approach to changing self-concept in elementary school children." Psychol Rec 26(1): 111-16, Winter, 1976. (12 References).
Describes the use of positive self-statements in promoting positive self-concepts in negative self-concept children.

582 Keat, Donald B. "Broad-spectrum behavior therapy with children: a case presentation." Behav Ther 3(3): 454-59, July, 1972. (21 References).
Illustrates the use of a wide variety of behavioral techniques, including training of the parents, in the treatment of an eleven-year-old boy, generally reported to be lacking in self-confidence and evincing social withdrawal.

583 Krop, H.; Calhoon, B.; Verrier, R. "Modification of the 'self-concept' of emotionally disturbed children by covert reinforcement." Behav Ther 2(2): 201-4, April, 1971. (12 References).
Compares overt and covert reinforcement of the self-concept of thirty-six children (mean age 10.5 years). Results indicate that covert reinforcement produced the more positive changes.

584 Lane, Jeffrey. "The effects of a self-concept enhancing operant reinforcement procedure on the self-concepts of selected elementary school students." For a summary see: Diss Abstr Int 36A(7): 4356, January, 1976.

585 Marsh, Helen Rome. "The effectiveness of conditioning in increasing children's self-esteem through identification with admired peers." For a summary see: Diss Abstr Int 34B(9): 4636, March, 1974.

586 Morena, Dorothy A., and Litrownik, Alan J. "Self-concept in educable mentally retarded and emotionally handicapped children: relationship between behavioral and self-report indices and an attempt at modification." J Abnorm Child Psychol 2(4): 281-92, December, 1974. (20 References).
Indicates that mentally retarded and emotionally handicapped children differ in self-concept development. Attempts to modify self-concept should include greater modeling exposure as well as increased opportunity for performance with its resultant feedback.

587 Phillips, Robert H. "The use of behavior modification to improve self-esteem in low income elementary school children." For a summary see: Diss Abstr Int 36A(3): 1400, September, 1975.

588 Sopina, Mary Victoria. "Self-concept changes in adolescents following behavior modification." For a summary see: Diss Abstr Int 31B(10): 6268, April, 1971.

589 Throckmorton, Kirby Lee. "Self-concept and reinforcement: two paths to achievement for black and white elementary school children." For a summary see: Diss Abstr Int 36B(7): 3683, January, 1976.

590 Washington, K. R. "Effects of systematic reinforcement and a self-awareness program on the self-concept of black preschool children." Child Study J 6(4): 199-208, 1976. (14 References).
Fifty-two black preschool children were subjects of a study which involved the use of positive reinforcement by teachers and parents. The program had significant effects on self-concepts, especially in the male subjects.

U. SELF-INJURY

591 Allen, K. Eileen, and Harris, Florence R. "Elimination of a child's excessive scratching by training the mother in reinforcement procedures." Behav Res Ther 4(2): 79-84, May, 1966. (9 References). (Reprinted in Item No. 27, 32).
Demonstrates the successful use of reinforcement procedures by the mother of a five-year-old girl whose excessive scratching was of almost a year's duration. The undesirable behavior was eliminated in six weeks; a follow-up at four months showed no recurrence.

592 Bachman, John A. "Self-injurious behavior: a behavioral analysis." J Abnorm Psychol 80(3): 211-24, December, 1972. (43 References).
Surveys the literature, discusses ethical and practical considerations, and proposes a discriminative stimulus-conditioned reinforcer hypothesis and an avoidance hypothesis to explain SIB in terms of learning principles.

593 Carr, Edward G.; Newsom, Crighton D.; Binkoff, Jody A. "Stimulus control of self-destructive behavior in a psychotic child." J Abnorm Child Psychol 4(2): 139-53, 1976. (16 References).
Documents two procedures which attempted to develop effective procedures for decreasing self-destruction and to discover new functional relationships relating to the motivation of self-destruction. The patient, an eight-year-old boy previously diagnosed as a childhood schizophrenic with mental retardation, had failed to respond to the usual behavioral interventions. Emphasis is placed on the need for a functional analysis of such behavior before instituting a corrective program.

594 Chandler, P. J.; Wilbur, Robert L.; Carpenter, Billy L. "Modification of self-mutilative behavior by aversive conditioning." Biomed Sci Instrum 11: 185-90, 1975. (14 References).
Evaluates instrumentation systems involving the use of electric shock.

595 Freeman, B. J.; Graham, Vicki; Ritvo, E. R. "Reduction of self-destructive behavior by overcorrection." Psychol Rep 37(2): 446, October, 1975. (4 References).
Briefly reports on the effectiveness of overcorrection in reducing nail-picking in a six-and-one-half-year-old aphasic girl.

596 Merbaum, Michael. "The modification of self-destructive behavior by a mother-therapist using aversive stimulation." Behav Ther 4(3): 442-47, May, 1973. (10 References).
Mild aversive shock was used effectively to reduce self-destructive behavior in a twelve-year-old boy. Procedures were effective in both the home and the school environment.

597 Mogel, Steven, and Schiff, William. "'Extinction' of a head-bumping symptom of eight years' duration in two minutes: a case report." Behav Res Ther 5(2): 131-32, May, 1967. (3 References).
Briefly describes the extinguishing of a head-bumping symptom in a ten-year-old girl by asking her to demonstrate the phenomena to the therapist. It is hypothesized that the patient had a high desire to please the therapist and experienced shame and embarrassment.

598 Romanczyk, Raymond G., and Goren, Elizabeth R. "Severe self-injurious behavior: the problem of clinical control." J Consult Clin Psychol 43(5): 730-39, October, 1975. (24 References).
Details the ten-month treatment of a six-and-one-half-year-old boy seen on an outpatient basis. Contingent electric shock and differential reinforcement were primary techniques used. Total suppression was eventually achieved in the clinical setting, but generalization to the natural environment was only moderately successful. Technical, ethical, and theoretical issues are discussed.

599 Ross, R. R.; Meichenbaum, D. H.; Humphrey, Carol. "Treatment of nocturnal headbanging by behavior modification techniques: a case report." Behav Res Ther 9(2): 151-54, May, 1971. (11 References).

Illustrates that sleep state maladaptive behavior is amenable to the same behavior modification techniques used during the waking state. The subject was a sixteen-year-old institutionalized female offender. The removal of staff attention following the occurrence of headbanging episodes resulted in a decrease in the headbanging. The second phase of treatment was concerned with the antecedent stimuli thought to be eliciting the headbanging behavior.

600 Williams, C., and Surtees, P. "Mannerisms, mutilation and management." In: Brengelmann, J. C., ed. Progress in behavior therapy. New York: Springer-Verlag, 1975. 1-12. (21 References).
Outlines current work with children exhibiting self-mutilating behavior. An experimental study, using a patient with limited behavioral repertoire, is also reported.

601 Woody, Robert H. "Controlling pica via an environmental-psychobehavioral strategy: with special reference to lead poisoning." J Sch Health 41(10): 548-55, December, 1971. (16 References).
Examines the development of pica from the behavioral point of view and advocates the use of behavior modification techniques (namely, aversion and positive reinforcement) in its control.

V. SEXUAL IDENTIFICATION

602 Bates, John E.; Skilbeck, William M.; Smith, Katherine V.; et al. "Intervention with families of gender-disturbed boys." Am J Orthopsychiatry 45(1): 150-57, January, 1975. (16 References).
Summarizes the treatment, based largely on behavior modification principles, of boys who demonstrated highly effeminate interests and a marked deficiency in social skills. Application was eventually in group settings for both the boys and their parents.

603 Dupont, Henry. "Social learning theory and the treatment of transvestite behavior in an eight-year-old boy." Psychotherapy 5(1): 44-45, Winter, 1968. (5 References).
Describes the successful treatment of a child who was not seen by the therapist. Only one interview was conducted with the father alone.

604 McCandless, Boyd R.; Bush, Carol; Carden, Ayse Ilgaz. "Reinforcing contingencies for sex-role behaviors in preschool children." Contemp Educ Psychol 1(3): 241-46, July, 1976. (3 References).
Reports on a study conducted with two groups of disadvantaged children in a day care center.

605 Parish, Thomas S., and Bryant, William T. "Reversing the effects of sexism in elementary school girls through the use of classical conditioning procedures." Paper presented at the Annual Meeting of the American Educational Research Association, San Francisco, April 19-23, 1976. (ED 126 375).
Girls who experienced conditioning procedures demonstrated more positive evaluations of females than did their control and placebo counterparts.

606 Rekers, George A., and Lovaas, O. Ivar. "Behavioral treatment and assessment of childhood cross-gender problems." Paper presented at the Western Psychological Association Meeting, Anaheim, California, April 13, 1973. 41p.

Feminine behaviors decreased and masculine behaviors increased in a four-year-eleven-month-old boy following behavior modification in the home and in the clinic setting.

607 ———. "Behavioral treatment of deviant sex-role behaviors in a male child." J Appl Behav Anal 7(2): 173-90, Summer, 1974. (48 References).
Demonstrates reinforcement control over pronounced feminine behaviors in a five-year-old boy. Both social reinforcers and token reinforcers were used in the clinic and in the home setting.

608 Rekers, George A.; Lovaas, O. Ivar; Low, Benson. "The behavioral treatment of a 'transsexual' preadolescent boy." J Abnorm Child Psychol 2(2): 99-116, June, 1974. (20 References).
Feminine sex-typed behaviors were reduced and masculine sex-typed behaviors were increased in an eight-year-old boy by means of a token economy program with back-up reinforcers used in the clinic, at home, and at school.

609 Rekers, George A., and Varni, James W. "Self-monitoring and self-reinforcement processes in a pre-transsexual boy." Behav Res Ther 15(2): 177-80, 1977. (14 References).
Suggests that self-regulation strategies were effective in producing the desired behavioral changes in a six-year-old boy who used a wrist counter to record his playing with boys' toys.

610 Winkler, R. C. "What types of sex-role behavior should behavior modifiers promote?" J Appl Behav Anal 10(3): 549-52, Fall, 1977. (11 References).
Criticizes the use of traditional sex-role concepts in forming target behaviors--as reported by Rekers and Lovaas, 1974 (Item No. 607)--and suggests androgenous behavior as an empirically based alternative.

W. SHYNESS/SOCIAL WITHDRAWAL

611 Allen, Richard; Safer, Daniel J.; Heaton, Ronald; et al. "Behavior therapy for socially ineffective children." J Am Acad Child Psychiatry 14(3): 500-509, Summer, 1975. (34 References).
Traces the implementation of a group treatment program which stressed the tangible reinforcement of graduated social tasks. Therapy sessions were held for one hour weekly with five groups (three for treatment; two for control) of fourth- and fifth-graders. The sociometric outcome for the treatment group showed significant gains, whereas the control group showed only a minimal change.

612 Clement, Paul W., and Milne, D. Courtney. "Group play therapy and tangible reinforcers used to modify the behavior of eight-year-old boys." Behav Res Ther 5(4): 301-12, November, 1967. (16 References). (Reprinted in Item No. 43).
Contrasts three play therapy techniques used with eleven eight-year-old boys referred by their teachers because of shy, withdrawn behavior. In the first group (the token group) the boys had a therapist and received tangible reinforcers for social approach behavior. In the second group (the verbal group) the boys had a therapist but no tangible reinforcers. The third (control) group met without a therapist. Each group met fourteen times. The token group demonstrated a greater increase in social

approach behavior than did the verbal group. The control group failed to demonstrate any change.

613 Patterson, Gerald R.; McNeal, Shirley; Hawkins, Nancy; et al. "Reprogramming the social environment." J Child Psychol Psychiatry 8(3/4): 181-95, December, 1967. (22 References). (Reprinted in Item No. 47).
Reports on a study conducted with a withdrawn five-year-old boy who sporadically displayed bizarre emotional outbursts. Following work with the parents, changes were effected in the child's social environment that resulted in changes in his behavior.

614 Potter, Ellis Brian. "The use of group operant techniques to modify shy boys' behavior." For a summary see: Diss Abstr Int 32B(6): 3623, December, 1971.

615 Ross, Dorothea M.; Ross, Sheila A.; Evans, Thomas A. "The modification of extreme social withdrawal by modeling with guided participation." J Behav Ther Exp Psychiatry 2(4): 273-79, December, 1971. (14 References).
Documents a successful seven-week treatment program conducted in a naturalistic setting. A model demonstrated social interactions, provided opportunities for practice, and participated with the subject in other social interactions.

616 Tosi, Donald; Upshaw, Kenneth; Lande, Angela; et al. "Group counseling with nonverbalizing elementary students." J Couns Psychol 18(5): 437-40, September, 1971. (7 References).
Compares two procedures--social reinforcement and the Premack Principle--in a group counseling setting with twenty-four reticent sixth- and seventh-grade students. Both groups showed significant gains but did not differ from each other.

X. SIBLING RELATIONSHIPS

617 Arnold, J. E.; Levine, A. G.; Patterson, G. R. "Changes in sibling behavior following family intervention." J Consult Clin Psychol 43(5): 683-88, October, 1975. (18 References).
Investigates the changes in behavior of the siblings of twenty-seven treated predelinquents. Results indicated significant reductions in rates of deviant behavior for the siblings and that these effects were maintained over a six-month period.

618 Lavigueur, Henry; Peterson, Robert F.; Sheese, Jan Gouse; et al. "Behavioral treatment in the home: effects on an untreated sibling and long-term follow-up." Behav Ther 4(2): 431-41, March, 1973. (18 References).
Time-out and differential reinforcement were employed to control the disruptive behavior of a three-year-old boy; similar changes resulted in the behavior of his five-year-old sibling.

619 Leitenberg, Harold; Burchard, John D.; Burchard, Sara N.; et al. "Using positive reinforcement to suppress behavior: some experimental comparisons with sibling conflict." Behav Ther 8(2): 168-82, March, 1977. (13 References).
Compares the relative suppressive effects of omission training (or DRO) and a specific reinforced alternative response procedure. One of the

major findings was that both procedures reduced the frequency of conflict by approximately 50 percent.

620 O'Leary, K. Daniel; O'Leary, Susan; Becker, Wesley C. "Modification of a deviant sibling interaction pattern in the home." Behav Res Ther 5(2): 113-20, May, 1967. (12 References). (Reprinted in Item Nos. 36, 43).
Describes the successful home modification of undesirable interactions between a six-year-old boy and his three-year-old brother. Methods used were a combination of a token system and a time-out procedure which were initiated by the therapist and gradually taken over by the mother.

621 Veenstra, Marjorie Shafer. "Behavior modification in the home with the mother as the experimenter: the effect of differential reinforcement on sibling negative response rates." Child Dev 42(6): 2079-83, December, 1971. (14 References).
Presents a case study in which a mother reduced negative sibling interaction at the dinner table by social reinforcement of positive interactions while extinguishing negative interactions.

Y. SLEEPING

622 Clement, Paul. "Elimination of sleepwalking in a seven-year-old boy." J Consult Clin Psychol 34(1): 22-26, February, 1970. (8 References).
A conditioning program, similar to that used in the behavioral treatment of enuresis, was carried out by the mother. A marked reduction of sleepwalking frequency resulted.

623 Shows, W. Derek. "A sleeping epidemic among first-grade children: crisis intervention." Community Ment Health J 10(3): 332-36, Fall, 1974.
Six first-grade girls, who had developed a pattern of going to sleep in school, were successfully treated by a removal of the reinforcing attention that had been directed toward this behavior.

624 Weil, Gabriel, and Goldfried, Marvin R. "Treatment of insomnia in an eleven-year-old child through self-relaxation." Behav Ther 4(2): 282-94, March, 1973. (4 References). (Reprinted in Item No. 35).
Describes the successful treatment of insomnia using tape recorded instructions for relaxation. Although the therapy was conducted over a period of two months, the therapist met with the child and her parents on only seven occasions.

625 Wright, Logan; Woodcock, James; Scott, Robert. "Treatment of sleep disturbance in a young child by conditioning." South Med J 63(2): 174-76, February, 1970. (11 References).
Presents a case study in which extinction and procedures of need reduction were used to control a combination of organically based hypersensitivity, phobic display, and tantrum behavior.

626 Yen, Sherman; McIntire, Roger W.; Berkowitz, Samuel. "Extinction of inappropriate sleeping behavior: multiple assessment." Psychol Rep 30(2): 375-78, April, 1972. (4 References).
The application of behavior modification eliminated an inappropriate sleeping pattern in a seventeen-year-old boy within a period of eight weeks.

Z. SPEECH

1. Miscellaneous Speech Problems

627 Acker, Loren E.; Kelley, William R.; Mason, Chris R.; et al. "Short-term team implemented behavior modification of speech in a young boy." Can J Behav Sci 5(2): 174-82, April, 1973. (8 References).
Describes the behavior therapy administered to a three-and-one-half year-old boy over a six-week period which resulted in substantial gains.

628 Borus, Judith F.; Greenfield, Sandra; Spiegel, Bernard; et al. "Establishing imitative speech employing operant techniques in a group setting." J Speech Hear Disord 38(4): 533-41, November, 1973. (11 References).
Advocates the use of group therapy as the most economical of manpower, space, and time. The description of a team approach with a group of four children is included.

629 Brookshire, Robert H. "Speech pathology and the experimental analysis of behavior." J Speech Hear Disord 32(3): 215-27, August, 1967. (19 References).
Reviews the use of operant conditioning procedures in the treatment of speech problems.

630 Daly, David A.; Cantrell, Robert P.; Cantrell, Mary Lynn; et al. "Structuring speech therapy contingencies with an oral apraxic child." J Speech Hear Disord 37(1): 22-32, February, 1972. (20 References).
Illustrates the use of the WGTA, an apparatus previously used in psychological research, to structure the treatment environment for maximally effective learning.

631 Fife, Betsy L. "The use of operant conditioning to increase the frequency of a child's verbal responses to questions." J Psychiatr Nurs 15(11): 31-34, November, 1977. (3 References).
A five-year-old boy's verbal interactions were increased by the use of role modeling, positive reinforcement with candy and attention, and the withholding of reinforcement for lack of response. Short-term treatment was carried out in a hospital psychiatric unit.

632 Holland, Audrey L. "Some applications of behavioral principles to clinical speech problems." J Speech Hear Disord 32(1): 11-18, February, 1967. (24 References).
Reviews basic behavioral principles and suggests ways in which they may be utilized effectively in treating speech problems. Behavioral analysis is applied to some successfully used clinical procedures; the extention of these findings is recommended.

633 McReynolds, Leija V. "Operant conditioning for investigating speech sound discrimination in aphasic children." J Speech Hear Res 9(4): 519-28, December, 1966. (7 References).
Candy and trinkets were used as reinforcers for correct sound discrimination in a study conducted with eight aphasic and eight normal children.

634 McReynolds, Leija V., and Huston, Kay. "Token loss in speech imitation training." J Speech Hear Disord 36(4): 486-95, November, 1971. (11 References).
Compares the use of tokens as positive reinforcers for correct responses with the loss of tokens for incorrect responses. Although it was con-

cluded that token loss could be an effective technique, related variables should be examined carefully.

635 Shprintzen, Robert J.; McCall, Gerald N.; Skolnick, M. Leon. "A new therapeutic technique for the treatment of velopharyngeal incompetence." J Speech Hear Disord 40(1): 69-83, February, 1975. (8 References).
Describes an operant procedure designed to utilize successive approximation to competent speech via competent blowing or whistling.

2. Articulation

636 Bailey, Jon S.; Timbers, Gary D.; Phillips, Elery L.; et al. "Modification of articulation errors of pre-delinquents by their peers." J Appl Behav Anal 4(4): 265-81, Winter, 1971. (18 References).
A speech correction procedure, involving modeling, peer approval, contingent points, and feedback, was successfully used by predelinquent peers who were themselves given points for their participation.

637 Costello, Janis, and Ferrer, Jami. "Punishment contingencies for the reduction of incorrect responses during articulation instruction." J Commun Disord 9(1): 43-61, March, 1976. (41 References).
Compares the effects of punishment combined with positive reinforcement, and reinforcement alone, on the articulation of six young children. The combination was found to be the more effective.

638 Johnston, James M., and Johnston, Gwendolyn T. "Modification of consonant speech-sound articulation in young children." J Appl Behav Anal 5(3): 233-46, Fall, 1972. (28 References).
Describes a series of three experiments performed in a classroom setting using small groups of young children with severe articulation problems. Variations on basic token reinforcement procedures were used.

639 Mumm, Myrna Neuman. "A comparison of the results of 'behavior-modification' versus 'traditional' approaches in the treatment of misarticulations in a public school setting." For a summary see: Diss Abstr Int 34B(11): 5734, May, 1974.

3. Stuttering

640 Floyd, Susan Ann. "Differential effects of contingent positive and negative listener response on the percentage of syllable disfluency of preschool boys." For a summary see: Diss Abstr Int 35B(4): 1970, October, 1974.

641 Ingham, Roger J., and Andrews, Gavin. "Behavior therapy and stuttering: a review." J Speech Hear Disord 38(4): 405-41, November, 1973. (145 References).
Reviews the literature with particular reference to measurement procedures, treatment design, and the adequacy of the measures of outcome.

642 Kondas, O. "The treatment of stammering in children by the shadowing method." Behav Res Ther 5(4): 325-29, November, 1967. (12 References). (Reprinted in Item No. 21).
Reports on the use of the "shadowing" technique with nineteen stammerers ranging in age from five to twenty years. Shadowing consists of the therapist reading from an unknown text and the stammerers repeating

exactly, one or two words later. Seventy percent of the cases were successfully treated, and relapses occurred in only 12 percent of the cases.

643 Manning, Walter H.; Trutna, Phyllis A.; Shaw, Candyce K. "Verbal versus tangible reward for children who stutter." J Speech Hear Disord 41(1): 52-62, February, 1976. (11 References).
Compares the effectiveness of verbal and tangible reinforcers in reducing the dysfluencies of three children (ages six, eight, and nine years). Results revealed that both forms of reward were equally effective. Possible explanations are discussed.

644 Martin, Richard R.; Kuhl, Patricia; Haroldson, Samuel. "An experimental treatment with two preschool stuttering children." J Speech Hear Res 15(4): 743-52, December, 1972. (13 References).
Describes the successful use of a "talking" puppet in reducing the stuttering frequencies of two preschool children with maintenance and carry-over to non-treatment situations.

645 Rickard, Henry C., and Mundy, Martha B. "Direct manipulation of stuttering behavior: an experimental-clinical approach." In: Ullmann, Leonard P., and Krasner, Leonard, eds. Case studies in behavior modification. New York: Holt, Rinehart & Winston, 1965. 268-74. (7 References).
Presents a case study of a nine-year-old boy whose stuttering was brought under control in the clinical setting by ignoring the stuttering behavior and reinforcing non-stuttering behavior.

646 Ryan, Bruce P. "Operant procedures applied to stuttering therapy for children." J Speech Hear Disord 36(2): 264-80, May, 1971. (12 References).
Describes various programs for five child stutterers ranging in age from six to nine years. The programs included desensitization, delayed auditory feedback, and gradual increase in the length and complexity of the speech utterances.

647 Shames, George H., and Egolf, Donald B. "Evaluation and therapy for children." In: Shames, George H., and Egolf, Donald B. Operant conditioning and the management of stuttering: a book for clinicians. Englewood Cliffs, New Jersey: Prentice-Hall, 1976. 77-101.
Presents an evaluation and management program for child stutterers and describes a program conducted with nine children, ranging in age from five to thirteen years, and their parents.

648 Shaw, Candyce K., and Shrum, William F. "The effects of response-contingent reward on the connected speech of children who stutter." J Speech Hear Disord 37(1): 75-88, February, 1972. (12 References).
The frequency of stuttering behaviors of three children (aged nine and ten years) was reduced by using a response-contingent reward of fluent verbal responses. Follow-up revealed a spontaneous carry-over of the fluent speech.

649 Verbal reinforcement during therapy with stutterers. 1972. 101p. For ordering information see: Government Reports Announcements 74(25): 36, December 13, 1974. Available from NTIS, Springfield, Virginia 22161. Order No. PB-235-235. (ED 117 902).

Presents a series of studies using verbal contingent stimuli in the clinical setting. Positive verbal reinforcers were found to be the most effective contingent stimuli, and time-out was an effective punishing contingent stimulus in group therapy.

650 Wahler, R. G.; Sperling, K. A.; Thomas, M. R.; et al. "The modification of childhood stuttering: some response-response relationships." J Exp Child Psychiatry 9(3): 411-28, June, 1970. (17 References).
The stuttering of two boys (ages nine and four years) was reduced when contingency management procedures were applied to their secondary, mildly deviant behavior problems.

AA. TANTRUMS

651 Ames, Sean McCurdy. "Four behavior therapy techniques for treating temper tantrums in young children: a comparative outcome study." For a summary see: Diss Abstr Int 37B(11): 5821, May, 1977.

652 Bernal, Martha E.; Duryea, John S.; Pruett, Harold L.; et al. "Behavior modification and the brat symdrome." J Consult Clin Psychol 32(4): 447-55, August, 1968. (10 References). (Reprinted in Item Nos. 27, 47).
Presents a case study of an eight-and-one-half-year-old boy demonstrating tantrums, physically abusive behavior, and other behavioral disturbances. The mother was instructed in behavior modification techniques and was able to effect a marked reduction in the disruptive behaviors within a period of twenty-five weeks.

653 Carlson, Constance S.; Arnold, Carole R.; Becker, Wesley C.; et al. "The elimination of tantrum behavior of a child in an elementary classroom." Behav Res Ther 6(1): 117-19, February, 1968. (Reprinted in Item Nos. 22, 39).
Briefly reports on the elimination of tantrum behavior in an eight-year-old girl of average intelligence. Instead of reinforcing the disruptive behavior by removing the child from the classroom, the attention of the rest of the children was withdrawn from her by giving candy reinforcers to those who ignored the tantrums. The child was able to earn a treat for the class by non-tantrum behavior.

654 Conway, John, and Bucher, Bradley D. "'Soap in the mouth' as an aversive consequence." Behav Ther 5(1): 154-56, January, 1974. (2 References).
Offers a brief report on the use of shaving cream squirted into the mouth of a child to control frequent tantrum behavior.

655 Kaufmann, Leon M., and Wagner, Bernard R. "Barb: a systematic treatment technology for temper control disorders." Behav Ther 3(1): 84-90, January, 1972. (8 References).
Describes an individual programming technique used to teach temper control. Special reference is made to adolescents.

656 Petty, Gary L. "Desensitization of parents to tantrum behavior." Am J Clin Hypn 19(2): 95-97, October, 1976. (8 References).
Documents two case studies in which mothers were desensitized to their children's temper tantrums in order to be able to apply contingency management principles at home.

657 Sailor, Wayne; Guess, Doug; Rutherford, Gorin; et al. "Control of tantrum behavior by operant techniques during experimental verbal training." J Appl Behav Anal 1(3): 237-43, Fall, 1968. (3 References). (Reprinted in Item Nos. 21, 29).
Discusses a technique of controlling disruptive behavior that was used during an ongoing program of verbal training with a nine-year-old retarded girl. The technique offers an alternative to procedures which require punishment or time-out.

658 Williams, Carl D. "The elimination of tantrum behavior by extinction procedures." J Abnorm Soc Psychol 59(2): 269, September, 1959. (Reprinted in Item Nos. 23, 42, 45).
Reports on the successful treatment of tyrant-like tantrums in a twenty-one-month-old boy by the removal of reinforcement, but without the use of aversive punishment.

BB. TEST ANXIETY

659 Barabasz, Arreed F. "Classroom teachers as paraprofessional therapists in group systematic desensitization of test anxiety." Psychiatry 38(4): 388-92, November, 1974. (13 References).
Describes a study conducted with test-phobic fifth-, sixth-, and seventh-grade students in which classroom teachers administered a structured systematic desensitization program. Significant improvements were noted.

660 ————. "Group desensitization of test anxiety in elementary school." J Psychol 83(2): 295-301, March, 1973. (26 References).
Eighty-seven fifth- and sixth-grade students were exposed to a group desensitization program for test anxiety. Those students who had demonstrated a high level of test anxiety showed a significant lessening of anxiety following the program. Those students who had demonstrated a low level of test anxiety showed no significant change.

661 Kondas, O. "Reduction of examination anxiety and 'stagefright' by group desensitization and relaxation." Behav Res Ther 5(4): 275-81, November, 1967. (20 References). (Reprinted in Item Nos. 21, 37).
Demonstrates the effective use of group desensitization, relaxation, and imagination of exam situations in the treatment of "stagefright" in twenty-three adolescents and thirteen psychology students.

662 Laxer, Robert M.; Quarter, Jack; Kooman, Ann; et al. "Systematic desensitization and relaxation of high-test-anxious secondary school students." J Couns Psychol 16(5): 446-51, September, 1969. (15 References).
Compares the effectiveness of relaxation and systematic desensitization on the test anxiety of eighty-nine students in grades nine through twelve. Results indicate no significant differences in the methods after two months.

663 Lott, Sarah Jane Bolden. "A study of covert reinforcement as a treatment of test anxiety in male and female fifth graders." For a summary see: Diss Abstr Int 36A(4): 2028, October, 1975.

664 Mann, Jay, and Rosenthal, Ted Lee. "Vicarious and direct counterconditioning of test anxiety through individual and group desensitization." Behav Res Ther 7(4): 359-67, November, 1969. (31 References).

Demonstrates the successful reduction of test anxiety in fifty seventh-grade students by means of desensitization techniques. Details of the method are not given in this article, but form part of the senior author's MA thesis, completed at the University of Arizona in 1969.

CC. THUMBSUCKING

665 Baer, Donald M. "Laboratory control of thumbsucking by withdrawal and representation of reinforcement." J Exp Anal Behav 5(4): 525-28, October, 1962. (7 References). (Reprinted in Item Nos. 27, 28, 41, 42, 45, 47).

Viewing cartoons by five-year-old boys was made contingent upon their refraining from thumbsucking. A reduction in thumbsucking behavior was noted.

666 Bishop, Barbara R., and Stumphauzer, Jerome S. "Behavior therapy of thumbsucking in children: a punishment (time-out) and generalization effect--what's a mother to do?" Psychol Rep 33(3): 939-44, December, 1973. (12 References).

Thumbsucking was reduced in nursery school children by the turning off of television cartoons contingent upon thumbsucking.

667 Kauffman, James M., and Scranton, T. R. "Parent control of thumbsucking in the home." Child Study J 4(1): 1-10, 1974. (11 References).

Reports on two studies conducted with a two-year-nine-month-old girl whose thumbsucking was controlled by the use of contingent reading and differential reinforcement of non-thumbsucking behavior.

668 Knight, Martha F., and McKenzie, Hugh S. "Elimination of bedtime thumbsucking in home settings through contingent reading." J Appl Behav Anal 7(1): 33-38, Spring, 1974. (14 References). (Reprinted in Item No. 35).

Describes the elimination of persistent bedtime thumbsucking in three girls (aged three, six, and eight years) by making reading of stories at bedtime contingent upon non-thumbsucking.

669 Martin, Duan. "A six-year-old 'behaviorist' solves her sibling's chronic thumbsucking behavior." Correct Soc Psychiatry 21(1): 19-21, 1975. (14 References).

Sets forth the procedure developed by a child to stop bed thumbsucking in her younger sister. The effectiveness of the procedure was evaluated by the use of a reversal design.

670 Skiba, Edward A.; Pettigrew, L. Eudora; Alden, Steven E. "A behavioral approach to the control of thumbsucking in the classroom." J Appl Behav Anal 4(2): 121-25, Summer, 1971. (4 References). (Reprinted in Item No. 27).

Praise and attention were made contingent upon behavior that was incompatible with thumbsucking for three eight-year-old girls.

DD. TICS

671 Alexander, A. Barney; Chai, Hyman; Creer, Thomas L.; et al. "The elimination of chronic cough by response suppression shaping." J Behav Ther Exp Psychiatry 4(1): 75-80, 1973. (8 References). (Reprinted in Item No. 35).

Presents a case report on the use of faradic aversive stimulation to reduce a chronic cough in a fifteen-year-old boy.

672 Cohen, Denise, and Marks, Frances M. "Gilles de la Tourette's syndrome treated by operant conditioning." [letter]. Br J Psychiatry 130: 315, March, 1977. (2 References).
Relates a case history of an eleven-year-old boy whose vocal tics were controlled by an operant conditioning program used by the parents in the home. After six weeks of treatment the vocal tics had disappeared, while the motor tics had not changed in frequency or severity.

673 Doleys, Daniel M., and Kurtz, Paul S. "A behavioral treatment program for the Gilles de la Tourette syndrome." Psychol Rep 35(1): 43-48, August, 1974. (14 References).
The reinforcement of incompatible behavior reduced the frequency of behavioral tics in a fourteen-year-old boy.

674 Feldman, Ronald B., and Werry, John S. "An unsuccessful attempt to treat a tiqueur by massed practice." Behav Res Ther 4(2): 111-17, May, 1966. (10 References).
Explores an attempt to reduce tics in a thirteen-year-old boy by the use of concentrated imitation of the tic behavior. The procedure was unsuccessful--probably due to the build-up of anxiety.

675 Miller, Arnold L. "Treatment of a child with Gilles de la Tourette's syndrome using behavior modification techniques." J Behav Ther Exp Psychiatry 1(4): 319-21, December, 1970. (3 References).
Symptoms of Gilles de la Tourette's syndrome in a five-year-old boy were curtailed by rewarding non-symptomatic behavior.

676 Rosen, Marvin, and Wesner, Chester. "A behavioral approach to Tourette's syndrome." J Consult Clin Psychol 41(2): 308-12, October, 1973. (13 References).
Outlines the reinforcement techniques used to modify the behavior of a twelve-year-old boy. Implications for classroom or home management are suggested.

677 Salkind, M. R. "The treatment of intractable hiccup by operant conditioning with negative incentive." Practitioner 206(234): 535-37, April, 1971. (6 References).
Presents a case history of a ten-year-old girl whose hiccuping of four month's duration was terminated by the aversive use of an ammonia solution.

678 Sand, Patricia L., and Carlson, Coldevin. "Failure to establish control over tics in the Gilles de la Tourette syndrome with behaviour therapy techniques." Br J Psychiatry 122(571): 665-70, June, 1973. (14 References).
Contingency management, self-recording, massed practice, and medication were used in the treatment of a nine-year-old boy. Medication appeared to be the most effective form of treatment.

679 Stevens, Janice R., and Blachly, Paul H. "Successful treatment of the Maladie des Tics." Am J Dis Child 112(6): 541-45, December, 1966. (18 References).
Describes the use of aversive conditioning and relaxation with a thirteen-year-old girl. The most successful type of treatment was the

administration of the drug Haloperidol. It is postulated that a metabolic disturbance is the primary cause of this disorder but that environmental factors modulate the physiologic dysfunction.

680 Walton, D. "Experimental psychology and the treatment of a ticqueur." J Child Psychol Psychiatry 2(2): 148-55, September, 1961. (15 References). (Reprinted in Item No. 30).
Explains in behavioral terms the development and modification of a number of diverse tics in an eleven-year-old boy. The tics consisted primarily of facial and explosive arm and leg movements. Thirty-six daily sessions of uninterrupted practice resulted in a measurable decline in the frequency of the tics.

EE. TOILET TRAINING

681 Azrin, Nathan H., and Foxx, Richard M. Toilet training in less than a day. New York: Simon & Schuster, 1974. 160p.
This simply written manual provides step-by-step instructions for rapid toilet training using positive reinforcement. Included are reminder lists and a question and answer section.

682 Benjamin, Lorna S.; Serdahely, William; Geppert, Thomas V. "Night training through parents' implicit use of operant conditioning." Child Dev 42(3): 963-66, September, 1971. (7 References).
Indicates that positive reinforcement was more successful than negative reinforcement in training children to stay dry at night. Data were gleaned from the answers to a questionnaire submitted to ninety parents.

683 Brown, Richard M., and Brown, Norma L. "The increase and control of verbal signals in the bladder training of a seventeen-month-old child--a case study." J Child Psychol Psychiatry 15(2): 105-9, April, 1974. (8 References).
Operant procedures, which were introduced by the parents, consisted of reinforcing signalling or signalled urinations with candy and praise. Under conditions of reinforcement the child withheld urination until she had signalled and was placed on her potty chair.

684 Carro, Geraldine. "Toilet training: reducing the anxieties." Ladies Home J 93: 186, October, 1976.
Briefly outlines the positive aspects of using behavior modification in toilet training, but advises that speed of training is not the only criterion to be considered.

685 Foxx, R. M., and Azrin, N. H. "Dry pants: a rapid method of toilet training children." Behav Res Ther 11(4): 435-42, November, 1973. (13 References). (Reprinted in Item No. 35).
Describes a method of toilet training, utilizing intensive learning experience and reinforcement procedures, that proved successful with thirty-four children who were experiencing toilet training problems. All thirty-four children were trained in an average of four hours.

686 Madsen, Charles H., Jr. "Positive reinforcement in the toilet training of a normal child: a case report." In: Ullmann, Leonard P., and Krasner, Leonard, eds. Case studies in behavior modification. New York: Holt, Rinehart & Winston, 1965. 305-7. (5 References).

Normal toilet training was accomplished in a short period of time with an eighteen-month-old child by the use of candy as a reward for appropriate toilet behavior.

687 Mahoney, Kurt; Van Wagenen, R. Keith; Meyerson, Lee. "Toilet training of normal and retarded children." J Appl Behav Anal 4(3): 173-81, Fall, 1971. (7 References).
Emphasizes the importance of the early elements in an operant chain of toilet behaviors in three normal infants and five retarded children. Subsequently, eliminative behaviors were conditioned by operant procedures using an auditory device.

688 Pumroy, Donald K., and Pumroy, Shirley S. "Systematic observation and reinforcement technique in toilet training." Psychol Rep 16(2): 467-71, April, 1965. (3 References). (Reprinted in Item No. 47).
Reports on the reinforcement techniques used by the authors in toilet training their own children--one male and one female.

FF. TOOTH-BRUSHING

689 Lattal, K. A. "Contingency management of toothbrushing behavior in a summer camp for children." J Appl Behav Anal 2(3): 195-98, Fall, 1969. (9 References).
Describes the maintenance of a high level of toothbrushing behavior when the opportunity to swim was used as a contingency.

690 Martens, Leslie V.; Frazier, P. Jean; Hirt, Katherine J.; et al. "Developing brushing performance in second graders through behavior modification." Health Serv Rep 88(9): 818-23, November, 1973. (3 References).
Advises the use of tokens, prizes, and individual contracts to develop toothbrushing skills and an awareness of dental hygiene in elementary school children.

GG. TRACHEOSTOMY DEPENDENCY

691 Wright, Logan; Nunnery, Arthur; Eichel, Berkley; et al. "Application of conditioning principles to problems of tracheostomy addiction in children." J Consult Clin Psychol 32(5, pt. 1): 603-6, October, 1968. (8 References). (Reprinted in Item No. 35).
Describes the treatment, by means of social reinforcement, of two eight-month-old infants with tracheostomy addiction. Sources of reinforcement were removed except when the cannula was occluded. Occlusion was extended from three minutes to thirty-six hours over a period of three weeks.

692 ————. "Behavioral tactics for reinstating natural breathing in infants with tracheostomy." Pediatr Res 3(4): 275-78, July, 1969. (13 References).
Documents the use of behavioral techniques over a three-week period in the treatment of two eight-month-old infants with apparent psychological dependence on breathing through a cannula. Techniques included exposure to pleasurable activities such as social contacts and playing with toys while breathing normally, and isolation from people and play objects while breathing through the cannulae.

HH. TRUANCY

693 Brooks, B. David. "Contingency management as a means of reducing school truancy." Paper presented at the Annual Meeting of the California Personnel and Guidance Association, San Francisco, February, 1974. (4 References). (ED 099 700).
Discusses truancy from the behavioral point of view. A program successfully employed in one high school is described in detail.

694 Gann, Olen Wayne. "The effect of selected reinforcement techniques on average daily attendance in a Mississippi high school." For a summary see: Diss Abstr Int 33A(7): 3190, January, 1973.

695 King, Larry W.; Cotler, Sherwin B.; Patterson, Kent. "Behavior modification consultation in a Mexican-American school: a case study." Am J Community Psychol 3(3): 229-35, September, 1975. (10 References).
Contingent rewards were ineffective in improving students' attendance. Reasons for the lack of success are discussed.

696 MacDonald, W. Scott; Gallimore, Ronald; MacDonald, Gwen. "Contingency counseling by school personnel: an economical model of intervention." J Appl Behav Anal 3(3): 175-82, Fall, 1970. (4 References).
Reports on two studies which involved the successful use of adult mediators who controlled reinforcement for chronic non-attenders.

697 Witkin-Weinstein, Lynn Michelle. "Peer reinforcement of school attendance." For a summary see: Diss Abstr Int 38B(8): 3921, February, 1978.

V.

Behavioral Techniques for the Handicapped Child

A. AUTISM

1. Behavioral Handling of the Autistic Child

698 Cowan, Philip A.; Hoddinott, B. A.; Wright, Barbara Anne. "Compliance and resistance in the conditioning of autistic children: an exploratory study." Child Dev 36(4): 913-23, December, 1965. (13 References).
Relates the findings of a two-part examination conducted with twelve autistic children between the ages of four and nine years. The study attempted to: (1) identify those children who were unwilling rather than unable to respond correctly; and (2) use operant conditioning methods to overcome that resistance.

699 Drabman, Ronald S. "An integrated approach to treating low-functioning children." Curr Psychiatr Ther 15: 45-50, 1975. (3 References).
Describes a program for the low-functioning child which stresses short-term hospitalization, coupled with parental instruction in behavior modification techniques and attendance at a special school. A case history of an eleven-year-old autistic boy is documented.

700 Ferster, Charles B. "Operant reinforcement of infantile autism." In: Lesse, Stanley, ed. An evaluation of the results of the psychotherapies. Springfield, Illinois: Thomas, 1968. 221-36. (16 References).
Emphasizes the reinforcement obtained by the autistic child from the aversive effects upon adults of his behavior. The general kinds of interactions that weaken a child's behavior are discussed.

701 ————. "Positive reinforcement and behavioral deficits of autistic children." Child Dev 32(3): 437-56, September, 1961. (12 References). (Reprinted in Item Nos. 31, 42).
Analyzes the basic variables determining the child's behavior that may operate to produce the particular kinds of behavioral problems seen in the autistic child.

702 ————. "The repertoire of the autistic child in relation to principles of reinforcement." In: Gottschalk, L., ed. Methods of research in psychotherapy. New York: Harper & Row, 1965. 312-30.
Recommends that the functional analysis of the autistic child's behavior will provide a framework for characterizing the repertoires of both the normal and the autistic child.

703 Frankel, Fred; Tymchuk, Alexander, J.; Simmons, James Q., III. "Operant analysis and intervention with autistic children: implications of current research." In: Ritvo, E. R., ed. Autism: diagnosis, current research and management. New York: Spectrum, 1976. 151-68. (62 References).
Reviews studies demonstrating the application of operant methods in the modification of a variety of behaviors such as language, perception, and social learning.

704 Geller, Jeffrey. "The development of behavior therapy with autistic children: a review." J Chronic Dis 25(1): 21-31, January, 1972. (72 References).
Traces the development of operant behavior therapy with autistic children, indicates the experimental evidence, and discusses the criticisms that have developed concerning its use with such children.

705 Graziano, Anthony M. Child without tomorrow. New York: Pergamon, 1974. 290p. (Bibliography). (Pergamon General Psychology Series, PGPS-36).
Reports on a program of group behavior therapy with severely emotionally disturbed children. Six case histories of autistic children are presented and, in addition to detailed descriptions of the rationales and procedures employed, there is a discussion of the sociopolitical factors involved in the establishment of this type of program.

706 Helm, David. "Psychodynamic and behavior modification approaches to the treatment of infantile autism: empirical similarities." J Autism Child Schizo 6(1): 27-41, March, 1976. (48 References).
Reviews the literature, draws parallels between the two approaches, and presents a case history of an eleven-year-old autistic boy.

707 Leff, Robert. "Behavior modification and the psychoses of childhood: a review." Psychol Bull 69(6): 396-409, June, 1968. (40 References).
Analyzes the research conducted into the use of operant training techniques with children labelled variously: childhood schizophrenic, early infantile autistic, and symbiotic autistic. Improvements are seen in controlling disruptive behavior and in the development of basic skills.

708 Lipman, L. "Management of the autistic child." S Afr Med J 44(36): 1028-32, September 12, 1970. (12 References).
Outlines the identifying characteristics of the autistic child and recommends behavioral therapy. Several day treatment centers are described briefly.

709 Lovaas, O. Ivar. "Behavioral treatment of autistic children." In: Spence, Janet T.; Carson, Robert C.; Thibaut, John W., eds. Behavioral approaches to therapy. Morristown, New Jersey: General Learning Press, 1976. 185-201. (34 References).
Summarizes research and treatment efforts with various behaviors labelled "autistic." The volume is intended for the undergraduate student.

710 ———. "Some studies on the treatment of childhood schizophrenia." In: Shlien, John M., ed. Research in psychotherapy, 3rd, Chicago, 1966. Proceedings. Washington, D.C.: American Psychological Association, 1968. 103-21. (25 References).

Reviews several studies conducted on the use of operant techniques in the treatment of autistic children. The target behaviors included self-destructive and tantrum behaviors, psychotic speech, self-stimulation, and verbal and nonverbal imitation.

711 Lovaas, O. Ivar, and Newsom, Crighton D. "Behavior modification with psychotic children." In: Leitenberg, Harold, ed. Handbook of behavior modification and behavior therapy. Englewood Cliffs, New Jersey: Prentice-Hall, 1976. 303-60. (159 References).
Presents a state-of-the-art review on research and methods in the behavior modification of psychotic children. Included is a behavioral description of psychotic children and a comparison of the more traditional approaches with behavioral treatment. Characteristics of the psychotic child, such as self-destructive and self-stimulatory behaviors, and deficiencies in language development, are discussed in detail, together with the methods used in the mediation of such behaviors. Current research on perception, motivation, and the training of parents and teachers is also covered.

712 Lovaas, O. Ivar; Schreibman, Laura; Koegel, Robert L. "A behavior modification approach to the treatment of autistic children." J Autism Child Schizo 4(2): 111-29, March, 1974. (29 References).
Traces the use of behavior modification in a program conducted over a twelve-year period. Each child who underwent treatment in the program described made measurable progress.

713 Margolies, Paul J. "Behavioral approaches to the treatment of early infantile autism: a review." Psychol Bull 84(2): 249-64, March, 1977. (91 References).
Surveys the reported attempts to modify a widely diverse group of autistic behaviors, discusses such issues as correct diagnosis, etiology, and generalization, and concludes that real behavior change has been documented.

714 Marshall, Nancy R., and Hegrenes, Jack R. "Programmed communication therapy for autistic mentally retarded children." J Speech Hear Disord 35(1): 70-83, February, 1970. (8 References).
Outlines a team approach toward the management of autistic children. The team included a clinician, one or more behavior analysts, observers, recorders, and parents. Four case histories are cited.

715 Ney, Philip. "Operant conditioning of schizophrenic children." Can Psychiatr Assoc J 12(1): 9-15, 1967. (58 References).
Reports on the experimental design and preliminary findings of a project which attempted to compare the results of operant conditioning and play therapy. The literature of the topic is briefly reviewed.

716 Ney, Philip G.; Palvesky, Audrey E.; Markely, John. "Relative effectiveness of operant conditioning and play therapy in childhood schizophrenia." J Autism Child Schizo 1(3): 337-49, July-September, 1971. (30 References).
Details a study conducted with schizophrenic boys ranging from three to fifteen years of age. Improvement was greater after operant conditioning than after play therapy, but the differences reached significant levels only after the second three months of treatment.

717 Rutter, Michael, and Sussenwein, Fraida. "A developmental and behavioral approach to the treatment of preschool autistic children." J Autism Child Schizo 1(4): 376-97, October-December, 1971. (34 References).
Describes an approach which emphasizes the positive development of normal functioning. It further stresses the elimination of abnormal behavior by a combination of behavioral modification and parental counseling and social work.

718 Shemesh, Sasson Sonny. "The use of operant procedures in the assessment of psychotic children." For a summary see: Diss Abstr Int 34B(6): 2953, December, 1973.

719 Weiland, I. Hyman. "Discussion of treatment approaches." In: Churchill, Don W.; Alpern, Gerald D.; DeMyer, Marian K., eds. Infantile autism: proceedings of the Indiana University Colloquium. Springfield, Illinois: Thomas, 1970. 200-211. (18 References).
Compares behavioral and psychoanalytic approaches to the treatment of infantile autism.

720 Wenar, Charles, and Ruttenberg, Bertram A. "Therapies of autistic children." Curr Psychiatr Ther 9: 32-42, 1969. (44 References).
Surveys the three major approaches for the treatment of the autistic child: (1) positive emotional relationship between child and therapist; (2) behavior therapy; and (3) body manipulation. The lack of scientific evidence in research is criticized.

721 Wetzel, Ralph J.; Baker, Jean; Roney, Marcia; et al. "Outpatient treatment of autistic behavior." Behav Res Ther 4(3): 169-77, August, 1966. (6 References).
Outlines a technique which relies upon the active involvement of the parents and other significant individuals in the child's environment. The treatment described resulted in significant changes in the child during a three-month period.

2. Elimination of Maladaptive Behaviors

722 Baroff, George S., and Tate, Bobby G. "The use of aversive stimulation in the treatment of chronic self-injurious behavior." J Am Acad Child Psychiatry 7(3): 454-70, July, 1968. (19 References).
Electric shock was used to reduce self-hitting in a nine-year-old autistic boy with a five-year history of such behavior.

723 Brown, Richard A.; Pace, Zietta S.; Becker, Wesley C. "Treatment of extreme negativism and autistic behavior in a six-year-old boy." Except Child 36(2): 115-22, October, 1969. (6 References).
Presents a case study in which the reinforcing consequences following the boy's negative responses to demands were removed. A subsequent increase in his social and verbal interaction with adults and peers was noted.

724 Bucher, Bradley, and King, Larry W. "Generalization of punishment effects in the deviant behavior of a psychotic child." Behav Ther 2(1): 68-77, January, 1971. (10 References).

Brief electric shock was used to suppress a specific form of destructive behavior in an eleven-year-old boy diagnosed as mentally retarded with childhood schizophrenia.

725 Davison, Gerald C. "A social learning therapy programme with an autistic child." Behav Res Ther 2(2): 149-59, May, 1964. (23 References).
Details the use of operant conditioning techniques to modify the behavior of a nine-year-old autistic girl. The program was administered by a team of trained undergraduates in a day-care center. Elimination of several phobias and maladaptive behaviors was accomplished.

726 Deatherage, Richard Marion. "Modifying appropriate and interfering behaviors in autistic children using a system of behavior modification therapeutic teaching." For a summary see: Diss Abstr Int 32A(12): 6827, June, 1972.

727 Ferster, Charles B., and DeMyer, Marian K. "A method for the experimental analysis of the behavior of autistic children." Am J Orthopsychiatry 32(1): 89-98, January, 1962. (8 References). (Reprinted in Item Nos. 23, 45).
The behavior of three hospitalized autistic children was brought under control by the use of food and candy as reinforcers; these were supplemented gradually by different reinforcing devices.

728 Foxx, R. M., and Azrin, N. H. "The elimination of autistic, self-stimulatory behavior by overcorrection." J Appl Behav Anal 6(1): 1-14, Spring, 1973. (24 References). (Reprinted in Item No. 35).
Reports on the use of overcorrection to eliminate self-stimulatory behavior, such as head-weaving, object-mouthing, hand-clapping, and hand-mouthing. Subjects were four retarded and/or autistic children in whom self-stimulatory behavior was reduced to a near zero level within ten days.

729 Freeman, B. J.; Somerset, Tom; Ritvo, E. R. "Effect of duration of time out in suppressing disruptive behavior of a severely autistic child." Psychol Rep 38(1): 124-26, February, 1976. (8 References).
A four-year-old child was exposed to three different durations of time-out (three minutes, one hour, and fifteen minutes). Disruptive behavior was best suppressed with the variable fifteen minute duration.

730 Graziano, Anthony M. "A group treatment approach to multiple problem behaviors of autistic children." Except Child 36(10): 765-70, Summer, 1970. (12 References).
Describes a program conducted with four autistic children treated in a group situation. Significant gains were noted in just under four years of therapy.

731 Jensen, Gordon D., and Womack, Marietta G. "Operant conditioning techniques applied in the treatment of an autistic child." Am J Orthopsychiatry 37(1): 30-34, January, 1967. (13 References).
Presents a case history of a six-year-old autistic boy whose temper tantrums and stereotypic and aggressive behaviors were reduced and whose peer interactions and language were increased by operant conditioning methods.

732 Koegel, Robert L.; Firestone, Paula B.; Kramme, Kenneth W.; et al. "Increasing spontaneous play by suppressing self-stimulation in autistic children." J Appl Behav Anal 7(4): 521-28, Winter, 1974. (24 References).
Documents an experiment conducted with two autistic children--an eight-year-old boy and a six-year-old girl--whose self-stimulatory behavior was suppressed by means of punishment or physical restraint. The level of appropriate play rose significantly when self-stimulatory behavior was reduced.

733 Lovaas, O. Ivar; Freitag, Gilbert; Gold, Vivian J.; et al. "Experimental studies in childhood schizophrenia: analysis of self-destructive behavior." J Exp Child Psychiatry 2(1): 67-84, March, 1965. (13 References). (Reprinted in Item No. 21).
Reports on three studies concerned with the investigation of variables which controlled self-destructive behaviors in a nine-year-old schizophrenic child. Data show the functional relationships between very specific environmental operations and the self-destruction.

734 Tate, B. G., and Baroff, George S. "Aversive control of self-injurious behavior in a psychotic boy." Behav Res Ther 4(4): 281-87, November, 1966. (10 References). (Reprinted in Item Nos. 32, 43).
Demonstrates successful control of self-injurious behavior in a nine-year-old psychotic blind boy by the use of withdrawal and reinstatement of human physical contact and electric shock.

735 Urry, Nellene. "Behaviour modification with an autistic child." Nurs Times 66(15): 456-58, April 9, 1970. (11 References).
Presents a case history in which head-banging was eliminated and eye contact and play were developed in a three-year-old autistic child.

736 Wolf, Montrose; Risley, Todd; Johnston, Margaret; et al. "Application of operant conditioning procedures to the behavior problems of an autistic child: a follow-up and extension." Behav Res Ther 5(2): 103-11, May, 1967. (5 References). (Reprinted in Item No. 36).
Follows up a case presented in a previous article (Item No. 737). The child was enrolled in a nursery school program for two years in order to prepare him for inclusion in a special education class. The program included elimination of problem behaviors such as tantrums and pinching, and the establishment of toilet training.

737 Wolf, Montrose M.; Risley, Todd R.; Mees, Hayden L. "Application of operant conditioning procedures to the behavior problems of an autistic child." Behav Res Ther 1(4): 305-12, November, 1964. (11 References). (Reprinted in Item Nos. 23, 45, 46).
Presents a case report on the use of operant conditioning techniques with a three-and-one-half-year-old autistic boy. Tantrum behavior was eliminated by a time-out procedure. Edible reinforcers were used to establish the wearing of essential corrective lenses and to generate a verbal repertoire.

3. Development of Specific Skills

a. Eye Contact

738 McConnell, Owen L. "Control of eye contact in an autistic child." J Child Psychol Psychiatry 8(3/4): 249-55, December, 1967. (8 References). (Reprinted in Item Nos. 21, 29).
Demonstrates the use of operant conditioning techniques in overcoming the visual avoidance of a five-and-one-half-year-old boy with infantile autism.

739 Ney, Philip G. "Effect of contingent and non-contingent reinforcement on the behavior of an autistic child." J Autism Child Schizo 3(2): 115-27, April-June, 1973. (18 References).
Covers an experimental study on the eye contact behavior of a four-and-one-half-year-old autistic boy.

b. Imitation

740 Hingtgen, Joseph N., and Churchill, Don W. "Differential effects of behavior modification in four mute autistic boys." In: Churchill, Don W.; Alpern, Gerald D.; DeMyer, Marian, eds. Infantile autism: proceedings of the Indiana University Colloquium. Springfield, Illinois: Thomas, 1970. 185-99. (12 References).
Imitative responses of three major types (use of body, use of objects, and vocalizations) were reinforced and followed by training on more complex behaviors.

741 ————. "Identification of perceptual limitations in mute autistic children: identification by the use of behavior modification." Arch Gen Psychiatry 21(1): 68-71, July, 1969. (8 References).
Four autistic boys were given food and social reinforcers in an intensive training program designed to develop imitative behavior.

742 Hingtgen, Joseph N.; Coulter, Susan K.; Churchill, Don W. "Intensive reinforcement of imitative behavior in mute, autistic children." Arch Gen Psychiatry 17(1): 36-43, July, 1967. (10 References).
Reports on a study which used edible reinforcers to encourage imitative use of body, use of objects, and vocalizations in two mute autistic children.

743 Lovaas, O. Ivar; Freitas, Lorraine; Nelson, Karen; et al. "The establishment of imitation and its use for the development of complex behavior in schizophrenic children." Behav Res Ther 5(3): 171-81, August, 1967. (Reprinted in Item Nos. 29, 38).
Describes a procedure for establishing nonverbal imitative behavior in schizophrenic children by means of edible reinforcers. Such behavior was then extended into the day-to-day functioning of the children.

744 Metz, J. Richard. "Conditioning generalized imitation in autistic children." J Exp Child Psychol 2(4): 389-99, December, 1965. (10 References). (Reprinted in Item No. 21).
Outlines methods used to teach two seven-year-old autistic children generalized imitative behavior or imitation of relatively new behavior on which training had not specifically been given.

745 Risley, Todd R., and Wolf, Montrose M. "Experimental manipulation of autistic behaviors and generalization into the home." In: Ulrich, Roger; Stachnik, Thomas; Mabry, John, eds. Control of human behavior. Glenview, Illinois: Scott, Foresman, 1966. 193-98.
Documents a study conducted with a six-year-old autistic boy exhibiting bizarre mannerisms and echolalia. Ice cream was used to elicit imitative behavior; parents were trained to continue the operant procedure at home.

c. Self-Help Skills

746 Ando, Haruhiko. "Training autistic children to urinate in the toilet through operant conditioning techniques." J Autism Child Schizo 7(2): 151-63, June, 1977. (16 References).
Evaluates the use of operant conditioning techniques with five children in the autism ward of a hospital for the developmentally disturbed. Appropriate urination was immediately rewarded with candy and/or verbal praise and physical affection; inappropriate urination was followed by verbal and physical punishment. Results were good for two subjects, fair for two subjects, and very poor for the fifth subject. The significance of the results is discussed.

747 Marshall, George R. "Toilet training of an autistic eight-year-old through conditioning therapy: a case report." Behav Res Ther 4(3): 242-45, August, 1966. (13 References).
Traces the successful toilet training of an autistic boy by using candy reinforcers over a period of forty-six days.

d. Social Skills

748 D'Alessandro, John G. "The influence of the reinforcing agent on the development of social behavior in schizophrenic children with autistic features." For a summary see: Diss Abstr Int 37B(8): 4133, February, 1977.

749 Hingtgen, Joseph N.; Sanders, Beverly J.; DeMyer, Marian K. "Shaping cooperative responses in early childhood schizophrenics." In: Ullmann, Leonard P., and Krasner, Leonard, eds. Case studies in behavior modification. New York: Holt, Rinehart & Winston, 1965. 130-38. (9 References).
Social interactions were developed between pairs of childhood schizophrenics by using food and candy as reinforcers.

750 Hingtgen, Joseph N., and Trost, Frank C., Jr. "Shaping cooperative responses in early childhood schizophrenics--II: reinforcement of mutual physical contact and vocal responses." In: Ulrich, Roger; Stachnik, Thomas; Mabry, John, eds. Control of human behavior. Glenview, Illinois: Scott, Foresman, 1966. 110-13.
Candy reinforcers were used to develop cooperative responses in four nonverbal early childhood schizophrenics. The social interactions developed were seen to extend beyond the test situation.

751 Kean, June M. "The development of social skills in autistic twins." NZ Med J 81(534): 204-7, February 26, 1975. (12 References).
Presents a case study describing the behavioral techniques employed to develop social skills in autistic twins during their year in kindergarten. A team approach was utilized in the program.

752 Maes, Jeannie. "Modifying behavior: the case of Alice." J Psychiatr Nurs 7: 89-90, March-April, 1969.
A system of rewards was effective in reducing the antisocial behavior of an autistic fourteen-year-old girl in an institutional setting.

753 Metz, J. Richard. "Conditioning social and intellectual skills in autistic children." In: Fisher, Jerome, and Harris, Robert E., eds. Reinforcement theory in psychological treatment: a symposium. Sacramento, California: Department of Mental Hygiene, 1966. 40-49. (7 References). (Research Monograph No. 8).
Describes the use of operant conditioning in the treatment of nine autistic children ranging in age from five to eight years. The children's lunch was used as reinforcement for demonstrating social and intellectual skills.

754 Romanczyk, Raymond G.; Diament, Charles; Goren, Elizabeth R.; et al. "Increasing isolate and social play in severely disturbed children: intervention and postintervention effectiveness." J Autism Child Schizo 5(1): 57-70, March, 1975. (20 References).
Cites two studies on the use of food and social reinforcement to increase play behavior in a group setting.

755 Shackel, Denis S. J. "A comparison of the effects of differential reinforcement and apparatus on cooperative behavior in two autistic children." Paper presented at the 2nd Annual Meeting of the Midwestern Association of Behavior Analysts, Chicago, May 1-4, 1976. (ED 138 839).
Documents an experiment which indicated that the use of novel apparatus was, at best, irrelevant to the establishment of cooperative behavior.

e. Speech/Language

756 Bartlett, Donald; Ora, John P.; Brown, Ellen; et al. "The effects of reinforcement on psychotic speech in a case of early infantile autism, age twelve." J Behav Ther Exp Psychiatry 2(2): 145-49, July, 1971. (13 References).
Provides details of procedures used in four experimental sessions in which the subject's verbal behavior was clearly controlled by the token reinforcement schedule, especially when a verbal statement of the contingencies was outlined.

757 Browning, Robert M. "Behavior therapy for stuttering in a schizophrenic child." Behav Res Ther 5(1): 27-35, February, 1967. (13 References).
Offers a case study which demonstrates the effective combination of several behavior modification techniques in the reduction of stuttering in a nine-year-old schizophrenic boy. Staff members in the residential setting were trained as modifiers.

758 Fineman, Kenneth R. "Shaping and increasing verbalizations in an autistic child in response to visual-color stimulation." Percept Mot Skills 27(2): 1071-74, December, 1968. (10 References).
Systematic visual-color consequences were effective in increasing the rate of verbalizations in a six-year-old autistic boy. However, food was found to be a more powerful contingency in shaping specific sounds.

759 ————. "Visual-color reinforcement in establishment of speech by an autistic child." Percept Mot Skills 26(3): 761-62, June, 1968. (5 References).
Summarizes a case report in which the verbalizations of a four-and-one-half-year-old girl were increased by the use of visual consequences.

760 Fineman, Kenneth R., and Ferjo, Juanita. "Establishing and increasing verbalizations in a deaf schizophrenic child through the use of contingent visual-color reinforcement." Percept Mot Skills 29: 647-52, October, 1969.
Describes a ten-session pilot study in which an eleven-year-old deaf schizophrenic boy was taught to verbalize by using visual-color contingencies.

761 Freeman, Betty Jo; Ritvo, Edward; Miller, Revel. "An operant procedure to teach an echolalic, autistic child to answer questions appropriately." J Autism Child Schizo 5(2): 169-76, June, 1975. (8 References).
Outlines a procedure involving the prevention of incorrect responses and the use of positive reinforcers for correct responses. The simplicity of the procedure allows it to be administered by various therapeutic personnel as well as by the parents in a variety of living situations.

762 Gottwald, P.; Redlin, W.; Ott, H.; et al. "Comparison among therapists attempting language training and generalization of punishment effects in the behavior modification of a schizophrenic child." In: Brengelmann, J. C., ed. Progress in behavior therapy. New York: Springer-Verlag, 1975. 23-34. (11 References).
Documents a number of behavior modification experiments conducted with a twelve-year-old girl previously diagnosed as a schizophrenic.

763 Hartung, Jurgen R. "A review of procedures to increase verbal imitation skills and functional speech in autistic children." J Speech Hear Disord 35(3): 203-17, August, 1970. (24 References).
Discusses the importance of developing verbal skills in the autistic child and presents an outline by which speech may be established. It is emphasized that imitation of verbal responses must be consistent before the initiation of verbal training.

764 Hewett, Frank M. "Teaching speech to an autistic child through operant conditioning." Am J Orthopsychiatry 35(5): 927-36, October, 1965. (13 References).
Candy was used as a reinforcer in developing speech and language in a four-and-one-half-year-old autistic boy. Following the establishment of a positive relationship between the child and the therapist, spontaneous vocalizations were shaped and reinforced to develop a thirty-two word vocabulary. When generalization and meaningful language were obtained, the parents were introduced into the program.

765 Lovaas, O. Ivar. "A behavior therapy approach to the treatment of childhood schizophrenia." In: Hill, John P., ed. Minnesota symposia on child development: Vol. I. Minneapolis, Minnesota: University of Minnesota Press, 1967. 108-59. (49 References).
Offers an overview of a research project which sought to develop speech and imitative behavior in ten schizophrenic children. A discussion of methodology and program implementation is included.

766 ————. "Considerations in the development of a behavioral treatment program for psychotic children." In: Churchill, Don W.; Alpern, Gerald D.; DeMyer, Marian, eds. Infantile autism: proceedings of the Indiana University Colloquium. Springfield, Illinois: Thomas, 1970. 124-44. (15 References).
Reports on a set of studies conducted with psychotic children using operant methods to establish language and beginning social and intellectual skills.

767 ————. "A program for the establishment of speech in psychotic children." In: Wing, J. K., ed. Early childhood autism: clinical, educational and social aspects. New York: Pergamon, 1966. 115-44.
Focuses on the use of behavior modification principles in the development of imitation, speech initiation, and discrimination in psychotic children. Parents must be instructed in these methods so that training can be carried out on a day-to-day basis.

768 Lovaas, O. Ivar; Berberich, John P.; Perloff, Bernard F.; et al. "Acquisition of imitative speech by schizophrenic children." Science 151: 705-7, 1966. (3 References). (Reprinted in Item Nos. 22, 38).
Imitative speech was developed in two mute, six-year-old schizophrenic boys by the use of reinforcement with food.

769 Park, David. "Operant conditioning of a speaking autistic child." J Autism Child Schizo 4(2): 189-91, March, 1974.
The parent of a thirteen-year-old girl briefly describes the use of a wrist counter and contracts to improve the girl's behavior and speech.

770 Risley, Todd R., and Wolf, Montrose M. "Establishing functional speech in echolalic children." Behav Res Ther 5(2): 73-88, May, 1967. (7 References). (Reprinted in Item Nos. 21, 32, 38).
Sets forth the techniques employed in reducing the echolalic responses and in encouraging more functional speech in children diagnosed as autistic. Edible reinforcers increased the desired responses and the removal of social reinforcers eliminated disruptive behavior.

771 Sailor, Wayne, and Taman, Trudie. "Stimulus factors in the training of prepositional usage in three autistic children." J Appl Behav Anal 5(2): 183-90, Summer, 1972. (13 References).
Examines the acquisition of prepositional usage by three speech deficient autistic children by employing ambiguous and unambiguous stimuli. The results suggest that training with unambiguous stimuli might enhance responding with ambiguous stimuli.

772 Schell, Robert E.; Stark, Joel; Giddan, Jane J. "Development of language behavior in an autistic child." J Speech Hear Disord 32(1): 51-64, February, 1967. (4 References).
Documents a systematic attempt to develop language in a nonverbal four-and-one-half-year-old autistic boy. The results show the relative effectiveness of the techniques used. There was an increase in the frequency and variety of his verbal and nonverbal behavior, as well as in his responsiveness to people.

773 Shaw, William H. "Treatment of a schizophrenic speech disorder by operant conditioning in play therapy." Can Psychiatr Assoc J 14(6): 631-34, December, 1969.
Describes a program of verbal conditioning used in a weekly play therapy situation with an eight-year-old boy. The boy was reinforced for appropriate verbal behavior by the therapist's participation in the boy's bizarre play. Generalization was effected by differential reinforcement administered by the parents in the home setting.

774 Stark, Joel; Giddan, Jane J.; Meisel, Joan. "Increasing verbal behavior in an autistic child." J Speech Hear Disord 33(1): 42-48, February, 1968. (3 References).
Provides details of the techniques used over a five-month period with a five-year-old autistic boy. Specific areas of attention were nonverbal imitation, vocal imitation, verbal labeling, and verbal discrimination.

775 Stevens-Long, Judith, and Rasmussen, Marilyn. "The acquisition of simple and compound sentence structure in an autistic child." J Appl Behav Anal 7(3): 473-79, Fall, 1974. (8 References).
Contingent edible reinforcers and imitative prompts were used to teach an eight-year-old autistic boy to use simple and compound sentences to describe a set of standard pictures. At the end of the training, the boy also used novel compound sentences to describe a set of pictures on which he had received no direct training.

776 Stevens-Long, Judith; Schwarz, Jane L.; Bliss, Deborah. "The acquisition and generalization of compound sentence structure in an autistic child." Behav Ther 7(3): 397-404, May, 1976. (10 References).
A six-year-old autistic boy was taught to describe verbally a set of pictures using simple and compound sentences by using imitative prompts, differential reinforcement, and time-out.

777 Sulzbacher, Stephen I., and Costello, Janis M. "A behavioral strategy for language training of a child with autistic behaviors." J Speech Hear Disord 35(3): 256-76, August, 1970. (19 References). (Reprinted in Item No. 43).
Examines the coordination of the efforts of a speech clinician, a teacher, a psychologist, and the parents in generalizing and maintaining vocal and other appropriate responses in a six-year-old boy displaying autistic behaviors.

778 Teaching language to autistic children. Springfield, Illinois: Media and Information Service, 1974. 48p. Available from Educational Media and Information Service, 100 North First Street, Springfield, Illinois 62777. (ED 140 543).
Furnishes information on the behavioral program for autistic children used in the Valley View School District in Illinois. Behavioral charts for eighteen subjects and sample record sheets are included.

4. Techniques with the Autistic Child

a. Specific Techniques

779 Brawley, Eleanor R.; Harris, Florence R.; Allen, K. Eileen; et al. "Behavior modification of an autistic child." Behav Sci 14(2): 87-97, March, 1969. (11 References). (Reprinted in Item No. 43).

Outlines a program for the systematic application of reinforcement procedures (adult attention and food), along with a carefully sequenced program of materials that resulted in marked increases in verbal, academic, and social skills.

780 Browning, Robert M. "Treatment effects of a total behavior modification program with five autistic children." Behav Res Ther 9(4): 319-27, November, 1971. (8 References). (Reprinted in Item No. 35).
Provides details of a modification project with five autistic children, each of whom had a specifically designed program. While all the children made progress, the results indicated that the children were trainable--but only by an expensive, intense, long-term program.

781 Churchill, Don W. "Psychotic children and behavior modification." Am J Psychiatry 125(11): 1585-90, May, 1969. (8 References).
Operant conditioning techniques were used in the treatment of fifteen autistic and/or schizophrenic children. Attention is drawn to the apparently limited response capability of some of the children even when motivation is high.

782 Colligan, Robert C., and Bellamy, Carol M. "Effects of a two year treatment program for a young autistic child." Psychotherapy 5(4): 214-19, December, 1968. (15 References).
Describes the use of behavior modification techniques in conjunction with playroom and milieu therapy in the treatment of a three-year-old autistic girl.

783 Ferster, Charles B. "The transition from the animal laboratory to the clinic." Psychol Rec 17(2): 145-50, April, 1967. (2 References). (Reprinted in Item No. 41).
Operant methods were used in a thirty-minute session to control the spontaneous behavior of a four-year-old autistic girl. No extrinsic reinforcement was used; rather, each desired behavior was allowed to become intrinsically rewarding.

784 Ferster, Charles B., and DeMyer, Marian K. "The development of performances in autistic children in an automatically controlled environment." J Chronic Dis 13(4): 312-45, April, 1961. (9 References). (Reprinted in Item No. 30).
Details the techniques employed in an experimental environment with two autistic children. The methods resulted in an increase of performances and a lessening of tantrums and atavistic behaviors, some of which appeared to be socially maintained.

785 Ferster, Charles B., and Simons, Jeanne. "Behavior therapy with children." Psychol Rec 16(1): 65-71, January, 1966. (7 References).
Contrasts the usual operant techniques in which food reinforcement is employed in animal studies with the use of natural reinforcers employed to modify the behavior of three autistic children. The procedures used are described in a functional analysis of behavior.

786 Gardner, James E.; Pearson, Douglas T.; Bercovici, Antonia N., et al. "Measurement, evaluation, and modification of selected social interactions between a schizophrenic child, his parents, and his therapist." J Consult Clin Psychol 32(5): 537-42, October, 1968. (16 References).

Following systematic observation, a training program was devised which enabled a schizophrenic child to be placed in a regular classroom within three months. The training was utilized by both the therapist and the parents. The program focussed on the decreasing of deviant behaviors and the increasing of appropriate behavior, attending behavior, and speech.

787 Graziano, Anthony M., and Kean, Jeffrey E. "Programmed relaxation and reciprocal inhibition with psychotic children." Behav Res Ther 6(4): 433-37, November, 1968. (13 References).
Four autistic children learned to perform muscular relaxation in highly structured brief daily sessions using verbal reinforcers. The relaxation training became a part of the regular program for these children, and the decrease in excitement was observed to generalize beyond the training session. Results were reflected in the children's responses during the rest of the day.

788 Howlin, Patricia; Marchant, Rosemary; Rutter, Michael; et al. "A home-based approach to the treatment of autistic children." J Autism Child Schizo 3(4): 308-36, October-December, 1973. (56 References).
Emphasizes the adequate assessment of the child and his family in the successful treatment of autism. The development of more normal social and linguistic behavior and the removal of maladaptive behaviors is illustrated with nine cases.

789 Lovaas, O. Ivar; Freitag, Gilbert; Kinder, Melvyn I.; et al. "Establishment of social reinforcers in two schizophrenic children on the basis of food." J Exp Child Psychol 4(2): 109-25, October, 1966. (15 References).
Four-year-old schizophrenic twins acquired social stimuli which were used as rewards in training new behaviors, and conditions were arranged so that these reinforcers maintained their effectiveness over extended periods of time.

790 Marr, John N.; Miller, Elizabeth B.; Straub, Richard R. "Operant conditioning of attention with a psychotic girl." Behav Res Ther 4(2): 85-87, May, 1966. (8 References).
Demonstrates the successful use of tape recordings in the modification of the behavior of an institutionalized twelve-year-old girl diagnosed as an acute schizophrenic. The techniques were used in conjunction with drugs and other forms of therapy. A need is indicated for similar research with control of other treatment variables.

791 Martin, Garry. "Brief time-outs as consequences for errors during training programs with autistic and retarded children: a questionable procedure." Psychol Rec 25(1): 71-89, Winter, 1975. (10 References).
Evaluates the effectiveness of brief time-outs as punishment for errors with four autistic and eight retarded children. The lack of significant results provokes questions as to the validity of the technique.

792 Martin, Garry L., and Pear, Joseph J. "Short-term participation by 130 undergraduates as operant conditioners in an ongoing project with autistic children." Psychol Rec 20(3): 327-36, Summer, 1970. (16 References).
Cites an effective program in which daily therapy sessions for autistic children were maintained by using undergraduate students who thereby gained experience in operant conditioning.

793 Mazik, Kenneth, and MacNamara, Roger. "Operant conditioning at the training school." Train Sch Bull 63(4): 153-58, February, 1967. (9 References).
Provides details of a pilot study which developed an effective program for the management of eight severely retarded schizophrenic children.

794 Moore, Benjamin L., and Bailey, Jon S. "Social punishment in modification of a preschool child's 'autistic-like' behavior with a mother as therapist." J Appl Behav Anal 6(3): 497-507, Fall, 1973. (21 References).
Examines the interactions between a mother and her three-year-old daughter. An improvement was achieved in the child's behavior by cueing the mother in systematic approval and disapproval via an FM wireless microphone.

795 Morrison, Delmont; Mejia, Berta; Miller, Dale. "Staff conflicts in the use of operant techniques with autistic children." Am J Orthopsychiatry 38(4): 647-52, July, 1968. (10 References).
Explores the problems encountered when an experimental design for a six-year-old child required that food be used as a reinforcer.

796 Nordquist, Vey Michael, and Wahler, Robert G. "Naturalistic treatment of an autistic child." J Appl Behav Anal 6(1): 79-87, Spring, 1973. (26 References). (Reprinted in Item No. 35).
Demonstrates the effectiveness of operant techniques used in the home setting by the parents of a four-year-old autistic child over a period of two years.

797 Rincover, Arnold; Newsom, Crighton D.; Lovaas, O. Ivar; et al. "Some motivational properties of sensory stimulation in psychotic children." J Exp Child Psychol 24(2): 312-23, October, 1977. (27 References).
Assesses the reinforcing properties of three types of sensory stimulation: music, visual flickering stimulation, and visual movement. Four autistic children participated in the study. Results indicated that: (1) sensory reinforcers can be used profitably with such children; (2) the effects were relatively durable over time; (3) the responses were idiosyncratic across children; (4) there was a substantial variability in daily response rates; and (5) a slight variation in the stimulus could prolong its effectiveness.

798 Schmidt, David C.; Franklin, Robert; Edwards, Joseph S. "Reinforcement of autistic children's responses to music." Psychol Rep 39(2): 571, October, 1976. (16 References).
Music served as an effective curriculum and as a context to shape and alter other individual and social behaviors in three autistic boys.

799 Steeves, Jan M.; Martin, Garry L.; Pear, Joseph J. "Self-imposed time-out by autistic children during an operant training program." Behav Ther 1(3): 371-81, August, 1970. (10 References).
Reports on a study conducted with two autistic boys (aged twelve and fifteen years) in which they voluntarily imposed thirty-second time-outs from the tasks in a verbal and printing training program.

800 Stilwell, William E. "Using behavioral techniques with autistic children." In: Krumboltz, John D., and Thoresen, Carl E., eds. Behavioral counseling: cases and techniques. New York: Holt, Rinehart & Winston, 1969. 193-99.

The peers of a hospitalized twelve-year-old autistic boy were used as models in a successful program to modify his behavior. A marked reduction in isolate behavior was noted in the results.

801 Tramontana, Joseph, and Stimbert, Vaughan E. "Some techniques of behavior modification with an autistic child." Psychol Rep 27(2): 498, October, 1970. (2 References).
Reports briefly on fifty twice-weekly training sessions with a seven-year-old boy.

802 Waizer, Jonas. "Effects of two parameters of visual reinforcement on the free-operant behavior of normal and autistic children." For a summary see: Diss Abstr Int 35B(5): 2417, November, 1974.

b. Aversion/Punishment

803 Breger, Louis. "Comments on 'building social behavior in autistic children by use of electric shock.'" J Exp Res Pers 1(2): 110-13, October, 1965. (5 References).
Criticizes the article by Lovaas, Schaeffer, and Simmons (Item No. 806) with reference to two specific areas: problems in the choice of autistic children as subjects, and the problem of transfer of effect.

804 Hobbs, Steven A., and Goswick, Ruth Ann. "Behavioral treatment of self-stimulation: an examination of alternatives to physical punishment." J Clin Child Psychol 6(1): 20-23, Spring, 1977. (24 References).
Reviews the research and concludes that the combination of positive reinforcement for functional responses with deceleration techniques--such as extinction or overcorrection--may provide effective methods of reducing self-stimulation and encouraging appropriate behavior.

805 Lichstein, Kenneth L., and Schreibman, Laura. "Employing electric shock with autistic children: a review of the side effects." J Autism Child Schizo 6(2): 163-73, June, 1976. (34 References).
Brings together information on the reported side effects of electric shock treatment. Generally, the side effects were positive in nature and included response generalization, increases in social behavior, and positive emotional behavior.

806 Lovaas, O. Ivar; Schaeffer, Benson; Simmons, James Q. "Building social behavior in autistic children by use of electric shock." J Exp Res Pers 1(2): 99-109, October, 1965. (10 References). (Reprinted in Item No. 38).
Demonstrates the use of painful electric shock to modify the behavior of two five-year-old identical twins diagnosed as childhood schizophrenics. Self-stimulatory and tantrum behaviors were eliminated, and positive interaction with adults was increased.

807 Risley, Todd R. "The effects and side effects of punishing the autistic behaviors of a deviant child." J Appl Behav Anal 1(1): 21-34, Spring, 1968. (10 References). (Reprinted in Item No. 21).
Reports on the successful use of electric shock to eliminate the dangerous climbing behavior of a severely deviant six-year-old girl. Less severe forms of punishment were used to eliminate the child's autistic rocking. Side effects in the form of behavioral contrasts or "symptom substitution" did occur; however, these side effects were primarily desirable ones.

808 Saposnek, Donald T., and Watson, Luke S., Jr. "The elimination of the self-destructive behavior of a psychotic child: a case study." Behav Ther 5(1): 79-89, January, 1974. (13 References). (Reprinted in Item No. 35).
Head-slapping was reduced in an institutionalized autistic ten-year-old boy by means of physical restraint and the shaping of hand-slapping.

809 Simmons, James Q., III, and Lovaas, O. Ivar. "Use of pain and punishment as treatment techniques with childhood schizophrenics." Am J Psychother 23(1): 23-36, January, 1969. (24 References). (Reprinted in Item No. 43).
Painful stimuli--consisting of electric shock and slapping paired with admonitory words--were used to achieve behavioral control over nine children diagnosed as childhood schizophrenics.

810 Solnick, Jay V.; Rincover, Arnold; Peterson, Christa R. "Some determinants of reinforcing and punishing effects of time-out." J Appl Behav Anal 10(3): 415-24, Fall, 1977. (29 References).
Offers data on two experiments which were initiated when time-out was found to be failing as an aversive technique in the reduction of tantrums in a six-year-old autistic girl, and in the reduction of spitting and the self-injurious behavior of a sixteen-year-old boy. In the case of the girl, the time-out was found to be providing an opportunity to engage in self-stimulatory behavior, and, in the case of the boy, it was necessary to "enrich" the time-in environment.

811 Webster, C. D. Letter to editor: "A negative reaction to the use of electric shock with autistic children." J Autism Child Schizo 7(2): 199-204, June, 1977. (17 References).
Refutes the argument on the use of physical punishment with autistic children propounded by Lichstein and Schreibman (Item No. 805). Details are given of several cases from the author's own experience.

B. BRAIN INJURY

812 Hall, Robert Vance. "Behavior modification of brain-injured youngsters through the application of principles of operant conditioning." For a summary see: Diss Abstr 27A(9): 2882, March, 1967.

813 Hall, R. Vance, and Broden, Marcia. "Behavior changes in brain-injured children through social reinforcement." J Exp Child Psychol 5(4): 463-79, December, 1967. (13 References). (Reprinted in Item No. 37, 41).
In a study conducted with three children diagnosed as having a central nervous system dysfunction, systematic reinforcement was applied by adults initially unfamiliar with such techniques.

814 Pascal, Charles E. "Application of behavior modification by parents for treatment of a brain damaged child." In: Ashem, Beatrice A., and Poser, Ernest G., eds. Adaptive learning: behavior modification with children. New York: Pergamon, 1973. 299-309. (16 References).
Presents a case report on the use of operant techniques with a brain-damaged nine-year-old boy. The program sought to eliminate bizarre vocal sounds and excessive hand-clapping and to develop functional speech. The program was conducted primarily by the mother but also involved other

members of the family. Included in the article is the "memo" which was directed to all people who spent more than ten hours a week with the boy. The memo explained the essential strategy of the modification program. Preliminary evaluation after two months indicated elimination of the maladaptive behaviors and progress in speech development.

C. EPILEPSY/SEIZURES

815 Balaschak, Barbara A. "Teacher-implemented behavior modification in a case of organically based epilepsy." J Consult Clin Psychol 44(2): 218-23, April, 1976. (13 References).
Significant reduction of seizures in an eleven-year-old epileptic girl was achieved by her teacher's positive reinforcement of seizure-free times.

816 Gardner, James E. "Behavior therapy treatment approach to a psychogenic seizure case." J Consult Psychol 31(2): 209-12, April, 1967. (8 References).
Psychogenic seizures in a ten-year-old girl were effectively controlled by the reinforcement of non-seizure behavior. Treatment consisted of three weekly counseling sessions with the parents who were instructed to give attention to appropriate behaviors and to withdraw attention for seizure behavior.

817 Wright, Logan. "Aversive conditioning of self-induced seizures." Behav Ther 4(5): 712-13, October, 1973. (3 References).
Electroshock was used to condition a five-year-old retarded boy to refrain from inducing seizures. Results from two separate three-to-four-day treatment periods, as well as from a seven-month follow-up, indicated a significant reduction in the number of self-induced seizures.

818 Zlutnick, Steven; Mayville, William J.; Moffat, Scott. "Behavioral control of seizure disorders: the interruption of chained behavior." In: Katz, Roger C., and Zlutnick, Steven, eds. Behavior therapy and health care: principles and applications. New York: Pergamon, 1975. 317-36. (22 References).
Focuses on an attempt to eliminate or decrease the rate of seizures in five epileptic children by contingent punishment and the reinforcement of behavior incompatible with seizures. Results indicated: (1) seizures of both organic and functional etiology appear sensitive to environmental manipulations; (2) seizures, particularly those of the minor motor variant, are more predictable than was previously assumed; (3) a strategy of seizure control on the interruption of pre-seizure behaviors is effective in some cases; (4) improved communication and cooperation between neurologists and behavioral scientists might improve the efficiency of treatment strategies.

819 ———. "Modification of seizure disorders: the interruption of behavioral chains." J Appl Behav Anal 8(1): 1-12, Spring, 1975. (24 References).
Investigates the effects of interruption and differential reinforcement on the seizures of five epileptic children. Seizures are conceptualized as being the terminal link in a behavioral chain. Parents and school personnel functioned as change agents. Seizures were reduced in four of the subjects.

D. HEARING IMPAIRMENTS

1. Behavioral Handling of the Hearing-Disabled Child

820 Bennett, Clinton W. "A four-and-a-half-year-old as a teacher of her hearing-impaired sister: a case study." J Commun Disord 6(2): 67-75, June, 1973. (7 References).
A four-and-one-half-year-old girl trained her three-year-old hearing-impaired sister to use correctly the plural allomorph/-s/ by rewarding her with candy.

821 Bennett, Clinton W., and Ling, Daniel. "Teaching a complex verbal response to a hearing-impaired girl." J Appl Behav Anal 5(3): 321-27, Fall, 1972. (16 References).
Operant conditioning techniques with edible reinforcers were successful in teaching a three-year-old hearing-impaired girl to use a present progressive sentence form in describing a picture.

822 Craig, Helen B., and Holland, Audrey L. "Reinforcement of visual attending in classrooms for deaf children." J Appl Behav Anal 3(2): 97-109, Summer, 1970. (11 References).
Examines the efficacy of immediate tangible reinforcement for entire classes of hearing-impaired children. Edible reinforcers or tokens were used, and in all classes an increase in visual attending was documented.

823 Garrard, Kay R., and Saxon, Samuel A. "Preparation of a disturbed deaf child for therapy: a case description in behavior shaping." J Speech Hear Disord 38(4): 502-9, November, 1973. (10 References).
Describes a treatment plan used to train the speech pathologist and the patient's mother in behavior modification. The initial steps of the plan are emphasized.

824 Gellens, Suzanne. "Behavior modification: a classroom technique." Volta Rev 75(2): 114-25, February, 1973. (5 References).
Discusses a behavior modification technique which can be used in classrooms to effect changes in social interactions, alter behavior, promote vocalizations, and teach content material. Case studies are used to illustrate the successful application of the technique.

825 Johnson, C. Merle, and Kaye, James H. "Acquisition of lipreading in a deaf multihandicapped child." J Speech Hear Disord 41(2): 226-32, May, 1976. (9 References).
Operant techniques were used to develop lipreading in a nine-year-old deaf boy who had failed to respond appropriately to previous attempts at speech-reading training.

826 Levine, Edna S., and Naiman, Doris W., eds. "Seminar on behavior modification methods for psychologists working with the deaf." Am Ann Deaf 115(4): 455-91, July, 1970.
Consists of four articles on the use of behavior modification methods in dealing with the specific problems of the deaf. Reports are included on a program for emotionally disturbed deaf boys and on the reinforcement of visual attending.

827 Maurer, James Frederick. "Sustaining and shaping vocal behavior in prelingually deaf pre-school children." For a summary see: Diss Abstr Int 29B(11): 4404, May, 1969.

828 Mira, Mary. "Behavior modification applied to training young deaf children." Except Child 39(3): 225-29, November, 1972. (3 References).
Demonstrates the facilitation of speech and language and the use of behavioral management methods in establishing effective discipline, aiding adjustment to prosthetic devices, and dealing with problems related to additional handicapping conditions.

829 Moore, Benjamin Luther. "Behavior management of the preschool deaf." For a summary see: Diss Abstr Int 34B(6): 2946, December, 1973.

830 Osborne, J. Grayson. "Free-time as a reinforcer in the management of classroom behavior." J Appl Behav Anal 2(2): 113-18, Summer, 1969. (10 References). (Reprinted in Item Nos. 27, 39, 41, 47).
In this study the amount of in-seat behavior was increased by making time away from school work contingent on remaining seated for specified periods of time. The subjects were six girls, aged eleven to thirteen years, attending a school for the deaf.

831 Webster, L. Michael, and Green, Walter B. "Behavior modification in the deaf classroom: current applications and suggested alternatives." Am Ann Deaf 118(4): 511-18, July, 1973. (14 References).
Outlines the advantages and disadvantages of using behavior modification techniques for deaf children. A sample program is provided.

832 Wilson, Michele Drisko, and McReynolds, Leija V. "A procedure for increasing oral reading rate in hard-of-hearing children." J Appl Behav Anal 6(2): 231-39, Summer, 1973. (18 References).
Investigates the effectiveness of a vibrotactile pulser and differential reinforcement to increase the reading rate of six children with moderate to severe hearing loss.

2. Behavioral Audiometry

833 Barraclough, B. M. "A method of testing hearing based on operant conditioning." Behav Res Ther 4(3): 237-38, August, 1966. (1 Reference).
Presents a case history describing a method of testing hearing in speechless and other difficult-to-test children. A comparison is made with a similar technique called "Peepshow" audiometry.

834 Bricker, Diane D., and Bricker, William A. "A programmed approach to operant audiometry for low-functioning children." J Speech Hear Disord 34(4): 312-20, November, 1969. (8 References).
Relates the general approach and a step-by-step procedure for dispensing reinforcements to a child when he emits a reliable response in the presence of a signal.

835 Bricker, William A., and Bricker, Diane D. "Four operant procedures for establishing auditory stimulus control with low-functioning children." Am J Ment Defic 73(6): 981-87, May, 1969. (6 References).
Investigates the use of operant procedures to obtain more reliable audiometric assessments of mentally retarded children. Thirty-six institutionalized retardates were tested; reliable testing assessments were obtained for thirty-three of the subjects.

836 Eger, Diane Levy. "The efficacy of auditory conditioning training for puretone testing with severely and profoundly retarded children." For a summary see: Diss Abstr Int 37B(5): 2146, November, 1976.

837 Freeman, Betty Jo; Leibowitz, J. Michael; Linseman, Mary Ann. "A study of an operant procedure: testing auditory deficits." Ment Retard 12(2): 14-17, April, 1974. (7 References).
Focuses on a simple procedure which was developed to test perceptual functioning in a twenty-six-month-old retarded child.

838 Fulton, Robert T.; Gorzycki, Pamela A.; Hull, Wilma L. "Hearing assessment with young children." J Speech Hear Disord 40(3): 397-404, August, 1975. (19 References).
Evaluates the efficacy and reliability of auditory stimulus-response control training and assessment procedures with children aged nine-months to twenty-five months.

839 Fulton, Robert T., and Graham, James T. "Conditioned Orientation Reflex audiometry with the mentally retarded." Am J Ment Defic 70(5): 703-8, March, 1966. (3 References).
Documents the successful use of Conditioned Orientation Reflex (COR) audiometry with seventy-one retarded children between the ages of five and ten years. COR relies on visual orientation responses to auditory stimuli. Retesting, after a one-year period, tended to indicate threshholds slightly more sensitive than those obtained originally.

840 Fulton, Robert T., and Spradlin, Joseph E. "Operant audiometry with severely retarded children." Audiology 10(4): 203-11, July-August, 1971. (5 References).
Furnishes the parameters of stimulus control in a procedure in which children are trained to press a response button in the presence of an auditory stimulus and to refrain from pressing the button in the absence of the stimulus.

841 Gerber, Sanford E.; Jones, Bronwyn L.; Costello, Janis M. "Behavioral measures." In: Gerber, Sanford E., ed. Audiometry in infancy. New York: Grune & Stratton, 1977. 85-97. (58 References).
Reviews the methods of audiologic testing that are dependent upon observable behavioral responses to auditory stimuli and that can be employed with very young children with a reasonable expectation of accuracy.

842 Hegrenes, Jack R.; Marshall, Nancy R.; Armas, Jess A. "Treatment as an extension of diagnostic function: a case study." J Speech Hear Disord 35(2): 182-87, May, 1970. (2 References).
Describes the extinguishing of an eight-year-old boy's inappropriate behavior by behavioral methods. His improved behavior enabled a more precise assessment of his hearing acuity and intellectual level to be made.

843 Lloyd, Lyle L. "Behavioral audiometry viewed as an operant procedure." J Speech Hear Disord 31(2): 128-36, May, 1966. (38 References).
Analyzes the more frequently used forms of pure-tone behavioral audiometry in terms of reinforcement and other operant principles.

844 Lloyd, Lyle L.; Spradlin, Joseph E.; Reid, Michael J. "An operant audiometric procedure for difficult-to-test patients." J Speech Hear Disord 33(3): 236-45, August, 1968. (26 References).

A tangible reinforcement operant conditioning audiometric procedure was used successfully with fifty profoundly retarded patients. It was also used successfully with three normal infants (seven, fifteen, and eighteen months old).

845 Lloyd, Lyle L., and Wilson, Wesley R. "Recent developments in the behavioral assessment of the infant's response to auditory stimulation." In: Loebell, E., ed. Sixteenth International Congress of Logopedics and Phoniatrics. Basel, Switzerland: Karger, 1976. 301-9. (19 References).
Surveys the use of operant behavior in the audiologic assessment of children under three years of age. Infants in the studies described received either a visual or a tangible reinforcer.

846 Martin, Frederick N., and Coombes, Sherry. "A tangibly reinforced speech reception threshold procedure for use with small children." J Speech Hear Disord 41(3): 333-38, April, 1976. (13 References).
Demonstrates the successful use of operant conditioning audiometry using tangible reinforcers with forty normal-hearing children between the ages of seventeen months and fifty-six months.

847 St. James-Roberts, I. "Why operant audiometry--a consideration of some shortcomings fundamental to the audiological testing of children." J Speech Hear Disord 37(1): 47-54, February, 1972. (19 References).
Indicates the importance of the variability in audiometric testing and recommends the development of operant procedures to remedy the deficiencies.

848 Thompson, G., and Weber, B. A. "Responses of infants and young children to Behavior Observation Audiometry (BOA)." J Speech Hear Disord 39: 140-47, May, 1974. (6 References).
Presents data on the testing of 190 children ranging from three months to fifty-nine months of age. Results indicated that Behavior Observation Audiometry (BOA) thresholds are influenced by chronological age. Children who could be tested by both BOA and play audiometry consistently demonstrated lower thresholds on the latter procedure.

849 Yarnall, G. D. "Comparison of operant and conventional audiometric procedures with deaf-blind, multiply-handicapped children." For a summary see: Diss Abstr Int 34B(11): 5313, May, 1974.

E. HYPERKINESIS

850 Alabiso, Frank. "Operant control of attention behavior: a treatment for hyperactivity." Behav Ther 6(1): 39-42, January, 1975. (12 References).
Token and social reinforcers were used to reinforce attention span, focus of attention, and selective attention in a group of eight, institutionalized, hyperactive retardates.

851 Allen, K. Eileen; Henke, Lydia B.; Harris, Florence R.; et al. "Control of hyperactivity by social reinforcement of attending behavior." J Educ Psychol 58(4): 231-37, August, 1967. (13 References). (Reprinted in Item No. 37).
The attention span of a hyperactive four-and-one-half-year-old boy was increased over a period of seven days by the use of adult social reinforcement.

852 Ayllon, Teodoro; Layman, Dale; Kandel, Henry J. "A behavioral-educational alternative to drug control of hyperactive children." J Appl Behav Anal 8(2): 137-46, Summer, 1975. (27 References).
Provides the results of a study in which the hyperactive behavior of three children--previously on drug therapy--was reduced by reinforcing correct academic responses.

853 Ayllon, Teodoro, and Rainwater, Nancy. "Behavioral alternatives to the drug control of hyperactive children in the classroom." Sch Psychol Dig 5(4): 33-39, Fall, 1976. (11 References).
Traces the development of the use of behavioral techniques with the hyperactive child and suggests their use as an alternative to drug control. Behavioral approaches that may be used by the classroom teacher are also provided.

854 Bower, K. Bruce, and Mercer, Cecil D. "Hyperactivity: etiology and intervention techniques." J Sch Health 45(4): 195-201, April, 1975. (8 References).
Recommends that drug intervention be considered only when other intervention methods--including behavior modification--have failed.

855 Brundage-Aguar, Dian; Forehand, Rex; Ciminero, Anthony R. "A review of treatment approaches for hyperactive behavior." J Clin Child Psychol 6(1): 3-10, Spring, 1977. (105 References).
Examines both medical and psychological treatment techniques. Chemotherapy with psychostimulant drugs was found to be the more frequently used treatment, although it was prone to negative side effects. Behavior modification has been the primary nonmedical technique but further research is needed--especially that which would furnish follow-up data.

856 Christensen, Donald Eugene. "The combined effects of methylphenidate (Ritalin) and a classroom behavior modification program in reducing the hyperkinetic behaviors of institutionalized mental retardates." For a summary see: Diss Abstr Int 34B(11): 5671, May, 1974.

857 ————. "Effects of combining methylphenidate and a classroom token system in modifying hyperactive behavior." Am J Ment Defic 80(3): 266-76, November, 1975. (36 References).
The results of a within-subject, placebo-controlled, double-blind design comparison study conducted with sixteen hyperactive, institutionalized, retarded children indicated that behavior modification is a viable alternative to drug therapy for hyperactivity in retarded children.

858 Christensen, Donald E., and Sprague, Robert L. "Reduction of hyperactive behavior by conditioning procedures alone and combined with methylphenidate (Ritalin)." Behav Res Ther 11(3): 331-34, August, 1973. (17 References).
Documents the results of a study conducted with twelve hyperactive children. Indications were that a combination of pharmacotherapy and behavior modification would be a very potent therapeutic approach.

859 Costello, William Henry. "The effectiveness of Ritalin and token economy in increasing hyperkinetic children's coloring behavior." For a summary see: Diss Abstr Int 35B(10): 5103, April, 1975.

860 Doubros, Steve G., and Daniels, Gary J. "An experimental approach to the reduction of overactive behavior." Behav Res Ther 4(4): 251-58, November, 1966. (12 References).

Reports on the successful use of operant conditioning techniques to establish control over the hyperactive behavior of six mentally retarded children. Appropriate behavior was rewarded by tokens.

861 Drash, Philip W. "Treatment of hyperactive two-year-old children." Paper presented at the 129th Annual Meeting of the American Psychiatric Association, Miami Beach, May 10, 1976. 19p. (ED 136 543).
Examines the use of behaviorally oriented treatment programs with two hyperactive boys. The class for the children was combined with a parent training program.

862 Firestone, Philip. "The effects of reinforcement contingencies and caffeine on hyperactive children." For a summary see: Diss Abstr Int 35B(10): 5109, April, 1975.

863 Firestone, Philip, and Douglas, Virginia. "The effects of reward and punishment on reaction times and autonomic activity in hyperactive and normal children." J Abnorm Child Psychol 3(3): 201-16, 1975. (33 References).
Reward, punishment, and reward plus punishment were all successful in improving reaction times for hyperactive and normal children. Reward led to a significant increase in impulsive responses in the hyperactive children.

864 Flynn, Nona Mitchell. "The effect of positive teacher reinforcement and classroom social structure on class behavior of boys diagnosed as hyperactive before and during medication." For a summary see: Diss Abstr Int 36A(4): 2109, October, 1976.

865 Gittelman, Rachel. "Preliminary report on the efficacy of methylphenidate and behavior modification in hyperkinetic children [proceedings]." Psychopharmacol Bull 13(2): 53-54, April, 1977. (2 References).
Furnishes the results of an ongoing study conducted with thirty-four children manifesting hyperactive behavior. Preliminary results indicated that behavior modification might prove to be a useful adjunct to medication, rather than a substitution for it.

866 Gittelman-Klein, Rachel; Klein, Donald F.; Abikoff, Howard; et al. "Relative efficacy of methylphenidate and behavior modification in hyperkinetic children: an interim report." J Abnorm Child Psychol 4(4): 361-79, December, 1976. (28 References).
Compares methylphenidate, behavior therapy and placebo, and behavior therapy and methylphenidate over an eight-week period with thirty-four children. The results indicate that although all methods of treatment were effective, methylphenidate was significantly superior to behavior therapy alone.

867 Jeffrey, Timothy Butler. "The effects of operant conditioning and the electromyographic biofeedback on the relaxed behavior of hyperkinetic children." For a summary see: Diss Abstr Int 37B(5): 2510, November, 1976.

868 Knowles, Patsy Livingston; Prutsman, Thomas D.; Raduege, Virginia. "Behavior modification of simple hyperkinetic behavior and letter discrimination in a hyperactive child." J Sch Psychol 6(2): 157-60, Winter, 1968. (6 References).

Uses a case history of a seven-year-old hyperactive boy to demonstrate the successful use of operant conditioning in the modification of two different types of behavior, i.e., habitual running in the hall, and letter reversals in writing. Candy was used as a reinforcer.

869 Krop, Harry. "Modification of hyperactive behavior of a brain-damaged emotionally disturbed child." Train Sch Bull 68(1): 49-54, May, 1971. (6 References).
Systematic reinforcement of non-hyperactive behavior resulted in a significant reduction of hyperactive behavior in an eight-year-old boy. Primary and secondary reinforcers contingent on non-hyperactive behavior were delivered by an occupational therapist. A follow-up at four weeks indicated that the reduction was maintained.

870 Moore, Craig Lee. "Behavior modification and electromyographic biofeedback as alternatives to drugs for the treatment of hyperkinesis in children." For a summary see: Diss Abstr Int 38B(6): 2872, December, 1977.

871 Nixon, Stewart B. "Increasing task-oriented behavior." In: Krumboltz, John D., and Thoresen, Carl E., eds. Behavioral counseling: cases and techniques. New York: Holt, Rinehart & Winston, 1969. 207-10. (Reprinted in Item No. 27).
Demonstrates the successful use of a filmed social model in reducing the hyperactive behavior of elementary school children. Candy was used to reinforce appropriate behavior.

872 O'Leary, K. Daniel; Pelham, William E.; Rosenbaum, Alan; et al. "Behavioral treatment of hyperkinetic children: an experimental evaluation of its usefulness." Clin Pediatr 15(6): 510-15, June, 1976. (19 References).
Analyzes a controlled evaluation of a ten-week program for hyperkinetic children attending normal or nonremedial classes. Behavioral methods are advocated as an alternative to drug therapy.

873 Parry, Penny Anna. "The effect of reward on the performance of hyperactive children." For a summary see: Diss Abstr Int 34B(12): 6220, June, 1974.

874 Patterson, G. R. "An application of conditioning techniques to the control of a hyperactive child." In: Ullmann, Leonard P., and Krasner, Leonard, eds. Case studies in behavior modification. New York: Holt, Rinehart & Winston, 1965. 370-75. (16 References). (Reprinted in Item Nos. 22, 27).
Presents a case report on the reduction of inappropriate classroom behavior in a hyperactive nine-year-old boy. Various rewards were used, including candy, pennies, and social approval of his peer group. Further research is recommended to determine the relative contributions of each of these variables.

875 Patterson, G. R.; Jones, R.; Whittier, J.; et al. "A behavior modification technique for the hyperactive child." Behav Res Ther 2(3): 217-26, May, 1965. (20 References). (Reprinted in Item Nos. 29, 36).
Summarizes the findings of a study--using an experimental and a control subject--on a procedure for conditioning the attending behavior of a

brain-injured, hyperactive ten-year-old boy. Conditioning took place over a three-month period in the classroom setting and utilized an auditory stimulus (previously paired with the delivery of candy or pennies) received by means of a radio-earphone device. The experimental subject showed a significant decrease in nonattending behavior which was maintained over a four-week extinction period.

876 Pelham, William E. Letter to editor: "Behavioral treatment of hyperkinesis." Am J Dis Child 130(5): 565, May, 1976. (10 References).
Details the successful treatment by behavioral methods of a nine-year-old hyperkinetic boy who had shown minimal improvement from the previous three years of pharmacotherapy.

877 Pihl, Robert O. "Conditioning procedures with hyperactive children." Neurology 17(4): 421-23, April, 1967. (7 References).
Provides the case histories of two hyperactive boys (age seven and fourteen) in which hyperactivity was controlled by means of a points system with the points exchangeable for money and privileges at home.

878 Pratt, Sandra J., and Fischer, Joel. "Behavior modification: changing hyperactive behavior in a children's group." Perspect Psychiatr Care 13(1): 37-42, January-March, 1975. (9 References).
Includes a review of the literature and describes a program used by a psychiatric nurse to reduce the hyperactivity of a nine-year-old boy in a therapy group.

879 Rosenbaum, Alan; O'Leary, K. Daniel; Jacob, Rolf G. "Behavioral intervention with hyperactive children: group consequences as a supplement to individual contingencies." Behav Ther 6(3): 315-23, May, 1975. (17 References).
Group reward and individual reward were compared during a four-week treatment and a four-week maintenance period. No significant difference was found between the two systems.

880 Ross, Dorothea M., and Ross, Sheila A. Hyperactivity: research, theory, and action. New York: Wiley, 1976. 148-75, 205-13. (Wiley Series on Personality Processes).
The chapter on psychotherapy in this comprehensive text includes a description of behavior therapy approaches. The principles of reinforcement and modeling are outlined with examples from the research literature. The training of nonprofessionals is also discussed. Included in the chapter on educational intervention is some discussion on the use of behavior modification procedures in the classroom.

881 Safer, Daniel J., and Allen, Richard P. Hyperactive children: diagnosis and management. Baltimore, Maryland: University Park Press, 1976. 256p. (Bibliography).
This text advocates a multimodal approach to the clinical management of the hyperactive child, with an emphasis on behavior modification methods. In addition to material on the general principles and methods of behavior therapy, there are chapters on behavior management in the classroom and in the home. Each chapter contains sample graphs and record charts.

882 Schofield, Leon J., Jr.; Hedlund, Carol; Worland, Julien. "Operant approaches to group therapy and effects on sociometric status." Psychol Rep 35(1): 83-90, August, 1974. (42 References).

Documents the use of a behavior modification approach with four hyperactive, unsocialized boys. Although there was improvement in behavior and an increase in social interactions, no improvement was noted in sociometric status.

883 Simmons, James Q., III. "Behavioral management of the hyperactive child." In: Cantwell, Dennis P., ed. The hyperactive child: diagnosis, management, current research. New York: Spectrum, 1975. 129-43. (21 References).
Briefly discusses the behavioral strategies suitable for use with the hyperactive child. Behavior therapy is suggested as only one of the possible strategies, although, perhaps, the most parsimonious. Three case histories are cited.

884 Stableford, William; Butz, Robert; Hasazi, Joseph; et al. "Sequential withdrawal of stimulant drugs and use of behavior therapy with two hyperactive boys." Am J Orthopsychiatry 46(2): 302-12, April, 1976. (34 References).
Compares the separate and combined effects of stimulant drugs, placebos, and behavior therapy with two hyperactive boys. Replacement of drugs with placebos has no observable effect. Behavior therapy, both alone and in combination with drugs, was effective in controlling hyperactive behavior.

885 Twardosz, Sandra, and Sajwaj, Thomas. "Multiple effects of a procedure to increase sitting in a hyperactive retarded boy." J Appl Behav Anal 5(1): 73-78, Spring, 1972. (10 References).
Describes the use of prompting and differential reinforcement procedure with a hyperactive, retarded four-year-old boy. The results indicated not only an increase in sitting, but desirable collateral changes--such as a decrease in posturing and an increase in the use of toys--were generated.

886 Vance, B. J. "Modifying hyperactive and aggressive behavior." In: Krumboltz, John D., and Thoresen, Carl E., eds. Behavioral counseling: cases and techniques. New York: Holt, Rinehart & Winston, 1969. 30-33. (Reprinted in Item No. 27).
Outlines the modification of a five-year-old boy's aggressive and hyperactive behavior. The improvement, which was accomplished in a two-week period, was brought about by teacher attention to appropriate behavior and the ignoring of inappropriate behavior.

887 Whitman, Thomas L.; Caponigri, Vicki; Mercurio, Joseph. "Reducing hyperactive behavior in a severely retarded child." Ment Retard 9(3): 17-19, June, 1971. (6 References).
A four-week training period--during which reinforcement was administered for sitting behavior--resulted in a marked reduction in hyperactivity in a six-year-old girl.

888 Worland, Julien. "Effects of positive and negative feedback on behavior control in hyperactive and normal boys." J Abnorm Child Psychol 4(4): 315-26, 1976. (28 References).
The results of this study imply that, while consistent negative feedback can reduce off-task behavior for hyperactivity, it can also decrease the accuracy of the work performed. The subjects--sixteen hyperactive boys and sixteen controls--were compared on two tasks.

889 ———. "Effects of reward and punishment on behavior control in hyperactive and normal boys." For a summary see: Diss Abstr Int 34B(12): 6227, June, 1974.

890 Wulbert, Margaret, and Dries, Robert. "The relative efficacy of methylphenidate (Ritalin) and behavior modification techniques in the treatment of a hyperactive child." J Appl Behav 10(1): 21-31, Spring, 1977. (21 References).
Contrasts drug and placebo effects with those of contingency management in the treatment of an eight-year-old boy. A multiple baseline design revealed the reinforcement contingencies to be the crucial variable controlling behavior within the clinic, but medication effects were significant within the home where reinforcement contingencies were not changed.

F. LEARNING DISABILITIES

891 Aikin, Paul Albert. "The effectiveness of a behavior oriented therapy and an insight oriented therapy on the academic achievement of educationally-disadvantaged students." For a summary see: Diss Abstr Int 30B(12, pt. 1): 5681, June, 1970.

892 Allen, K. Eileen. "Behavior modification: what teachers of young exceptional children can do." Teach Except Child 4: 119-27, Winter, 1972. (13 References).
Examines the uses that can be made of positive reinforcement to prevent the development of learning disabilities. Five case studies are provided that demonstrate the effectiveness of behavioral techniques with various types of learning disabilities, including social withdrawal, short attention span, and low verbal output.

893 Axelrod, Saul. "Token reinforcement programs in special classes." Except Child 37(5): 371-79, January, 1971. (19 References).
Surveys various token reinforcement programs that have been implemented in the special classroom. Positive results were obtained across a wide variety of target behaviors and populations, including handicapped teenagers, urban underachievers, dropouts, and learning and reading disabled, and the emotionally disturbed. Implications for further research are discussed.

894 Bradfield, Robert H., and Criner, Jane. "Precision teaching the learning-disabled child." In: Bradfield, Robert H., ed. Behavioral modification of learning disabilities. San Rafael, California: Academic Therapy, 1971. 147-70. (3 References).
Studies a program which utilized precision teaching methods to modify the behavior of emotionally disturbed and learning disabled children ranging in age from six to nine years.

895 Broden, Marcia; Hall, R. Vance; Dunlap, Ann; et al. "Effects of teacher attention and a token reinforcement system in a junior high school special education class." Except Child 36(5): 341-49, January, 1970. (12 References). (Reprinted in Item Nos. 21, 37).
Teacher attention and/or a token point system were used in a study involving thirteen disruptive and academically retarded junior high school students. The program was implemented by a first year teacher lacking prior teaching experience.

896 Case, Charleen. "A comparison of the differential effects of mother-child client-centered counseling and behavior therapy in terms of the academic achievement, behavior and personality characteristics of the educationally handicapped child." For a summary see: Diss Abstr Int 36A(1): 183, July, 1975.

897 Cooke, Thomas P., and Apolloni, Tony. "Developing positive social-emotional behaviors: a study of training and generalization effects." J Appl Behav Anal 9(1): 65-78, Spring, 1976. (29 References).
Four handicapped children (mean age 8.6 years) were taught smiling, sharing, positive physical contacting, and verbal complimenting by the use of instructions, modeling, and praise. Follow-up at four weeks indicated that improvements had generally been maintained.

898 Gardner, William L. Children with learning and behavior problems: a behavior management approach. Boston: Allyn & Bacon, 1974. 353p. (Bibliography).
This text is designed primarily for the classroom teacher. The first chapters are devoted to the general principles and possible applications of behavior modification techniques. Later sections deal with the specifics of setting up programs in the classroom and contain many examples. One chapter concentrates on home and home/school programs. Appendices contain supplementary readings and lists of audio-visual aids.

899 Glavin, John P. "Behaviorally oriented resource rooms: a follow-up." J Spec Educ 8(4): 337-47, Winter, 1974. (28 References).
Evaluates the academic and behavioral gains made by 208 second and sixth grade students after one or two years of part-time placement in a behaviorally oriented resource room and full-time attendance in a regular class for two or three years. The results indicated no significant differences between the experimental and control groups.

900 Gray, Burl B. "A behavioral strategy for reading training." In: Bradfield, Robert H., ed. Behavioral modification of learning disabilities. San Rafael, California: Academic Therapy, 1971. 73-89. (14 References).
Presents a behavioral approach to training in reading and includes a detailed description of a reading program (Performance Determined Instruction) which utilizes tangible reinforcers.

901 Grieger, Russell M., II. "Behavior modification with a total class: a case report." J Sch Psychol 8(2): 103-6, 1970. (13 References). (Reprinted in Item No. 26).
Reports on the successful implementation of a combined social, object, and token reward system with a class of nine children (mean age 9.3 years) enrolled in a school for the learning disabled.

902 Haring, Norris G., and Hauck, Mary Ann. "Improved learning conditions in the establishment of reading skills with disabled readers." Except Child 35(5): 341-52, January, 1969. (19 References). (Reprinted in Item No. 29).
A token reinforcement program was used to increase the reading skills of four reading disabled elementary school boys. Tokens were exchangeable for toys, trinkets, and store items.

903 Haring, Norris G., and Whelan, Richard J. "The learning environment: relationship to behavior modification and implications for special education." Kan Stud Educ 16(2): 1-68, June, 1966.

Furnishes the complete transcript of symposium proceedings, including four original papers with discussion and question-and-answer sessions.

904 Hewett, Frank M.; Taylor, Frank D.; Artuso, Alfred A. "The engineered classroom: an innovative approach to the education of children with learning problems." In: Bradfield, Robert H., ed. Behavior modification: the human effort. San Rafael, California: Dimensions Press, 1970. 77-78.
Sets forth a detailed description of a three-year demonstration project involving an engineered classroom model in eight classrooms for the educationally handicapped. The classrooms were located in five separate schools. Samples are included of floor plans, daily schedules, and materials used in the program.

905 Hewett, Frank M.; Taylor, Frank D.; Artuso, Alfred A.; et al. "The learning center concept." In: Bradfield, Robert H., ed. Behavioral modification of learning disabilities. San Rafael, California: Academic Therapy, 1971. 127-37. (8 References).
Advocates the use of behavior modification techniques in a learning center program which was established to provide a mechanism whereby a learning disabled child could function within the regular classroom.

906 Hobbs, Steven A., and Lahey, Benjamin B. "The behavioral approach to learning disabled children." J Clin Child Psychol 6(1): 10-14, Spring, 1971. (62 References).
Reviews the research on the use of behavior modification procedures as a treatment approach to the academic problems of learning disabled children. It is concluded that, although more research is required in this area, no other approach shows as much promise.

907 Hotchkiss, James Merel. "The modification of maladaptive behavior of a class of educationally handicapped children by operant conditioning techniques." For a summary see: Diss Abstr 27A(12): 4129, June, 1967.

908 Karraker, R. J. "Self versus teacher selected reinforcers in a token economy." Except Child 43(7): 454-55, April, 1977.
Higher rates of performance were achieved by students who were allowed to select their own reinforcers in a study conducted with twelve children (ages eight to twelve years) suspected of having learning disabilities.

909 Lahey, Benjamin. "Behavior modification with learning disabilities and related problems." In: Hersen, Michel; Eisler, Richard M.; Miller, Peter M., eds. Progress in behavior modification: Vol. 3. New York: Academic Press, 1976. 173-205. (70 References).
Defines the characteristics, outlines the traditional approaches to treatment, and examines the experimental literature on the use of behavioral techniques with the learning disabled child.

910 ————. "Therapy of learning disabilities." Curr Psychiatr Ther 16: 29-32, 1976. (9 References).
Briefly reviews the uses made of behavior modification techniques in the treatment of language and cognition disabilities.

911 Lahey, Benjamin B.; Busemeyer, Mary Kay; O'Hara, Christiane; et al. "Treatment of severe perceptual-motor disorders in children diagnosed as learning disabled." Behav Modif 1(1): 123-40, January, 1977. (12 References).

Evaluates a procedure using positive reinforcement in the remediation of severe perceptual-motor disorders affecting the handwriting of four learning disabled boys. Reinforcement and corrective feedback resulted in substantial increases in the frequency of correct printings. A significant degree of generalization to handwriting in the classroom was found in one student.

912 Lovitt, Thomas C. "Assessment of children with learning disabilities." Except Child 34(4): 233-39, December, 1967. (21 References). (Reprinted in Item No. 24).
Advocates the use and describes in detail methods of thorough behavioral assessment for children with learning disabilities. Assessments of this kind are considered to be an essential step in the formulation of teaching plans for children exhibiting this type of school problem.

913 ———. "Operant conditioning techniques for children with learning disabilities." J Spec Educ 2(3): 283-89, Spring, 1968.
Briefly describes the methods of putting operant procedures into practice in public schools. Emphasis is placed on the necessity for establishing objectives and methods for each child before beginning a program. It may be necessary to involve other potential resources such as speech therapists, school psychologists, parents, and the children themselves.

914 McKenzie, Hugh S.; Clark, Marilyn; Wolf, Montrose M.; et al. "Behavior modification of children with learning disabilities using grades as tokens and allowances as backup reinforcers." Except Child 34(10): 745-52, Summer, 1968. (12 References). (Reprinted in Item No. 24).
Familiar rewards (grades and money) were used as reinforcers for academic improvement in learning disabled children. This type of system has the advantage of being simple to run and can also involve the participation of the parents.

915 Martin, Garry L., and Powers, Richard B. "Attention span: an operant conditioning analysis." Except Child 33(8): 565-70, April, 1967. (28 References). (Reprinted in Item No. 24).
Presents an analysis of attention span in behavioral terms which considers only the time spent engaged in a task and uses reinforcement variables to account for task persistence. Using this analysis as a basis, methods are indicated by which attention span may be increased.

916 Nolen, Patricia A.; Kunzelmann, Harold P.; Haring, Norris G. "Behavioral modification in a junior high learning disabilities classroom." Except Child 34(3): 163-68, November, 1967. (11 References). (Reprinted in Item No. 24).
Rewards--in the form of highly desirable activities--were made contingent upon academic performance in an educational program conducted with twelve- to sixteen-year-old children exhibiting severe learning and behavior disorders. Significant academic gains were noted over a teaching period of approximately 100 days.

917 Novy, Pamela; Burnett, Joseph; Powers, Maryann; et al. "Modifying attending-to-work behavior of a learning disabled child." J Learn Disabil 6(4): 217-21, April, 1973. (12 References).
A token reinforcement system was used to modify the study habits of a nine-year-old learning disabled boy. His attending-to-work behavior increased from 60 percent to 88 percent in a thirty-minute period.

918 Philage, Mary Lou; Kuna, Daniel J.; Becerril, Gloria. "A new family approach to therapy for the learning disabled child." J Learn Disabil 8(8): 490-99, October, 1975. (1 Reference).
A treatment program, developed over a three-year period and derived from a parent questionnaire, resulted in increase in independent functioning of learning disabled children. Positive results were seen in both remediation and socialization.

919 Schoonover, Robert J. Handbook for parents of children with learning disabilities. Danville, Illinois: Interstate, 1976. 55p. (Bibliography).
This simply written text outlines the characteristics of the learning disabled child. Numerous exercises, based on behavioral principles, are offered to help develop learning skills in children.

920 Skinner, Michael George. "Contingency management with the learning disabled child." For a summary see: Diss Abstr Int 37A(5): 2790, November, 1976.

921 Staats, Arthur W. "A general apparatus for the investigation of complex learning in children." Behav Res Ther 6(1): 45-50, February, 1968. (10 References). (Reprinted in Item No. 21).
Describes a learning apparatus that facilitates the dispensation of rewards while maintaining good experimental behavior and voluntary participation over long periods of time. The apparatus can be employed with such tasks as reading, writing, number concept learning, concept formation, complex discrimination learning, and speech acquisition. A schematic drawing is included.

922 Staats, Arthur W.; Minke, Karl A.; Butts, Priscilla. "A token-reinforcement remedial reading program administered by black therapy-technicians to problem black children." Behav Ther 1(3): 331-53, August, 1970. (16 References).
Gives details of a four-to-five-month program involving thirty-two black ghetto children. Results indicated the procedures and reinforcement system to be significantly effective in producing improved attention and work behaviors. The program was administered by black, subprofessional therapy-technicians supervised by a behaviorally trained teacher.

923 Staats, Arthur W.; Minke, Karl A.; Goodwin, William; et al. "Cognitive behavior modification: 'motivated learning' reading treatment with subprofessional therapy-technicians." Behav Res Ther 5(4): 283-99, November, 1967. (11 References). (Reprinted in Item Nos. 21, 29).
Outlines a method of treating reading deficits with a token reinforcement system. The procedure was used successfully with eighteen junior high school students, using adult volunteers and high school seniors as the therapy-technicians.

924 Stiavelli, Richard E., and Shirley, Donald T. "The Citizenship Council: a technique for managing behavior disorders in the educationally handicapped class." J Sch Psychol 6(2): 147-56, 1968. (9 References).
A program, utilizing both social and concrete reinforcers, was successfully used to modify disruptive behaviors in a class of educationally handicapped boys aged eleven and twelve years. Results showed: (1) the group gained in cohesiveness; (2) the frustration tolerance threshold

rose; (3) there were gains in self-control; (4) the students were better able to deal with frustration and failures; and (5) the teacher found it easier to work with the class.

925 Wadsworth, H. G. "A motivational approach toward the remediation of learning disabled boys." Except Child 38(1): 33-42, September, 1971. (18 References).
This study, conducted with ten learning disabled boys, used rate of learning (based on past learning speed) to measure progress against their own performance. Significant improvements were noted in both reading and social behaviors.

926 Wagner, Rudolph F., and Guyer, Barbara P. "Maintenance of discipline through increasing children's span of attending by means of a token economy." Psychol Sch 8(3): 285-89, July, 1971. (5 References).
Reports on a study conducted with the entire population of a school serving children with specific learning disabilities. Significant differences were noted for attention span and on a behavioral rating scale. The number of disciplinary problems decreased, but no improvement in academic skills was noted.

927 Wetzel, Ralph J. "Therapeutic engineering in the natural environment." In: Bradfield, Robert H., ed. Behavior modification of learning disabilities. San Rafael, California: Academic Therapy, 1971. 19-29. (8 References).
Proposes an administrative design for programs utilizing behavioral techniques. Emphasis is placed on the involvement of all personnel who could become effective behavior modifiers.

928 Wolf, Montrose M.; Giles, David K.; Hall, R. Vance. "Experiments with token reinforcement in a remedial classroom." Behav Res Ther 6(1): 51-64, February, 1968. (6 References). (Reprinted in Item No. 38).
Contains a detailed description--including procedures, financial costs, and results of the first year--of an after school, remedial education program for low-achieving fifth and sixth grade children in an urban poverty area. A token reinforcement system using trading stamps was established with the stamps redeemable for a wide range of rewards, including snacks, trinkets, field trips, and clothing. Various contingencies were also built into the program for the teachers and the families of the students. The effects on academic achievement were found to be significant when compared with the gains of a control group.

G. MENTAL RETARDATION/DELAYED DEVELOPMENT/ DEVELOPMENTAL DISABILITIES

1. Behavioral Handling of the Mentally Retarded Child

929 Barrett, Beatrice. "Behavior analysis." In: Wortis, Joseph, ed. Mental retardation and developmental disabilities: an annual review: Vol. 9. New York: Brunner/Mazel, 1977. 141-202. (440 References).
Provides an outline of the general principles of behavioral analysis with more specific information on those aspects having direct application to the severely retarded. Suggestions for future research are given and an extensive bibliography accompanies the article.

930 Behaviour modification with the retarded child. Edited by John Comley. London: Heinemann Medical Books, 1975. 208p. (Bibliography).
Provides an introduction to the principles and methods of behavior modification for parents, teachers, and nurses. Emphasis is placed on the elimination of antisocial behavior patterns and the encouragement of more acceptable behavior. The text is illustrated with numerous case histories.

931 Bijou, Sidney W. "Behavior modification in the mentally retarded: application of operant conditioning principles." Pediatr Clin North Am 15(4): 969-87, November, 1968. (23 References).
Contains a brief review of a functional analysis of retardation and a discussion of current research. Characteristics of behavior modification programs conducted with the retarded child are also covered.

932 Birnbrauer, Jay S. "Mental retardation." In: Leitenberg, Harold, ed. Handbook of behavior modification and behavior therapy. Englewood Cliffs, New Jersey: Prentice-Hall, 1976. 361-404. (186 References).
This review of research is divided into five sections: (1) research strategies; (2) research in educational settings; (3) research in institutional wards; (4) research in vocational settings; and (5) appraisal and recommendations. Several tables are included which summarize the methods and results of studies conducted in each of several subareas, e.g., the development of self-help skills and the suppression of aggressive behavior. In the final section attention is drawn to recurring methodological and research design errors; recommendations are made for improvements in future research.

933 Block, James D. "Operant conditioning." In: Wortis, Joseph, ed. Mental retardation: an annual review: Vol. 3. New York: Brunner/Mazel, 1971. 128-45. (173 References).
Presents a state-of-the-art review on the use of operant conditioning techniques with both institutionalized and noninstitutionalized retarded populations. Areas needing further investigation are indicated.

934 Callias, Maria; Carr, Janet; Corbett, John; et al. "Use of behaviour modification techniques in a community service for mentally handicapped children." Proc R Soc Med 66(11): 1140-42, November, 1973. (6 References).
Furnishes details on the implementation of behavior modification techniques in a London suburb using community workers and parents as change agents. Two case histories are cited.

Comley, John, ed.
see Behaviour modification with the retarded child. (Item No. 930).

935 Frair, Cheryl Mayo. "Behavioral modification of trainable mentally retarded children." For a summary see: Diss Abstr Int 30B(8): 3885, February, 1970.

936 Gardner, James M. "Behavior modification in mental retardation: a review of research and analysis of trends." In: Rubin, Richard D.; Lazarus, Arnold A.; Fensterheim, Herbert; et al. Advances in behavior therapy: Vol. 3. New York: Academic Press, 1971. 37-59. (79 References).

Analyzes trends and reviews clinical findings with special reference to self-care and social skills. Included is an examination of the research methodologies, together with a summary table of studies concerned with the elimination of undesirable behavior in the mentally retarded. Areas needing further research are indicated.

937 ———. "Behavior modification research in mental retardation: search for an adequate paradigm." Am J Ment Defic 73(6): 844-51, May, 1969. (41 References).
Although not particularly related to children, this review of research provides a criticism of the lack of methodological precision in the reported studies on the use of operant conditioning with the mentally retarded. Noticeable deficiencies are: (1) exact specifications of all relevant independent variables; (2) proper sampling techniques; (3) adequate controls; and (4) proper assessment of the dependent variable. Suggestions are made for future research.

938 Gardner, William I. Behavior modification in mental retardation: the education and rehabilitation of the mentally retarded adolescent and child. Chicago: Aldine, 1971. 379p. (Bibliography).
This text, which assumes no previous knowledge of behavior modification techniques, is divided into four sections: (1) the types of problems encountered in the education and rehabilitation of the mentally retarded; (2) the concepts and principles of behavior modification; (3) the psychological evaluation of the mentally retarded; and (4) the methods of producing behavior change. The volume includes many examples drawn from the research literature.

939 Kazdin, Alan E. "Issues in behavior modification with mentally retarded persons." Am J Ment Defic 78(2): 134-40, September, 1973. (56 References). (Reprinted in Item No. 35).
Recognizing that behavior modification techniques have proven successful with the mentally retarded, the author advocates that greater attention be paid to such salient issues as effective training of staff, developing performance which is not situation specific, unresponsiveness to the program, and maintenance of behavior change.

940 Kiernan, C. C., and Woodford, F. Peter, eds. Behavior modification with the severely retarded. New York: Associated Scientific, 1975. 332p.
Presents papers, commentaries, and discussions of a study group of the Institute for Research into Mental and Multiple Handicap. The interest of the group was particularly directed toward responsibility for the planning and implementation of programs. The topics covered include fundamental research, existing programs in various settings, definition of goals, and ethical issues.

941 Nawas, M. Mike, and Braun, Stephen H. "The use of operant techniques for modifying the behavior of the severely and profoundly retarded--Part I: Introduction and initial phase." Ment Retard 8(2): 2-6, April, 1970. (32 References).
Outlines the initial steps that must be taken to ensure the success of a program for the severely and profoundly retarded.

942 ———. "The use of operant techniques for modifying the behavior of the severely and profoundly retarded--Part II: The techniques." Ment Retard 8(3): 18-24, June, 1970. (53 References).

Reviews behavioral procedures and techniques as they apply to the severely retarded. Also discussed are positive reinforcement, avoidance and escape procedures, imitation, extinction, punishment, and time-out.

943 ———. "The use of operant techniques for modifying the behavior of the severely and profoundly retarded--Part III: Maintenance of change and epilogue." Ment Retard 8(4): 4-11, August, 1970.
Discusses methods for expanding the individual's repertoire of behaviors, maintaining those behaviors, and helping them to become self-sustaining. Future directions for research are also indicated.

944 Neisworth, John T., and Smith, Robert M. Modifying retarded behavior. Boston: Houghton Mifflin, 1973. 220p. (Bibliography).
This introductory text covers basic behavioral principles and practice and is intended for teachers, parents, and para-professionals dealing with children who exhibit retarded behavior. Each chapter contains illustrative examples and a set of topics to discusss or questions to answer. Emphasis is placed on the educable mentally retarded in the classroom situation.

945 O'Neil, Sally M.; McLaughlin, Barbara Newcomer; Knapp, Mary Beth, eds. Behavioral approaches to children with developmental delays. St. Louis, Missouri: Mosby, 1977. 210p. (Bibliography).
Although this text is intended primarily for nursing personnel, it is also suitable for parents and teachers. Basic principles of behavior modification are outlined and details are given on the promotion of specific motor, self-help, verbal, and social skills.

946 Terdal, Leif; Jackson, Russell H.; Garner, Ann M. "Mother-child interactions: a comparison between normal and developmentally delayed groups." In: Mash, Eric J.; Hamerlynck, Leo A.; Handy, Lee C., eds. Behavior modification and families. Banff International Conference on Behavior Modification, 6th, 1974. New York: Brunner/ Mazel, 1976. 249-64. (15 References).
Reports on the observations conducted on the interactions between forty normal children and their mothers and forty-two developmentally delayed children and their mothers. The implications for behavior modification are discussed and, in particular, it is noted that the mother may receive impaired and confusing feedback from the retarded child.

947 Thompson, Travis, and Grabowski, John, eds. Behavior modification of the mentally retarded. New York: Oxford University Press, 1972. 297p. (Bibliography).
Sets forth detailed information on methods of behavior modification with a retarded population. Although most of the examples given are of the adult retardate, one section deals with the application of behavioral principles with the retarded child in a special education classroom and with the parents.

948 Thurman, S. Kenneth. "Environmental maintenance of retarded behavior: a behavioral perspective." Education 97(2): 121-25, Winter, 1976.
Suggests that retarded behavior may be maintained in the child by the reinforcement prevalent in the child's environment. Several examples are given to substantiate this theory.

949 Wehman, Paul. Helping the mentally retarded to acquire play skills: a behavioral approach. Springfield, Illinois: Thomas, 1977. 231p. (Bibliography).
Describes methods of developing play and leisure skills in the retarded since these are frequently not spontaneous activities in the mentally deprived. Information is provided on program implementation and the selection of suitable activities, materials, and toys. Emphasis throughout is placed on the positive reinforcement of appropriate responses and activities.

950 Weisberg, Paul. "Operant procedures with the retardate: an overview of laboratory research." In: Ellis, Norman R., ed. International review of research in mental retardation: Vol. 5. New York: Academic Press, 1971. 113-45. (69 References).
Reviews studies carried out with retarded subjects, including several with retarded children. All the studies were conducted under traditional experimental limitations and utilized operant procedures such as reinforcement and punishment.

951 Yamaguchi, Kaoru. "Application of operant principles to mentally retarded children." In: Thompson, Travis, and Dockens, William S., Ill, eds. Applications of behavior modification. New York: Academic Press, 1975. 365-84. (5 References).
Presents six case histories in which operant principles were applied to modify the behavior of mentally retarded children. Target behaviors included toilet training, self-help skills, walking, and various deviant behavior patterns.

2. Elimination of Maladaptive Behaviors

a. Miscellaneous Behavior Problems

952 Ausman, James; Ball, Thomas S.; Alexander, Dean. "Behavior therapy of pica with a profoundly retarded adolescent." Ment Retard 12(6): 16-18, December, 1974. (2 References).
A time-out procedure was used in the successful treatment of a nonverbal, fourteen-year-old, severely retarded boy with a lengthy history of pica.

953 Baker, Bruce L., and Ward, Michael H. "Reinforcement therapy for behavior problems in severely retarded children." Am J Orthopsychiatry 41(1): 124-35, January, 1971. (23 References). (Reprinted in Item No. 29).
Details the use of behavioral techniques with six severely retarded childreb in a small home-like living unit. Although treatment was generally effective, less success was obtained with those children who also displayed psychotic behavior.

954 Barker, P. "'Changing image': the reduction of self-stimulatory behavior in four profoundly retarded males." Int J Nurs Stud 13(3): 179-86, 1976. (14 References).
Describes the use of edible reinforcers to modify the stereotypic and maladaptive behaviors of four profoundly retarded males, two of whom were of adolescent age. The treatment took place over a period of twelve weeks.

955 Barton, Elizabeth Spindler; Guess, Doug; Garcia, Eugene; et al. "Improvement of retardates' mealtime behaviors by timeout proce-

cedures using multiple baseline techniques." J Appl Behav Anal 3(2): 77-84, 1970. (9 References). (Reprinted in Item No. 38).
Reports on a program conducted with sixteen severely and profoundly retarded male cottage residents. Undesirable mealtime behaviors were reduced by the use of time-out procedures or by the removal of the food tray for a fifteen-second period.

956 Carson, Peter, and Morgan, Sam B. "Behavior modification of food aversion in a profoundly retarded female: a case study." Psychol Rep 34(3): 954, June, 1974. (1 Reference).
Summarizes a treatment approach which successfully used a secondary reinforcer to establish a primary reinforcer. The subject was a seventeen-year-old girl suffering from phenylketonuria.

957 Doke, Larry A., and Epstein, Leonard H. "Oral overcorrection: side effects and extended applications." J Exp Child Psychol 20(3): 496-511, December, 1975. (13 References).
Documents three experiments in which contingent toothbrushing with an oral antiseptic was used to correct persistent hand-mouthing.

958 Doleys, Daniel M.; Wells, Karen C.; Hobbs, Steven A.; et al. "The effects of social punishment on noncompliance: a comparison with timeout and positive practice." J Appl Behav Anal 9(4): 471-82, Winter, 1976. (40 References).
Interprets the effects of social punishment, positive practice, and time-out on the noncompliant behavior of four mentally retarded children. The results indicated that social punishment was the most effective method of control.

959 Flavell, Judith E. "Reduction of stereotypies by reinforcement of toy play." Ment Retard 11(4): 21-23, August, 1973. (5 References).
Stereotypic behavior was reduced in three retarded boys, aged eight to fourteen years, by the use of prompting and positive reinforcement of toy play. The results were confirmed by two single-subject experimental design studies.

960 Henriksen, Kerm., and Doughty, Richard. "Decelerating undesired mealtime behavior in a group of profoundly retarded boys." Am J Ment Defic 72(1): 40-44, July, 1967. (9 References).
Operant conditioning techniques were used to decelerate the disruptive mealtime behavior of four profoundly retarded boys. Undesirable behavior was rewarded with verbal or facial disapproval or by physical interruption of movement; desired behavior was rewarded with verbal and facial approval and pats on the back.

961 Hogg, J., and Maier, I. "Transfer of operantly conditioned visual fixation in hyperactive severely retarded children." Am J Ment Defic 79(3): 305-10, November, 1974. (4 References).
Presents a follow-up to Item No. 971 and documents the transfer of increased visual attention from a controlled environment to a variety of situations in hyperactive, severely retarded children. Results showed consistent improvement for most subjects.

962 Hollis, John H. "Body-rocking: effects of sound and reinforcement." Am J Ment Defic 75(5): 642-44, March, 1971. (11 References).

Intense noise increased the rate of body-rocking in two mentally retarded children. Variable-interval and fixed-ratio schedules of reinforcement produced cumulative records similar to those obtained for lever-pressing with retardates.

963 ————. "'Superstition': the effects of independent and contingent events on free operant responses in retarded children." Am J Ment Defic 77(5): 585-96, March, 1973. (29 References).
Explores the effect of response-independent delivery of candy on high probability stereotyped behavior. Three experiments were conducted with six institutionalized, developmentally retarded girls. The results indicated that a reinforcer delivered independently of behavior accelerated baseline response rates for dominant free-operant behavior.

964 Husted, John R.; Hall, Patricia; Agin, Bill. "The effectiveness of time-out in reducing maladaptive behavior of autistic and retarded children." J Psychol 79(2): 189-96, November, 1971. (12 References).
Examines a fourteen-month intensive behavior therapy program implemented with four profoundly retarded girls. It is recommended that time-out procedures can best be utilized as part of a comprehensive self-help development program or after most of the basic self-help skills have been developed.

965 Kauffman, James; Hallahan, Daniel P.; Ianna, Susan. "Suppression of a retardate's tongue protrusion by contingent imitation: a case study." Behav Res Ther 15(2): 196-97, 1977. (4 References).
A twelve-year-old retarded boy's tongue protrusion was rapidly brought under his control by contingent imitation by adults. The technique was accompanied by intermittment contingent praise for keeping his tongue in his mouth.

966 Knapczyk, Dennis R., and Yoppi, Judith O. "Development of cooperative and competitive play responses in developmentally disabled children." Am J Ment Defic 80(3): 245-55, November, 1975. (24 References).
Provides details on a study conducted with five educable mentally retarded children with marked behavior and communication disorders. A behavior management program was used for training cooperative and competitive social play.

967 Lemke, Haru, and Mitchell, Robert D. "Controlling the behavior of a profoundly retarded child." Am J Occup Ther 26(5): 261-64, July-August, 1972. (3 References).
A profoundly retarded, self-abusive, and assaultive twelve-year-old boy was motivated to feed himself and to modify his undesirable behavior. The program, which used bites of his meals as a reinforcer, was successful within a period of eight days.

968 Levine, Bruce A. "Use of response-contingent withdrawal of reinforcement in reducing inappropriate behavior in a retarded child." Psychol Rep 35(2): 1015-18, October, 1974. (14 References).
The brief withdrawal of reinforcing events reduced four classes of perseverative behavior in a thirteen-year-old noninstitutionalized boy. The four classes of behavior were rocking, eye-rolling, giggling, and mouthing.

969 Luiselli, James K. "The effects of multiple contingencies on the rocking behavior of a retarded child." Psychol Rec 25(4): 559-65, Fall, 1975. (12 References).
Indicates that time-out was the most effective method of reducing the frequency of self-stimulatory rocking behavior in a mentally retarded fourteen-year-old boy. There is a discussion of the efficacy of this method in institutional settings.

970 Luiselli, James K.; Helfen, Carol S.; Pemberton, Bruce W.; et al. "Elimination of a child's in-class masturbation by overcorrection and reinforcement." J Behav Ther Exp Psychiatry 8(2): 201-4, June, 1977. (9 References).
Describes the successful use of an overcorrection procedure with an eight-year-old mentally retarded behaviorally disturbed child. All masturbation was eliminated after eight days. Follow-ups at one, six, and twelve months showed no recurrence.

971 Maier, I., and Hogg, J. "Operant conditioning of sustained visual fixation in hyperactive severely retarded children." Am J Ment Defic 79(3): 297-304, November, 1974. (14 References).
Demonstrates the effective use of operant procedures to increase visual fixation on items of known preference in hyperactive, severely retarded children. (See Item No. 901 for a follow-up study.)

972 Martin, Garry L.; McDonald, Stewart; Omichinski, Marna. "An operant analysis of response interactions during meals with severely retarded girls." Am J Ment Defic 76(1): 68-75, July, 1971. (18 References). (Reprinted in Item No. 33).
Describes a program in which undergraduate students served as operant conditioners on a short-term basis. The students effectively treated the undesirable mealtime behaviors of four severely retarded, institutionalized girls.

973 Paluck, Robert J., and Esser, Aristide H. "Controlled experimental modification of aggressive behavior in territories of severely retarded boys." Am J Ment Defic 76(1): 23-29, July, 1971. (9 References). (Reprinted in Item No. 33).
Charts the spatial patterning of three groups of institutionalized severely retarded boys. The experiment measured the degree to which territorial behavior can be modified by punishment, coupled with positive reinforcement for incompatible behavior.

974 Paul, Howard A., and Miller, Joel R. "Reduction of extreme deviant behaviors in a severely retarded girl." Train Sch Bull 67(4): 193-97, February, 1971. (6 References).
A combination of reinforcing positive behaviors and a time-out procedure was effective in reducing deviant behavior and increasing appropriate behavior in a twelve-year-old girl.

975 Pendergrass, Virginia E. "Time-out from positive reinforcement following persistent, high-rate behavior in retardates." J Appl Behav Anal 5(1): 85-91, Spring, 1972. (10 References).
The suppression of misbehavior in two very withdrawn retarded children was accomplished by time-out procedures in spite of the fact that their participation in group activities was minimal.

976 Provencal, Gerald, and MacCormak, J. Paul. "Using a token economy to modify incorrigible behavior on a school bus: a case report." SALT: Sch Appl Learn Theory 4(1): 27-32, October, 1971.
Verbal praise and tokens were dispensed by the bus driver for appropriate behavior in a ten-year-old mongoloid girl. Backup reinforcers were provided by the parents.

977 Salzberg, Bernard, and Napolitan, James. "Holding a retarded boy at a table for two minutes to reduce inappropriate object contact." Am J Ment Defic 78(6): 748-51, May, 1974. (5 References).
Cites the use of mild physical restraint in modifying the behavior of a profoundly retarded twelve-year-old boy. The need for extensive research is indicated.

978 Tait, Tom; Brookes, Margerie; Firth, Hugh. "Sleep problems in mental subnormality." Nurs Mirror 143(3): 69-70, July 15, 1976.
Provides a case history of an eighteen-year-old retarded girl whose disturbed sleep patterns were modified by the removal of the attention caused by her waking.

979 Talkington, Larry W., and Altman, Reuben. "Effects of film-mediated aggressive and affectual models on behavior." Am J Ment Defic 77(4): 420-25, January, 1973. (24 References).
Investigates the effects, on 144 retarded male students, of modelling procedures using two films contrasting aggressive and affectual responses. Results indicated that aggressive models exerted considerable influence, but affectual modelling had little effect.

980 Wells, Patricia. "Getting control of Wayne." Nursing 5(11): 6, November, 1975.
Presents a case history of a retarded, seriously overweight twelve-year-old boy. His disruptive behavior was brought under control and a weight-loss program established by means of a combination of behavior modification techniques.

981 White, Geoffry D.; Nielsen, Gary; Johnson, Stephen M. "Timeout duration and the suppression of deviant behavior in children." J Appl Behav Anal 5(2): 111-20, Summer, 1972. (39 References).
Compares different time-out durations in the suppression of such behaviors as aggression, tantrums, self-destruction, and running away. In a group of twenty retarded, institutionalized children, the range of effects in all time-out conditions was seen to vary widely.

982 Whitman, Thomas L.; Caponigri, Vicki; Mercurio, Joseph. "Reducing hyperactive behavior in a severely retarded child." Ment Retard 9(3): 17-19, June, 1971. (6 References). (Reprinted in Item No. 33).
Describes the four-week training period undertaken with a six-year-old girl using edibles and praise as reinforcers for sitting down. A three-week follow-up indicated a substantial improvement had been maintained.

983 Wiesen, Allen E., and Watson, Edith. "Elimination of attention seeking behavior in a retarded child." Am J Ment Defic 72(1): 50-52, July, 1967. (5 References). (Reprinted in Item No. 33).
Reports on the elimination of highly disruptive behavior in an institutionalized six-year-old boy. The procedures used were a combination of aversive consequences--primarily time-out accompanied by verbal disapproval--and positive reinforcement of compatible behavior.

984 Wolf, Montrose; Birnbrauer, Jay; Lawler, Julia; et al. "The operant extinction, reinstatement, and re-extinction of vomiting behavior in a retarded child." In: Ulrich, Roger; Stachnik, Thomas; Mabry, John, eds. Control of human behavior: Vol. 2. From cure to prevention. Glenview, Illinois: Scott, Foresman, 1970. 146-49.
Discusses the experimental analysis of the vomiting behavior of a nine-year-old, nonverbal, retarded girl. The behavior was brought under control by means of eliminating the reinforcing contingencies that had attended the vomiting.

985 Wolf, Montrose M.; Birnbrauer, Jay S.; Williams, Tom; et al. "A note on apparent extinction of the vomiting behavior of a retarded child." In: Ullmann, Leonard P., and Krasner, Leonard, eds. Case studies in behavior modification. New York: Holt, Rinehart & Winston, 1965. 364-66.
Documents the reduction of vomiting in a nine-year-old retarded girl. The contingencies which were acting as reinforcement for the vomiting behavior were removed, and non-vomiting behavior was reinforced with M & M's and praise.

b. Self-Injurious Behavior

986 Adams, Kenneth M.; Klinge, Valerie; Keiser, Thomas W. "The extinction of self-injurious behavior in an epileptic child." Behav Res Ther 11(2): 351-56, August, 1973. (12 References).
Presents a case report of a fourteen-year-old girl with a history of grand mal and petit mal seizures. Her non-epileptic falling was brought under control by the use of behavior modification techniques.

987 Bailey, Jon, and Meyerson, Lee. "Effect of vibratory stimulation on a retardate's self-injurious behavior." Psychol Aspect Disabil 17(3): 133-37, November, 1970. (10 References). (Reprinted in Item No. 21).
Briefly describes the use of vibratory stimulation in the modification of self-destructive behavior in a profoundly retarded, crib-bound child. Free continuous vibration reduced the behavior to a near zero level.

988 Birnbrauer, J. S. "Generalization of punishment effects--a case study." J Appl Behav Anal 1(3): 201-11, Fall, 1968. (21 References).
Aversion therapy, including electric shock, was successful in reducing the destructive behavior of a fourteen-year-old profoundly retarded male. Although the results were initially dramatic, no internalized control was developed. The limitations of this form of therapy are enumerated, and careful assessment is advised prior to initiating such a program.

989 Comley, Reinlinde. "Self-injurious behaviour in a retarded child." Nurs Mirror 142(12): 66-68, March 18, 1976. (8 References).
The self-injurious behavior of a fifteen-year-old retarded girl was controlled by reinforcing socially desirable behavior and withdrawing reinforcement for nonacceptable behavior.

990 Corbett, J. "Aversion for the treatment of self-injurious behaviour." J Ment Defic Res 19(2): 79-95, June, 1975. (78 References).
Reviews research covering aversion and various other forms of treatment. Caution is advised in the use of aversive procedures.

991 Corte, Henry Edward. "The use of punishment in the modification of self-destructive behavior of retarded children." For a summary see: Diss Abstr Int 30B(12, pt. 1): 5685, June, 1970.

992 Corte, Henry E.; Wolf, Montrose M.; Locke, Bill J. "A comparison of procedures for eliminating self-injurious behavior of retarded adolescents." J Appl Behav Anal 4(3): 201-13, Fall, 1971. (16 References). (Reprinted in Item No. 28).
Compares the effects of elimination of social consequences, differential reinforcement of other behavior, and punishment in the elimination of self-injurious behavior. The subjects were four institutionalized, profoundly retarded adolescents. The results indicated that punishment was the most effective means, but that the effects of punishment were usually specific to the setting in which it was administered.

993 Duker, P. "Behaviour control of self-biting in a Lesch-Nyhan patient." J Ment Defic Res 19(1): 11-19, March, 1975. (12 References).
Ignoring self-biting and reinforcing more appropriate behavior resulted in a reduction of self-biting but failed to achieve control over head-banging. The patient was eight years of age at the time of treatment. It is recommended that behavioral intervention be instigated at an early age to deal with the self-mutilation that is a frequent concomitant of the Lesch-Nyhan syndrome.

994 ———. "Intra-subject controlled time-out (social-isolation) in modification of self-injurious behaviour." J Ment Defic Res 19(2): 107-12, June, 1975. (8 References).
Socialization was effective in reducing self-injurious behavior to a near zero level in a profoundly retarded fifteen-year-old girl. The socialization was used under normal ward conditions.

995 Frankel, Fred; Moss, Debra; Schofield, Susan; et al. "Case-study: use of differential reinforcement to suppress self-injurious and aggressive behavior." Psychol Rep 39(3, pt. 1): 843-49, December, 1976. (18 References).
Rapid reduction of aggressive behavior and head-banging was achieved in a six-year-old profoundly retarded girl by the use of differential reinforcement of other behaviors.

996 Frankel, Fred, and Simmons, James Q., III. "Self-injurious behavior in schizophrenic and retarded children." Am J Ment Defic 80(5): 512-22, March, 1976. (61 References).
Reviews the literature which has considered the possible operant and respondent paradigms instrumental in the acquisition and maintenance of self-injurious behavior. The implications for treatment and future research are outlined.

997 Geiger, Jane K.; Sindberg, Ronald M.; Barnes, Charles M. "Head hitting in severely retarded children." Am J Nurs 74(10): 1822-25, October, 1974. (5 References).
Nursing strategies--based on behavior modification--were used to replace destructive with more constructive behavior. Two case histories are cited.

998 Greene, Robert J., and Hoats, David L. "Aversive tickling: a simple conditioning technique." Behav Ther 2(3): 389-93, July, 1971. (11 References).

Attendants and teachers used aversive tickling to reduce self-destructive head-banging in two blind, retarded, adolescent girls.

999 Harmatz, Morton, and Rasmussen, Warren A. "A behavior modification approach to head banging." Ment Hyg 53(4): 590-93, October, 1969. (1 Reference).
Presents a case study of a retarded eight-year-old boy whose head-banging behavior was extinguished by removing the social reinforcement that had been attendant upon such behavior.

1000 Harris, Sandra L., and Romanczyk, Raymond G. "Treating self-injurious behavior of a retarded child by overcorrection." Behav Ther 7(2): 235-39, March, 1976. (7 References).
Overcorrection procedures applied both at school and at home resulted in a rapid suppression of self-injurious behavior in an eight-year-old retarded boy. Results suggest that this simple procedure can be applied consistently by both parents and teachers.

1001 Lovaas, O. Ivar, and Simmons, James Q. "Manipulation of self-destruction in three retarded children." J Appl Behav Anal 2(3): 143-57, Fall, 1969. (12 References). (Reprinted in Item Nos. 38, 41).
Documents a study, conducted with three severely retarded and psychotic children, of the variables that control self-destructive behavior. An extinction program in which the subjects were isolated, and a punishment program involving the use of electric shock, were both effective in lessening the undesirable behaviors.

1002 Lucero, William J.; Frieman, Jeanne; Spoering, Kathy; et al. "Comparison of three procedures in reducing self-injurious behavior." Am J Ment Defic 80(5): 548-54, March, 1976. (12 References).
Compares the effects of withdrawal of food, withdrawal of attention, and the simultaneous withdrawal of food and attention on the rate of self-injurious behavior in three profoundly retarded girls. The removal of food was found to be the most successful method.

1003 McPherson, Lynne, and Joachim, Ron. "The use of electric shock to reduce head-banging in a mentally retarded boy--a case study." Aust J Ment Retard 3(1): 20-24, March, 1974. (13 References).
Aversive stimulation was combined with positive reinforcement to reduce head-banging in a nine-year-old retarded boy. The self-destructive behavior decreased dramatically in a relatively short period of time.

1004 Measel, C. Julius, and Alfieri, Peter A. "Treatment of self-injurious behavior by a combination of reinforcement for incompatible behavior and overcorrection." Am J Ment Defic 81(2): 147-53, September, 1976. (13 References).
Reports on related studies with two profoundly retarded boys exhibiting severe head-banging and slapping. The results were markedly different in the two studies and possible reasons for this disparity are discussed. Areas needing further research are indicated.

1005 Muttar, A. K.; Peck, D.; Whitlow, D.; et al. "Reversal of a severe case of self-mutilation." J Ment Defic Res 19(1): 3-9, March, 1975. (10 References).

Presents a case report in which self-injurious behavior was eliminated in a ten-year-old retarded girl by the use of response-contingent shock combined with rewards. The treatment was effective within three months.

1006 Myers, David V. "Extinction, DRO, and response-cost procedures for eliminating self-injurious behavior: a case study." Behav Res Ther 13(2/3): 189-91, June, 1975. (12 References).
A response-cost procedure was significantly more effective than either DRO or extinction in eliminating severe finger and nail-biting in a retarded twelve-year-old boy.

1007 Nunes, Dennis L.; Murphy, Robert J.; Ruprecht, Michael L. "Reducing self-injurious behavior of severely retarded individuals through withdrawal of reinforcement procedures." Behav Modif 1(4): 499-516, October, 1977. (22 References).
Reports on a study conducted with two severely retarded adolescents exhibiting self-injurious behavior. The results indicated that vibratory stimulation can serve as an effective reinforcer for the severely retarded and that its contingent withdrawal can result in response suppression similar to that found under an application of aversive stimulus procedures.

1008 Peterson, Robert F., and Peterson, Linda R. "The use of positive reinforcement in the control of self-destructive behavior in a retarded boy." J Exp Child Psychiatry 6(3): 351-60, September, 1968. (8 References). (Reprinted in Item Nos. 21, 38).
Explores the use of positive reinforcement--primarily by the presentation and withdrawal of a blanket--in the control of self-destructive behavior in an eight-year-old retarded boy.

1009 Prochaska, James; Smith, Nelson; Marzilli, Robert; et al. "Remote-control aversive stimulation in the treatment of head-banging in a retarded child." J Behav Ther Exp Psychiatry 5(3/4): 285-89, December, 1974. (6 References).
Demonstrates the use of portable, remotely-controlled aversive stimulation to reduce head-banging in a profoundly retarded nine-year-old girl. In the case reported, the equipment was successful in effecting generalization.

1010 Ragain, Ronnie D., and Anson, John E. "The control of self-mutilating behavior with positive reinforcement." Ment Retard 14(3): 22-25, June, 1976. (5 References).
Food reinforcement was used to reduce scratching and head-banging in a twelve-year-old severely retarded, institutionalized girl.

1011 Repp, Alan C., and Deitz, Samuel M. "Reducing aggressive and self-injurious behavior of institutionalized retarded children through reinforcement of other behaviors." J Appl Behav Anal 7(2): 313-25, Summer, 1974. (29 References).
Aggressive and self-injurious behaviors were reduced in four retarded children by combining differential reinforcement of other behaviors with either mild verbal punishment, brief time-out, or response cost.

1012 Smolev, Susan Roth. "Use of operant techniques for the modification of self-injurious behavior." Am J Ment Defic 76(3): 295-305, November, 1971. (16 References).

Reviews the research conducted with various operant techniques. A discussion of the ethical issues involved is included, together with the problems of maintenance and generalization, and implications for the future.

1013 Tate, B. G. "Case study: control of chronic self-injurious behavior by conditioning procedures." Behav Ther 3(1): 72-83, January, 1972. (8 References).
Describes the use of a combination of edible and social reinforcers and electric shock in the reduction of chronic self-injury in a blind, retarded nineteen-year-old girl. The behavior was brought under control within one month.

1014 Thomas, Richard L., and Howard, Gail A. "A treatment program for a self-destructive child." Ment Retard 9(6): 16-21, December, 1971. (2 References). (Reprinted in Item No. 33).
Traces the reduction of self-destructive behavior in a retarded boy by the removal of attention and physical contact for the duration of the self-destructive action.

1015 Weiher, Richard G., and Harman, Roger E. "The use of omission training to reduce self-injurious behavior in a retarded child." Behav Ther 6(2): 261-68, March, 1975. (17 References).
A response-elimination technique was used to control head-banging behavior in a severely retarded fourteen-year-old boy.

1016 Whaley, Donald L., and Tough, Jerry. "Treatment of a self-injuring mongoloid with shock-induced suppression and avoidance." In: Ulrich, Roger; Stachnik, Thomas; Mabry, John, eds. Control of human behavior: Vol. 2. From cure to prevention. Glenview, Illinois: Scott, Foresman, 1970. 154-55.
Describes the modification of self-injurious head-banging and ear-pounding in a severely retarded six-year-old boy by the use of aversive electric shock.

3. Development of Specific Skills

a. Motor Skills

1017 Friedlander, Bernard Z.; Kamin, Phyllis; Hesse, Gary W. "Operant therapy for prehension disabilities in moderately and severely retarded young children." Train Sch Bull 71(2): 101-8, August, 1974. (14 References).
Prehension was improved in thirty retarded children by the use of audiovisual reinforcers for correct responses.

1018 Levy, Joseph. "Social reinforcement and knowledge of results as determinants of motor performance among EMR children." Am J Ment Defic 78(6): 752-58, May, 1974. (24 References).
Cites a study, conducted with eighty EMR children, that indicated that motor performance improved in all social reinforcement conditions to a greater degree when knowledge of results was present than when it was not.

1019 Loynd, Jenni, and Barclay A. "A case study in developing ambulation in a profoundly retarded child." Behav Res Ther 8(2): 207, May, 1970.

Presents a case report of the successful development of walking in an eight-year-old microcephalic, profoundly retarded girl. M & M candies and a variety of other primary reinforcers were used. Independent walking was acquired in approximately eighty-four sessions.

1020 O'Brien, F.; Azrin, N. H.; Bugle, C. "Training profoundly retarded children to stop crawling." J Appl Behav Anal 5(2): 131-37, Summer, 1972. (14 References).
Outlines a successful program employed with four retarded children (ages five through seven years) in a day care nursery school. The program utilized response priming for walking and restraint for crawling.

1021 Peterson, Rolf A., and McIntosh, Eranell I. "Teaching tricycle riding." Ment Retard 11(5): 32-34, October, 1973. (3 References). (Reprinted in Item No. 33).
Eight retarded children were taught to ride regular tricycles following training on a stationary vehicle. Food, social- and rest-play were used as reinforcers for successful attempts.

1022 Piper, Terence J., and MacKinnon, Ronald C. "Operant conditioning of a profoundly retarded individual reinforced via a stomach fistula." Am J Ment Defic 73(4): 627-30, January, 1969. (2 References).
Documents the case of a profoundly retarded, tube-fed fifteen-year-old girl who was conditioned to raise her arm. The reinforcement schedule consisted of the delivery of her eight-ounce fluid evening meal--one-half ounce at a time--directly into the stomach by means of a cannula through a fistula in the abdominal wall. The implications for the conditioning of profoundly retarded individuals are discussed.

1023 Schack, Frederick Kurt. "The effects of varying types of reinforcement on gross motor skill learning and retention in trainable mentally retarded boys." For a summary see: Diss Abstr Int 37A(8): 4963, February, 1976.

1024 Sylvis, James. "Effect of operant conditioning on the motor performance of educable mentally retarded boys." For a summary see: Diss Abstr Int 37A(5): 2723, November, 1976.

1025 Whitman, Thomas L.; Zakaras, Michael; Chardos, Stephen. "Effects of reinforcement and guidance procedures on instruction-following behavior of severely retarded children." J Appl Behav Anal 4(4): 283-90, Winter, 1971. (15 References).
Edible reinforcers, physical guidance, and fading procedures were used to teach two severely retarded children motor responses to a variety of verbal instructions. There was some evidence of generalization of instruction-following behavior.

b. Self-Help Skills

1026 Abramson, Edward E., and Wunderlich, Richard A. "Dental hygiene training for retardates: an application of behavioral techniques." Ment Retard 10(3): 6-8, June, 1972. (1 Reference).
Describes the use of behavioral techniques to train nine severely retarded boys to brush their teeth. Details are given on: (1) the creation of the program, during which a behavior checklist of nineteen requisite behaviors was constructed; (2) the implementation, using modelling and re-

inforcement of successive approximations; and (3) the evaluation of the program.

1027 Ball, Thomas S. "Behavior shaping of self-help skills in the severely retarded child." In: Fisher, Jerome, and Harris, Robert E., eds. Reinforcement theory in psychological treatment: a symposium. Sacramento, California: Department of Mental Hygiene, 1966. 15-24. (2 References). (Research Monograph Series No. 8).
Records the establishment of self-help skills in profoundly retarded boys using edible reinforcers. In some cases, breakfast and lunch trays were withheld and the contents used as reinforcement.

1028 Ball, Thomas S.; Seric, Kathy; Payne, Lawrence E. "Long-term retention of self-help skill training in the profoundly retarded." Am J Ment Defic 76(3): 378-82, November, 1971. (5 References). (Reprinted in Item No. 33).
Offers a follow-up study conducted with six profoundly retarded boys after a ninety-day intensive training period. Attention is called to the implications for program planning and administration.

1029 Bensberg, Gerard J.; Colwell, Cecil N.; Cassel, Robert H. "Teaching the profoundly retarded self-help activities by behavior shaping techniques." Am J Ment Defic 69(5): 674-79, March, 1969. (3 References).
Describes the use of behavior modification with edible reinforcers to improve self-help skills--primarily toilet training, dressing, and washing--in six profoundly retarded children. The program was conducted in a special unit for seven months and was judged to be successful. Mention is made of the increased job satisfaction derived by the attendant using this system.

1030 Copeland, Mildred; Ford, Lana; Solon, Nancy. Occupational therapy for mentally retarded children: guidelines for occupational therapy aides and certified occupational therapy assistants. Baltimore, Maryland: University Park Press, 1976. 226p. (Bibliography).
Provides an introduction to mental retardation and to occupational therapy and is intended for use in the training of occupational therapy aides and assistants. Detailed instructions, with photographs, are given for the teaching of self-help skills. The emphasis throughout is on the use of behavior modification techniques in the development of those skills.

1031 Edwards, Marion, and Lilly, Robert T. "Operant conditioning: an application to behavioral problems in groups." Ment Retard 4(4): 18-20, August, 1966. (7 References).
Traces the training in mealtime behavior by reinforcement and management procedures of a group of twenty-six adolescent and older brain damaged and/or emotionally impaired females.

1032 Ford, Lana Jean. "Teaching dressing skills to a severely retarded child." Am J Occup Ther 29(2): 87-92, February, 1975. (11 References).
An eight-year-old severely retarded boy was taught to remove his polo shirt by using edible reinforcers.

1033 Gross, Steven Charles. "Behavioral engineering procedures in a self-feeding maintenance program for institutionalized, severely mentally retarded children by higher functioning institutionalized maintenance tutors." For a summary see: Diss Abstr Int 36A(4): 2100, October, 1975.

1034 Groves, Ivor D., and Carroccio, Dennis F. "A self-feeding program for the severely and profoundly retarded." Ment Retard 9(3): 10-12, June, 1971. (4 References). (Reprinted in Item No. 33).
Sixty institutionalized females were taught to eat with spoons in a ward-wide program. The ages of the patients ranged from thirteen to fifty-nine years and the program was completed within a period of fourteen weeks.

1035 Horner, R. Don, and Keilitz, Ingo. "Training mentally retarded adolescents to brush their teeth." J Appl Behav Anal 8(3): 301-9, Fall, 1975. (7 References).
Evaluates a program designed to teach eight retarded adolescents to brush their teeth. The comprehensive program included a detailed task analysis and a systematic training strategy.

1036 Karen, Robert L., and Maxwell, Sandra. "Strengthening self-help behavior in the retardate." Am J Ment Defic 71(4): 546-50, January, 1967. (16 References).
Details the successful training of a seven-year-old retarded boy in the buttoning of his shirt. A vest with buttons of varying sizes was used, together with reinforcers of praise and M & M candies. The skill was generalized to daily dressing situations.

1037 Kierman, C. C., and Wright, E. C. "Behavior modification with the severely mentally handicapped. The F6 Project--a preliminary report." Proc R Soc Med 66(11): 1137-40, November, 1973. (3 References).
Provides details of a two-year project using behavior modification with profoundly retarded children. Gains were noted in several self-help areas. The implications of setting up this type of program are discussed.

1038 Leibowitz, J. Michael, and Holcer, Paulette. "Building and maintaining self-feeding skills in a retarded child." Am J Occup Ther 28(9): 545-48, October, 1974. (13 References).
A four-year-eleven-month-old girl was taught self-feeding skills and the acceptance of a wider variety of foods in a fifteen-day period. Progress was also noted in other self-help areas and had been maintained at a five-month follow-up.

1039 Martin, Garry L.; Kehoe, Bonnie; Bird, Elizabeth; et al. "Operant conditioning in dressing behavior of severely retarded girls." Ment Retard 9(3): 27-31, June, 1971. (9 References).
Records in detail the training procedures utilized to teach eleven girls to dress with several clothing items. The program was conducted by psychiatric nurses and nurses' aides.

1040 Miller, Harold R.; Patton, Mary E.; Henton, Karel R. "Behavior modification in a profoundly retarded child: a case report." Behav Ther 2(3): 375-84, July, 1971. (11 References).
Examines the results of three behavior modification programs designed to increase self-sufficiency in a profoundly retarded seven-year-old boy. The program developed a self-feeding skill, taught the child to respond appropriately to a verbal command, and greatly increased his ability to stand without support.

1041 Minge, M. Ronald, and Ball, Thomas S. "Teaching of self-help skills to profoundly retarded patients." Am J Ment Defic 71(5): 864-68, March, 1967. (3 References). (Reprinted in Item No. 33).
Focuses on the training in self-help skills of six profoundly retarded children. The skills developed included attention, standing up, and dressing. The training was given over a two-month period by psychiatric technicians who used food and praise as reinforcers. The results indicate the feasibility of teaching self-help skills to profoundly retarded patients.

1042 Moore, Pat, and Carr, Janet. "Behaviour modification programme." Nurs Times 72(35): 1356-59, September 2, 1976. (6 References).
Presents a case history which demonstrates the development of self-dressing skills in a fifteen-and-one-half-year-old retarded boy. Edible reinforcers were used.

1043 Murphy, Michael J., and Zahm, David. "Effects of improved ward conditions and behavioral treatment of self-help skills." Ment Retard 13(6): 24-27, December, 1975. (9 References).
Furnishes the results of a study on the effects of enhanced physical and social environment and behavior modification training on the acquisition of self-help skills. The subjects were eight institutionalized retarded males. The results indicate that an adequate resident-to-staff ratio is a necessary condition for training and maintenance.

1044 Nelson, Gary L.; Cone, John D.; Hanson, Christopher R. "Training correct utensil use in retarded children: modeling vs. physical guidance." Am J Ment Defic 80(1): 114-22, July, 1975. (15 References).
Twenty-four retarded males (mean age thirteen-and-one-half years; mean IQ 25.3) were taught to use a knife, fork, and spoon. Methods involving physical guidance produced significant improvement while modelling did not.

1045 O'Brien, F.; Bugle, C.; Azrin, N. H. "Training and maintaining a retarded child's proper eating." J Appl Behav Anal 5(1): 67-72, Spring, 1972. (11 References).
Demonstrates the necessity for establishing continuous motivational procedures, in addition to training, for the maintenance of proper eating skills in a profoundly retarded child.

1046 Singh, Nirbhay. "Modification of self-feeding behaviours of a retarded child with nurses as therapists." NZ Nurs J 70(2): 4-5, February, 1977. (5 References).
Briefly describes the procedures used to increase self-feeding with a severely retarded six-year-old boy. Three staff nurses, trained in behavior modification techniques, carried out the program and provided manual guidance when necessary.

1047 Song, A. Y., and Gandhi R. "An analysis of behavior during the acquisition and maintenance phases of self-spoon feeding skills of profound retardates." Ment Retard 12(1): 25-28, February, 1974. (12 References).
Analyzes the problems encountered in teaching self-feeding skills to four profoundly retarded children. There is a discussion of such factors as maintenance, choice of procedure, use of physical restraints, and motivation of the trainers.

1048 Treffry, Doug; Martin, Garry; Samels, Jerry; et al. "Operant conditioning of grooming behavior of severely retarded girls." Ment Retard 8(4): 29-33, August, 1970. (11 References).
Seven out of eleven retarded girls were taught to wash their hands and faces without any physical guidance.

1049 Zeiler, Michael D., and Jervey, Susan S. "Development of behavior: self-feeding." J Consult Clin Psychol 32(2): 164-68, April, 1968. (5 References).
A profoundly retarded fifteen-year-old girl was taught to feed herself by making food available when she responded appropriately.

c. Toilet Training

1050 Barrett, Beatrice H. "Behavior modification in the home: parents adapt laboratory-developed tactics to bowel-train a five-and-one-half-year-old." Psychotherapy 6(3): 172-76, Summer, 1969. (10 References).
The parents of a retarded, hyperactive five-and-one-half-year-old boy successfully treated his encopresis by using operant methods. They received only short periods of instruction in the methods.

1051 Baumeister, Alfred, and Klosowski, Raymond. "An attempt to group toilet train severely retarded patients." Ment Retard 3(6): 24-26, December, 1965. (1 Reference).
Summarizes a program to group toilet train eleven retarded patients. An attempt was made to provide a relatively constant environment with reinforcement of appropriate responses.

1052 Connolly, John A., and McGoldrick, Maureen. "Behaviour modification: toilet training procedures in a special care unit." Child Care Health Dev 2(5): 267-72, September-October, 1976.
Two out of nine retarded subjects were successfully toilet trained by the use of behavior modification procedures. Details are included on the program design and implementation.

1053 Doleys, Daniel M., and Arnold, Susan. "Treatment of childhood encopresis: Full Cleanliness Training." Ment Retard 13(6): 14-16, December, 1975. (10 References).
Demonstrates the use of operant procedures and Full Cleanliness Training to establish appropriate toileting behavior in a retarded eight-year-old boy. Full Cleanliness Training consists of requiring the subject to correct the results of his inappropriate behavior by cleaning himself and his clothing.

1054 Edgar, Clara Lee; Kohler, Hugh F.; Hardman, Scott. "A new method for toilet training developmentally disabled children." Percept Mot Skills 41(1): 63-69, August, 1975. (12 References).
Relaxation training was combined with operant methods to develop appropriate urination in twenty profoundly retarded children.

1055 Ellis, Norman R. "Toilet training the severely defective patient: an S-R reinforcement analysis." Am J Ment Defic 68(1): 98-103, July, 1963.
Offers a theoretical analysis of "toilet behavior" and a training program based on this analysis.

1056 Giles, David K., and Wolf, Montrose M. "Toilet training institutionalized, severe retardates: an application of operant behavior modification techniques." Am J Ment Defic 70(5): 766-80, March, 1966. (15 References). (Reprinted in Item No. 32).
Records the successful toilet training of five severely retarded males ranging in chronological age from six to twenty-two years. Positive reinforcers such as food, drink, and hugs were used contingent upon appropriate elimination behavior. The program was successfully completed within a period of eight weeks.

1057 Hundziak, Marcel; Maurer, Ruth A.; Watson, Luke S., Jr. "Operant conditioning in toilet training of severely mentally retarded boys." Am J Ment Defic 70(1): 120-24, July, 1965. (2 References).
This controlled study involved twenty-nine severely retarded boys, ranging in chronological age from seven to fourteen years. The subjects were assigned to one of three groups: (1) operant conditioning (received candy for appropriate toilet behavior); (2) conventional (received scolding for inappropriate and praise for appropriate behavior); and (3) control (received no consistent toilet training). The first group advanced more in training than did the other two groups, and the improvement carried over into the living cottage.

1058 Kimbrell, Don L.; Luckey, Robert E.; Barbuto, Paul F.; et al. "Operation Dry Pants: an intensive habit-training program for severely and profoundly retarded." Ment Retard 6(2): 32-36, April, 1967. (6 References). (Reprinted in Item No. 33).
Outlines a study conducted with forty severely and profoundly retarded females. The twenty girls who were exposed to a combination of behavior shaping techniques required only half the amount of laundry used by the control group.

1059 Levine, Martin N., and Elliott, Charles B. "Toilet training for profoundly retarded with a limited staff." Ment Retard 8(3): 48-50, June, 1970. (5 References). (Reprinted in Item No. 33).
Describes an attempt to toilet train 103 profoundly retarded institutionalized residents in a ten-week program. A successive approximations model, using M & M candies as reinforcement, was utilized.

1060 McNamara, Edward. "Dora: or how they met their Waterloo." Spec Educ 61(3): 9-11, September, 1972. (1 Reference).
Reports on the use of candy in the attempt to toilet train a retarded seven-year-old girl. Although not entirely successful, some progress was noted.

1061 Osarchuk, Michael. "Operant methods of toilet behavior training of the severely and profoundly retarded: a review." J Spec Educ 7(4): 423-37, Winter, 1973. (34 References).
Critically surveys the reported research and discusses future avenues of investigation. It is noted that progress usually disappears when the trainee is returned to his pretraining environment; possible explanations for this regression are discussed.

1062 Rentfrow, Robert K., and Rentfrow, Doris K. "Studies related to toilet training of the mentally retarded." Am J Occup Ther 23(5): 425-30, September-October, 1969. (10 References).
Provides a review and discusses the limitations of past research. New directions for future investigation are indicated.

1063 Sloop, Edgar Wayne. "Conditioning treatment of nocturnal enuresis among the institutionalized mentally retarded." For a summary see: Diss Abstr Int 30B(11): 5244, May, 1970.

1064 Sloop, Edgar Wayne, and Kennedy, Wallace A. "Institutionalized retarded nocturnal enuretics treated by a conditioning technique." Am J Ment Defic 77(6): 717-21, May, 1973. (10 References).
Relates the results of a study conducted with twenty-one enuretic retardates in which a commercially available warning device was used. Eleven of the subjects were conditioned successfully, and one subject showed a spontaneous recovery. Results at a follow-up were disappointing.

1065 Tierney, Alison J. "Toilet training." Nurs Times 69(51): 1740-45, December 20, 1973. (14 References).
Furnishes a detailed description of a toilet training procedure used with thirty-six retarded persons. The age range of the subjects was from six to twenty-one years.

1066 Van Wagenen, R. Keith; Meyerson, Lee; Kerr, Nancy J.; et al. "Field trials of a new procedure for toilet training." J Exp Child Psychiatry 8(1): 147-59, August, 1969. (13 References).
Nine profoundly retarded children were successfully toilet trained. The procedure utilized a quick sequence of events prompted by an auditory signal.

1067 Yoder, James W., Jr. "Toilet training the profoundly defective patient at Greene Valley Hospital and School using an S-R reinforcement analysis." Mind Matter 11: 28-34, 1966.
Edible reinforcers were used in a successful training program conducted with sixty-four individuals.

d. Speech/Language

1068 Ausman, James O., and Gaddy, Michael R. "Reinforcement training for echolalia: developing a repertoire of appropriate verbal responses in an echolalic girl." Ment Retard 12(1): 20-21, February, 1974. (3 References).
Briefly reports on the use of edible reinforcers with a seventeen-year-old functionally blind, retarded girl.

1069 Barton, Elizabeth Spindler. "Inappropriate speech in a severely retarded child: a case study in language conditioning and generalization." J Appl Behav Anal 3(4): 299-307, Winter, 1970. (14 References).
Demonstrates the use of candy reinforcers in the modification of bizarre and inappropriate speech in a severely retarded eleven-year-old boy. The procedure was also used to develop more appropriate language.

1070 Bennet, Fay W. "Ward language development program for institutionalized retardates." Train Sch Bull 66(1): 23-31, May, 1969. (7 References).
Significant gains in language skills were noted in retarded children when their attendants were rewarded for attempts to stimulate these skills.

1071 Bricker, William A., and Bricker, Diane D. "Development of receptive vocabulary in severely retarded children." Am J Ment Defic 74(5): 599-607, March, 1970. (9 References). (Reprinted in Item No. 33).

Describes two procedures for facilitating the development of word control over object choice. Both procedures used edible reinforcers. Structured approaches were more successful in those subjects identified as learners.

1072 Eddy, James Bruce, II. "Application of the Premack hypothesis to the verbal behavior of retardates." For a summary see: Diss Abstr Int 35B(9): 4647, March, 1975.

1073 Frisch, Sue Ann, and Schumaker, Jean B. "Training generalized receptive prepositions in retarded children." J Appl Behav Anal 7(4): 611-21, Winter, 1974. (14 References).
Three retarded children were taught to follow prepositional instructions by means of reinforcement and prompting procedures.

1074 Garcia, Eugene E.; Bullet, John; Rust, Frank P. "An experimental analysis of language training generalization across classroom and home." Behav Modif 1(4): 531-50, October, 1971. (20 References).
Attempts to extend the systematic investigation of language generalization. Two retarded children were taught--using imitation and reinforcement--to label a series of pictures with complex sentences containing five-word chains. Generalization was not effected to the classroom until some training was instituted in that setting. There is some discussion of the implications for speech therapy and future research.

1075 Garcia, Eugene; Guess, Doug; Byrnes, Jim. "Development of syntax in a retarded girl using procedures of imitation, reinforcement, and modelling." J Appl Behav Anal 6(2): 299-310, Summer, 1973. (13 References).
Demonstrates the use of edible reinforcers, imitation, and modelling to encourage the development of the use of simple declarative sentences. The subject was a ten-year-old retarded girl.

1076 Guess, Doug. "A functional analysis of receptive language and productive speech: acquisition of the plural morpheme." J Appl Behav Anal 2(1): 55-64, Spring, 1969. (11 References).
Operant conditioning procedures were applied to two retarded boys in order to establish auditory comprehension of plurals. The subjects did not generalize to expressive plurals.

1077 Guess, Doug; Sailor, Wayne; Rutherford, Gorin; et al. "An experimental analysis of linguistic development: the productive use of the plural morpheme." J Appl Behav Anal 1(4): 297-306, Winter, 1968. (17 References).
Operant conditioning procedures, which used edible reinforcers, helped establish a generative use of the plural morpheme in the speech of a severely retarded ten-year-old institutionalized girl.

1078 Guess, Doug; Smith, James O.; Ensminger, E. Eugene. "The role of nonprofessional persons in teaching language skills to mentally retarded children." Except Child 37(6): 447-53, February, 1971. (10 References).
Reports on a two-year language development program conducted by nonprofessionals. The program was implemented in an institutional setting and was supervised by a professional speech clinician.

1079 Guralnick, Michael. "A language development program for severely handicapped children." Except Child 39(1): 45-49, September, 1972. (14 References).

A successful language program was conducted by undergraduate students with eight children who had received varied diagnoses, including autism and brain damage. The implications of such use of undergraduates with respect to the shortage of technical personnel in institutions and treatment centers is examined.

1080 Jackson, Donald A., and Wallace, R. Frank. "The modification and generalization of voice loudness in a fifteen-year-old retarded girl." J Appl Behav Anal 7(3): 461-71, Fall, 1974. (25 References).
A fifteen-year-old mildly retarded and severely withdrawn aphasic girl was conditioned in a laboratory setting to speak more loudly. Although there was no generalization to the classroom setting, voice loudness was achieved there also by reintroducing the token reinforcement system.

1081 Jacobson, Leonard I.; Bernal, Guillermo; Lopez, Gerardo N. "Effects of behavioral training on the functioning of a profoundly retarded microcephalic teenager with cerebral palsy and without language or verbal comprehension: a case study." Behav Res Ther 11(1): 143-45, February, 1973. (2 References).
Documents the use of behavior modification methods to develop some behavioral, conceptual, and language skills in a seventeen-year-old boy previously diagnosed as uneducable.

1082 MacCubrey, Jean. "Verbal operant conditioning with young institutionalized Down's syndrome children." Am J Ment Defic 75(6): 696-701, May, 1971. (15 References).
Results of this study with eighteen children indicate that functional speech can be increased by means of employing behavior modification techniques in group sessions.

1083 Nelson, Rosemery O.; Peoples, Arthur; Hay, Linda R.; et al. "The effectiveness of speech training techniques based on operant conditioning: a comparison of two methods." Ment Retard 14(3): 34-38, June, 1976. (21 References).
Four retarded speech-deficient children were taught imitative verbal responses by two methods. Both methods were effective although progress was slow. The training required one year.

1084 Odom, Richard D.; Liebert, Robert M.; Fernandez, Luis E. "Effects of symbolic modeling on the syntactical productions of retardates." Psychon Sci 17(2): 104-5, October 25, 1969. (2 References).
Cites an experiment conducted with thirty retarded children. The results indicate that a very brief period of symbolic modelling can increase children's production of certain grammatical constructions.

1085 Rubin, Beverly Kam, and Stolz, Stephanie B. "Generalizations of self-referent speech established in a retarded adolescent by operant procedures." Behav Ther 5(1): 93-106, January, 1974. (15 References).
A thirteen-year-old retarded boy demonstrated increased competence in pronoun usage in his spontaneous speech following training. Food and praise were used as reinforcers.

1086 Sailor, Wayne. "Reinforcement and generalization of productive plural allomorphs in two retarded children." J Appl Behav Anal 4(4): 305-10, Winter, 1971. (4 References).

Demonstrates the use of edible reinforcers to develop plurals in two retarded children. The results indicate that "rules" of grammar may be acquired through differential reinforcement in the presence of verbal models.

1087 Snyder, Lee K.; Lovitt, Thomas C.; Smith, James O. "Language training for the severely retarded: five years of behavior analysis research." Except Child 42(1): 7-15, September, 1975. (30 References).
Reviews twenty-three behavior analysis studies, all of which employed positive reinforcement. The implications for the classroom teacher and the speech clinician are analyzed, and avenues for future research are indicated.

1088 Straughan, James H.; Potter, Warren K., Jr.; Hamilton, Stephen H., Jr. "The behavioral treatment of an elective mute." J Child Psychol Psychiatry 6(2): 125-30, November, 1965. (5 References).
Elective mutism in a fourteen-year-old retarded boy was successfully treated in the classroom. A signalling device was used that had previously been employed in the treatment of hyperactive children.

1089 Wheeler, Andrew J., and Sulzer, Beth. "Operant training and generalization of a verbal response form in a speech-deficient child." J Appl Behav Anal 3(2): 139-47, Summer, 1970. (13 References). (Reprinted in Item No. 38).
Traces the use of a token reinforcement system to train a speech-deficient retarded eight-year-old boy to use a particular sentence form. The child had previously spoken in "telegraphic" style.

e. Social Skills

1090 Baer, Donald M.; Peterson, Robert F.; Sherman, James A. "The development of imitation by reinforcing behavioral similarity to a model." J Exp Anal Behav 10(5): 405-16, September, 1967. (10 References). (Reprinted in Item No. 22).
Documents the use of edible reinforcers to develop imitation in three retarded children. The children had previously demonstrated no imitative behavior whatsoever.

1091 Brownfield, E. Dorothy, and Keehn, Jack D. "Operant eyelid conditioning in Trisomy-18." J Abnorm Psychol 71(6): 413-15, December, 1966. (9 References).
Two profoundly retarded children were conditioned to emit eyeblinks in conformity with continuous and extinction schedules of reinforcement. Conditioning with each child was undertaken at normal mealtimes, and eyeblinks were rewarded with spoonfuls of food.

1092 Bry, Peter Michael. "The role of reinforcement in the development of a generalized imitation operant in severely and profoundly retarded children." For a summary see: Diss Abstr Int 30B(10): 4786, April, 1970.

1093 Burchard, John D. "Systematic socialization: a programmed environment for the habilitation of antisocial retardates." Psychol Rec 17(4): 461-76, October, 1967. (29 References).
Provides the results of two experiments conducted with mildly retarded boys. Systematic reinforcement and punishment were effective in controlling antisocial behavior.

1094 Criticos, Anne Katherine. "Imitation training for developmentally delayed children: the effects of reinforcement and nonreinforcement on gestural accommodation." For a summary see: Diss Abstr Int 37B(8): 4180, February, 1977.

1095 Goldenberg, Edward Elliott. "The effects of reinforcement on the social approach behaviors with children of low and average intellectual ability." For a summary see: Diss Abstr Int 34B(10): 5189, April, 1974.

1096 Hopkins, B. L. "Effects of candy and social reinforcement, instructions, and reinforcement schedule learning on the modification and maintenance of smiling." J Appl Behav Anal 1(2): 121-29, Summer, 1968. (17 References). (Reprinted in Item No. 29).

Describes the use of candy and social reinforcement to encourage and maintain smiling in two mentally retarded boys exhibiting abnormally low rates of smiling. Signs were employed to regulate social interactions, and the rate of smiling was shown to be controlled by these interactions serving as reinforcers.

1097 Lachenmeyer, Charles W. "Systematic socialization: observations on a programmed environment for the habilitation of antisocial retardates." Psychol Rec 19(2): 247-57, April, 1969. (5 References).

Analyzes the use of a token system and the problems attendant upon several uncontrolled contingencies.

1098 Lawrence, Wayne, and Kartye, Joseph. "Extinction of social competency skills in retarded and profoundly retarded females." Am J Ment Defic 75(5): 630-34, March, 1971. (16 References).

Investigates the effects of discontinuation of an operant conditioning program with twenty-one severely and profoundly retarded females between the chronological ages of eight and eleven. No significant decrease in self-help skills were observed, but significant decreases were seen in communication, initiative, and social skills.

1099 Lloyd, Kenneth E.; Russell, Harry K.; Garmize, Lewis M. "Operant eyelid conditioning in Trisomy-18: replication and extension." J Abnorm Psychol 75(3): 338-41, June, 1970. (12 References).

A profoundly retarded child was conditioned to emit operant eyeblinks and to maintain a head position by using spoonfuls of food as reinforcers.

1100 McClure, Robert F. "Reinforcement of verbal social behavior in moderately retarded children." Psychol Rep 23(2): 371-76, October, 1968. (7 References).

Verbal social responses increased in a group with contingent reinforcement and verbal instructions about the reinforcement contingency. No improvement was seen in groups when only one of these contingencies was employed.

1101 Maus, Michael Earl. "The use of contingent observation to increase the peer interaction of three mentally retarded adolescents." For a summary see: Diss Abstr Int 38B(6): 2870, December, 1977.

1102 Nelson, Rosemery; Gibson, Frank, Jr.; Cutting, D. Scott. "Videotaped modeling: the development of three appropriate social responses in a mildly retarded child." Ment Retard 11(6): 24-28, December, 1973. (33 References).

A seven-year-old boy was successfully taught to ask grammatically correct questions, to smile, and to talk about appropriate topics. Modelling was used, together with instructions and social reinforcement.

1103 Paloutzian, Raymond F.; Hasazi, Joseph; Streifel, John; et al. "Promotion of positive social interaction in severely retarded young children." Am J Ment Defic 75(4): 519-24, January, 1971. (12 References). (Reprinted in Item No. 33).
Provides the results of a study involving twenty retarded institutionalized children. Prompting and reinforcement were used with ten of the children to encourage initiation of social responses. The other ten children were designated as a control group and received no reinforcement. The experimental group showed a significantly higher level of social behavior which then generalized to the ward setting.

1104 Sewell, Edith; McCoy, James F.; Sewell, William R. "Modification of an antagonistic social behavior using positive reinforcement for other behavior." Psychol Rec 23(4): 499-504, Fall, 1973. (17 References).
Socially inappropriate target behaviors were reduced in four retarded boys through differential reinforcement of other behavior.

1105 Teel, Sidney Kreider. "Operant conditioning of social behaviors in educably mentally retarded children in a free-field setting." For a summary see: Diss Abstr Int 31B(7): 4347, January, 1971.

1106 Whitman, Thomas L.; Mercurio, J. R.; Caponigri, Vicki. "Development of social responses in two severely retarded children." J Appl Behav Anal 3(2): 133-38, Summer, 1970. (11 References).
Demonstrates the use of food and praise in the development of social interaction in two severely retarded, withdrawn children. Social behavior decreased markedly following the removal of reinforcement procedures.

f. Vocational Skills

1107 Brown, Lou; Johnson, Sylvester; Gadberry, Eve; et al. "Increasing individual and assembly line production rates of retarded students." Train Sch Bull 67(4): 206-13, February, 1971. (5 References).
Work arrangements and reinforcement were manipulated to increase the work production of six trainable retarded students in an envelope stuffing task.

1108 Karen, Robert L.; Eisner, Melvin; Endres, Robert W. "Behavior modification in a sheltered workshop for severely retarded students." Am J Ment Defic 79(3): 338-47, November, 1974. (12 References).
Studies the effects of a token system on the work behavior of ten severely retarded adolescents. Data reveals differences in work difficulty, a reduction in average error, and an increase in average production following the implementation of the program.

1109 Lent, James R.; Leblanc, Judith; Spradlin, Joseph E. "Designing a rehabilitative culture for moderately retarded adolescent girls." In: Ulrich, Roger; Stachnik, Thomas; Mabry, John, eds. Control of human behavior: Vol. 2. From cure to prevention. Glenview, Illinois: Scott, Foresman, 1970. 121-45.
Reports on an attempt to train twenty-seven moderately retarded girls for life outside an institution. The girls ranged in age from fifteen to

twenty-one. There is an endeavor to answer the most frequently asked questions concerning such a program.

1110 Logan, Daniel L.; Kinsinger, John; Shelton, Gene; et al. "The use of multiple reinforcers in a rehabilitation setting." Ment Retard 9(3): 3-6, June, 1971.
Visual and verbal reinforcements were found to be as effective as monetary reinforcement in this study conducted in a sheltered workshop. The subjects were six mentally retarded trainees between the ages of sixteen and nineteen.

1111 O'Hara, E. A. "Using pay to change mentally retarded students' work behavior." Teach Except Child 2: 163-69, 1970.
Examines both the effectiveness of operant techniques in the teaching of work and social skills, and the effectiveness of pay as an incentive for achieving those skills. The subjects were mentally retarded high school students.

1112 Trybus, Raymond J., and Lacks, Patricia B. "Modification of vocational behavior in a community agency for mentally retarded adolescents." Rehabil Lit 33(9): 258-66, September, 1972.
Operant conditioning techniques were successful in raising the production rates and in eliminating or reducing work-interfering behaviors in nineteen noninstitutionalized adolescents.

1113 Underwood, T. Lon. "A vocationally oriented token reinforcement program." Pointer 16(1): 53-57, Fall, 1971.
Describes a system employed with educable mentally retarded adolescents to acquaint them with practical job experience.

4. Techniques with the Mentally Handicapped

a. Specific Techniques

1114 Altman, Reuben, and Talkington, Larry W. "Modeling: an alternative behavior modification approach for retardates." Ment Retard 9(3): 20-23, June, 1971. (63 References).
Reviews the reported research and suggests that maximum gains in the therapeutic milieu would be realized by a combination of modelling and conventional operant procedures.

1115 Apolloni, Tony; Cooke, Sharon A.; Cooke, Thomas P. "Establishing a normal peer as a behavioral model for developmentally delayed toddlers." Percept Mot Skills 44(1): 231-41, February, 1977.
Outlines a teaching procedure employed with three children exhibiting delayed development. The training consisted of adult prompting and social reinforcement contingent upon the imitation of the material use and motor responses of a normal peer. Results indicated success and generalization across settings and responses.

1116 Bailey, Jon, and Meyerson, Lee. "Vibration as a reinforcer with a profoundly retarded child." J Appl Behav Anal 2(2): 135-37, Summer, 1969. (3 References).
Investigates the use of vibration as a reinforcer for the lever-pressing behavior of a profoundly retarded seven-year-old crib-bound child. Suggestions are made for further use of this technique with the retarded.

1117 Baumeister, Alfred A., and Ward, L. Charles, III. "Effects of rewards upon the reaction times of mental defectives." Am J Ment Defic 71(5): 801-5, March, 1967. (9 References).
Documents the results of three experiments which investigated the efficacy of different kinds of rewards, and the superiority of one reward over an extended period of time. The target behavior was the reaction times of sixty institutionalized male mental retardates ranging in age from twelve to thirty-five years. Verbal praise and money facilitated performance about equally; money proved to be the more effective reward over a long period of time.

1118 Bijou, Sidney W., and Orlando, Robert. "Rapid development of multiple-schedule performances with retarded children." J Exp Anal Behav 4(1): 7-16, January, 1961. (9 References). (Reprinted in Item Nos. 23, 30, 45).
Provides details on the modification of simple operant behavior in eight, institutionalized retarded children. Such modification is a prerequisite for the development of multiple schedules.

1119 Bricker, William A. "Identifying and modifying behavioral deficits." Am J Ment Defic 75(1): 16-21, July, 1970. (24 References). (Reprinted in Item No. 35).
Advocates changes in behavior modification technology--especially in the areas of generalization of repertoires, establishment of validity, and the replicability and efficiency of training programs--so that this approach can be used to full advantage with the mentally retarded.

1120 Buchan, L. Gerald; Teed, Sally; Peterson, Craig. "Role playing and behavior modification: a demonstration with mentally retarded children." Clearing House 50(2): 77-80, October, 1976. (9 References).
Recommends the combining of role-playing and behavior modification techniques in the training of the mentally retarded. Two procedures, skill training and problem solving, are examined, and the classroom application of them are outlined.

1121 Burchard, John D., and Barrera, Francisco. "An analysis of time out and response cost in a programmed environment." J Appl Behav Anal 5(3): 271-82, Fall, 1972. (23 References).
Analyzes the effectiveness of several values of time-out and response cost in the suppression of undesirable behavior in eleven mildly retarded adolescents.

1122 Clark, Hewitt B.; Rowbury, Trudylee; Baer, Ann M.; et al. "Timeout as a punishing stimulus in continuous and intermittent schedules." J Appl Behav Anal 6(3): 443-55, Fall, 1973. (31 References).
Reports on the use of time-out in continuous and intermittent schedules to reduce the disruptive behaviors of an eight-year-old retarded girl in a preschool setting. Results indicate that some schedules of intermittent punishment may be as effective as continuous punishment, at least in the case of the continued suppression of a response that has already been reduced to a low frequency.

1123 Daley, Marvin F. "The 'reinforcement menu': finding effective reinforcers." In: Krumboltz, John D., and Thoresen, Carl E., eds. Behavioral counseling: cases and techniques. New York: Holt, Rinehart & Winston, 1969. 42-45. (5 References).

Describes the use, with five retarded children, of a "menu" containing illustrations of preferred activities from which the children were allowed to select their reinforcement.

1124 De Csipkes, Robert A.; Smouse, Albert D.; Hudson, Bobbye A. "Influence of reinforcement on the paired-associate learning of retarded and nonretarded children." Am J Ment Defic 80(3): 357-59, November, 1975. (9 References).
Investigates the effects of tangible and social reinforcement on the paired-associate learning of twenty-four retarded and twenty-four nonretarded children (aged eleven to fourteen years). The results indicated that the influence of reinforcement was highly significant.

1125 Gardner, William I., and Briskin, Alan S. "Use of punishment procedures in management of behavioral difficulties of the severely retarded." J Psychiatr Nurs 7: 5-16, January-February, 1969. (25 References).
Describes punishment procedures, reviews studies, and discusses the ethical-humanitarian issues involved.

1126 Haring, Norris G. "Aversive conditioning and the severely/profoundly handicapped." Paper presented at the 54th Annual International Convention, The Council for Exceptional Children, Chicago, April 4-9, 1976. 24p. (24 References). (ED 122 552).
Reviews the reported research and advocates caution in the employment of aversive techniques with the retarded population.

1127 Harris, Lawrence M., and Tramontana, Joseph. "Discrimination learning of retarded children as a function of positive reinforcement and response cost." Am J Ment Defic 78(2): 216-19, September, 1973. (16 References).
Indicates that intellectual level is an important factor in determining which reinforcement contingency is the more effective. The study was conducted with sixteen male and eight female children.

1128 Kircher, Alfred S.; Pear, Joseph J.; Martin, Garry L. "Shock as punishment in a picture-naming task with retarded children." J Appl Behav Anal 4(3): 227-33, Fall, 1971. (19 References).
Two severely retarded children were used as subjects for experiments in which electric shock was employed as a punishment for inattentive behavior and incorrect responses in a picture-naming task. Inattentive behavior was reduced and more correct responses were elicited.

1129 Kurtzberg, Evelyn Claire. "Hierarchies of reinforcement effectiveness in older retarded and younger bright normal children of the same mental age." For a summary see: Diss Abstr Int 33A(10): 5553, April, 1973.

1130 Lambert, Jean-Luc. "Extinction by retarded children following discrimination learning with and without errors." Am J Ment Defic 80(3): 286-91, November, 1975. (13 References).
Documents the results of a study conducted with sixteen retarded noninstitutionalized children. Conclusions are drawn concerning the continuity of reinforcers. The major implication is that the responses to stimulus in errorless discrimination must not be continuously reinforced.

1131 Locke, Bill J. "Verbal conditioning with retarded subjects: establishment or reinstatement of effective reinforcing consequences." Am J Ment Defic 73(4): 621-26, January, 1969. (4 References).
Presents the results of a follow-up study to Item No. 1132 in which attempts were made to develop a mean whereby an ineffective social reinforcer might acquire reinforcing properties by pairing it to an already established reinforcing agent (tokens). Conditioning via "good" consequences was greatly enhanced by both direct and inverse association of the two classes of reinforcement, but some conditioning also occurred with no prior token association.

1132 ———. "Verbal conditioning with the retarded: reinforcer, sex of subject, and stimulus pacing." Am J Ment Defic 73(4): 616-20, January, 1969. (14 References).
Compares the reinforcing properties of the statement "Good" with tokens exchangeable for money and trinkets. The subjects were fifty-four mildly to moderately retarded children in whom it was sought to stimulate verbal behavior. The monetary-based tokens were more effective, and no significant results were associated with the social reinforcement, the sex of the subject, or stimulus exposure rate.

1133 McCreary, Richard Duerr. "An investigation of time-out procedures with the severely and profoundly retarded." For a summary see: Diss Abstr Int 35B(8): 4187, February, 1975.

1134 Macht, Joel. "Operant measurement of subjective visual acuity in non-verbal children." J Appl Behav Anal 4(1): 23-36, Spring, 1971. (24 References).
Demonstrates the successful use of edible reinforcers to reward correct responses to visual stimuli in retarded children. Additionally, the procedure enabled a successful evaluation of the prosthetic lenses previously prescribed for two of the children.

1135 McManis, Donald L., and Bell, Donald R. "Retardate reward seeking or punishment avoiding under three types of incentives." Am J Ment Defic 72(6): 844-50, May, 1968. (8 References).
A significantly greater number of the subjects of this study indicated a preference for rewards, but one-fourth to one-third preferred punishment avoidance. Significant test-retest correlations were found under symbolic and monetary incentives.

1136 McManis, Donald L.; Bell, Donald R.; Pike, Earl O. "Performance of reward-seeking and punishment-avoiding retardates under reward and punishment." Am J Ment Defic 73(6): 906-11, May, 1969. (5 References).
Presents the results of a comparative study conducted with thirty-seven institutionalized retardates who had been categorized as reward-seeking or punishment-avoiding. Both groups persisted in tasks under the reinforcement contingency consistent with their prior classification. The target behavior was the enhancement of performance in work situations.

1137 Marburg, Carol Colenda. "Generalized imitation as a behavior therapy technique with retarded children." For a summary see: Diss Abstr Int 35B(5): 2440, November, 1974.

1138 Orlando, Robert, and Bijou, Sidney W. "Single and multiple schedules of reinforcement in developmentally retarded children." J Exp

Anal Behav 3(4): 339-48, October, 1960. (10 References). (Reprinted in Item No. 42).
Demonstrates characteristic performance under four basic schedules for forty-six institutionalized retarded children.

1139 Redd, William H., and Birnbrauer, J. S. "Adults as discriminative stimuli for different reinforcement contingencies with retarded children." J Exp Child Psychol 7(3): 440-47, June, 1969. (Reprinted in Item No. 47).
Details a study in which the same adults functioned as agents of both contingent and noncontingent reinforcement for ten severely retarded boys. The adults acquired discriminative properties when paired with specific reinforcement contingencies.

1140 Reynolds, Carolyn Lois Buchanan. "An investigation of the efficacy of a hierarchy system of reinforcement used in modifying the behavior of trainable mentally retarded children." For a summary see: Diss Abstr Int 33A(7): 3444, January, 1973.

1141 Scott, Patsy Lou. "Contingency contracting techniques with junior high school educable mentally retarded." For a summary see: Diss Abstr Int 36A(3): 1402, September, 1975.

1142 Stephens, Carl E.; Pear, Joseph J.; Wray, Lyle D.; et al. "Some effects of reinforcement schedules in teaching picture names to retarded children." J Appl Behav Anal 8(4): 435-47, Winter, 1975.
Compares the effectiveness of several different schedules of primary reinforcement in a picture-naming task with retarded children. Learning rates were generally low, and little difference was noted between the effects of the schedules.

1143 Stephens, Wyatt E.; Holder, Loreta O.; Ludy, Isa E. "Action-concept usage by nonretarded and retarded children on structured tasks with praise for performance." Am J Ment Defic 79(6): 659-65, May, 1975. (10 References).
Demonstrates the combined use of structured tasks and praise for performance in increasing the use of action-concepts in both retarded and nonretarded children. The mildly retarded were found to respond more favorably than did the moderately retarded. Recommendations are made for further research.

1144 Terrell, Catherine and Stevenson, Harold W. "The effectiveness of normal and retarded peers as reinforcing agents." Am J Ment Defic 70(3): 373-81, November, 1965. (8 References).
Investigates the relationship existing between normal and retarded peers. The results indicated that normal children are more effective reinforcers than are retarded children.

1145 Thor, Donald H. "Sex differences in extinction of operant responding by educable retarded and nonretarded children." Am J Ment Defic 77(1): 100-106, July, 1972. (15 References).
Provides details of two experiments conducted with third-grade children. There were indications of a greater resistance to extinction among retarded children than among nonretarded children. Boys were found to respond longer than girls during extinction.

1146 Tramontana, Joseph. "Social versus edible rewards as a function of intellectual level and socio-economic class." Am J Ment Defic 77(1): 33-38, July, 1972. (27 References).
Compares the effects of praise and candy on seventy-two middle and lower socioeconomic level children who were further subdivided into three intellectual groups (average, mildly retarded, and severely retarded). Candy was the more effective reinforcer, regardless of intellectual level. There were no differential reward effects related to socioeconomic class.

1147 Watson, Luke S., Jr. "Reinforcement preferences of severely retarded children in a generalized reinforcement context." Am J Ment Defic 72(5): 748-56, March, 1968. (11 References).
Furnishes the results of a study conducted with seventeen boys with a mean age of 10.10 years. The results indicated that candy was the preferred reinforcer.

1148 Whalen, Carol K., and Henker, Barbara A. "Creating therapeutic pyramids using mentally retarded patients." Am J Ment Defic 74(3): 331-37, November, 1969. (21 References).
Describes procedures for teaching adolescent retardates to use behavior modification techniques with younger patients. Three brief case histories are documented.

b. Token Economies

1149 Axelrod, Saul. "Token reinforcement programs in special classes." Except Child 37(5): 371-79, January, 1971.
Presents a review of programs indicating that positive results were obtained with different types of target behaviors and various kinds of populations. The suggestions made for future research concentrate on developing means of withdrawing tokens.

1150 Baer, Ann Middlemas. "Token economies: an incomplete technology?" For a summary see: Diss Abstr Int 38B(7): 3426, January, 1978.

1151 Baer, Richard; Ascione, Frank; Casto, Glendon. "Relative efficacy of two token economy procedures for decreasing the disruptive classroom behavior of retarded children." J Abnorm Child Psychol 5(2): 135-45, 1977. (27 References).
Describes a study which sought to compare the effectiveness of token delivery with a combination of token delivery and removal when the children were given no instructions regarding the contingencies. Four disruptive retarded children served as the subjects and, while token delivery was not effective in decreasing disruptive behavior in any of the children, a combination of token delivery and removal was effective for three of the four children. The results indicate that the combined procedure may be effective with certain populations that are not readily controlled by instructions.

1152 Baker, J. Garry; Stanish, B.; Fraser, B. "Comparative effects of a token economy in nursery school." Ment Retard 10(4): 16-19, August, 1972. (9 References).
Demonstrates the effective use of reinforcement, with tokens and time-out procedures, in controlling maladaptive behavior in nine retarded nursery school children. Lay volunteers were used as technicians.

1153 Birnbrauer, J. S.; Wolf, M. M.; Kidder, J. D.; et al. "Classroom behavior of retarded pupils with token reinforcement." J Exp Child Psychol 2(2): 219-35, June, 1965. (18 References). (Reprinted in Item No. 38).

Reports on the effects of discontinuing a token system for a period of twenty-one days and then reinstating it. The study was conducted in a classroom of seventeen mildly and moderately retarded pupils. The wide variability in the results is discussed.

1154 Cataldo, Michael F. "The effects of systematically applying a token program on a residential unit for retarded boys." For a summary see: Diss Abstr Int 35B(9): 4622, March, 1975.

1155 Dalton, A. J.; Rubino, C. A.; Hislop, M. W. "Some effects of token rewards on school achievement of children with Down's syndrome." J Appl Behav Anal 6(2): 251-59, Summer, 1973. (14 References).

Outlines the effectiveness of a token economy in improving the arithmetic and language performance of seven children with Down's syndrome. No measured generalization on the conduct was noted.

1156 Hill, Freda C. "Using token reinforcements to change behavior in a class of adolescent retardates." Spec Educ Can 44(3): 9-18, March, 1970.

Documents the successful use of tokens with twelve students, aged thirteen to eighteen years. The program was administered by only one teacher who did not receive any additional help.

1157 Hislop, M. W.; Moore, C.; Stanish, B. "Remedial classroom programming: long-term transfer effects from a token economy system." Ment Retard 11(2): 18-20, April, 1973. (6 References).

Records the use of a token economy program for the control of disruptive classroom behaviors. Methods are suggested for enhancing the longevity of the successful transfer of effects.

1158 Jenkins, Joseph R., and Gorrafa, Sheila. "Academic performance of mentally handicapped children as a function of token economies and contingency contracts." Educ Train Ment Retarded 9(4): 183-86, December, 1974.

Investigates several incentive systems and their effects on the reading and arithmetic performances of twelve educable mentally retarded children.

1159 Jones, Russell, and Kazdin, Alan. "Programming response maintenance after withdrawing token reinforcement." Behav Ther 6(2): 153-64, March, 1975. (37 References).

A token reinforcement program produced marked improvement in the behavior of four educable, mentally retarded children who had previously exhibited undesirable behaviors in the classroom. The improvement in behavior was maintained after the removal of the token system.

1160 Kreitman, Leon; Corbin, Gretchen; Bell, Mary. "The use of operant learning principles with retarded children." Educ Train Ment Retarded 4(3): 109-12, October, 1969. (9 References).

Describes the establishment of a token economy system in a class of eight retarded children. Tokens were exchangeable for items in a class store and for cookies.

1161 Lazar, Alfred L., and Stadden, Robert. "Suggestions for using token economy." Pointer 19(2): 154-56, Winter, 1974.
Delineates the necessary components for programs designed to change behavior in mentally retarded and educationally handicapped children.

1162 Mielzarek, Rolf Herbert. "An investigation of token and social reinforcement with moderately retarded teenagers." For a summary see: Diss Abstr Int 38B(7): 3438, January, 1978.

1163 Orlando, Robert. "Tokens as reinforcers: classroom applications by teachers of the retarded." IMRID Papers Rep 4(14): 1-26, 1967.
Tokens were used first to gain behavioral control, then to establish and strengthen academic skills. Appendices cover the kinds of tokens, the establishment and operation of a token exchange store, and stock items for the store.

1164 Repp, Alan C.; Klett, Sylvia Z.; Sosebee, Lynn H.; et al. "Differential effects of four token conditions on rate and choice of responding in a matching-to-sample task." Am J Ment Defic 80(1): 51-56, July, 1975. (26 References).
Compares the effects on simple task performance of four different token programs. Results show that response cost decreased errors but did not influence correct responding.

1165 Ribes-Inesta, E.; Duran, L.; Evans, B.; et al. "An experimental evaluation of tokens as conditioned reinforcers in retarded children." Behav Res Ther 11(1): 125-28, February, 1973. (14 References).
Indicates that the reinforcing effects of tokens seem to depend, in some cases, on the social reinforcement being presented simultaneously. The study was conducted with four retarded children.

1166 Tymchuk, Alexander J. "Token economy and motivating environment for mildly retarded adolescent boys." Ment Retard 9(6): 8, December, 1971.
Briefly reports on a token economy conducted with twenty institutionalized retarded adolescent boys.

1167 Van Osdol, B. M.; Gulick, G.; Johnson, Dale. "The effects of a token reinforcement system on arithmetic achievement and short-term retention by educable mentally retarded students in a public school setting." J Ment Defic Res 17(3/4): 247-54, September-December, 1973. (10 References).
Focuses on the results of a study, conducted with ninety-six subjects, which revealed no significant difference in the retention of arithmetic material. The experimental group was rewarded with tokens for performance, whereas the other two groups did not receive extrinsic rewards.

1168 Westphal, Carl R. "Variables affecting the efficacy of a token economy." Ment Retard 13(6): 32-34, December, 1975. (6 References).
Presents the results of a longitudinal study conducted with sixteen institutionalized mentally retarded boys, all of whom exhibited disruptive behavior. Four variables were investigated: staff/resident ratio; consistency of reinforcement; immediacy of reinforcement; and location of tokens. Manipulation of the variables, coupled with increased staff-to-resident ratio, resulted in an increased efficiency of the token system.

1169 Zimmerman, Elaine H.; Zimmerman, J.; Russell, C. D. "Differential effects of token reinforcement on instruction-following behavior in retarded students instructed as a group." J Appl Behav Anal 2(2): 101-12, Summer, 1969. (6 References). (Reprinted in Item No. 21).
Examines a classroom procedure designed for use with a group of retarded students, aged eight to fifteen years. All of the children displayed severe attention deficits and/or disruptive behaviors. Tokens exchangeable for tangible reinforcers were used to improve instruction-following behaviors. Emphasis is placed on the gathering of objective quantative data.

c. Residential Programs

1170 Baker, Bruce L. "Camp Freedom: behavior modification for retarded children in a therapeutic camp setting." Am J Orthopsychiatry 43(3): 418-27, April, 1973. (13 References).
Compares the progress of twenty-five children in an experimental camp, based on behavioral principles with fifteen children who did not attend the camp. The campers showed significantly greater progress in preselected target areas.

1171 Carr, Janet; Hutchinson, Ian; Corbett, John. "Rehabilitation in Camberwell." Nurs Mirror 139(20): 49-52, November 14, 1974.
Details are given of the methods employed at a residential center situated in a London suburb. The patients are predominantly those with severe behavior disorders, and the aim of the center is to keep institutionalization to a minimum.

1172 Doubros, Steve G. "Behavior therapy with high level, institutionalized, retarded adolescents." Except Child 33(4): 229-33, December, 1966. (7 References).
Two cases are presented in which instrumental, nonverbal behavior was modified by systematic conditioning of verbal behavior. Verbal aggression, when extinguished during therapy, will lead to the extinction of overt motor aggression, since an individual's actions reinforce his verbal expression.

1173 Fingado, Marta L.; Kini, Joanne F.; Stewart, Kathryn; et al. "A thirty-day residential training program for retarded children." Ment Retard 8(6): 42-45, December, 1970. (9 References).
Reports on an interview program conducted by nursing and psychology personnel in which parents receive training and guidance in carrying out behavior modification programs with their retarded children.

1174 Girardeau, Frederic L., and Spradlin, Joseph E. "Token rewards in a cottage program." Ment Retard 2(6): 345-51, December, 1964. (3 References).
Provides the details of a token program designed to improve behavior in trainable adolescent girls. Tokens were redeemable for food, soft drinks, jewelry, clothing, and novelties. Socially acceptable behavior increased significantly.

1175 Marburg, Carol C.; Houston, B. Kent; Holmes, David S. "Influence of multiple models on the behavior of institutionalized retarded children: increased generalization to other models and other behaviors." J Consult Clin Psychol 44(4): 514-19, August, 1976. (7 References).

Thirty-two institutionalized retarded children (aged nine to fourteen years) were reinforced for imitating a model in nine training sessions. The results are discussed, together with the implications for maintenance and generalized effectiveness of social intervention. Results indicate that: (1) the subjects learned to imitate; and (2) the subjects generalized and imitated nonreinforced behaviors.

1176 Paluck, Robert James. "Territoriality and operant conditioning of institutionalized severely retarded boys." For a summary see: Diss Abstr Int 32B(3): 1856, September, 1971.

1177 Roos, Philip. "Development of an intensive habit-training unit at Austin State School." Ment Retard 3(3): 12-15, June, 1965. (6 References).
Traces the establishment of a habit-training unit and the development and implementation of efficient training procedures. The unit is used to train attendants, develop innovative procedures and equipment, and to provide service to the children.

1178 Roos, Philip, and Oliver, Margaret. "Evaluation of operant conditioning with institutionalized retarded children." Am J Ment Defic 74(3): 325-30, November, 1969. (19 References). (Reprinted in Item No. 29).
The effectiveness of operant conditioning procedures implemented by attendants was evaluated by comparing the development of self-help skills in three groups of severely and profoundly retarded institutionalized children. In addition to the experimental and control groups, a placebo group, which received classroom-type training, was included in the study. Results indicated a significantly greater improvement in the group trained by operant conditioning methods.

1179 Sigelman, Carol K., ed. Behavior modification in three settings. Lubbock, Texas: Texas Technical University, Research and Training Center in Mental Retardation, 1974. 64p. (Monograph No. 2). (ED 105 693).
Presents three conference papers describing the implementation of behavior modification principles with three separate and distinct population groups: (1) severely and profoundly retarded, institutionalized children; (2) predelinquents in a group home; and (3) educable mentally retarded children in a special education secondary school program.

1180 Watson, Luke S., Jr. "Application of operant conditioning techniques to institutionalized severely and profoundly retarded children." Ment Retard Abstr 4(1): 1-18, January-March, 1967. (36 References).
Discusses the principles of operant conditioning and their application in training programs. Each principle is illustrated with examples. Special attention is drawn to those self-help and social skills that may be developed by using these methods.

1181 ————. "Applications of behavior-shaping devices to training severely and profoundly mentally retarded children in an institutional setting." Ment Retard 6(6): 21-23, December, 1968. (7 References). (Reprinted in Item No. 33).
Advocates the use of automated behavior-shaping devices and describes an ongoing automated toilet training program.

1182 Whalen, Carol K., and Henker, Barbara A. "Pyramid therapy in a hospital for the retarded: methods, program evaluation, and long-term effects." Am J Ment Defic 75(4): 414-34, January, 1971. (18 References).
Summarizes the procedures and results of a nine-month training program for the retarded patients in an institution. The program attempted to: (1) extend the use of nonprofessional therapists to include the retarded patients; (2) develop procedures that could be taught to the retarded; and (3) evaluate the effectiveness of such a program. Follow-up indicated that the effects of the program were durable.

H. MINIMAL BRAIN DYSFUNCTION

1183 Bradbard, Gail Susan. "Minimal brain dysfunction with hyperactivity: a comparison of the behavioral and cognitive effects of pharmacological and behavioral treatments." For a summary see: Diss Abstr Int 35B(1): 496, July, 1974.

1184 Hewett, Frank M. "Conceptual models for viewing brain dysfunction: developmental psychology and behavioral modification." Ann NY Acad Sci 205: 38-45, February 28, 1973. (20 References).
Reviews the literature in the fields of developmental psychology and behavior modification relevant to the problems of the child with minimal brain dysfunction. A blending is advocated of developmentally-oriented, competency-based approaches with behavioral technology in devising programs for the child with these problems.

I. MULTIPLE HANDICAPS

1185 Banik, Sambhu N., and Mendelson, Martin A. "A comprehensive program for multi-handicapped, mentally retarded children." J Spec Educ Ment Retarded 11(1): 44-49, Fall, 1974.
Describes a hospital program for approximately forty multiply-handicapped and retarded children. A token economy is used to reward appropriate social, self-care, and play behaviors.

1186 Benassi, Barbara J., and Benassi, Victor A. "Behavioral strategies for a deaf and cerebral palsied child." J Commun Disord 6(3): 165-74, September, 1973. (12 References).
Presents a program designed for the treatment of a six-year-old nonverbal boy diagnosed as mentally retarded, cerebral palsied, and deaf. Quantitative data suggested the efficacy of the procedures used.

1187 Chandler, Lynette S., and Adams, Marjorie A. "Multiply handicapped child motivated for ambulation through behavior modification." Phys Ther 52(4): 399-401, April, 1972. (5 References).
Furnishes the details of a case report of a multiply handicapped eight-year-old boy who became an independent walker following a twenty-eight day program of behavior modification using candy as reinforcers.

1188 Friedlander, Bernard Z., and Knight, Marcia S. "Brightness sensitivity and preference in deaf-blind retarded children." Am J Ment Defic 78(3): 323-30, November, 1973. (16 References).
Documents the investigation of light sensitivity in sixteen deaf-blind, retarded children by the use of an operant procedure which allowed them to select preferred illumination feedback.

1189 Gallagher, Patricia A., and Heim, Ruth E. "The classroom application of behavior modification principles for multiply handicapped blind students." New Outlook Blind 68(10): 447-53, December, 1974. (5 References).
Reports on three studies conducted with adolescent or preadolescent blind children with additional handicaps. The children were able to achieve independence in specific responses.

1190 Goldblatt, Michael, and Steisel, Ira M. "Behavior modification with multihandicapped blind children." In: American Psychological Association, Montreal, Canada, 81st, 1973. Proceedings. 805-6.
Presents three case reports in which blind, multi-handicapped children responded to behavior modification techniques. The target behaviors were aggressive acting out, rumination, and "hysterical" sleeping.

1191 Hopper, Christine; York, Robert; Simmons, Penny; et al. "Reduction of hand-mouthing behavior of a profoundly retarded, multiply-handicapped student." Child Study J 6(3): 113-26, 1976. (7 References).
Hand-mouthing was mildly punished and various developmentally valuable skills were reinforced by behavioral means. The child, a nine-year-old residential patient, was profoundly retarded and visually handicapped. The modification procedures, conducted by three teachers in three different educational settings, were within a period of six weeks.

1192 Larsen, Lawrence A. "Behavior modification with the multihandicapped." New Outlook Blind 64(1): 6-15, January, 1970. (27 References).
Summarizes the most important steps that must be taken to ensure the success of a behavior modification project.

1193 Lennan, Robert K. "The deaf multihandicapped unit at the California School for the Deaf, Riverside." Am Ann Deaf 118(3): 439-45, June, 1975. (12 References).
Describes the physical facilities, staffing, and programs of the California School for the Deaf. Particular emphasis is placed on classroom organization and behavior modification strategies utilized.

1194 Murphy, Robert J., and Doughty, Neil R. "Establishment of controlled arm movements in profoundly retarded students using response contingent vibratory stimulation." Am J Ment Defic 82(2): 212-16, September, 1977. (10 References).
Depicts the use of a vibratory mechanism to establish coordinated arm movement in seven nonambulatory, profoundly retarded, multi-handicapped male students attending a public school program. It is suggested that the technique could have physical therapy applications and that it could be instrumental in preparing such students to participate in educational activities requiring manipulative interaction with their environment.

1195 Patterson, Gerald R., and Brodsky, G. "A behavior modification programme for a child with multiple problem behaviors." J Child Psychol Psychiatry 7(3/4): 277-95, 1966. (29 References). (Reprinted in Item Nos. 21, 36).
Social and nonsocial reinforcers were employed in the treatment of a preschool boy with multiple behavior problems. Most of the conditioning procedures were introduced in the schoolroom and in the home.

1196 Rice, Harold K.; McDaniel, Martha W.; Denney, Sarah L. "Operant conditioning techniques for use in the physical rehabilitation of the multiply handicapped retarded patient." Phys Ther 48(4): 342-46, April, 1968. (15 References).
Discusses the techniques and methods used with a six-year-old retarded boy. The advantages of operant conditioning techniques are that they can be used effectively with the mentally retarded; that the patient need not be verbal or even particularly motivated; and that the practice can be continued by an untrained person.

1197 Smeets, Paul M., and Striefel, Sebastian. "The effects of different reinforcement conditions on the test performance of multihandicapped deaf children." J Appl Behav Anal 8(1): 83-89, Spring, 1975. (16 References).
Compares the effectiveness of four types of reinforcement on the audiometric test performance of multiply-handicapped deaf children. Immediate reinforcement was demonstrably more effective than end-of-session, noncontingent, or delayed reinforcement.

1198 Writer, Jan. "Behavior management for the deaf-blind." In: Baud, Hank, and Garrett, Jeff, eds. Multi-dimensional models for teaching deaf-blind children. Raleigh, North Carolina: North Carolina State Department of Public Instruction, 1975. 26-34. (ED 123 815).
Brings together five papers which discuss the basic techniques, assessment and program planning for the deaf-blind child. Appropriate reinforcers for such children are suggested.

1199 Yarnall, Gary Dean. "Comparison of operant and conventional audiometric procedures with deaf-blind, multiply-handicapped children." For a summary see: Diss Abstr Int 34B(11): 5313, May, 1974.

J. PHYSICAL DISABILITIES

1200 Ball, Thomas S.; McCrady, Richard E.; Hart, Archibald D. "Automated reinforcement of head posture in two cerebral palsied retarded children." Percept Mot Skills 40(2): 619-22, April, 1975. (3 References).
A transistor radio was used to control the head posture of two cerebral palsied retarded children. Dropping the head forward automatically terminated the music.

1201 Bank, Stephen Paul. "Behavior therapy with a boy who had never learned to walk." Psychotherapy 5(3): 150-53, Fall, 1968. (3 References).
Failure of development could probably be ascribed to a peculiar set of reinforcement contingencies and the use of behavior modification techniques resulted in the rapid, and apparently lasting, acquisition of walking behavior.

1202 Bhattacharya, D. D., and Singh, Ratan. "Operant manipulation of a behaviour problem." Indian J Pediatr 38(282): 309-12, July, 1971. (5 References).
Presents a case report describing the control of chronic drooling in a nine-year-old boy.

1203 Bijou, Sidney W., and Grimm, Jeffrey A. "Behavioral diagnosis and assessment in teaching young handicapped children." In: Thompson,

Travis, and Dockens, William S., III, eds. Applications of behavior modification. New York: Academic Press, 1975. 161-80. (28 References).

Emphasizes the careful diagnosis and the ongoing assessment necessary for the development of effective treatment plans. The necessity of knowledge and systematic application of behavioral principles is also underlined.

1204 Bragg, Janice H.; Houser, Carolyn; Schumaker, Jean. "Behavior modification: effects on reverse tailor sitting in children with cerebral palsy." Phys Ther 55(8): 860-68, August, 1975. (14 References).

Desirable sitting positions in six cerebral palsied children were rewarded with praise, affection, and food. It is suggested that behavior modification techniques can be combined effectively with physical therapy techniques.

1205 Creer, Thomas L., and Christian, Walter P. Chronically ill and handicapped children: their management and rehabilitation. Champaign, Illinois: Research Press, 1976. 183p. (Bibliography).

This text, intended for professionals in the field, discusses general principles of behavior modification, the techniques derived from them, and their applicability to the chronically ill and handicapped child. Many examples, culled from the reported research, are included. There is also a discussion of the roles of the various professionals who may deal with the ill or handicapped child, together with a discussion of the role of the institution.

1206 Garber, Norman B. "Operant procedures to eliminate drooling behavior in a cerebral palsied adolescent." Dev Med Child Neurol 13(5): 641-44, October, 1971. (2 References).

Positive reinforcement through a penny reward system was used to increase non-drooling behavior in a fourteen-year-old boy.

1207 Goldfarb, Robert, and Guglielmo, Hope. "The efficacy of an overcorrection procedure in the management of tongue thrust and drooling behavior." Paper presented at the 54th Annual International Convention, The Council for Exceptional Children, Chicago, April 4-9, 1976. 19p. (7 References). (ED 125 202).

A verbal warning, paired with positive reinforcement, was effective in eliminating one child's drooling and reducing another child's tongue thrusting behavior.

1208 Grove, David N., and Dalke, Bruce A. "Contingent feedback for training children to propel their wheelchairs." Phys Ther 56(7): 815-20, July, 1976. (8 References).

Describes the use of verbal praise and food to establish self-movement of their wheelchairs in three handicapped children.

1209 Horner, R. D. "Establishing use of crutches by a mentally retarded spina bifida child." J Appl Behav Anal 4(3): 183-89, Fall, 1971. (4 References).

The use of crutches was established and maintained through a combination of successive approximation sequences, fading of modelled and physical prompts, and contingent scheduling of natural reinforcers.

1210 Johnston, Margaret K.; Kelley, C. Susan; Harris, Florence R.; et al. "An application of reinforcement principles to development of

motor skills of a young child." Child Dev 37(2): 379-87, June, 1966. (5 References). (Reprinted in Item No. 37).
An unusually low rate of physical activity in a three-year-old child was changed to a normal rate through systematic social reinforcement of climbing behavior.

1211 Knapp, Mary Elizabeth; O'Neil, Sally M.; Allen, K. Eileen. "Teaching Suzi to walk by behavior modification of motor skills." Nurs Forum 13(2): 158-83, 1974. (5 References).
Presents a detailed case history of a four-year-old girl with a neuromuscular impairment whose walking skills were reinforced by a nurse working in a special education setting.

1212 Kolderie, Mary L. "Behavior modification in the treatment of children with cerebral palsy." Phys Ther 51(10): 1083-90, October, 1971. (15 References).
Reviews the literature and provides a case history of a ten-year-old girl with whom behavior modification was successfully used by physical, occupational, and speech therapists.

1213 Morris, Richard J. Behavior modification with children: a systematic guide. Cambridge, Massachusetts: Winthrop, 1976. 229p. (Bibliography).
This text is intended for those who work with the handicapped child and for students preparing to enter the field. It assumes no previous knowledge of behavior modification or theories of learning. Each chapter is preceded by a summary and is concluded with study questions. There are appendices with checklists, behavior charts, lists of apparatus, and film guides.

1214 Rugel, Robert P.; Mattingly, Joseph; Eichinger, Marjorie; et al. "The use of operant conditioning with a physically disabled child." Am J Occup Ther 25(5): 247-49, July-August, 1971. (5 References).
Operant conditioning techniques were used with an eight-year-old cerebral palsied boy to increase the amount of time the child could stand with his weight on his feet.

1215 Stone, Martin C. "Behavior shaping in a classroom for children with cerebral palsy." Except Child 36(9): 674-77, May, 1970. (5 References).
Describes the use of positive reinforcement in the development of appropriate behaviors in a group of seven boys. There was an overall improvement in behavior, but it is noted that the boys needed continuing tangible rewards to motivate their learning.

1216 Yeatts, Linda M., and Brantley, John C. "Improving a cerebral palsied child's typing with operant techniques." Percept Mot Skills 42(1): 197-98, February, 1976. (3 References).
A seven-year-old girl was taught correct responses on two typing tasks using raisins as reinforcers.

K. VISUAL IMPAIRMENTS

1217 Caetano, Anthony P., and Kauffman, James M. "Reduction of rocking mannerisms in two blind children." Educ Vis Handicap 7(4): 101-5, December, 1975. (8 References).
Describes the use of feedback and reminders to reduce rocking behavior in two blind third-grade girls.

1218 Coyne, Peggy H.; Peterson, Linda W.; Peterson, Robert F. "The development of spoon-feeding behaviors in a blind child." Int J Educ Blind 18(4): 108-12, December, 1968.
A three-year-old blind child was taught independent spoon-feeding by the use of operant learning methods. The entire program was conducted in the child's home during mealtimes.

1219 Greene, Robert J.; Hoats, David L.; Hornick, Adelbert J. "Music distortion: a new technique for behavior modification." Psychol Rec 20(1): 107-9, Winter, 1970. (4 References).
Distorted music was made contingent upon the disruptive rocking behavior of a fifteen-year-old blind, retarded boy. Conditioning, extinction, reconditioning, and intermittent reinforcement demonstrated the aversive nature of music distortion.

1220 Groffman, Sidney. "Operant conditioning and vision training." Am J Optom 46(8): 583-94, August, 1969. (7 References).
Outlines basic principles and describes optometric applications for individuals and groups.

1221 Guess, Doug, and Rutherford, Gorin. "Experimental attempts to reduce stereotyping among blind retardates." Am J Ment Defic 71(6): 984-86, May, 1967. (4 References).
Reports on a study conducted with thirteen blind retardates, aged eight to sixteen years. Results indicate that specific objects and sound-producing apparatus can significantly decrease the rate of stereotypy.

1222 Letourneau, Jacques E. "Application of biofeedback and behavior modification techniques in visual training." Am J Optom Physiol Opt 53(4): 187-90, April, 1976. (21 References).
Describes apparatus and techniques using music or movement of toys as reinforcers.

1223 McClennen, Sandra. "Teaching techniques for institutionalized blind retarded children." New Outlook Blind 63(10): 322-25, December, 1969.
Provides details of programs using the token system of motivation which stresses language, speech, and acceptable social behavior.

1224 Macht, Joel. "Examination and reevaluation of prosthetic lenses employing an operant procedure for measuring subjective visual acuity in a retarded child." J Exp Child Psychiatry 10(2): 139-45, October, 1970. (7 References).
Gives information on the procedure employed to evaluate corrective lenses that had been prescribed for a six-year-old retarded child.

1225 Roades, Sue-ann; Pisch, Lillian; Axelrod, Saul. "Use of behavior modification procedures with visually handicapped students." Educ Vis Handicap 6(1): 19-26, March, 1974. (10 References).
Reviews the few articles on the topic and describes two cases in which behavior modification techniques were used to further the tactile and motor development of visually-handicapped students.

1226 Stolz, Stephanie B., and Wolf, Montrose M. "Visually discriminated behavior in a 'blind' adolescent retardate." J Appl Behav Anal 2(1): 65-77, Spring, 1969. (17 References).

The visual discrimination of a sixteen-year-old male retardate (previously diagnosed as organically blind) was increased by means of edible reinforcers for correct responses.

1227 Swanson, H. Lee. "Effect of positive reinforcement on visual academic performance with a partially sighted child." Educ Vis Handicap 9(3): 72-76, Fall, 1977. (7 References).
Academic accuracy was increased by the use of candy, and candy combined with praise. Candy combined with praise was the most effective mode of treatment (in the classroom setting). The implications for teachers are discussed.

1228 Ulan, Howard; Juris, Antoinette; Dornback, Fred. "Keeping that patch on: the application of behavior modification techniques in orthoptic practice." Am Orthopt J 24: 60-62, 1974. (4 References).
Briefly describes the methods of dealing with the problem of young amblyoptic patients' resistence to wearing eye patches. Examples of written instructions to mothers are included.

VI.

Educational Applications of Behavior Modification

A. NORMAL SCHOOL SETTINGS

1. Preschool/Kindergarten

a. Behavioral Handling of the Preschool/Kindergarten Child

1229 Baer, Donald M. "Effect of withdrawal of positive reinforcement on an extinguishing response in young children." Child Dev 32(1): 67-74, March, 1961. (9 References). (Reprinted in Item No. 30).
Sixteen six-year-old children were conditioned to press a bar to receive a reward of peanuts. This response was then extinguished by means of withdrawing the reinforcement.

1230 Baer, Donald M., and Wolf, Montrose M. "The reinforcement contingency in preschool and remedial education." In: Hess, Robert D., and Baer, Roberta Meyer, eds. Early education. Chicago: Aldine, 1968. 119-29.
Summarizes those studies which have endeavored to evaluate the effects of teacher attention on preschool children's behavior.

1231 Barkley, Russell A., and Routh, Donald K. "Reduction of children's locomotor activity by modeling and the promise of contingent reward." J Abnorm Child Psychol 2(2): 117-31, June, 1974. (14 References).
The locomotor and toy-switching activities of sixty children, aged four and five years, were reduced by the use of modelling by an adult male and by the promise of monetary reward.

1232 Beecher, Ronnie. "Teacher approval and disapproval of classroom behavior in pre-kindergarten, kindergarten, and first grade." For a summary see: Diss Abstr Int 35B(2): 1015, August, 1974.

1233 Betancourt, Francella W., and Zeiler, Michael D. "The choices and preferences of nursery school children." J Appl Behav Anal 4(4): 299-304, Winter, 1971. (3 References).
The choices of and preferences among kindergarten jobs were influenced by the awarding of tokens exchangeable for play activities. The subjects were twenty-four four-to-five-year-old children. When tokens were dependent on choosing the nonpreferred jobs, those jobs came to be preferred. When tokens were dependent on choosing the preferred jobs, the preferences were strengthened.

1234 Bijou, Sidney W. "Patterns of reinforcement and resistance to extinction in young children." Child Dev 28(1): 47-54, March, 1957. (20 References).

Reports on two experiments involving operant or instrumental conditioning techniques used with thirty-nine preschool children. Results indicated that intermittent reinforcement showed more resistance to extinction than did continuous reinforcement.

1235 Bushell, Don; Wrobel, Patricia A.; Michaelis, Mary Louise. "Applying 'group' contingencies to the classroom study behavior of preschool children." J Appl Behav Anal 1(1): 55-61, Spring, 1968. (3 References). (Reprinted in Item Nos. 21, 39).
Provides the details of a study conducted with twelve preschool children. The children's levels of study behavior were increased by the use of group contingencies earned under a token system.

1236 Endsley, Richard C., and Clarey, Susan A. "Answering young children's questions as a determinant of their subsequent question-asking behavior." Dev Psychol 11(6): 863, November, 1975. (2 References).
Answers to children's questions served a dual function: as a discriminative cue and as a reinforcer to elicit and maintain inquiry behavior patterns in preschool children.

1237 Grayson, Joann Hess. "The effects of social reinforcement in interaction with intrinsic reward." For a summary see: Diss Abstr Int 36B(12): 6380, June, 1976.

1238 Hanson, Paul Gilbert. "The effects of a behavior modification workshop in a pre-school setting." For a summary see: Diss Abstr Int 35B(8): 4174, February, 1975.

1239 Harris, Florence R.; Johnston, Margaret K.; Kelley, C. Susan; et al. "Effects of positive social reinforcement on regressed crawling of a nursery school child." J Educ Psychol 55(1): 35-41, February, 1964. (3 References). (Reprinted in Item No. 45).
Demonstrates the use of teacher attention to reward standing behavior in a three-year-old child. Attention was withheld for crawling, and normal standing was reestablished within five weeks.

1240 Harris, Florence R.; Wolf, Montrose M.; Baer, Donald M. "Effects of adult social reinforcement on child behavior." Young Child 20(1): 8-17, 1964. (16 References). (Reprinted in Item Nos. 22, 23, 36, 46).
Provides an account of the procedures and results of five studies on the effect of adult social reinforcement on the behavior of preschool children. Behaviors successfully modified included crawling, excessive crying, excessive passivity, and isolate play.

1241 Homme, L. E.; de Baca, P. C.; Devine, J. V.; et al. "Use of the Premack Principle in controlling the behavior of nursery school children." J Exp Anal Behav 6(4): 544, October, 1963. (1 Reference). (Reprinted in Item No. 46).
The Premack Hypothesis (if behavior B is of higher probability than behavior A, then behavior A can be made more probable by making behavior B contingent upon it) proved to be a practical means of controlling the behavior of three three-year-old children.

1242 Kelly, Richard. "Comparison of the effects of positive and negative vicarious reinforcement in an operant learning task." J Educ Psychol 57(5): 307-10, October, 1966. (13 References).

This study, conducted with 120 kindergarten children, compared the effects of positive, negative, and no reinforcement in both direct and vicarious reinforcement situations. Negative reinforcement resulted in the highest operant rates in both direct and vicarious reinforcement groups. Lowest operant rates were recorded in the no reinforcement situation.

1243 Kelso, Robert R. "A study of reinforcement hierarchies of children using a free operant technique." For a summary see: Diss Abstr Int 34B(8): 4046, February, 1974.

1244 King, Karen. "You can prepare for good behavior--and get it!" Parents Mag 50: 40, 60-62, February, 1975.
Advocates the use of role-playing techniques to anticipate appropriate behavior in preschool children.

1245 Lovaas, O. Ivar. "Interaction between verbal and nonverbal behavior." Child Dev 32(2): 329-36, June, 1961. (7 References). (Reprinted in Item No. 30).
Examines the effect on a class of nonverbal responses of strengthening a class of verbal responses. The study was conducted with nineteen nursery school children.

1246 Mandelker, Annabel V.; Brigham, Thomas A.; Bushell, Don, Jr. "The effects of token procedures on a teacher's social contracts with her students." J Appl Behav Anal 3(3): 169-74, Fall, 1970. (4 References).
Describes a study, conducted with six kindergarten children, in which it was observed that the teacher's rate of social contact was higher with children receiving contingent tokens than with those who received non-contingent tokens.

1247 Miller, L. Keith, and Schneider, Richard. "The use of a token system in Project Head Start." J Appl Behav Anal 3(3): 213-20, Fall, 1970. (8 References). (Reprinted in Item No. 43).
Reports on the successful use of tokens to develop and maintain writing skills in a group of thirty underprivileged four- and five-year-old children. The tokens were exchangeable for snacks and play activities.

1248 Moore, Shirley. "Behavior modification in early childhood classrooms." Contemp Educ 45(4): 261-65, Summer, 1974. (3 References).
Discusses the use of behavioral methods (primarily positive reinforcement) in establishing acceptable behavior in the preschool classroom.

1249 Okovita, Hymie Wolf, and Bucher, Bradley. "Attending behavior of children near a child who is reinforced for attending." Psychol Sch 13(2): 205-11, April, 1976. (7 References).
Investigates the effects of a token program for one child on the attending behavior of two unrewarded children. No disturbing effects were found in the behavior of the unrewarded children.

1250 Redd, William H., and Winston, Andrew S. "The role of antecedent positive and negative comments in the control of children's behavior." Child Dev 45(2): 540-46, June, 1974. (13 References).
An adult's antecedent negative comments exerted greater control of the children's behavior than did positive comments. The subjects were three four-year-old boys.

1251 Risley, Todd R., and Twardosz, Sandra. "The preschool as a setting for behavioral intervention." In: Leitenberg, Harold, ed. Handbook of behavior modification and behavior therapy. Englewood Cliffs, New Jersey: Prentice-Hall, 1976. 453-74. (97 References).
Reviews research on the involvement of the preschool in applied behavior analysis as: (1) a source of subjects; (2) a child development laboratory; (3) a clinical setting; and (4) a day care living environment. Emphasis is placed on the potential of the preschool as an effective setting for behavioral intervention.

1252 Salzberg, Bernard H.; Wheeler, Andrew J.; Devar, Linda Taylor; et al. "The effect of intermittent feedback and intermittent contingent access to play on printing of kindergarten children." J Appl Behav Anal 4(3): 163-71, Fall, 1971. (25 References).
Demonstrates the efficacy of intermittently applied observation and contingencies in increasing the accuracy of kindergarten children's printing responses. Intermittent grading alone failed to produce an increase in accuracy but when grading was paired with access to play, accuracy increased for every child.

1253 Sherman, James A. "Modification of nonverbal behavior through reinforcement of related verbal behavior." Child Dev 35(3): 717-23, September, 1964. (8 References).
Investigates the effects of approval and candy, following the children's verbal statements about a play situation, on subsequent nonverbal behaviors. The subjects were twenty preschool children.

1254 Stokes, Trevor Francis. "Training preschool children to recruit natural communities of reinforcement." For a summary see: Diss Abstr Int 38B(7): 3441, January, 1978.

1255 Tawney, James W. "Training letter discrimination in four-year-old children." J Appl Behav Anal 5(4): 455-65, Winter, 1972. (15 References).
Reports on a study designed to compare the effects of two training procedures on subsequent letter discrimination. Results indicated that reinforcement (with toys and edibles) in the training period reduced the frequency of the most common letter confusions.

1256 Ward, William D., and Ward, Wanda L. "In vivo transfer of behavioral control from tangible to conditioned social reinforcers." Psychol Rep 35(2): 747-51, October, 1974. (9 References).
Provides the details of a study conducted with twenty-five kindergarten children. The children received tangible rewards for inhibiting inappropriate responses and for engaging in appropriate behavior. They were able to maintain desired behavior for a period of two months following the removal of the tangible rewards.

1257 Weiner, Elliot A.; Weiner, Barbara J.; Hartsough, Don M. "Effects of indirect reinforcement on performance of kindergarten children." J Sch Psychol 9(3): 284-91, 1971. (11 References).
Investigates the effects of indirect reinforcement on the performance of kindergarten children. Results indicate that indirect negative reinforcement produced the greatest amount of improvement in performance. Possible classroom implications are discussed.

1258 Yawkey, Thomas D., and Jones, Dawn M. "Application of behavior modification to learning center choices in a kindergarten open education classroom." Psychol Sch 11(3): 321-28, July, 1974. (39 References).
Furnishes the details of an investigation, conducted in an open classroom kindergarten, of the effects of teacher attention on the choice of activity by the children. The results indicate that teacher attention can produce a more frequent choice of academically oriented activities.

b. Elimination of Maladaptive Behaviors

(1) Noncompliant Behavior

1259 Drash, Philip W., et al. "Hyperactivity in preschool children as non-compliance: a new conceptual basis for treatment." Paper presented at the 29th meeting of the Florida Psychological Association, Clearwater Beach, Florida, May 9, 1976. (ED 138 000).
Presents a multifaceted behavioral treatment program which brought noncompliant behavior and hyperactivity to within normal limits in five hyperactive preschoolers.

1260 Goetz, Elizabeth M.; Holmberg, Margaret C.; LeBlanc, Judith M. "Differential reinforcement of other behavior and noncontingent reinforcement as control procedures during the modification of a preschooler's compliance." J Appl Behav Anal 8(1): 77-82, Spring, 1975. (21 References).
Compares two reversal control procedures. The subject was a three-year-old girl who demonstrated marked noncompliance in a preschool setting.

1261 Scarboro, M. Eugene, and Forehand, Rex. "Effects of two types of response-contingent time-out on compliance and oppositional behavior of children." J Exp Child Psychol 19(2): 252-64, April, 1975. (18 References).
Examines the effects of within-room and out-of-room time-out procedures on the compliance and oppositional behavior of twenty-four five-year-old children. Results indicate that, while the methods were equally effective, the within-room approach required significantly more administrations of time-out than did the out-of-room technique.

1262 Schutte, R. C., and Hopkins, B. L. "The effects of teacher attention on following instructions in a kindergarten class." J Appl Behav Anal 3(2): 117-22, Summer, 1970. (15 References).
Demonstrates the effective use of teacher attention on increasing compliance. Verbal instructions were employed in a kindergarten class of five girls.

(2) Disruptive Behavior

1263 Abbott, Martha S. "Modification of the classroom behavior of a 'disadvantaged' kindergarten boy by social reinforcement and isolation." J Educ 151(4): 31-45, April, 1969.
The disruptive behavior of a kindergarten boy was modified by the teacher using social reinforcement for desirable behavior and ignoring, or using time-out procedures, for undesirable behavior.

1264 Baucum, Don G.; Smith, Andrea E.; Weisberg, Paul. "Elimination of disturbing naptime behaviors of preschool children through with-

drawal and re-presentation of TV audio reception." Psychol Rep 35(1): 51-56, August, 1974. (7 References).
Disturbing naptime behaviors were successfully controlled in three preschool children. TV reception was made audible during appropriate behavior and was eliminated for the duration of disruptive behavior.

1265 Briskin, Alan S., and Gardner, William I. "Social reinforcement in reducing inappropriate behavior." Young Child 24(2): 84-89, December, 1968. (16 References).
Evaluates a time-out procedure employed with contingent nonattention in an attempt to reduce the frequency of inappropriate behavior in a three-year-old child. Social reinforcement was used to promote appropriate behavior.

1266 Culbertson, Frances M. "An effective, low-cost approach to the treatment of disruptive school children." Psychol Sch 11(2): 183-87, April, 1974. (7 References).
Describes the successful integration of behavior modification and relationship therapy. The therapeutic measures were employed over a period of one year with six disruptive children of kindergarten age.

1267 Herman, Steven H., and Tramontana, Joseph. "Instructions and group versus individual reinforcement in modifying disruptive group behavior." J Appl Behav Anal 4(2): 113-19, Summer, 1971. (13 References).
Traces the modification of disruptive behavior of Head Start children using either individual or group token reinforcement procedures. Results suggest that: (1) a combination of instructions and reinforcement is more effective than either used alone; (2) behavior change is specific to the environmental contingencies; and (3) group reinforcement is as effective as individual reinforcement.

1268 Holt, Wilma J. "Problems in aggression: three case studies." Paper presented at the Annual meeting of the National Association for the Education of Young Children, Minneapolis, Minnesota, November 5, 1971. (ED 135 474).
Reviews three studies demonstrating the use of different modification techniques to control aggression in the preschool setting. The two procedures examined were time-out, employed as a mild punishment, and extinction paired with reinforcement. All three studies reported success in the use of these two techniques.

1269 Lahey, Benjamin; Gendrich, John G.; Gendrich, Susan I.; et al. "An evaluation of daily report cards with minimal teacher and parent contacts as an efficient method of classroom intervention." Behav Modif 1(3): 381-94, July, 1977. (14 References).
The use of daily report cards resulted in marked changes in the classroom behavior of two classes of disruptive kindergarten children. No special training or assistance was given to the parents or the teachers.

1270 Porterfield, Janet K.; Herbert-Jackson, Emily; Risley, Todd R. "Contingent observation: an effective and acceptable procedure for reducing disruptive behavior of young children in a group setting." J Appl Behav Anal 9(1): 55-64, Spring, 1976. (14 References).
Provides the details of a study conducted with preschool children to determine whether the contingent observation procedure was more or less

effective than the more commonly recommended procedure of directing a child to an alternative activity when disruptions occur. Contingent observation, combined with a brief time-out, proved effective in maintaining low levels of disruptions and was considered, by both parents and teachers, to be an acceptable form of restraint.

1271 Salzberg, Bernard H.; Hopkins, B. L.; Wheeler, Andrew J.; et al. "Reduction of kindergarten children's disruptive behavior with delayed feedback and delayed contingent access to play." J Sch Psychol 12(1): 24-30, Spring, 1974. (7 References).
Nine kindergarten children were used to demonstrate that substantial changes in behavior occurred as a result of events that were as much as thirty minutes removed from the behavior itself.

1272 Sibley, Sally A.; Abbott, Martha S.; Cooper, Betty P. "Modification of the classroom behavior of a disadvantaged kindergarten boy by social reinforcement and isolation." J Exp Child Psychol 7(1): 203-19, April, 1969. (8 References).
Contingent teacher attention was used to promote desirable behavior and to reduce disruptive behavior in a five-and-one-half-year-old boy.

1273 Spencer, Richard J., and Gray, David F. "A time-out procedure for classroom behavioral change within the public school setting." Child Study J 3(1): 29-38, 1973. (25 References).
Time-out from positive reinforcement was used successfully to decrease inappropriate behavior in a classroom setting. The subjects were two kindergarten boys.

1274 Strong, Catherine; Sulzbacher, Stephen I.; Kirkpatrick, Marjorie A. "Use of medication versus reinforcement to modify a classroom behavior disorder." J Learn Disabil 7(4): 214-18, April, 1974. (14 References).
The facial grimacing of a five-year-old boy was reduced more effectively by the use of behavior modification methods than by the use of drugs.

1275 Wilson, Claire V. "The use of rock music as a reward in behavior therapy with children." J Music Ther 13(1): 39-48, Spring, 1976.
Describes the use of rock music with four preschool children (three boys and one girl). Response-contingent withdrawal of the music and a time-out procedure were effective in reducing inappropriate or disruptive behavior in the classroom.

c. Development of Specific Skills

(1) Imitation

1276 Baer, Donald M., and Sherman, James A. "Reinforcement control of generalized imitation in young children." J Exp Child Psychol 1(1): 37-49, April, 1964. (3 References). (Reprinted in Item No. 46).
An animated talking puppet served both as a model and as a source of social reinforcement in an experiment designed to develop imitation in eleven children.

1277 Bandura, Albert. "Behavior theory and identificatory learning." Am J Orthopsychiatry 33(4): 591-601, July, 1963. (21 References).

Reports on a series of experiments on the imitative process. The indications were that much of a child's behavioral repertoire is acquired through imitation of adult models, but that these patterns can be strengthened and maintained by direct reinforcement procedures.

1278 Peterson, R. F., and Whitehurst, G. J. "A variable influencing the performance of generalized imitative behaviors." J Appl Behav Anal 4(1): 1-9, Spring, 1971. (14 References).
Two experiments, conducted with four preschool children, indicated that the presence of the experimenter increased imitative behavior.

(2) Social Interactions

1279 Allen, K. Eileen; Hart, Betty M.; Buell, Joan S.; et al. "Effects of social reinforcement on isolate behavior of a nursery school child." Child Dev 35(2): 511-18, June, 1964. (7 References). (Reprinted in Item Nos. 27, 45).
Demonstrates the use of adult attention to promote social interaction with her peers on the part of a shy preschool girl. Teacher attention was given contingent upon interaction with another child. Social contacts with other children increased markedly and were maintained throughout the school year.

1280 Baer, Donald M., and Wolf, Montrose M. "Recent examples of behavior modification in preschool settings." In: Neuringer, Charles, and Michael, Jack L., eds. Behavior modification in clinical psychology. New York: Appleton-Century-Crofts, 1970. 10-25. (5 References).
Summarizes the results of four studies on the use of behavior modification to increase social interaction in preschool children.

1281 Brown, David; Reschly, Daniel; Sabers, Darrell. "Using group contingencies with punishment and positive reinforcement to modify aggressive behaviors in a Head Start classroom." Psychol Rec 24(4): 491-96, Fall, 1974. (15 References).
Results of this study suggest that group contingencies enhance the effectiveness of other modification techniques. A progressive plan, using rewards and punishment, followed by the addition of group contingencies, may lead to the eventual fading out of the former modification techniques.

1282 Brown, Paul, and Elliott, Rogers. "Control of aggression in a nursery school class." J Exp Child Psychol 2(2): 103-7, June, 1965. (10 References). (Reprinted in Item Nos. 22, 27, 32).
Reports on the successful modification of aggressive behavior in twenty-seven three- and four-year-old boys. The results were achieved by the systematic ignoring, by the teachers, of aggressive behavior and the giving of attention to nonaggressive behavior.

1283 Buell, Joan; Stoddard, Patricia; Harris, Florence; et al. "Collateral social development accompanying reinforcement of outdoor play in a preschool child." J Appl Behav Anal 1(2): 167-73, Summer, 1968. (5 References). (Reprinted in Item Nos. 27, 38).
Social reinforcement was used to increase both the social and motor skills of a three-year-old girl. The improvement in motor skills was noted by an increase of the use of outdoor play equipment. Changes in these two areas were accompanied by a decrease in one category of baby-like behavior.

1284 Doland, Dilman J., and Adelberg, Kathryn. "The learning of sharing behavior." Child Dev 38(3): 695-700, September, 1967. (5 References). (Reprinted in Item No. 32).
Sharing behavior was enhanced in preschool age children by the use of social reinforcement. The subjects were two groups of children drawn from a private nursery school and a child welfare center for dependent and neglected children. A newly devised technique for studying sharing behavior is described in detail.

1285 Evers-Pasquale, Wendy, and Sherman, Mark. "The reward value of peers. A variable influencing the efficacy of filmed modeling in modifying social isolation in preschoolers." J Abnorm Child Psychol 3(3): 179-89, 1975. (10 References).
A study conducted with preschool children indicated that those children who watched a peer-oriented modelling film increased their peer social interactions significantly more than did the children who watched a modelling film that was not peer-oriented.

1286 Hart, Betty M.; Reynolds, Nancy J.; Baer, Donald M.; et al. "Effect of contingent and noncontingent social reinforcement on the cooperative play of a preschool child." J Appl Behav Anal 1(1): 73-76, Spring, 1968. (5 References). (Reprinted in Item Nos. 27, 37, 40).
Presents a study on the effect of adult social reinforcement on the cooperative play of a five-year-old girl in a preschool setting. Only when reinforcement was presented contingent upon cooperative play did the cooperative play increase.

1287 Kirby, Frank D., and Toler, Hayward C., Jr. "Modification of preschool isolate behavior: a case study." J Appl Behav Anal 3(4): 309-14, Winter, 1970. (4 References).
Social interaction with nursery school classmates was increased in a five-year-old isolate boy by inducing him to pass out candy to them.

1288 O'Connor, Robert D. "Modification of social withdrawal through symbolic modeling." J Appl Behav Anal 2(1): 15-22, Spring, 1969. (36 References). (Reprinted in Item Nos. 28, 39).
Investigates the use of symbolic modelling to enhance the social interactions of isolate nursery school children. The method used was the showing of a film demonstrating positive social interactions.

1289 ————. "Relative efficacy of modeling, shaping, and the combined procedures for modification of social withdrawal." J Abnorm Psychol 79(3): 327-34, June, 1972. (25 References). (Reprinted in Item No. 35).
Reports on a study conducted with socially withdrawn nursery school children. A comparison was made between the effects of viewing a modelling film, with and without social reinforcement, and viewing a control film, with and without social reinforcement. Peer interaction increased following the viewing of the modelling film.

1290 Parish, Thomas S. "The enhancement of altruistic behaviors in children through the implementation of language conditioning procedures." Behav Modif 1(3): 395-404, July, 1977. (23 References).
Presents the findings of an experiment that demonstrated that both male and female children's altruistic behaviors could be enhanced through

the systematic use of language conditioning procedures. The procedure described was relatively easy to administer to a large number of children simultaneously and required little or no special training.

1291 Perry, James Samuel. "The effectiveness of modeling and reinforcement on generosity in young children." For a summary see: Diss Abstr Int 33A(3): 1026, September, 1972.

1292 Pinkston, Elsie M.; Reese, Nancy M.; LeBlanc, Judith M.; et al. "Independent control of a preschool child's aggression and peer interaction by contingent teacher attention." J Appl Behav Anal 6(1): 115-24, Spring, 1973. (12 References).
Demonstrates the successful technique of largely ignoring the subject's aggressive behavior and attending instead to whatever child he was attacking. A notable increase in subject interaction with peers was functionally related to teacher attention contingent upon that behavior.

1293 Quilitch, H. Robert, and Risley, Todd R. "The effects of play materials on social play." J Appl Behav Anal 6(4): 573-78, Winter, 1973. (22 References).
Cites the effective use, in the preschool setting, of access to toys as a reinforcer in the development of social play. "Social" toys produced markedly better results than did "isolate" toys.

1294 Rogers-Warren, Ann; Warren, Steven, F.; Baer, Donald M. "A component analysis: modeling, self-reporting, and reinforcement of self-reporting in the development of sharing." Behav Modif 1(3): 307-22, July, 1977. (26 References).
Analyzes the components of procedure designed to encourage sharing behavior in young children. When examined with two groups of four-year-old children, modelling, in combination with self-reporting, was sufficient to increase sharing in some children. The combined use of modelling, self-reporting, and reinforcement for true reports of sharing was most effective for all subjects.

1295 Scott, Phyllis M.; Burton, Roger V.; Yarrow, Marian Radke. "Social reinforcement under natural conditions." Child Dev 38(1): 53-63, March, 1967. (2 References). (Reprinted in Item No. 32).
Unacceptable behavior toward peers was changed in a four-year-old boy when adult attention was redirected toward his positive interactions with peers.

1296 Spencer, Margaret Beale, and Horowitz, Frances. "Effects of systematic social and token reinforcement on the modification of racial and color concept attitudes in black and in white preschool children." Dev Psychol 9(2): 246-54, September, 1973.
Describes a study conducted with twenty-four black and twenty-four white preschool children which attempted to change the minority members' view of their race and the view of the dominant majority. Methods used included stimulus cards and puppets.

1297 Strain, Philip S., and Timm, Matthew A. "An experimental analysis of social interaction between a behaviorally disordered preschool child and her classroom peers." J Appl Behav Anal 7(4): 583-90, Winter, 1974. (10 References).
The social interaction between a three-year-eight-month-old girl and her classmates was increased by the use of contingent adult attention.

1298 Strain, Philip S., and Wiegerink, Ronald. "The social play of two behaviorally disordered preschool children during four activities: a multiple baseline study." J Abnorm Child Psychol 3(1): 61-69, 1975. (7 References).
Demonstrates that contingent teacher attention can increase the social play of behaviorally disordered children. The subjects were two three-year-old boys. The changes were effected with only minor alterations in classroom programming and a minimal amount of teacher time and effort.

1299 Titus, Richard Meredith. "Environmental behavior modification: responses of 'isolate' preschool children to a cooperation-contingent treatment environment and associated changes in free play behavior." For a summary see: Diss Abstr Int 37B(2): 677, August, 1976.

1300 Whitehurst, Carol, and Miller, Edward. "Behavior modification of aggressive behavior on a nursery school bus: a case study." J Sch Psychol 11(2): 123-28, Summer, 1973. (6 References).
Aggressive behavior of two preschool boys was modified by the use of a negative punishment contingency in the form of a delayed return to their homes.

(3) Creativity

1301 Goetz, Elizabeth M., and Baer, Donald M. "Social control of form diversity and the emergence of new forms in children's blockbuilding." J Appl Behav Anal 6(2): 209-17, Summer, 1973. (7 References).
Sets forth the results of a study on the use of social reinforcement to encourage the development of diversity and creativity in the block building of three preschool children. The production of new forms of block building was increased during periods of reinforcement of different forms.

1302 Goetz, Elizabeth M.; Jones, Karen; Weamer, Katherine. "The generalization of creativity 'training' in easel painting to blockbuilding." Paper presented at the 81st meeting of the American Psychological Association, Montreal, Canada, August 27-31, 1973. 12p. (ED 086 324).
Verbal reinforcement for the painting of different forms by two preschool boys increased the number of forms and generalized the form diversity to block building. No generalization was noted in the appearance of new forms.

d. The Culturally Deprived Preschool/Kindergarten Child

1303 Allen, K. Eileen. "Behavior modification principles with disadvantaged and deprived." In: Cull, John G., and Hardy, Richard E., eds. Behavior modification in rehabilitation settings: applied principles. Springfield, Illinois: Thomas, 1974. 89-129. (3 References).
Reviews the literature and deduces a set of general principles for the application of behavioral methods with the disadvantaged child. A case report is included which describes the successful use of such methods to bring under control the violently disruptive behavior of a three-and-one-half-year-old girl.

1304 Risley, Todd. "Learning and lollipops." Psychol Today 1(8): 28-31; 62-65, January, 1968.
Reports on the use of behavior modification techniques in two programs for culturally deprived preschool children. One program involved the teaching of the techniques to the mothers of the children.

1305 Risley, Todd; Reynolds, Nancy; Hart, Betty. "Behavior modification with disadvantaged preschool children." In: Bradfield, R. H., ed. Behavior modification: the human effort. San Rafael, California: Dimensions, 1970. 123-57. (12 References).
Furnishes the results of a pilot research program conducted over a period of two years with a group of disadvantaged preschool children. Emphasis is placed on the development of speech and language skills and the changing of the child-rearing practices of the mothers in the poverty group.

2. Elementary/High School

a. Behavioral Handling of the Elementary/ High School Student

1306 Ackerman, John Mark. Operant conditioning techniques for the classroom teacher. Glenview, Illinois: Scott, Foresman, 1972. 143p. (Bibliography).
This text was used originally in teaching classes of practicing teachers. It presents the principles of learning and the operant conditioning techniques derived from those principles. Included are instructions for observing and recording behavior, reinforcing desirable behavior, and using the peer group to modify behavior.

1307 Altman, K. I., and Linton, T. E. "Operant conditioning in the classroom setting: a review of the research." J Educ Res 64(6): 277-86, February, 1971. (38 References).
Surveys the reported research and discusses problems within the following categories: (1) teacher attention; (2) peer attention; (3) token reinforcement; and (4) vicarious reinforcement. Implications for the classroom teacher and future research are also discussed.

1308 Archer, D. K. Humane atmosphere within the school. Dubuque, Iowa: Kendall/Hunt, 1976. 90p. (Bibliography).
Advocates the use of behavior modification techniques to establish a learning environment which will foster an atmosphere of trust, confidence, and cooperation. The basic principles of behavior modification are outlined, and chapters are included on such aspects as accountability, decision making, and leadership. Each chapter contains case histories.

1309 Axelrod, Saul. Behavior modification for the classroom teacher. New York: McGraw-Hill, 1977. 190p. (Bibliography).
Provides detailed descriptions of how behavior modification techniques can be applied in classroom settings. The basic principles are covered, as well as measurement and research design, and typical school problems. Each chapter contains questions and suggested activities, and one chapter is devoted to the frequently expressed questions and concerns about the use of behavior modification.

1310 Baer, Paul E., and Goldfarb, Garry E. "A developmental study of verbal conditioning in children." Psychol Rep 10(1): 175-81, February, 1962. (7 References).

Documents an experiment conducted with children in the third, sixth, and tenth grades using verbal conditioning. Results revealed significant differences between age and sex subgroups.

1311 Baltes, Margret M. "Operant principles applied to the acquisition and generalization of nonlittering behavior in children." For a summary see: Diss Abstr Int 34B(11): 5700, May, 1974.

1312 Becker, Wesley C. "Applications of behavior principles in typical classrooms." In: Thoresen, Carl E., ed. Behavior modification in education. National Society for the Study of Education, Yearbook, 72, pt. 1. Chicago: University of Chicago Press, 1973. 77-106. (48 References).
Examines the potential importance to teachers of behavioral techniques. Examples of possible application are given, together with suggestions pointing out the importance of knowledge in this area for all practicing teachers.

1313 Becker, Wesley C.; Thomas, Don R.; Carnine, Douglas. Reducing behavior problems: an operant conditioning guide for teachers. Urbana, Illinois: Educational Resources Information Center, 1969. 36p. (28 References). (Reprinted in Item No. 22).
Outlines the possible applications of learning principles in elementary and preschool classrooms. Details, together with supportive research, are given of three procedures that can be employed by teachers, as well as typical circumstances under which the procedures would be effective.

1314 Broughton, Sam F. "The unwitting behavior modifier." Elem Sch J 75(3): 143-51, December, 1974. (20 References).
Illustrates how various teacher behaviors can effect pupil behaviors. The constructive use of reinforcement is advocated.

1315 Buys, Christian J. "Effects of teacher reinforcement on elementary pupils' behavior and attitudes." Psychol Sch 9(3): 278-88, July, 1972. (29 References).
Describes a study which attempted to change overt behaviors by means of teacher reinforcement and to assess attitudes following the behavioral changes. The students involved were eighteen third- and fourth-graders.

1316 Christiansen, Gary Allen. "Minicourse 23: classroom management through positive reinforcement--a preliminary field study." For a summary see: Diss Abstr Int 37A(7): 4295, January, 1976.

1317 Christie, Lu, et al., eds. "A very special education for all children." In: Convention for Behavioral Educators, 3rd, Montpelier, Vermont, 1973. Proceedings. 1-206. (ED 097 785).
Contains twenty-seven case studies of educational programs which applied behavior therapy across a wide variety of school settings.

1318 Clarizio, Harvey F. Toward positive classroom discipline. New York: Wiley, 1971. 159p. (Bibliography).
This text, intended for both prospective and experienced teachers, emphasizes that student behavior--or misbehavior--is closely related to teacher behavior. The techniques of reward, modelling, extinction, punishment, and desensitization are examined in detail with many examples taken from classroom situations.

1319 Clarizio, Harvey F., and Yelon, Stephen L. "Learning theory approaches to classroom management: rationale and intervention techniques." J Spec Educ 1(3): 267-74, Spring, 1967. (43 References). (Reprinted in Item No. 25).
Outlines the reasons for focusing on the changing of deviant classroom behavior rather than on its causes. A brief description is given of some of the techniques that can be used.

1320 Copeland, Rodney, and Hall, R. Vance. "Behavior modification in the classroom." In: Hersen, Michel; Eisler, Richard M.; Miller, Peter M., eds. Progress in behavior modification: Vol. 3. New York: Academic Press, 1976. 45-78. (107 References).
Traces the progress of behavior modification from the laboratory to the classroom, outlines the development of teacher training programs, and suggests directions for research and applications in education. The moral and ethical issues are discussed, together with the changing roles of teachers, principals, school psychologists, and teacher aides.

1321 Crandall, Virginia C.; Good, Suzanne; Crandall, Vaughn J. "Reinforcement effects of adult reactions and nonreactions on children's achievement expectations: a replication study." Child Dev 35(2): 485-97, June, 1964. (12 References).
The results of this study provided evidence that high expectancy children changed their expectancies more as the result of negative adult reactions, while low expectancy children responded more to positive adult reactions. The subjects were fourth-grade boys.

1322 Dickinson, Donald J. "But what happens when you take that reinforcement away?" Psychol Sch 11(2): 158-60, April, 1974. (9 References).
Presents the results of a two-year follow-up study of fifty students who had been enrolled in a token reinforcement program. The program had been conducted in the fifth and sixth grades and had then been discontinued. The indications were that natural reinforcers take over and serve the function of the original reinforcement program.

1323 Dollar, Barry. Humanizing classroom discipline: a behavioral approach. New York: Harper & Row, 1972. 114p.
This text, which is intended primarily for beginning teachers, presents the conceptual framework for establishing effective discipline. Practice exercises and numerous examples complete the volume.

1324 Drabman, Ronald S. "Behavior modification in the classroom." In: Craighead, W. Edward; Kazdin, Alan E.; Mahoney, Michael J., eds. Behavior modification: principles, issues, and applications. Boston: Houghton Mifflin, 1976. 227-42.
Looks at the systematic use of teacher attention, token economies, and punishment procedures. The discussion of current areas of research includes peer reinforcement, self-control, sociometric changes, and generalization of treatment effects.

1325 Fargo, George A.; Behrns, Charlene; Nolen, Patricia, eds. Behavior modification in the classroom. Belmont, California: Wadsworth, 1970. 344p. (Bibliography).
Brings together thirty-nine articles that deal with ethical and theoretical issues, as well as the practical application of behavioral principles. Examples are drawn from various settings such as normal and special classrooms, mental health and speech clinics, and the home.

1326 Ferinden, William E., Jr. Classroom management through the application of behavior modification techniques. Linden, New Jersey: Remediation Associates, 1970. 62p. (51 References). (ED 073 392).
Surveys behavior modification techniques for the teacher. Specialized techniques are discussed for dealing with such common classroom problems as hyperactivity, aggression, and negativism.

1327 Fontana-Durso, Barbara. "The effects of behavior modification on locus of control, self-concept, reading achievement, math achievement, and behavior in second grade children." For a summary see: Diss Abstr Int 36B(8): 4197, February, 1976.

1328 Forness, Steven R. "Behavioristic approach to classroom management and motivation." Psychol Sch 7(4): 356-63, 1970. (22 References).
Reviews the possible application of behavioral principles. Special attention is paid to the use of reinforcement and desensitization in the classroom situation.

1329 ———. "The reinforcement hierarchy." Psychol Sch 10(2): 168-77, April, 1973. (57 References).
Advocates movement along continuum from lower-level reinforcers, such as edibles, toward high-level reinforcers, such as competence. The rationale for such an approach is that the child is thus prepared for the motivational system of the regular classroom.

1330 Gallagher, Patricia A. Positive classroom performance: techniques for changing behavior. Denver, Colorado: Love, 1971. 62p. (Education Series).
This volume, which is intended for both the prospective and the practicing teacher, contains a brief explanation of reinforcement principles. It provides many examples of classroom situations and appropriate methods of handling them.

1331 Graubard, Paul S., and Rosenberg, Harry. Classrooms that work: prescriptions for change. New York: Dutton, 1974. 214p.
Recommends behavior modification to improve instructional programs for children with learning and behavioral problems. The basic principles are outlined, as well as such topics as the setting of goals, individualized instruction programs, parental involvement, discipline, and motivation.

1332 Haring, Norris G., and Phillips, E. Lakin. Analysis and modification of classroom behavior. Englewood Cliffs, New Jersey: Prentice Hall, 1972. 196p. (Bibliography). (Special Education Series).
Covers basic methodology, research, and program implementation. Chapters are included on the roles of various school personnel and the involvement of the parents to ensure program success.

1333 Harris, Mary B. Classroom uses of behavior modification. Columbus, Ohio: Merrill, 1972. 440p. (Bibliography).
This volume is intended for psychology and education students, as well as for the practicing teacher. It provides an introduction to principles and methods, and includes a series of reprinted articles dealing with the practical application of the principles.

1334 Hazzard, James Curtis. "Effects of behavioral consultation on teacher application and transfer of behavior management principles." For a summary see: Diss Abstr Int 38A(5): 2557, November, 1977.

1335 Hirsch, Benjamin. "Reinforcer effectiveness with negro and white children." For a summary see: Diss Abstr Int 35B(4): 1889, October, 1974.

1336 Keller, Fred Simmons, and Ribes-Inesta, Emilio. Behavior modification: applications to education. New York: Academic Press, 1974. 211p. (Bibliography).
Presents a series of conference papers dealing with the problems attendant on the use of behavior modification in the educative process. The focus is on grade school and university education.

1337 McColloch, Michael Arnold. "The relationship of locus of control to behavior and achievement in open education and behavior modification classrooms." For a summary see: Diss Abstr Int 36B(9): 4699, March, 1976.

1338 McCullough, James P.; Cornell, John E.; McDaniel, Max H.; et al. "Utilization of the simultaneous treatment design to improve student behavior in a first-grade classroom." J Consult Clin Psychol 42(2): 288-92, April, 1974. (7 References).
Presents a single-case study of a program which allowed a statistical comparison of the treatment effects of two contingency programs administered simultaneously. The program was conducted by a teacher and an aide.

1339 MacDonald, Willard Scott, and Tanabe, Gilfred, eds. Focus on classroom behavior: readings and research. Springfield, Illinois: Thomas, 1973. 162p. (Bibliography).
Furnishes a collection of fifteen papers covering three primary areas: (1) understanding pupil behavior through behavioral analysis; (2) altering the behavior of students; and (3) the role of the teacher.

1340 MacMillan, Donald L. Behavior modification in education. New York: Macmillan, 1973. 238p. (Bibliography).
This text, which is intended for both student and practicing teachers, covers principles of learning theory and practical methods for utilizing them. Examples are taken from settings with normal and handicapped children.

1341 Madsen, Charles H., Jr., and Madsen, Clifford. Teaching/discipline: a positive approach for educational development. 2nd ed. Boston: Allyn & Bacon, 1974. 265p. (Bibliography).
This text is intended for prospective or practicing teachers. It is divided into three sections which deal with: (1) the central issues relating to discipline; (2) the application of behavioral principles with eighty-seven examples; and (3) the effect of teacher responses on student behavior. A bibliography and a glossary are included.

1342 Marholin, David, II, and Steinman, Warren M. "Stimulus control in the classroom as a function of the behavior reinforced." J Appl Behav Anal 10(3): 465-78, Fall, 1977. (35 References).
Documents research which sought to demonstrate a means by which academic and social behavior can become less dependent on the teacher's direct supervision. The study was conducted in a special classroom with children ranging in age from ten to twelve years. By providing contingencies for the products of the children's activities, rather than for on-task behavior, their behaviors came more under the influence of the academic materials themselves.

1343 Martin, David L. "Your praise can smother learning." Learning 5(6): 43-51, February, 1977.
Cautions that the overuse of praise can weaken a child's self-motivation, perpetuate unequal treatment based on race or ethnic background, and result in sabotaging the learning process.

1344 Martin, William John. "Fiedler's contingency model in classroom teaching situations." For a summary see: Diss Abstr Int 38A(4): 1792, October, 1977.

1345 Miller, D. Merrily. "How can the teacher manage the system, rather than the system manage the teacher?" Paper presented at the 55th Annual International Convention, The Council for Exceptional Children, Atlanta, Georgia, April 11-15, 1977. 20p. (ED 139 193).
Outlines ten stages involved in guiding teachers through the development and implementation of behavior modification projects.

1346 O'Leary, Susan G., and O'Leary, K. Daniel. "Behavior modification in the school." In: Leitenberg, Harold, ed. Handbook of behavior modification and behavior therapy. Englewood Cliffs, New Jersey: Prentice-Hall, 1976. 475-515. (163 References).
Reviews research which has focused primarily on the normal kindergarten through grade twelve classrooms. Studies are grouped according to the method of reinforcement employed (teacher attention, peer attention, punishment, etc.). One section is devoted to teacher training. The final chapter criticizes, among other things, the lack of research in junior high schools, and advocates investigation of such factors as classroom environment, the teaching of self-evaluation, and self-reinforcement.

1347 Patterson, Joseph Russell. "Applied behavior analysis in the classroom: issues and techniques." For a summary see: Diss Abstr Int 38A(3): 1307, September, 1977.

1348 Phillips, David. "Application of behavioral principles to classroom settings." In: Becker, Wesley C., ed. An empirical basis for change in education: selections on behavioral psychology for teachers. Palo Alto, California: Science Research Associates, 1971. 333-57.
Presents a brief outline of typical procedures used in dealing with behavior problems in the classroom. Seven studies, conducted by elementary school teachers, are cited.

1349 Presbie, Robert J., and Brown, Paul L. Behavior modification. What research says to the teacher. Washington, D.C.: National Education Association, 1976. 39p. (100 References). (ED 118 563).
Surveys research findings and summarizes the procedures shown to be effective in the classroom.

1350 ————. Physical education: the behavior modification approach. Washington, D.C.: National Education Association, 1977. 122p. (Bibliography). (The Curriculum Series).
Outlines methods of improving athletic skills, sports behaviors, and physical fitness for both students and adults. Some background in psychology or learning theory would be useful, but the examples given are all accompanied by references to the published literature.

1351 Presland, John. "Modifying behavior now." Spec Educ Forward Trends 1(3): 20-22, September, 1974. (12 References).
Briefly outlines the possible uses of behavior modification techniques in the classroom.

1352 Rhinard, Larry Dean. "A comparison of the effectiveness of non-directive play therapy and behavior modification approaches." For a summary see: Diss Abstr Int 30B(12, pt. 1): 5696, June, 1970.

1353 Sarason, Irwin G.; Glaser, Edward M.; Fargo, George A. Reinforcing productive classroom behavior: a teacher's guide to behavior modification. New York: Behavioral Publications, 1972. 43p. (Bibliography).
Presents a guide to the use of behavior modification techniques by teachers, counselors, and others working with children on a day-to-day basis. The types of behavioral and academic problems amenable to treatment are delineated, as well as appropriate methods. Four case histories are included, together with a glossary and an annotated bibliography of sixteen items.

1354 Schultz, Charles B., and Sherman, Roger H. "Social class, development, and differences in reinforcer effectiveness." Rev Educ Res 46(1): 25-59, Winter, 1976. (110 References).
Analyzes research from the standpoint of the comparative effectiveness of various reinforcers as related to social class. The conclusion is reached that the determination of reinforcer preference should be made on an individual basis rather than by a priori judgments of the experimenter.

1355 Sherman, James A., and Bushell, Don, Jr. "Behavior modification as an educational technique." In: Horowitz, Frances Degen, ed. Review of child development research: Vol. 4. Chicago: University of Chicago Press, 1975. 409-62.
Reviews procedures and methods of implementation, specifies standards, and discusses the ethical implications of using behavior modification in the classroom.

1356 Skinner, B. F. "Contingency management in the classroom." Education 90(2): 93-100, November-December, 1969.
Considers a number of topics relating to the classroom use of contingency management, including why students go to school, behave appropriately or inappropriately, and learn or do not learn. The discussion includes comments on programmed instruction, punishment, token systems, and teacher training.

1357 ———. The technology of teaching. New York: Appleton-Century-Crofts, 1968. 271p. (Bibliography). (The Century Psychology Series).
This reference and resource volume presents the basic operant principles developed by Skinner, together with their application to the educational process.

1358 Snow, David L., and Brooks, Robert B. "Behavior modification techniques in the school setting." J Sch Health 44(4): 198-205, April, 1974. (205 References).
Reviews general procedures and methods that can be used in the school setting, including reinforcement, extinction, time-out, and punishment. Issues related to the selection of appropriate reinforcers, group contingencies, and modelling techniques are also discussed.

1359 Sulzer, Beth, and Mayer, G. Roy. Behavior modification procedures for school personnel. Hinsdale, Illinois: Dryden Press, 1972. 316p. (Bibliography).
Covers basic principles, procedures for increasing and decreasing existing behaviors, teaching new behaviors, maintenance, and program evaluation. Each chapter is preceded by special learning objectives and contains practical exercises.

1360 Sunshine, Phyllis M. Approaches to school discipline. A selected review of the literature: No. 2. Reviews of research. Baltimore, Maryland: Maryland State Department of Education, Division of Research, Evaluation and Information Systems, 1973. 39p. (60 References). (ED 087 084).
Compares psychoanalytical and behavior modification models for dealing with classroom discipline.

1361 Tinsley, David G., and Ora, John P. "Catch the child being good." Todays Educ 59: 24-25, January, 1970.
Briefly outlines the use of social reinforcement in the classroom.

1362 Van Cara, Flora Wallace. "The effects of different types of positive extrinsic reinforcement on high and low intrinsic motivation in young children." For a summary see: Diss Abstr Int 38B(4): 1963, October, 1977.

1363 Vernon, Walter M. Motivating children: behavior modification in the classroom. New York: Holt, Rinehart & Winston, 1972. 88p. (Bibliography).
This volume, which is intended for the practicing teacher, contains the basic principles of behavior modification, together with examples taken primarily from elementary school classrooms.

1364 Ward, James. "Behaviour modification in education: an overview and a model for programme implementation." Bull Br Psychol Soc 29: 257-68, 1976.
Reviews literature, discusses issues, and outlines procedures for the implementation of a program.

1365 Whelan, Richard J., and Haring, Norris G. "Modification and maintenance of behavior through systematic application of consequences." Except Child 32(5): 281-89, January, 1966. (23 References). (Reprinted in Item No. 25).
Covers the basic principles of behavior modification and indicates their application in the classroom. Precision is encouraged, and the dangers of random or haphazard application emphasized.

1366 Whitman, Myron, and Whitman, Joan. "Behavior modification in the classroom." Psychol Sch 8(2): 176-86, April, 1971. (16 References).
Presents the rationale for behavior modification and suggests some techniques for the classroom management of maladaptive behavior.

1367 Winett, Richard A. "Behavior modification and open education." J Sch Psychol 11(3): 207-13, Fall, 1973. (44 References).
Compares behavior modification and open education and suggests a merging of techniques and procedures. Similarities are discussed, e.g., both methods stress a direct relationship of the class environment to the child's behavior.

b. Behavior Problems in the Classroom

(1) Maladaptive Behaviors

1368 Argast, Terry Lee. "The effects of self-observation and self-reinforcement on deviant classroom behavior." For a summary see: Diss Abstr Int 36B(1): 432, July, 1975.

1369 Becker, Wesley C.; Madsen, Charles H., Jr.; Arnold, Carole Revelle; et al. "The contingent use of teacher attention and praise in reducing classroom behavior problems." J Spec Educ 1(3): 287-307, Spring, 1967. (5 References). (Reprinted in Item Nos. 36, 39, 48).
Presents the findings of a group of studies involving five elementary school teachers whose classes contained a high percentage (95 percent) of black children. The studies demonstrated the successful use of ignoring deviant behavior while reinforcing productive behaviors. A discussion is also included on methods of teacher training.

1370 Broden, Marcia; Bruce, Carl; Mitchell; Mary A.; et al. "Effects of teacher attention on attending behavior of two boys at adjacent desks." J Appl Behav Anal 3(3): 199-203, Fall, 1970. (8 References). (Reprinted in Item Nos. 27, 39).
Demonstrates the effectiveness of teacher attention being paid to attentive behavior while ignoring disruptive behavior. The subjects were two second-grade boys.

1371 Dickinson, Donald J. "Changing behavior with behavioral techniques." J Sch Psychol 6(4): 278-83, Summer, 1968. (8 References).
Presents a case study of an eight-year-old boy whose classroom behavior was improved by the use of a combination of punishment for undesirable behavior and a reinforcement system to maintain the new behavior.

1372 Eleftherios, Christos P.; Shoudt, John T.; Strang, Harold R. "The game machine: a technological approach to classroom control." J Sch Psychol 10(1): 55-60, March, 1972. (11 References).
The out-of-seat behavior of twenty-two rural first graders was controlled through the use of common classroom rewards. The teacher was thus freed from the usual disciplinary chores, and the students' academic productivity was increased.

1373 Flowers, John V. "A behavior modification technique to reduce the frequency of unwarranted questions by target students in an elementary classroom." Behav Ther 5(5): 665-67, October, 1974. (2 References).
A significant decrease in unwarranted questions was accomplished in eight target subjects and twenty-one non-target subjects by the use of a token system.

1374 Grandy, Gordon S.; Madsen, Charles H., Jr.; de Mersseman, Lois M. "The effects of individual and interdependent contingencies on inappropriate classroom behavior." Psychol Sch 10(4): 488-93, October, 1973. (13 References).
Individual and group contingencies were found to be equally effective in reducing talking-out and out-of-seat behaviors in twenty-eight students. Indications are given of the need for further research.

1375 Hall, R. Vance; Axelrod, Saul; Foundopoulos, Marlyn; et al. "The effective use of punishment to modify behavior in the classroom." Educ Technol 11(4): 24-26, April, 1971. (6 References). (Reprinted in Item No. 39).
Reports on four experiments dealing with the effects of punishment procedures on specific behaviors that the teacher wished to reduce or eliminate and which did not result in strong emotional responses.

1376 Keesee, Joseph Thornton, II. "The effects of a behavioral management class on students exhibiting a high rate of unsatisfactory conduct." For a summary see: Diss Abstr Int 36A(5): 2538, November, 1975.

1377 Kent, Ronald N., and O'Leary, K. Daniel. "A controlled evaluation of behavior modification with conduct problem children." J Consult Clin Psychol 44(4): 586-96, August, 1976. (21 References).
Sets forth a comprehensive evaluation of the use of behavioral techniques with elementary school children exhibiting behavior problems. The thirty-two children were also seen at a nine-month follow-up. Although no differences were noted between treated and untreated children at the termination of treatment, the treated children fared better in achievement scores and grades at the nine-month follow-up.

1378 Lahey, Benjamin B.; McNees, M. Patrick; McNees, Margaret C. "Control of an obscene 'verbal tic' through timeout in an elementary school classroom." J Appl Behav Anal 6(1): 101-4, Spring, 1973. (11 References).
Cites the use, by a classroom teacher, of the "massed practice" technique followed by a time-out procedure to reduce the use of an obscene "verbal tic" in a ten-year-old boy.

1379 Lovitt, Thomas C.; Lovitt, Althea O.; Eaton, Marie D.; et al. "The deceleration of inappropriate comments by a natural consequence." J Sch Psychol 11(2): 148-54, Summer, 1973. (5 References).
The inappropriate comments of a nine-year-old boy were brought under control by a ten-year-old "manager" who moved away from the subject to another desk following each inappropriate remark.

1380 McAllister, Loring W.; Stachowiak, James G.; Baer, Donald M.; et al. "The application of operant conditioning techniques in a secondary school classroom." J Appl Behav Anal 2(4): 277-85, Winter, 1969. (13 References). (Reprinted in Item Nos. 27, 28, 37, 43).
Describes the effective use of teacher praise and disapproval in the reduction of inappropriate talking and turning around in a high school class.

1381 McGovern, Lois Maryanne. "The assessment and treatment of behavior problems in the classroom." For a summary see: Diss Abstr Int 36B(12): 6102, June, 1975.

1382 McLaughlin, Thomas, and Malaby, John. "Reducing and measuring inappropriate verbalizations in a token classroom." J Appl Behav Anal 5(3): 329-33, Fall, 1972. (11 References).
Describes a successful program conducted with fifth and sixth grade students. The aim of the program was to reduce inappropriate verbalizations using reinforcers in the natural school setting and using students from within to act as data recorders.

1383 McLaughlin, T. F., and Scott, John W. "The use of response cost to reduce inappropriate behavior in educational settings." Correct Soc Psychiatry J Behav Technol 22(2): 32-34, 1976. (20 References).
Reviews the reported literature and evaluates the effectiveness of response cost programs. Teacher and pupil preferences are noted, together with adverse effects. Recommendations are made for future research.

1384 McNaughton, S. Stuart. "Some implications of a technique designed to produce rapid and generalized modification of out-of-seat behaviour." NZ J Educ Stud 10(2): 120-27, November, 1975. (14 References).
Presents a case report in which the out-of-seat behavior of a nine-year-old boy was controlled within three days. The method used was a points system with a back-up reinforcer of a preferred activity.

1385 Madsen, Charles H.; Becker, Wesley C.; Thomas, Don R.; et al. "An analysis of the reinforcing function of 'sit down' commands." In: Parker, Ronald K., ed. Readings in educational psychology. Boston: Allyn & Bacon, 1968. 265-78. (19 References).
Documents an experiment conducted with forty-eight first-grade children. The purpose of the study was to show that giving disapproval to inappropriate behavior serves to increase that behavior.

1386 Marlowe, Roy Hilding. "A comparison of teacher use of behavior modification and two group counseling techniques in the change of inappropriate classroom behavior of low achieving seventh grade students." For a summary see: Diss Abstr Int 32A(11): 6273, May, 1972.

1387 O'Keefe, Maureen, and Smaby, Marlowe. "Seven techniques for solving classroom discipline problems." High Sch J 56(4): 190-99, January, 1973. (23 References).
Outlines seven behavior modification techniques used successfully by the authors in a high school setting.

1388 Quay, Herbert C.; Sprague, Robert L.; Werry, John S.; et al. "Conditioning visual orientation of conduct problem children in the classroom." J Exp Child Psychol 5(4): 512-17, December, 1967. (8 References).
Five hyperactive, aggressive children were reinforced, by candy and social reinforcement, for looking at the teacher. The results indicated an increase in orienting responses under conditions of combined primary and social reinforcement.

1389 Ross, Joel A., and Levine, Bruce A. "Identification of reinforcement for talking-out in the classroom." Psychol Rep 38(2): 363-67, April, 1976. (6 References).
Tokens were removed when children responded to verbal outbursts directed at them by peers. Such specifically directed verbal behavior decreased in frequency, while verbal outbursts of a more general nature did not.

1390 Schirmer, Gene Jerome. "The use of behavior modification techniques to reduce out of seat behaviors in two regular classrooms." For a summary see: Diss Abstr Int 32A(11): 6223, May, 1972.

1391 Shier, David A. "Applying systematic exclusion to a case of bizarre behavior." In: Krumboltz, John D., and Thoresen, Carl E., eds. Behavioral counseling: cases and techniques. New York: Holt, Rinehart & Winston, 1969. 114-23.
A systematic exclusion from school as a result of deviant behavior in a third-grade boy is described. The program was effective in modifying his classroom behavior, but had little effect on behavior outside the classroom. Drug therapy was also employed toward the end of the school year.

1392 Spencer, Richard J. "An empirical study of elementary teacher's attention as reinforcement for student behavior." Child Study J 3(3): 145-58, 1973. (21 References).
Demonstrates that a teacher's verbal disapproval can function as a positive social reinforcement for inappropriate behavior. It is suggested that a more effective method of behavior change is to give verbal approval to appropriate behavior and ignore the inappropriate behavior.

1393 Valett, Robert E. "A social reinforcement technique for the classroom management of behavior disorders." Except Child 33(3): 185-89, November, 1966. (5 References).
Discusses a model social reinforcement program applicable to both regular and special classrooms. A key element in the program was the maintenance of weekly work and reward records by each student.

1394 Walker, Hill M.; Hops, Hyman; Fiegenbaum, Edward. "Deviant classroom behavior as a function of combinations of social and token reinforcement and cost contingency." Behav Ther 7(1): 76-88, January, 1976. (19 References).
Evaluates a series of program variables in modifying classroom behavior within an experimental class setting. The subjects were children between six and nine years of age. Combinations of variables were less effective in controlling behavior than simultaneous application of all treatment variables.

1395 Webster, Raymond E. "A time-out procedure in a public school setting." Psychol Sch 13(1): 72-76, 1976. (16 References).
Presents a case study which demonstrates the successful use of time-out as the primary therapeutic intervention. The subject was a thirteen-year-old highly aggressive male in a public school setting.

1396 Wilson, Cheryl Wright, and Hopkins, B. L. "The effects of contingent music on the intensity of noise in junior high home economics classes." J Appl Behav Anal 6(2): 269-75, Summer, 1973. (17 References).
Quiet contingent music was used to reduce the noise level in four classes of seventh and eighth-grade girls.

(2) Disruptive Behavior

1397 Ayllon, Teodoro; Garber, Stephen; Pisor, Kim. "The elimination of discipline problems through a combined school-home motivational system." Behav Ther 6(5): 616-26, October, 1975. (12 References).
The classroom behavior of twenty-three students was linked to consequences provided at home by the parents. The procedure was effective in reducing disruptive behavior in the classroom and in maintaining appropriate conduct.

1398 Ayllon, Teodoro, and Roberts, Michael D. "Eliminating discipline problems by strengthening academic performance." J Appl Behav Anal 7(1): 71-76, Spring, 1974. (9 References). (Reprinted in Item No. 35).
Reports on the elimination of disruptive classroom behavior in five fifth-grade boys. The boys received systematic reinforcement of their reading performance.

1399 Barrish, Harriet; Saunders, Muriel; Wolf, Montrose M. "Good Behavior Game: effects of individual contingencies for group consequences on disruptive behavior in a classroom." J Appl Behav Anal 2(2): 119-24, Summer, 1969. (11 References). (Reprinted in Item Nos. 27, 37, 39).
Outlines a technique designed to reduce disruptive classroom behavior. The device was used in a fourth-grade classroom and involved a team game with competition for privileges. The rewards employed were those generally available in classrooms. (See Item No. 1420 for a replication study).

1400 Boardman, William K. "Rusty: a brief behavior disorder." J Consult Psychol 26(4): 293-97, August, 1962.
The application of simple learning theory principles were quickly effective in modifying disruptive behavior in a six-year-old boy. The behavior was of recent origin.

1401 Bolstad, Orin D., and Johnson, Stephen M. "Self-regulation in the modification of disruptive behavior." J Appl Behav Anal 5(4): 443-54, Winter, 1972. (19 References).
Compares the effectiveness of self and externally managed reinforcement systems in first- and second-grade children. Low rates of disruptive behavior were reinforced. Self-regulation procedures were found to be slightly more effective in reducing disruptiveness than were the externally administered procedures.

1402 Bornstein, Philip H.; Hamilton, Scott B.; Quevillo, N. Randall P. "Behavior modification by long-distance: demonstration of functional control over disruptive behavior in a rural classroom setting." Behav Modif 1(3): 369-80, July, 1977. (18 References).
Presents the results of a program of positive practice for out-of-seat classroom behavior in a nine-year-old boy. Since both teacher and pupil lived in an isolated rural area, professional involvement was restricted to a long-distance consultation-type format.

1403 Chan, Adrian; Chiu, Ada; Mueller, Donald J. "An integrated approach to the modification of classroom failure and disruption: a case study." J Sch Psychol 8(2): 114-21, 1970. (17 References).
An eleven-year-old black youth, in a predominantly white elementary school, was successfully treated by a combined behavior modification and counseling approach.

1404 Dietz, Samuel M., and Repp, Alan C. "Decreasing classroom misbehavior through the use of DRL schedules of reinforcement." J Appl Behav Anal 6(3): 457-63, Fall, 1973. (15 References).
Provides the data on three studies that demonstrates the efficacy and manageability of differential reinforcement of low rates of responding (DRL) in reducing disruptive classroom behaviors. One experiment dealt with the talking-out behavior of an eleven-year-old trainable mentally

retarded boy; the second experiment involved the talking-out of an entire class; and the third experiment reduced the off-task verbalizations of fifteen high school girls.

1405 Drabman, Ronald S.; Spitalnik, Robert; O'Leary, K. Daniel. "Teaching self-control to disruptive children." J Abnorm Psychol 82(1): 10-16, August, 1973. (17 References). (Reprinted in Item No. 35).
Reports on a study conducted with eight nine-to-ten-year-old boys experiencing academic and emotional problems. The study attempted to teach accurate self-evaluative behavior, and to evaluate the generalization of improved behavior from the token program situation to other situations. Shaping procedures appeared to be effective and generalization was significant.

1406 Edwards, Clifford Hazen. "Modification of disruptive and nonacademic behaviors of junior high school students in the natural school setting: a token reinforcement program." For a summary see: Diss Abstr Int 29A(8): 2560, February, 1969.

1407 Goodlet, George R.; Goodlet, Margaret M.; Dredge, Karen. "Modification of disruptive behavior of two young children and follow-up one year later." J Sch Psychol 8(1): 60-63, 1970. (6 References).
Praise and attention were used as reinforcers with two children, aged five and seven years. A marked improvement was noted in their behavior.

1408 Greenberg, David J., and O'Donnell, William J. "A note on the effects of group and individual contingencies upon deviant classroom behavior." J Child Psychol Psychiatry 13(1): 55-58, March, 1972. (6 References).
The disruptive behavior of a six-year-old boy was modified by a combination of time-out for tantrum behavior and candy for his entire class as a reward for periods of non-tantrum behavior.

1409 Hackett, Regina. "In praise of praise." Am Educ 11(2): 11-15, March, 1975.
Describes a program, Contingencies for Learning Academic and Social Skills (CLASS), which works within the regular classroom to modify the disruptive behavior of individual children.

1410 Harris, V. William, and Sherman, James A. "Use and analysis of the 'Good Behavior Game' to reduce disruptive classroom behavior." J Appl Behav Anal 6(3): 405-17, Fall, 1973. (13 References).
The use of group contingencies in a team game setting resulted in a reduction of disruptive behavior in two fifth- and sixth-grade classrooms.

1411 Heaton, Ronald C.; Safer, Daniel J.; Allen, Richard P.; et al. "A motivational environment for behaviorally deviant junior high school students." J Abnorm Child Psychol 4(3): 263-75, 1976. (24 References).
A contingency management program, with both school and home-based reinforcers, was successful in reducing negative school behavior in eighth-grade boys who had histories of severe misconduct.

1412 Holms, David S. "The application of learning theory to the treatment of a school behavior problem: a case study." Psychol Sch 3(4): 355-59, October, 1966. (14 References).

Presents a case report on the modification of the disruptive classroom and antisocial behavior of a nine-year-old boy. Since class attention was discerned as the "reward" that he was seeking, this "reward" was withdrawn by paying minimum attention to his outbursts. Attention was, instead, directed to him during periods of good behavior. Following a period of increased disruptions, there was a lessening and eventual elimination of this type of behavior.

1413 Hummel, John H., et al. "Misbehavior in the classroom: a comparison of two reinforcement-based behavior-reducing procedures (DRO and DRL)." Paper presented at the Annual Meeting of the American Educational Research Association, New York, April 4-8, 1977. 11p. (ED 139 513).
Details two experiments which demonstrated the effectiveness of two methods of scheduling reinforcement: differential reinforcement of other behaviors (DRO) and differential reinforcement of low rates of responding (DRL). The target behaviors were classroom misbehavior of various kinds.

1414 Keelin, Peter W. "Case analysis: consultation and counseling, the case of Michael." Elem Sch Guid Couns 7(3): 231-33, March, 1973.
A time-out procedure was successfully used to modify the disruptive behavior of a second-grade boy. The procedures involved approximately ten hours of consultation as well as additional hours of observation, planning, and parent counseling.

1415 Kubany, Edward S.; Weiss, Leslie, E.; Sloggett, Barbara B. "The good behavior clock: a reinforcement/time out procedure for reducing disruptive classroom behavior." J Behav Ther Exp Psychiatry 2(3): 173-79, September, 1971. (8 References).
Documents a study conducted with a first-grade boy whose deviant behavior was brought under control by means of a clock which recorded his good behavior. The good behavior earned treats for himself and his peers.

1416 Lobitz, W. Charles. "A simple stimulus cue for controlling disruptive classroom behavior. Methodological implications for behavior change procedures." J Abnorm Child Psychol 2(2): 143-52, June, 1974. (13 References).
A red light, which had no specific consequences, was used to reduce talking-out and out-of-seat behavior in two elementary classrooms.

1417 McNamara, J. Regis. "Teacher and students as sources for behavior modification in the classroom." Behav Ther 2(2): 205-13, April, 1971. (11 References).
Examines the methods of controlling the teacher's attention-dispensing behavior. It was found necessary to introduce punishment to bring disruptive student behavior under control.

1418 MacPherson, Evelyn M.; Candee, Benjamin L.; Hohman, Robert J. "A comparison of three methods for eliminating disruptive lunchroom behavior." J Appl Behav Anal 7(2): 287-97, Summer, 1974. (15 References).
Presents the findings of a comparison study which reveal that the use of behavior modification procedures plus the copying of a "meditation essay" was an effective technique in reducing disruptive behavior. The technique was found to be more effective than either behavior modification procedures used alone or behavior modification procedures used with a

"punishment essay." The subjects were fourth and fifth graders who were exhibiting disruptive behavior in a lunchroom.

1419 Madsen, Charles H.; Becker, Wesley C.; Thomas, Don R. "Rules, praise and ignoring: elements of elementary classroom control." J Appl Behav Anal 1(2): 139-50, Summer, 1968. (6 References). (Reprinted in Item Nos. 28, 29, 39, 40, 46).
Offers confirmation of the hypotheses that rules alone exert little effect on classroom behavior and that the ignoring of disruptive behavior and showing approval of appropriate behavior are the most effective means of classroom control. The study cited involved three elementary school children, two in one classroom and one in another. The report contains behavior coding categories for both children and teachers.

1420 Medland, M. B., and Stachnik, T. J. Good Behavior Game: a replication and systematic analysis." J Appl Behav Anal 5(1): 45-51, Spring, 1972. (12 References).
Evaluates the efficacy of the Good Behavior Game (See Item No. 1399) in controlling disruptive behaviors in two reading groups of fifth-grade children. The evaluations were carried out in both independent study and teacher-directed lessons.

1421 Meyers, Joel. "Consultee-centered consultation with a teacher as a technique in behavior management." Am J Community Psychol 3(2): 111-21, June, 1975. (12 References).
The consultation technique was effective in helping a teacher to decrease one child's disruptive behavior and improve classroom control generally.

1422 Mitchell, Dewayne W., and Crowell, Phyllis J. "Modifying inappropriate behavior in an elementary art class." Elem Sch Guid Couns 8(1): 34-42, October, 1973. (7 References).
A technique of "praise and ignore" was used successfully with three nine-year-old boys to modify their disruptive behavior. Guidelines for establishing similar programs of modification are presented.

1423 Muller, Adler J.; Hasazi, Susan E.; Pierce, Mary M.; et al. "Modification of disruptive behavior in a large group of elementary school students." In: Ramp, Eugene, and Semb, George, eds. Behavior analysis: areas of research and application. Englewood Cliffs, New Jersey: Prentice-Hall, 1975. 269-76.
Relates the findings of a study conducted with 455 elementary school children. The study investigated the modification of noise and disruptive behavior in such settings as the school cafeteria and auditorium.

1424 O'Leary, K. Daniel, and Becker, Wesley C. "The effects of the intensity of a teacher's reprimands on children's behavior." J Sch Psychol 7(1): 8-11, 1968. (5 References).
Analyzes the disruptive behavior of first-grade children and relates the findings to experimentally controlled variations in the teacher's responses. Loud reprimands increased disruptive behavior, while a combination of ignoring disruptions and praising appropriate behavior resulted in a reduction of the disruptive behavior.

1425 O'Leary, K. Daniel; Drabman, Ronald S.; Kass, Ruth E. "Maintenance of appropriate behavior in a token program." J Abnorm Child Psychol 1(2): 127-38, 1973. (18 References).

A token program, using free-time in an activity area as a reward, was effective in reducing disruptive behavior in three classrooms. Reasons for the maintenance of the low rate of disruptions in one of the classrooms are discussed.

1426 O'Leary, K. Daniel; Kaufman, Kenneth F.; Kass, Ruth E.; et al. "The effects of loud and soft reprimands on the behavior of disruptive students." Except Child 37(2): 145-55, October, 1970. (9 References). (Reprinted in Items Nos. 25, 37).

In a study with two disruptive second-grade boys, the mean level of disruptive behavior was consistently higher when loud reprimands were used.

1427 Patterson, Gerald R.; Shaw, David A.; Ebner, Michael J. "Teachers, peers, and parents as agents of change in the classroom." In: Benson, F. Arthur M., ed. Modifying deviant social behaviors in various classroom settings. Eugene, Oregon: University of Oregon, Department of Special Education, College of Education, 1969. 13-47. (60 References).

Presents a detailed description of a set of procedures designed to modify hyperactive and disruptive behavior. The techniques may be employed without removing the child from the classroom and involve the teacher, the peer group, and the parents in the change process.

1428 Pratt, Teressa Marjorie. "A positive approach to disruptive behavior." Todays Educ 64(2): 60-62, March-April, 1975.

Briefly reports on the use of contingency management techniques with a group of ten intermediate grade boys.

1429 Pyle, Patricia L. "Behaviour modification." Nurs Times 71(17): 665-67, April 24, 1975.

Describes the use of social and nonsocial reinforcers in the modification of the disruptive behavior of a ten-year-old boy.

1430 Ramp, Eugene; Ulrich, Roger; Dulaney, Sylvia. "Delayed timeout as a procedure for reducing disruptive classroom behavior: a case study." J Appl Behav Anal 4(3): 235-39, Fall, 1971. (2 References).

A nine-year-old boy's disruptive classroom behavior was reduced by the use of a time-out procedure. A loss of free time later in the day was signalled by a light on the boy's desk.

1431 Rosen, Dennis C., and Piper, Terrence J. "Individualized instruction with and without a token economy in a class for disruptors." Educ Train Ment Retarded 7(1): 22-25, February, 1972.

Reports on the use of an inexpensive token economy with disruptive junior high school boys.

1432 Ryan, Robert Gordon. "An evaluation of a program for the modification of disruptive student behavior." For a summary see: Diss Abstr Int 36A(11): 7309, May, 1976.

1433 Sachs, Patricia. "The use of behavior modification techniques in an urban classroom." In: Winters, Stanley A., and Cox, Eunice, eds. Behavior modification techniques for the special educator. New York: MSS Information Corporation, 1972. 35-41.

Behavioral techniques were used to modify the disruptive behavior and improve the learning habits of eight boys, aged seven to twelve years. The program took place in a special education class.

1434 Santsaver, H. E. "Behavior modification paired with TA." Trans Anal J 5(2): 137-38, April, 1975. (4 References).
Contracts were used to reduce disruptive behavior in twenty-one grade school children. A back-up points system was used with points awarded for the successful completion of a contract. It was felt that by focusing on internal "OK feelings" as self-reinforcers, a dependence on points might be avoided.

1435 Siggers, Walter Woodward. "Intervention in an elementary school with aversive and positive contingencies: the effect upon disruption and teacher correcting behavior." For a summary see: Diss Abstr Int 37A(7): 4246, January, 1976.

1436 Solomon, Robert W., and Wahler, Robert G. "Peer reinforcement control of classroom problem behavior." J Appl Behav Anal 6(1): 49-56, Spring, 1973. (12 References).
The peers of five disruptive sixth-grade boys were found to be attentive almost exclusively to the deviant behavior. By the use of control peers, less attention was paid to the deviant behavior which subsequently lessened.

1437 Thomas, Don R.; Becker, Wesley C.; Armstrong, Marianne. "Production and elimination of disruptive classroom behavior by systematically varying teacher's behavior." J Appl Behav Anal 1(1): 35-45, Spring, 1968. (8 References). (Reprinted in Item Nos. 38, 40).
Emphasizes the role of the teacher in producing, maintaining, and eliminating disruptive behavior, as well as pro-social classroom behavior. In this study, conducted with a class of twenty-eight middle-primary level students, approving teacher responses served a positive reinforcing function in maintaining appropriate behavior. Disruptive behaviors increased each time approving teacher responses were withdrawn.

1438 Thomas, Don R.; Nielsen, Loretta J.; Kuypers, David S.; et al. "Social reinforcement and remedial instruction in the elimination of a classroom behavior problem." J Spec Educ 2(3): 291-305, Spring, 1968. (4 References).
Presents a case report of a six-year-old boy whose disruptive behavior was brought under control and whose academic performance improved following the institution of a combined program of social reinforcement and remedial tutoring.

1439 Walker, Hill M.; Mattson, Robert H.; Buckley, Nancy K. "Special class placement as a treatment alternative for deviant behavior in children." In: Benson, F. Arthur M., ed. Modifying deviant social behaviors in various classroom settings. Eugene, Oregon: University of Oregon, Department of Special Education, College of Education, 1969. 49-80. (40 References).
Describes the development and evaluation of a treatment model designed to modify disruptive classroom behavior by establishing a token culture classroom. The problems of producing generalization of effects when the child is returned to his own classroom are also discussed.

1440 Ward, J. "Modification of deviant classroom behaviour." Br J Educ Psychol 41(3): 304-13, November, 1971. (13 References).
Documents three case studies of elementary school children exhibiting disruptive behavior. In the two cases where the teachers were able to apply reinforcement techniques consistently, a marked improvement in behavior was noted.

1441 Ward, Michael H., and Baker, Bruce L. "Reinforcement therapy in the classroom." J Appl Behav Anal 1(4): 323-28, Winter, 1968. (12 References). (Reprinted in Item Nos. 22, 28, 39).
Reports on the systematic use of attention and praise by the teacher to reduce the disruptive behavior of four first-grade children. No adverse changes in the target children or the rest of the class were noted.

1442 Whitley, A. Dan, and Sulzer, Beth. "Reducing disruptive behavior through consultation." Pers Guid J 48(10): 836-41, June, 1970. (19 References).
The disruptive classroom behavior of a nine-year-old boy was brought under control by the teacher's use of positive reinforcement for nondisruptive behavior.

c. Development of Specific Behaviors

(1) Academic Behavior

1443 Academic and social behavior change in a public school setting: PICA final report: project year four. Silver Springs, Maryland: Educational Facility Press, 1974. 125p.
Presents a detailed report of a four-year contingency management program directed particularly to junior high school students with scholastic problems that were part of larger behavior patterns. Objectives were developed in four areas of interest: (1) student academic learning; (2) student interpersonal learning; (3) family interaction learning; and (4) public school personnel training.

1444 Atkinson, Donald R.; Davis, Jerry L.; Sanborn, Marshall P. "Behavioral techniques: effective with superior high school students?" Sch Couns 19(4): 254-60, March, 1972. (10 References).
Relates the details of a study conducted with seventy-one superior high school seniors. The results indicated that verbal reinforcers were effective in increasing the number of questions students asked professors during information-seeking interviews.

1445 Bogue, Carole Jo Hoffman. "The effect of a token system on reading achievement and attitude toward reading." For a summary see: Diss Abstr Int 36A(8): 5193, February, 1976.

1446 Brigham, Thomas A.; Graubard, Paul S.; Stans, Aileen. "Analysis of the effects of sequential reinforcement contingencies on aspects of composition." J Appl Behav Anal 5(4): 421-29, Winter, 1972. (7 References).
A point system, with points redeemable for privileges within the classroom, was used in a fifth-grade remedial classroom. The target behavior was composition writing and, among the results noted, were an increase in the length of the compositions and an improvement in quality.

1447 Brooks, Robert B., and Snow, David L. "Two case illustrations of the use of behavior-modification techniques in the school setting." Behav Ther 3(1): 100-103, January, 1972. (1 Reference).
Offers two case histories illustrating different behavior modification techniques. The first example demonstrates the use of positive reinforcement to increase the academic performance of a low-achieving boy. The second case documents the use of a group contingency to modify deviant behavior in a fourth-grade student.

1448 Brophy, Jere E., and Good, Thomas L. "Teachers' communications of differential expectations for children's classroom performance: some behavioral data." J Educ Psychol 61(5): 365-74, October, 1970. (12 References).
Deals with a study conducted in four first-grade classrooms. It was demonstrated that the teachers expected more and gave more encouragement to those children for whom they had higher academic expectations.

1449 Brown, Joe H. "The differential effects of monitoring procedures on achievement behavior." J Educ Res 68(8): 318, April, 1975. (5 References).
Suggests that peer and self-monitored contingency managed programs were more effective than teacher-monitored programs. The study was conducted with forty-eight sixth-grade children.

1450 Camp, Bonnie W., and Van Doorninck, William J. "Assessment of 'motivated' reading therapy with elementary school children." Behav Ther 2(2): 214-22, April, 1971. (12 References).
Evaluates a reading therapy program conducted with third- to sixth-grade children. Nonprofessional aides were used as tutors, and tokens (exchangeable for money) were awarded for successful reading.

1451 Chadwick, Bruce, and Day, Robert C. "Systematic reinforcement: academic performance of underachieving students." J Appl Behav Anal 4(4): 311-19, Winter, 1971. (12 References).
Tangible and social reinforcers were used to increase work-time, rate of output, and accuracy in twenty-five underachieving students. The higher levels of performance were maintained following the removal of the tangible reinforcers.

1452 Cheuvront, Herbert Leroy. "Use of behavior modification concepts with adolescent underachievers to improve school achievement through attitude change." For a summary see: Diss Abstr Int 36B(4): 1940, October, 1975.

1453 Fauke, Joyce; Burnett, Joseph; Powers, Mary Ann; et al. "Improvement of handwriting and letter recognition skills: a behavior modification procedure." J Learn Disabil 6(5): 296-300, May, 1973. (11 References).
Primary and social reinforcers were used, together with several instructional procedures, to improve the letter identification and handwriting skills of a six-year-old boy. The improvement took place over a three-week period.

1454 Ferritor, D. E., Buckholdt, D.; Hamblin, R. L.; et al. "The non-effects of contingent reinforcement for attending behavior on work accomplished." J Appl Behav Anal 5(1): 7-17, Spring, 1972. (14 References).
Investigates the relationship between the elimination of disruptive behavior and academic performance in an inner-city third-grade classroom. Emphasis is placed on the importance of designing specific contingencies for specific target behaviors.

1455 Fisher, Robert. "An investigation of self-reinforcement behavior and locus of control of achieving readers and two types of mildly underachieving readers." For a summary see: Diss Abstr Int 38A(4): 1995, October, 1977.

1456 Flexibrod, Jeffrey J., and O'Leary, K. Daniel. "Effects of reinforcement on children's academic behavior as a function of self-determined and externally imposed contingencies." J Appl Behav Anal 6(2): 241-50, Summer, 1973. (6 References).
Demonstrates the effectiveness of contingent reinforcement when performance standards were self-determined. Over a period of six sessions the twelve second-grade subjects became progressively more lenient in their self-imposed demands.

1457 Glynn, E. L. "Classroom applications of self-determined reinforcement." J Appl Behav Anal 3(2): 123-32, Summer, 1970. (13 References).
Compares self-determined, experimenter-determined, chance-determined token reinforcement and no-token treatment. The target behavior was the learning of history and geography in ninth-grade girls. Self-determined and experimenter-determined token procedures were found to be superior to the other methods.

1458 Gray, Burl B.; Baker, Richard D.; Stancyk, Susan E. "Performance Determined Instruction for training in remedial reading." J Appl Behav Anal 2(4): 255-63, Winter, 1969. (14 References).
Outlines a methodological tactic for training in remedial reading called Performance Determined Instruction (PDI). The system incorporates aspects of binary logic, instrumental conditioning, and programmed instruction.

1459 Greer, R. Douglas. "Behavioral psychology in first chair." Teach Coll Rec 77(1): 123-27, September, 1975. (14 References).
Advocates the incorporation of elements of positive reinforcement into a program of music education.

1460 Hall, R. Vance; Lund, Diane; Jackson, Deloris. "Effects of teacher attention on study behavior." J Appl Behav Anal 1(1): 1-12, Spring, 1968. (8 References). (Reprinted in Item Nos. 21, 32).
Reports on the successful increase of study behavior in one first-grade pupil and five third-grade pupils, all of whom had high rates of disruptive or dawdling behaviors. Reinforcement for desirable behavior was provided by increased teacher attention. Follow-up indicated a continuance of the improved performance.

1461 Hanley, Edward M. "Review of research involving applied behavior analysis in the classroom." Rev Educ Res 40(5): 597-625, December, 1970. (64 References).
Surveys and evaluates the published research on the use of applied behavioral analysis in various classroom settings. The emphasis is on academic behaviors, but nonacademic behaviors are also included.

1462 Harris, Cleveland J. "Social reinforcement to increase the utilization of library books by sixth grade pupils." Paper presented at the Annual Meeting of the Mid-South Educational Research Association, Jackson, Mississippi, November 12-14, 1975. 10p. (5 References). (ED 117 689).
Praise by the librarian was used to increase the number of books checked out and to encourage the proper care and prompt return of the books.

1463 Harris, V. William, and Sherman, James A. "Effects of peer tutoring and consequences on the math performance of elementary classroom students." J Appl Behav Anal 6(4): 587-97, Winter, 1973. (12 References).

Evaluates the effects of unstructured peer-tutoring on the math behavior of fourth- and fifth-grade students. The use of consequences for accurate performance seemed to enhance the effects of tutoring.

1464 Hasazi, Joseph E., and Hasazi, Susan E. "Effects of teacher attention on digit-reversal behavior in an elementary school child." J Appl Behav Anal 5(2): 157-62, Summer, 1972. (6 References).
Describes the successful use of praise and attention by the teacher to reinforce correct responses from an eight-year-old boy who demonstrated habitual digit-reversal.

1465 Hawkins, James Lester. "A comparison of the effects of two types of reinforcement techniques on academic and non-academic classroom behaviors of underachieving elementary students." For a summary see: Diss Abstr Int 35B(5): 2404, November, 1974.

1466 Heitzman, Andrew J. "Effects of a token reinforcement system on the reading and arithmetic skills learning of migrant primary school pupils." J Educ Res 63(10): 455-58, July-August, 1970. (6 References).
A token reinforcement system, using candy, toys, and trinkets as back-ups, was effective in improving arithmetic and reading skills in a group of migrant primary school students. The program was conducted throughout a six-week summer school session.

1467 ———. "Effects of a token reinforcement system on the reading behavior of black migrant primary school pupils." J Educ Res 67(7): 299-302, March, 1974. (16 References).
Positive effects accrued from the use of a token reinforcement system in a summer school reading program. Varying effects were noted on the learning of black and white students.

1468 Hopkins, B. L.; Schutte, R. C.; Garton, Kathleen L. "The effects of access to a playroom on the rate and quality of printing and writing of first- and second-grade students." J Appl Behav Anal 4(2): 77-87, Summer, 1971. (9 References).
Documents a study conducted with fourteen first- and second-grade students. The children were allowed to go to a playroom when they had completed their writing or printing assignments instead of waiting for the rest of the class to finish. The results indicated an increase in the rate of writing and printing.

1469 Hops, Hyman, and Cobb, Joseph A. "Survival behaviors in the educational setting: their implications for research and intervention." In: Hamerlynck, Leo A.; Handy, Lee C.; Mash, Eric J., eds. Behavior change: methodology, concepts, and practice. Banff International Conference on Behavior Modification, 4th, 1972. Champaign, Illinois: Research Press, 1974. 193-208. (45 References).
Illustrates the use of an empirical model to investigate the possible causal relationship between specific academic survival skills and reading achievement in a regular first-grade classroom. The results confirmed the main hypothesis and indicated that first-grade teachers can be trained to increase the students' survival skills so that reading achievement can be enhanced.

1470 Hundert, Joel; Bucher, Bradley; Henderson, Michael. "Increasing appropriate classroom behaviour and academic performance by

reinforcing correct work alone." Psychol Sch 13(2): 194-200, April, 1976. (7 References).
Furnishes details on a study conducted with five disruptive elementary school boys. Reinforcement of arithmetic performance not only increased correct work, but also resulted in a high rate of appropriate behavior.

1471 Kirby, Frank D., and Shields, Frank. "Modification of arithmetic response rate and attending behavior in a seventh-grade student." J Appl Behav Anal 5(1): 79-84, Spring, 1972. (6 References). (Reprinted in Item No. 28).
The use of an adjusting fixed-ratio schedule of praise and immediate correctness feedback produced an increase in the arithmetic response rate of a seventh-grade student. A collateral effect of an increase in attending behavior was also noted.

1472 Lahey, Benjamin B., and Drabman, Ronald S. "Facilitation of the acquisition and retention of sight-word vocabulary through token reinforcement." J Appl Behav Anal 7(2): 307-12, Summer, 1974. (13 References).
Presents the findings of a study conducted with two groups of second-grade children. The group receiving verbal consequences plus token reinforcement acquired and retained a sight-word vocabulary more successfully than did the group receiving only verbal consequences.

1473 Lahey, Benjamin B.; McNees, Michael P.; Brown, Cathy C. "Modification of deficits in reading for comprehension." J Appl Behav Anal 6(3): 475-80, Fall, 1973. (11 References).
Cites an attempt to improve reading comprehension in two six-grade students. Praise and pennies were used to reward correct answers. The percentage of correct answers increased to approximately the same level as other children at the same grade level.

1474 Langford, Ken, and Johnson, Terry D. "Behavior modification and beginning reading." Acad Ther 10(1): 53-63, Fall, 1974. (12 References).
Outlines a tutorial procedure based on behavioral principles for teaching beginning reading. Emphasis is placed on constant feedback. Two case histories are included.

1475 Levenkron, Jeffrey; Santogrossi, David A.; O'Leary, Daniel. "Increasing academic performance through contingent access to tutoring." Psychol Sch 11(2): 201-7, April, 1974. (19 References).
Focuses on a program which uses individualized tutoring as a naturally available reinforcer. It is pointed out, however, that when tutoring is made contingent upon poor academic achievement, it may inadvertently encourage "helpless" behavior.

1476 Lovitt, Thomas C.; Guppy, Tal E.; Blattner, James E. "The use of a free-time contingency with fourth graders to increase spelling accuracy." Behav Res Ther 7(2): 151-56, May, 1969.
Records the results of a comparison study, conducted with thirty-two fourth-grade students, to assess spelling performance as a function of three conditions. Group I functioned under traditional procedures; Group II earned free time on an individual basis; Group III operated under a group contingency with radio-listening added to the individually earned free time. The results indicated that the use of contingent free time and radio-listening were effective reinforcers.

1477 McKerracher, D. W. "Alleviation of reading difficulties by a simple operant conditioning technique." J Child Psychol Psychiatry 8(1): 51-56, May, 1967. (9 References). (Reprinted in Item No. 21).
Presents a case report on the use of an operant conditioning technique employing both reward conditioning and avoidance conditioning. The subject was an eight-year-old boy experiencing reading difficulties. An almost immediate improvement was noted after the institution of the conditioning program, although the boy had failed to respond to three months of remedial teaching and supportive therapy in a child guidance clinic.

1478 McLaughlin, Rodney Eugene. "Behaviorially oriented techniques for the remediation of academic underachievers in high potential intermediate school students." For a summary see: Diss Abstr Int 37A(11): 7046, May, 1976.

1479 Madsen, Clifford K. "How reinforcement techniques work." Music Educ J 57(8): 38-41, April, 1971.
Looks at both the use of music to reinforce nonmusical behaviors and the use of behavioral principles in the reinforcement of specific musical experiences.

1480 Madsen, Clifford K., and Forsythe, Jere L. "Effect of contingent music listening on increases of mathematical responses." J Res Music Educ 21(2): 176-81, Summer, 1973. (9 References).
Investigates, with sixth-grade students, the effect of earned music listening. Further examination of several variables is indicated.

1481 Madsen, Clifford K.; Greer, R. Douglas; Madsen, H., Jr. Research in music behavior: modifying music behavior in the classroom. New York: Teachers College Press, 1975. 277p. (Bibliography).
This text deals with contingent music used as reinforcement and the use of behavioral techniques in music instruction. An annotated bibliography is included.

1482 Noffsinger, Thomas. "The effects of reward and level of aspiration on students with deviant behavior." Except Child 37(5): 355-64, January, 1971. (22 References).
Covers a study conducted with forty-five junior high school students classified, by a behavior problem checklist, as potential dropouts. The results suggest that setting a high level of aspiration had a significantly positive effect.

1483 Rickard, Henry C.; Clements, Carl B.; Willis, Jerry W. "Effects of contingent and noncontingent token reinforcement upon classroom performance." Psychol Rep 27(3): 903-8, December, 1970. (5 References).
Five boys attending a therapeutic summer camp were awarded tokens contingent upon classroom productivity. The program was judged successful in producing increased work levels.

1484 Roets, Lois F. "Behavior modification program for first graders to improve study skills and habits in relation to reading." Paper presented at the Annual Meeting of the American Educational Research Association, New York, April, 1977. 24p. (ED 142 951).
Describes the successful use of a reinforcement program with twenty-two first graders to increase the on-task performance during reading periods.

1485 Rollins, Howard A.; McCandless, Boyd R.; Thompson, Marion; et al. "Project Success Environment: an extended application of contingency management in inner-city schools." J Educ Psychol 66(2): 167-78, April, 1974. (24 References).
Positive behavior contingencies were used for one academic year by sixteen teachers in inner-city schools. Significant academic and behavioral achievements were noted during the year.

1486 Rosen, Paul Michael. "The effects of reasons and positive reinforcement on the maintenance of academic behavior." For a summary see: Diss Abstr Int 38A(5): 2730, November, 1977.

1487 Rosenfeld, George Walker. "Some effects of reinforcement on achievement and behavior in a regular classroom." J Educ Psychol 63(3): 189-93, June, 1972. (7 References).
Reports on a study on the passing of arithmetic tests by sixty sixth-grade students. A comparison was made between those students receiving chart reinforcement, those receiving monetary reinforcement, and those receiving both chart and monetary reinforcement. It was found that the results differed according to I.Q. level, leading to the conclusion that the addition of reinforcement results in improved performance for many students, but that improvement was positively related to I.Q.

1488 Ross, James Michael. "The effect of free-time contingency on arithmetic and problem behavior in the classroom." For a summary see: Diss Abstr Int 37B(6): 3093, December, 1976.

1489 Sloggett, Barbara B. "Use of group activities and team rewards to increase individual classroom productivity." Teach Except Child 3(1): 54-66, Fall, 1971. (22 References).
Describes the use of a token system to reward group rather than individual effort in order to promote academic achievement. The subjects were low-achieving adolescent boys.

1490 Taffel, Suzanne Johnson; O'Leary, K. Daniel; Armel, Sandra. "Reasoning and praise: their effects on academic behavior." J Educ Psychol 66(3): 291-95, June, 1974. (11 References).
Verbalizing reasons for studying arithmetic was as effective or more effective than praising second-grade children for maintaining arithmetic task behavior.

1491 Walker, Hill M., and Buckley, Nancy K. "Effects of reinforcement, punishment, and feedback upon academic response rate." Psychol Sch 9(2): 186-93, April, 1972. (31 References).
Evaluates the effects, on academic response rate, of various combinations of positive reinforcement, feedback, and punishment. The subjects were two behaviorally disruptive children.

1492 Walker, Hill M., and Hops, Hyman. "Increasing academic achievement by reinforcing direct academic performance and/or facilitative nonacademic responses." J Educ Psychol 68(2): 218-25, April, 1976. (18 References).
Compares the effects of three intervention procedures with groups of primary-grade children. Some received treatment in an experimental class setting while others were treated within the regular classroom. No significant differences were found between the groups.

1493 Whitlock, Carolyn, and Bushell, Don, Jr. "Some effects of 'back-up' reinforcers on reading behavior." J Exp Child Psychol 5(1): 50-57, March, 1967. (12 References).
In a study conducted with a six-year-old girl, classified as a "slow reader," a greater increase in reading rate was noted when counters were used with back-up reinforcers rather than when counters were used alone.

1494 Yarbrough, Cornelia; Charboneau, Margaret; Wapnick, Joel. "Music as reinforcement for correct math and attending in ability assigned math classes." J Music Ther 14(2): 77-88, Summer, 1977. (13 References).
Contingent access to music listening was found to reinforce attentiveness and correct math problem solving. The subjects were divided into three ability groups. The low ability group was found to be more responsive to the reinforcement than either of the other two groups.

(2) Attending Behavior

1495 Cossairt, Ace; Hall, R. Vance; Hopkins, B. L. "The effects of experimenter's instructions, feedback, and praise on teacher praise and student attending behavior." J Appl Behav Anal 6(1): 89-100, Spring, 1973. (11 References).
Examines the causal factors in increasing teacher praise by measuring and recording behaviors of all concerned, including teachers, the students, and the experimenters.

1496 Crandall, Judith Ann. "Control of off-task behavior by pacing and reinforcement." For a summary see: Diss Abstr Int 36A(4): 2095, October, 1975.

1497 Jamarillo, Patricio Thomas. "The use of reinforcement techniques by elementary school students to increase teacher attending behavior." For a summary see: Diss Abstr Int 36A(1): 131, July, 1975.

1498 Kennedy, Daniel A., and Thompson, Ina. "Use of reinforcement technique with a first grade boy." Pers Guid J 46(4): 366-70, December, 1967. (13 References).
The attending and assignment completion behaviors of a six-year-old boy were improved by the use of candy reinforcers.

1499 Walker, Hill M., and Buckley, Nancy K. "The use of positive reinforcement in conditioning attending behavior." J Appl Behav Anal 1(3): 245-50, Fall, 1968. (10 References). (Reprinted in Item No. 38).
Reports on the successful modification of the attending behavior of a nine-year-old underachieving boy. His behavior was improved by a token system in a controlled setting and was then generalized to the classroom situation.

1500 Willis, Jerry, and Crowder, Jeane. "A portable device for group modification of classroom attending behavior." J Appl Behav Anal 5(2): 199-202, Summer, 1972. (4 References).
Describes an inexpensive, portable signalling device which was adapted from a wireless switch and used successfully in a classroom to increase student attention.

(3) Creativity

1501 Chambers, Kathy; Goldman, Laurie; Kovesdy, Peter. "Effect of positive reinforcement on creativity." Percept Mot Skills 44(1): 322, February, 1977.
Documents a study conducted with twenty children on the effects of immediate, nondirective verbal reinforcement on the number of novel block-building configurations. The subjects were six to eight years of age. Verbal reinforcement appeared to enhance diversity.

1502 Glover, John A., and Gary, Albert L. Behavior modification: enhancing creativity and other good behaviors. Pacific Grove, California: Boxwood Press, 1975. 135p. (Bibliography).
Introduces the theory and practice of behavior modification and is intended for parents and teachers without an extensive background in psychology. Emphasis is placed on the promotion of good behaviors rather than on the suppression of inappropriate behaviors.

1503 ————. "Procedures to increase some aspects of creativity." J Appl Behav Anal 9(1): 79-84, Spring, 1976. (13 References).
Instructions, reinforcement, and practice were applied to four behaviorally defined creative behaviors. The subjects were eight fourth- and fifth-grade students. Increases were noted in each of the four behaviors.

1504 Henson, Ferris Owen, II. "A preliminary investigation into the effects of token reinforcement on one aspect of creativity: as measured by the Wallach-Kogan creativity test." For a summary see: Diss Abstr Int 35B(8): 4145, April, 1974.

1505 Hutchison, Bruce Delbert. "A comparison of instructions and social reinforcement as related to 'creativity' in children's drawings." For a summary see: Diss Abstr Int 34B(6): 2899, December, 1973.

1506 Maloney, Karen Blase, and Hopkins, B. L. "The modification of sentence structure and its relationship to subjective judgements of creativity in writing." J Appl Behav Anal 6(3): 425-33, Fall, 1973. (14 References). (Reprinted in Item No. 35).
Relates an attempt to define and manipulate some compositional variables in stories written by fourth-, fifth-, and sixth-grade children and to relate these operationally defined variables to subjective ratings of creativity.

1507 Milgram, Roberta M., and Feingold, Sarah. "Concrete and verbal reinforcement in creative thinking of disadvantaged children." Percept Mot Skills 45(2): 675-78, October, 1977. (7 References).
Documents an investigation conducted with ninety disadvantaged seventh-grade Israeli children. Both concrete and verbal incentives enhanced creative thinking, but concrete reinforcement--in the form of candy--was more effective than verbal reinforcement.

1508 Peterson, Nancy Laraine. "Behavior modification technology: its application to the development of creativity in elementary school children." For a summary see: Diss Abstr Int 30A(9): 3861, March, 1970.

(4) Social Interactions

1509 Adams, Gerald R. "Classroom aggression: determinants, controlling mechanisms, and guidelines for the implementation of a behavior modification program." Psychol Sch 10(2): 155-68, April, 1973. (42 References).
Reviews the literature on causes and various methods of control of aggression. Those methods examined include stimulus control, punishment, and induction. The use of behavioral methods is advocated, and outlines of the methods of setting up such a program are given.

1510 Arwood, Barbara; Williams, Robert L.; Long, James D. "The effects of behavior contracts and behavior proclamations on social conduct and academic achievement in a ninth grade English class." Adolescence 9(35): 425-36, Fall, 1974. (6 References).
Provides the details of a study conducted with twenty-eight ninth-grade students. Indications are that contracting produced a greater improvement in classroom behavior and academic performance than did behavior proclamation.

1511 Azrin, Nathan H., and Lindsley, Ogden R. "The reinforcement of cooperation between children." J Abnorm Soc Psychol 52(1): 100-102, January, 1956. (4 References). (Reprinted in Item Nos. 23, 25, 27, 45).
Describes the use of edible reinforcers to foster cooperation between two game players. No instructions were given that would encourage or discourage cooperation but the reinforcement was dependent upon evidence of it.

1512 Barclay, James R. "Effecting behavior change in the elementary classroom: an exploratory study." J Couns Psychol 14(3): 240-47, 1967. (16 References).
Presents the findings of a comparison study conducted with three fifth-grade classrooms. The aim was to increase social acceptance of minimally accepted students. Differential treatments included planned interventions, selective reinforcement, and a change of teacher.

1513 Clement, Paul W.; Fazzone, Roger A.; Goldstein, Bertram. "Tangible reinforcers and child group therapy." J Am Acad Child Psychiatry 9(3): 409-27, July, 1970. (31 References).
Token reinforcement for social approach behaviors were used successfully with second- and third-grade shy and withdrawn boys.

1514 Fleischman, Diane Hernandez, et al. "Increasing interactive behavior of withdrawn children in the regular classroom." Paper presented at the 84th Annual Convention of the American Psychological Association, Washington, D.C., September 3-7, 1976. 18p. (ED 143 446).
A series of four studies examined the effects of both antecedent and consequent events on the social interactions of four primary grade withdrawn children. The results indicated that joint task procedure was the most effective method in a classroom setting, and individual reinforcement with a group back-up was most effective during recess.

1515 Hauserman, Norma; Walen, Susan R.; Behling, Maxine. "Reinforced racial integration in the first grade: a study in generalization." J Appl Behav Anal 6(2): 193-200, Summer, 1973. (15 References).

Reports on the use of reinforcement techniques, with tokens exchangeable for edibles, to promote "sitting with a new friend" in the school cafeteria. The results indicated a significant generalization to integrated free play.

1516 McClain, W. A. "The modification of aggressive classroom behavior through reinforcement, inhibition and relationship therapy." Train Sch Bull 65(4): 122-25, February, 1969.
The aggressive classroom behavior of a ten-year-old boy was modified by an individualized program conducted by a classroom teacher and a behavior therapist.

1517 Meyer, Mary E., and Berg-Cross, Linda. "Helping the withdrawn child." Theory Pract 15(5): 332-36, December, 1976. (2 References).
Outlines several strategies, including positive reinforcement, to enable the teacher to deal with the shy or withdrawn child within the classroom setting.

1518 Patterson, G. R.; Cobb, J. A.; Ray, R. S. "Director intervention in the classroom: a set of procedures for the aggressive child." In: Clark, F. W.; Evans, D. R.; Hamerlynck, L. A., eds. Implementing behavioral programs for schools and clinics. Banff International Conference on Behavior Modification, 3rd, 1971. Champaign, Illinois: Research Press, 1972. 151-201. (78 References).
Demonstrates the successful direct intervention approach in the modification of the hyperaggressive behavior of eleven boys in elementary classrooms.

1519 Thomas, Carroll Ray. "Systematic desensitization as a self-control technique for developing socially relevant behavior in children." For a summary see: Diss Abstr Int 38B(3): 1425, September, 1977.

1520 Vahey, Harry M. "Classroom management of socially withdrawn behavior through vicarious reinforcement." For a summary see: Diss Abstr Int 37A(12): 7654, June, 1976.

1521 Walker, Hill M., and Hops, Hyman. "The use of group and individual reinforcement contingencies in the modification of social withdrawal." In: Hamerlynck, Leo A.; Handy, Lee C.; Mash, Eric J., eds. Behavior change: methodology, concepts, and practice. Banff International Conference on Behavior Modification, 4th, 1972. Champaign, Illinois: Research Press, 1974. 269-307. (15 References).
Investigates the effects of a symbolic modelling training procedure, combined with three different reinforcing contingencies, for modifying social withdrawal. The subjects were twelve elementary school children selected for their low rate of social interaction with their peers. The data indicate that a combined individual/group reinforcement contingency is the most effective method.

1522 ———. The use of group and individual reinforcement contingencies in the modification of social withdrawal. Eugene, Oregon: University of Oregon, Department of Special Education, College of Education, Report No. 6, 1972. 61p. (ED 069 096).

Documents an experiment with three socially withdrawn first- and second-graders. The indications were that individual token reinforcement and group reinforcement were both effective but that a combination produced the most dramatic changes in rate of interaction.

1523 Williams, Robert L.; Cormier, William H.; Sapp, Gary L.; et al. "The utility of behavior management techniques in changing interracial behaviors." J Psychol 77(1): 127-38, January, 1971. (8 References).
Evaluates several behavior management procedures, including contingent teacher reinforcement, peer reinforcement, role modelling, and group counseling. The subjects were junior high school students. A main effect positive change was obtained on both sociometric and behavioral measures.

d. Specific Techniques

(1) Use of Classroom Peers

1524 Briskin, Alan S., and Anderson, Donna M. "Students as contingency managers." Elem Sch Guid Couns 7(4): 262-68, May, 1973. (17 References).
Sixth-grade students were used as an integral part of a behavior modification program designed to reduce the disruptive behavior of third-grade students.

1525 Christy, Pauline Richter. "Does use of tangible rewards with individual children affect peer observers?" For a summary see: Diss Abstr Int 34B(11): 5672, May, 1974.

1526 ————. "Does use of tangible rewards with individual children affect peer observers?" J Appl Behav Anal 8(2): 187-96, Summer, 1975. (19 References).
Presents the data on a study conducted with two classes of children, aged three-and-one-half to six years. It was demonstrated that the use of verbal contingencies and food rewards with individual children was an effective managerial procedure that did not decrease performance in the observing children.

1527 Edwards, Clifford H. "Variable delivery systems for peer associated token reinforcement." Ill Sch Res 12(1): 19-28, Fall, 1975. (9 References).
Reports on the effects of teacher and peer delivery of token reinforcement for appropriate classroom behavior. The subjects were junior high school students.

1528 Evans, Gary W., and Oswalt, Gaylon L. "Acceleration of academic progress through the manipulation of peer influence." Behav Res Ther 6(2): 189-95, May, 1968. (5 References). (Reprinted in Item No. 39).
Describes four experiments designed to test the effectiveness of peer approval in accelerating the academic performance of underachievers. The test subjects were fourth- and sixth-graders, and the academic subjects tested were spelling, arithmetic, social science, and general science. Early dismissal or story reading for the entire class were made contingent upon the performance of the underachievers. Results were mixed: some underachievers continued their accelerated progress after the experimental period, and in one test situation, the performance of the entire class declined. The possible reasons for the discrepancies are discussed.

1529 Hartup, Willard W. "Friendship status and the effectiveness of peers as reinforcing agents." J Exp Child Psychol 1(2): 154-62, July, 1964. (13 References).
Continuous attention and verbal approval were more effective as reinforcers when delivered by liked peers than when delivered by disliked peers.

1530 Lawther, Jane Wilcoxon. "The differential influence of peer behavior modification and class discussions on selective child characteristics of middle school students." For a summary see: Diss Abstr Int 37A(10): 6278, April, 1976.

1531 McLaughlin, T. F., and Malaby, J. E. "Elementary school children as behavioral engineers." In: Ramp, Eugene, and Semb, George, eds. Behavior analysis: areas of research and application. Englewood Cliffs, New Jersey: Prentice-Hall, 1975. 319-28.
Outlines methods of maintaining records, observation, recording, and tutoring that can involve pupil participation in classroom programs.

1532 Patterson, G. R., and Anderson D. "Peers as social reinforcers." Child Dev 35(3): 951-60, September, 1964. (13 References).
Peers were effective in making significant changes in preference behavior. They dispensed social reinforcers to condition thirty boys and thirty-two girls for a simple motor response.

1533 Pines, Michael Bruce. "An investigation of the effectiveness of contingency contracting using teachers and peers as contract managers." For a summary see: Diss Abstr Int 38A(1): 184, July, 1977.

1534 Scott, John W., and McLaughlin, T. F. "Use of peers in classroom behavior change." Contemp Educ Psychol 1(4): 384-92, October, 1976. (25 References).
Discusses research conducted on the use of children to modify the behavior of other children. Ethical problems and avenues of future research are outlined.

1535 Siegel, Lawrence J., and Steinman, Warren M. "The modification of a peer-observer's classroom behavior as a function of his serving as a reinforcing agent." In: Ramp, Eugene, and Semb, George, eds. Behavior analysis: areas of research and application. Englewood Cliffs, New Jersey: Prentice-Hall, 1975. 329-40.
Describes a study conducted with two ten-year-old boys in a residential treatment program in which one child served as a reinforcing agent for the other.

1536 Solomon, Robert Wolfe. "Peers as behavior modifiers for problem classmates." For a summary see: Diss Abstr Int 33A(8): 4189, February, 1973.

1537 Strain, Phillip S.; Cooke, Thomas P.; Apolloni, Tony. "Role of peers in modifying classmates' social behavior: review." J Spec Educ 10(4): 351-56, Winter, 1976. (51 References).
Reviews the reported research on peer behavior modification strategies and discusses the ethical implications of such procedures.

1538 Surratt, Paul R.; Ulrich, Roger E.; Hawkins, Robert P. "An elementary student as a behavioral engineer." J Appl Behav Anal 2(2): 85-92, Summer, 1969. (12 References). (Reprinted in Item Nos. 39, 47).

Cites the modification of the non-study behaviors of four first-grade children by a fifth-grade student. Tokens were awarded which were exchangeable for desired activities within the school setting.

(2) Group Contingencies

1539 Billingsley, Felix F., and Smelser, Sandra J. "A group approach to classroom management: the Behavior Game." Teach Except Child 7(1): 30-33, Fall, 1974.
Traces the development of a game that facilitates academic achievement, improves attendance, and reduces disruptive behavior.

1540 Coleman, R. "A conditioning technique application to elementary school classrooms." J Appl Behav Anal 3(4): 293-97, Winter, 1970. (16 References). (Reprinted in Item No. 27).
Reports on the use of candy reinforcement contingent upon the working behavior of one child. The candy reward was divided equally among the entire class.

1541 Devine, Vernon T., and Tomlinson, Jerry R. "'The Workclock': alternative to token economies in the management of classroom behaviors." Psychol Sch 13(2): 163-70, April, 1976. (8 References).
Outlines a set of procedures for modifying the behavior of an entire class by the use of contingent free time for attending behavior.

1542 Greenwood, Charles R.; Hops, Hyman; Delquadri, Joseph; et al. "Group contingencies for group consequences in classroom management: a further analysis." J Appl Behav Anal 7(3): 413-25, Fall, 1974. (26 References).
Reveals that a total intervention package (rules plus feedback plus group and individual consequences) was effective in increasing appropriate behavior. Rules plus feedback produced increased appropriate behavior in two of the three classrooms. Rules alone produced no change in classroom behavior.

1543 Litow, Leon, and Pumroy, Donald K. "A brief review of classroom group-oriented contingencies." Behav Res Ther 8(3): 341-47, Fall, 1975. (96 References).
Surveys the literature on three types of group-oriented contingencies: (1) dependent; (2) independent; and (3) interdependent. Further research is advocated in order to determine more clearly the limitations of each method.

1544 Long, James D., and Williams, Robert L. "The comparative effectiveness of group and individually contingent free time with inner-city junior high school students." J Appl Behav Anal 6(3): 465-74, Fall, 1973. (14 References).
Compares the use of group and individually contingent free time to establish classroom control. The subjects were thirty-two inner-city junior high school students. Group reinforcement appeared to be slightly more effective than individual reinforcement.

1545 McInnis, Elizabeth T., and Marholin, David, II. "Individualizing behavior therapy for children in group settings." Child Welfare 56(7): 449-63, July, 1977. (17 References).
Outlines the procedures involved in generating an individualized program within a group setting. Examples are included of scoring charts that may be used in such a program.

1546 McLaughlin, T. F. "A review of applications of group-contingency procedures used in behavior modification in the regular classroom: some recommendations for school personnel." Psychol Rep 35(3): 1299-1303, December, 1974. (13 References).
Reviews the use of group contingencies and discusses specific studies. A comparison is made between individual and group contingencies. Questions are posed for future research and recommendations made for the teacher.

1547 Packard, Robert G. "The control of 'classroom attention:' a group contingency for complex behavior." J Appl Behav Anal 3(1): 13-28, Spring, 1970. (22 References).
Documents a study conducted in four classrooms (kindergarten, third, fifth, and sixth grades). Both individual and group reinforcers were used in order to increase "paying attention behavior."

1548 Quesenberg, Billy Grant, Jr. "Contingency management in the classroom: a demonstration of a no-cost plan and investigation of interval reinforcement effects on a group operant." For a summary see: Diss Abstr Int 32B(10): 6038, April, 1972.

1549 Schaeffer, Benson; Harris, Alice; Greenbaum, Marvin. "The treatment of socially oriented underachievers: a case study." J Sch Psychol 7(4): 70-73, 1968. (1 Reference).
This successful treatment employed behavior modification techniques and consisted, essentially, of rewarding the entire class for academic improvement demonstrated by the sixth-grade underachievers.

1550 Schmidt, Gilbert W., and Ulrich, Roger E. "Effects of group contingent events upon classroom noise." J Appl Behav Anal 2(3): 171-79, Fall, 1969. (4 References). (Reprinted in Item No. 40).
Investigates the utilization of a group control procedure for the suppression of excessive noise and out-of-seat behavior in a fourth-grade classroom. Reinforcement consisted of an addition to the class gym period and a two-minute break period.

1551 Shigley, Ralph Hal. "A comparison of group administered punishment and individually administered punishment to suppress inappropriate classroom behavior." For a summary see: Diss Abstr Int 34B(8): 4028, February, 1974.

1552 Simmons, Joyce T., and Wasik, Barbara H. "Use of small group contingencies and special activity times to manage behavior in a first-grade classroom." J Sch Psychol 11(3): 228-38, Fall, 1973. (7 References).
Access to a special activity was used to decrease the frequency with which first-grade children left small instructional centers. Following the institution of the program, the teacher spent less time in responding to inappropriate behavior.

1553 Turnbull, Elizabeth Wendy. "The effects of group versus individual reinforcement on individual and cooperative tasks in a special education class." For a summary see: Diss Abstr Int 37B(8): 4172, February, 1977.

1554 Wilson, Sandra H., and Williams Robert L. "The effects of group contingencies on first graders' academic and social behaviors." J Sch Psychol 11(2): 110-17, Summer, 1973. (8 References).

Group-contingent free time was effective in increasing the percentage of work completed and in reducing disruptive responses. A check after one year showed that the teachers were continuing to make use of group-contingent free time.

1555 Winett, Richard A., and Vachon, Edith M. "Group feedback and group contingencies in modifying behavior of fifth graders." Psychol Rep 34(3): 1283-92, June, 1974. (15 References).
Feedback and a contingency system produced significant changes in a fifth grade art class. The results are discussed with reference to the open classroom setting.

1556 Wolf, Montrose M.; Hanley, Edward L.; King, Louise A.; et al. "The timer game: a variable interval contingency for the management of out-of-seat behavior." Except Child 37(2): 113-18, October, 1970. (10 References). (Reprinted in Item No. 25).
Cites two experiments which evaluated a technique for decreasing out-of-seat behavior in the students of a remedial classroom. Such behavior resulted in a loss of tokens for the entire group.

1557 Woolfolk, Anita E., and Woolfolk, Robert L. "A contingency management technique for increasing student attention in a small group setting." J Sch Psychol 12(3): 204-12, Fall, 1974. (12 References).
A token system resulted in a significant increase in attending behavior in elementary school children. Changes did not transfer to the regular classroom and training for the teachers did not affect in-class attention scores.

(3) Home/School Interactions

1558 Bernal, Martha E.; Delfini, Leo F.; North, Juel Ann; et al. "Comparison of boys' behaviors in homes and classrooms." In: Mash, Eric J.; Hamerlynck, Leo A.; Handy, Lee C., eds. Behavior modification and families. Banff International Conference on Behavior Modification, 6th, 1974. New York: Brunner/Mazel, 1976. 204-27. (14 References).
Reports on a study conducted with twenty-one kindergarten and first-grade boys. A comparison was made between school and home behaviors using naturalistic observation data in a multivariate scoring system. The results indicate that behavior tends to be setting-specific.

1559 Cantrell, Robert P.; Cantrell, Mary Lynn; Huddleston, Clifton M.; et al. "Contingency contracting with school problems." J Appl Behav Anal 2(3): 215-20, Fall, 1969. (11 References). (Reprinted in Item Nos. 29, 43).
Contingency contracting procedures were used in managing problems with school-age children. The written contracts were dictated by an analysis of teacher and/or parental reports of behavior problem situations.

1560 Csapo, Marg. "Parent-teacher intervention with inappropriate behavior." Elem Sch Guid Couns 7(3): 198-203, March, 1973. (7 References).
A greater reduction of inappropriate behavior was achieved through the use of a combined teacher and parent intervention. The study was conducted with twelve emotionally disturbed pupils from four large inner-city elementary schools.

1561 Dickerson, Dave; Spellman, C. R.; Larsen, Steve; et al. "Let the cards do the talking--a teacher-parent communication program." Teach Except Child 5(4): 170-78, Summer, 1973.
A card system was used by which the parents were notified that home privileges, for acceptable academic and school behavior in school, might be awarded.

1562 Edlund, Calvin V. "Rewards at home to promote desirable school behavior." Teach Except Child 1(4): 121-27, Summer, 1969. (7 References).
Reinforcers available in most home environments were used to enhance appropriate classroom behaviors. The organization of the parent-teacher collaboration is discussed.

1563 Fairchild, Thomas N. "Home-school token economies: bridging the communication gap." Psychol Sch 13(4): 463-67, October, 1976. (14 References).
Discusses the benefits accruing from the use of home-school token systems. Two case histories of elementary-age children are included.

1564 Hall, R. Vance; Cristler, Connie; Cranston, Sharon S.; et al. "Teachers and parents as researchers using multiple baseline designs." J Appl Behav Anal 3(4): 247-55, Winter, 1970. (14 References). (Reprinted in Item No. 38).
Presents three studies illustrating the use of multiple baseline designs (across situations, across individuals, and across behaviors). In each of the cases a teacher or a parent acted in the dual role of experimenter and observer.

1565 Heaton, Ronald C.; Safer, Daniel J.; Allen, Richard P.; et al. "A motivational environment for behaviorally deviant junior high school students." J Abnorm Child Psychol 4(3): 263-75, 1976. (24 References).
A contingency management program with reinforcers provided both at school and at home resulted in significant reductions in negative school behavior and increases in academic achievement for a group of junior high school students.

1566 Keirsey, David W. "Systematic exclusion: eliminating chronic classroom disruptions." In: Krumboltz, John D., and Thoresen, Carl E., eds. Behavioral counseling: cases and techniques. New York: Holt, Rinehart & Winston, 1969. 89-114.
Outlines methods of enforcing systematic exclusion from school in order to eliminate disruptive classroom behavior. The need for parental cooperation is emphasized and a sample educational contract, that can be signed by pupil, teacher, principal, and parents, is included.

1567 Patterson, G. R. "Parents as dispensers of aversive stimuli." J Pers Soc Psychol 2(6): 844-51, December, 1965. (19 References).
Describes an experiment conducted with sixty families to test the effect of the parent dispensing social disapproval for a simple motor response. A correlation was found between those children who were most responsive to parental disapproval and those who were described by their teachers as immature, inefficient, tense, or angry.

1568 Patterson, G. R.; Littman, R. A.; Hinsey, W. C. "Parental effectiveness as reinforcers in the laboratory and its relation to

child rearing practices and child adjustment in the classroom." J Pers 32(2): 180-99, June, 1964. (16 References).
Investigates the effect of parental approval on the child's performance of a simple task. The study was conducted with forty-one pairs of parents and children. Approval by the parents produced significant changes in the preferences of their children.

1569 Sluyter, David J., and Hawkins, Robert P. "Delayed reinforcement of classroom behavior by parents." J Learn Disabil 5(1): 16-24, January, 1972. (11 References).
Academic standing and/or inappropriate classroom behavior were modified in three children by the use of reinforcers dispensed by the parents in the home. The parents were alerted by a note from the teacher indicating that the reinforcement had been earned.

1570 Tyler, James L., and Larsen, Stephen C. "HSCP: a boon for teachers." Acad Ther 9(3): 215-20, Winter, 1974. (3 References).
Provides the details of the Home-School Communication Program (HSCP) which utilized desired home activities as rewards for acceptable school behavior.

1571 Wahler, Robert G. "Setting generality: some specific and general effects of child behavior therapy." J Appl Behav Anal 2(4): 239-46, Winter, 1969. (6 References). (Reprinted in Item Nos. 27, 29).
Presents an evaluation of deviant child behavior in school settings as a function of contingency changes in the children's home settings. Contingency operations carried out in the home resulted in changes in behavior in the home, but not in the school setting.

(4) Self-Management

1572 Bandura, Albert, and Perloff, Bernard. "Relative efficacy of self-monitored and externally imposed reinforcement systems." J Pers Soc Psychol 7(2): 111-16, October, 1967. (6 References). (Reprinted in Item No. 39).
Furnishes the results of an experiment conducted with eighty elementary school children. The indications were that self-monitored and externally applied reinforcement were equally efficacious, but both reinforcement systems sustained more responsivity than did the control conditions.

1573 Broden, Marcia; Hall, R. Vance; Mitts, Brenda. "The effect of self-recording on the classroom behavior of two eighth-grade students." J Appl Behav Anal 4(3): 191-99, Fall, 1971. (12 References). (Reprinted in Item No. 39).
The self-monitoring of study behavior in an eighth-grade girl improved that behavior as did increased teacher praise. Both methods of reinforcement were phased out without loss of high level performance. The self-recording of an eighth-grade boy's "talk-outs" decreased that activity.

1574 Downing, Charles J. "Teaching children behavior change techniques." Elem Sch Guid Couns 11(4): 277-83, April, 1977. (11 References).
Discusses a group program designed to teach children specific behavior change techniques for use in altering their own behavior. Children who participated in the program made greater academic achievement gains than those children who did not participate. The participants were judged by their teachers to behave as though they felt better about themselves.

1575 Duricko, Allen John. "The free-choice free-time approach to management of classroom behavior: a replication and introduction of self-control features." For a summary see: Diss Abstr Int 35B(5): 2425, November, 1974.

1576 Flowers, John V. "Behavior modification of cheating in an elementary school student: a brief note." Behav Ther 3(2): 311-12, April, 1972.
Cheating behavior in a sixth-grade girl was eliminated by the reinforcement of accurate self-evaluation. A follow-up at fourteen weeks showed no further cheating.

1577 Fo, Walter Shen On. "Behavioral self-control: training students in the self-improvement of studying." For a summary see: Diss Abstr Int 37B(1): 458, July, 1976.

1578 Glynn, E. L.; Thomas, J. D.; Shee, Seok M. "Behavioral self-control of on-task behavior in an elementary classroom." J Appl Behav Anal 6(1): 105-13, Spring, 1973. (23 References).
Describes the training of second-grade children in the techniques of behavioral self-control in order to maintain high rates of on-task behavior. The rates of behavior had been established by externally administered reinforcement procedures.

1579 Goshko, Robert. "Self-determined behavior change." Pers Guid J 51(9): 629-32, May, 1973. (5 References).
Sixteen fifth-grade children were taught to modify their own behavior using videotape feedback and behavior modification techniques.

1580 Harris, Mary B., and Trujillo, Amaryllis E. "Improving study habits of junior high school students through self-management versus group discussion." J Couns Psychol 22(6): 513-17, November, 1975. (12 References).
A self-management approach, which included an understanding of the principles of behavior modification and a group discussion technique, was successful in improving study habits in low-achieving junior high school students.

1581 Johnson, Stephen M., and Martin, Sander. "Developing self-evaluation as a conditioned reinforcer." In: Ashem, Beatrice A., and Poser, Ernest G., eds. Adaptive learning: behavior modification with children. New York: Pergamon, 1973. 69-78. (13 References).
Compares the effects of self-monitored and externally monitored reinforcement systems. The subjects were sixty second-grade children engaged in a visual discrimination task. The results indicate that self-reinforcement procedures can serve to establish positive self-evaluation as a conditioned reinforcer.

1582 Kurtz, P. David, and Neisworth, John T. "Self control possibilities for exceptional children." Except Child 42(4): 212-17, January, 1976. (31 References).
Investigates the possibilities of developing self-control through: (1) cue regulation; (2) self-reinforcement; and (3) self-observation. The discussion is limited to those techniques that appear to be applicable to the problems of handicapped children.

1583 Lovitt, Thomas C. "Self-management projects with children with behavioral disabilities." J Learn Disabil 6(3): 138-50, March, 1973. (2 References). (Reprinted in Item No. 35).
Reports on seven projects, conducted in elementary schools, that investigated various aspects of pupil self-management among children exhibiting academic or social disabilities.

1584 Lovitt, Thomas C., and Curtiss, Karen A. "Academic response rate as a function of teacher- and self-imposed contingencies." J Appl Behav Anal 2(1): 49-53, Spring, 1969. (5 References). (Reprinted in Item Nos. 28, 29, 39).
Demonstrates that self-imposed contingencies were more successful in increasing academic response rate than were contingencies imposed by the teacher. The subject was a twelve-year-old girl.

1585 McNamara, Edward, and Heard, Christine. "Self-control through self-recording." Spec Educ: Forward Trends 3(2): 21-23, June, 1976. (2 References).
Self-recording was used as a technique to improve the classroom adjustment of two adolescent girls.

1586 Meisels, Linda. "The student's social contract: learning social competence in the classroom." Teach Except Child 7(1): 34-35, Fall, 1974. (7 References).
Describes an "alternative behavior model" in which the child is given responsibility for making a choice when the consequences of that choice are clearly understood.

1587 Turkewitz, Hillary; O'Leary, K. Daniel; Ironsmith, Marsha. "Generalization and maintenance of appropriate behavior through self-control." J Consult Clin Psychol 43(4): 577-83, August, 1975. (13 References).
Outlines a program in which eight disruptive children evaluated their academic and social behavior.

1588 Wall, Shavaun Mary. "Behavioral self-management: an effective classroom technique." For a summary see: Diss Abstr Int 38A(5): 2678, November, 1977.

(5) Token Economies

1589 Boegli, R. Glen, and Wasik, Barbara H. "Use of the token economy system to intervene on a school-wide level." Psychol Sch 15(1): 72-78, January, 1978. (8 References).
Traces the implementation of a token economy system with 459 students in a kindergarten to sixth-grade elementary school. A major decrease in classroom disruptions was noted, together with favorable results in the areas of student suspensions, achievement test scores, and teacher turnover rates.

1590 Clark, Marilyn; Lachowicz, Joe; Wolf, Montrose. "A pilot basic education program for school dropouts incorporating a token reinforcement system." Behav Res Ther 6(2): 183-88, May, 1968. (6 References).
A two-month program was conducted with five female school dropouts between the ages of sixteen and twenty-one. The subjects were paid, by means of a token system, for workbook assignments correctly completed. The results indicated a substantial increase in academic skills.

1591 Drabman, Ronald; Spitalnik, Robert; Spitalnik, Karen. "Sociometric and disruptive behavior as a function of four types of token reinforcement programs." J Appl Behav Anal 7(1): 93-101, Spring, 1974. (20 References).
Presents the findings of a comparison study of four different types of token economies used in first-grade classrooms. All four methods were successful in reducing disruptive behavior. The feasibility was also demonstrated of manipulating a child's sociometric status without directly reinforcing sociometric selection. A comparison is made between the effects of token systems on well-behaved and disruptive children.

1592 Drabman, Ronald S., and Tucker, Richard D. "Why classroom token economies fail." J Sch Psychol 12(3): 178-88, Fall, 1974. (20 References).
Discusses three possible problem areas that may hinder the successful implementation of a token program: (1) the token program itself; (2) the teacher; and (3) the specific population. Methods of circumventing these problems are outlined.

1593 Elardo, Richard. "Implementing behavior modification procedures in an elementary school: problems and issues." Paper presented at the Annual Meeting of the American Educational Research Association, New York, April 4-8, 1977. 27p. (ED 135 762).
Provides the details of a year-long case study of the implementation of a token economy in an entire elementary school. The evolution is traced of the school justice system that was the eventual outcome of the project.

1594 Fjellstedt, Nancy, and Sulzer-Azároff, Beth. "Reducing the latency of a child's responding to instructions by means of a token system." J Appl Behav Anal 6(1): 125-30, Spring, 1973. (6 References).
Token reinforcement, using play periods and toys, was used with an eight-year-old boy. The method resulted in a prompt and effective reduction of the time it took him to follow instructions.

1595 Groh, Linda A., and Groh, Thomas R. "Token reinforcement with an eight-year-old for learning number games." Read Improv 14(2): 131-36, Summer, 1977. (8 References).
Reports on the use of a token reinforcement program which employed a multiple baseline design to teach number games to a learning disabled second-grade boy. Rapid improvement was noted with a demonstration of 100 percent accuracy at a six-week follow-up.

1596 Iwata, Brian A., and Bailey, Jon S. "Reward versus cost token systems: an analysis of the effects on students and teacher." J Appl Behav Anal 7(4): 567-76, Winter, 1974. (13 References).
Examines a study conducted in a special education classroom with fifteen elementary school children. The results indicated no appreciable difference in the effectiveness of reward and cost token systems. Small differences were found in the teacher's behavior.

1597 Knapczyk, Dennis R., and Livingston, Gary. "Self-recording and student teacher supervision: variables within a token economy structure." J Appl Behav Anal 6(3): 481-86, Fall, 1973. (16 References).
A token system was effective in increasing the accuracy with which thirteen junior high students, in a special education program, answered

questions about reading assignments. Only slight changes in accuracy of student performance were noted when the recording was done by a student teacher rather than by the students themselves.

1598 Koch, Larry, and Breyer, Norman L. "A token economy for the teacher." Psychol Sch 11(2): 195-200, April, 1974. (15 References).
An inexperienced teacher was successful in implementing a simple token economy system in a regular class setting. A group contingency was employed.

1599 Krasner, Leonard, and Krasner, Miriam. "Token economies and other planned environments." In: Thoresen, Carl E., ed. Behavior modification in education. National Society for the Study of Education, Yearbook, 72nd, pt. 1. Chicago: University of Chicago Press, 1973. 351-81. (85 References).
Reviews token economy procedures and examines their relationship to other planned environments such as the "open classrooms."

1600 Kurash, Frieda. "The relation between children's participation in a token economy classroom and changes in their locus of control and test anxiety." For a summary see: Diss Abstr Int 36B(12): 6359, June, 1976.

1601 Kuypers, David S.; Becker, Wesley C.; O'Leary, K. Daniel. "How to make a token system fail." Except Child 35(2): 101-9, October, 1968. (4 References). (Reprinted in Item Nos. 25, 37, 38).
Clarifies the important components of effective token systems. The examination focuses on the use of a token system in a classroom in which no other modifications were made in the teacher's handling of the class. A full understanding of the basic principles and supplementary procedures before embarking upon such a program is advocated.

1602 McLaughlin, T. F., and Malaby, J. E. "An analysis of assignment completion and accuracy across time under fixed, variable, and extended token exchange periods in a classroom token economy." Contemp Educ Psychol 1(4): 346-55, October, 1976. (8 References).
Records the data on an experiment conducted with fifth- and sixth-grade classes in a low socioeconomic area. The effects of fixed, variable, and extended token exchange periods were investigated. The results indicated a higher percentage of assignments were completed when the number of days between point exchanges was variable.

1603 ———. "The effects of various token reinforcement contingencies on assignment completion and accuracy during variable and fixed token exchange schedules." Can J Behav Sci 7(4): 411-19, October, 1975. (14 References).
Provides details of a study conducted in a combined fifth- and sixth-grade classroom. The data indicated that the token program maintained assignment completion and controlled the accuracy of performance for the entire class.

1604 ———. "Intrinsic reinforcers in a classroom token economy." J Appl Behav Anal 5(3): 263-70, Fall, 1972. (12 References). (Reprinted in Item No. 28).
Furnishes the results of a year-long investigation of the effects of an inexpensive token economy system on assignment completion. The study was conducted in a combined fifth- and sixth-grade classroom.

1605 ————. "The utilization of an individual contingency program to control assignment completion in a token classroom: a case study." Psychol Sch 11(2): 191-94, April, 1974. (10 References).
Presents a case study of a ten-year-old girl who failed to respond to a class-wide token system. An individualized reinforcement program was devised and later proved successful in modifying the girl's behavior.

1606 O'Leary, K. Daniel. Establishing token programs in schools: issues and problems. Stony Brook, New York: The State University of New York, 1969. 10p. (10 References). (ED 039 020).
Answers some of the questions asked by teachers and principals when considering the implementation of a token economy program. Among other topics examined are the questions of cost in time and money.

1607 O'Leary, K. Daniel; Becker, W. C.; Evans, M. B.; et al. "A token reinforcement program in a public school: a replication and systematic analysis." J Appl Behav Anal 2(1): 3-13, Spring, 1969. (17 References). (Reprinted in Item Nos. 21, 22, 39).
Seeks to evaluate generalization and to analyze the separate effects of such variables as classroom rules, educational structure, teacher praise and a token reinforcement program. The target behaviors were the classroom disruptions caused by second-grade children.

1608 O'Leary, K. Daniel, and Drabman, Ronald. "Token reinforcement programs in the classroom: a review." Psychol Bull 75(6): 379-98, June, 1971. (68 References).
Reviews the development and effectiveness of classroom token economies. Methodological and generalization problems associated with the implementation of such programs are also considered.

1609 Payne, James S.; Polloway, Edward A.; Kauffman, James M.; et al. Living in the classroom: the currency-based token economy. New York: Human Sciences Press, 1976. 202p. (Bibliography).
This text is intended as a resource for methods courses in education, practicing teachers, supervisors, and principals. Chapters are included on the justification for token currency programs with suggestions for suitable reinforcers. Detailed instructions on establishment and maintenance are provided.

1610 Richardson, Wayne Donald. "The effects of tokens, praise, and tangibles on academic and conduct behaviours." For a summary see: Diss Abstr Int 36B(10): 5278, April, 1976.

1611 Robertson, Stephen J.; Dereus, Denise M.; Drabman, Ronald S. "Peer and college-student tutoring as reinforcement in a token economy." J Appl Behav Anal 9(2): 169-77, Summer, 1976. (24 References).
No significant difference was found in the level of disruptive behavior of eighteen second-grade students whether they were tutored by fifth-graders or by college students. Contingent tutoring was found to be effective in reducing disruptive classroom behavior.

1612 Sattler, Howard E., and Swoope, Karen E. "Token systems: a procedural guide." Psychol Sch 7(4): 383-86, 1970. (6 References).
Outlines ten steps to be followed in setting up a token system in a classroom. An understanding is assumed of the basic principles of operant procedures.

1613 Schwarz, Michael L., and Hawkins, Robert P. "Application of delayed conditioning procedures to the behavior problems of an elementary school child." In: Ulrich, Roger; Stachnik, Thomas; Mabry, John, eds. Control of human behavior: Vol. II. From cure to prevention. Glenview, Illinois: Scott, Foresman, 1970. 271-83.
Token reinforcers exchangeable for such items as bracelets, pens, and dresses, were used to modify the deviant classroom behavior of a self-conscious, maladjusted twelve-year-old girl.

1614 Stainback, William C.; Stainback, Susan B.; Payne, James S.; et al. Establishing a token economy in the classroom. Columbus, Ohio: Merrill, 1973. 124p. (Bibliography). (The Charles E. Merrill Series on Behavioral Techniques in the Classroom).
This volume is intended as a resource for prospective and practicing teachers. It contains instructions on the implementation of token economy systems in classrooms for both normal and retarded children.

1615 Wegman, Thomas Joseph. "Reinforcement schedules and social maturity in an inexpensive token motivation program." For a summary see: Diss Abstr Int 34B(10): 5178, April, 1974.

e. The Culturally Deprived Elementary/High School Student

1616 Clark, Carl A., and Walberg, Herbert J. "The use of secondary reinforcement in teaching inner-city school children." J Spec Educ 3(2): 177-85, Summer, 1969. (6 References).
Covers the results of seven studies which dealt with the school achievement of retarded and culturally deprived students. The inference is drawn that all teachers need to be trained in the systematic application of reward and that behavior modification should form a part of the basic professional skills of the teacher.

1617 Copeland, Rodney E.; Brown, Ronald E.; Hall, R. Vance. "The effects of principal-implemented techniques on the behavior of pupils." J Appl Behav Anal 7(1): 77-86, Spring, 1974. (6 References).
Investigates the effects of various procedures, initiated by a school principal, on the behaviors of children in an overcrowded inner-city school. Target behaviors included nonattendance and academic skills. In all three experiments the target behavior improved when the principal applied the treatment contingencies.

1618 Gutkin, Terry B. "The modification of locus of control among lower class, minority, elementary school students: an operant approach." For a summary see: Diss Abstr Int 36A(10): 6551, April, 1976.

1619 Wasik, Barbara H. "The application of Premack's Generalization on reinforcement to the management of classroom behavior." J Exp Child Psychol 10(1): 33-43, August, 1970. (23 References).
Behavior management procedures were successfully employed to increase appropriate behavior in a second-grade classroom of twenty culturally deprived children.

1620 Wasik, Barbara H.; Senn, Kathryn; Welch, Roberta H.; et al. "Behavior modification with culturally deprived school children: two case studies." J Appl Behav Anal 2(3): 181-94, Fall, 1969. (9 References). (Reprinted in Item Nos. 28, 29).

Describes the increase in appropriate classroom behavior and the decrease in inappropriate behavior of two culturally deprived seven-year-old girls. The method employed was positive social reinforcement.

1621 Wodarski, John Stanley. "The effects of different reinforcement contingencies on peer-tutoring, studying, disruptive, and achievement behaviors: a study of behavior modification in a ghetto school." For a summary see: Diss Abstr Int 32A(2): 683, August, 1971.

1622 Zimmerman, Barry J., and Pike, Earl O. "Effects of modeling and reinforcement on the acquisition and generalization of question-asking behavior." Child Dev 43(3): 892-907, September, 1972.
The question-asking behavior of disadvantaged Mexican-American second-grade children was found to be readily modified by using an adult model offering contingent praise.

f. Miscellaneous Techniques

1623 Ascare, Donald, and Axelrod, Saul. "Use of a behavior modification procedure in four 'open' classrooms." Psychol Sch 10(2): 243-48, April, 1973. (6 References).
Demonstrates a combination of the British primary school system and behavior modification techniques. The subjects were twenty fifth- and sixth-grade children. Free playtime was used as a reinforcer.

1624 Baer, Donald M. "A technique of social reinforcement for the study of child behavior: behavior avoiding reinforcement withdrawal." Child Dev 33: 847-58, March-December, 1962. (8 References).
A mechanized talking puppet was used to present social reinforcement. The method allows for standardization of responses, and there is less complexity than in interactions with an adult.

1625 Baucum, Don Gardner. "Control of observer accuracy in classroom behavior modification research." For a summary see: Diss Abstr Int 36B(12): 6408, June, 1976.

1626 Breyer, Norman L., and Calchera, David J. "A behavioral observation schedule for pupils and teachers." Psychol Sch 8(4): 330-37, October, 1971. (12 References).
Describes an observation technique for recording classroom behavior. The technique was used easily by paraprofessionals with minimal training.

1627 Clement, Paul W., and Richard, Robert C. "Identifying reinforcers for children: a children's reinforcement survey." In: Mash, Eric J., and Terdal, Leif G., eds. Behavior-therapy assessment: diagnosis, design, and evaluation. New York: Springer, 1976. 207-16. (9 References). (Springer Series in Behavior Modification).
Presents a tool which may be used in performing a functional analysis of a child's behavior. The therapist is enabled to identify potentially reinforcing events.

1628 Cobb, Joseph A., and Ray, Roberta S. "The classroom behavior observation code." In: Mash, Eric J., and Terdal, Leif G., eds. Behavior-therapy assessment: diagnosis, design, and evaluation.

New York: Springer, 1976. 286-94. (Springer Series in Behavior Modification).
This manual is to be used in conjunction with the behavior coding system presented in Item No. 1652. Definitions of the behaviors are provided.

1629 Coleman, Richard G. "An operant technique for elementary classrooms." For a summary see: Diss Abstr Int 31B(11): 6872, May, 1971.

1630 Crow, Frances; Johnston, Dede; Meeks, Margery; et al. "Punch me, I earned it." Teach Except Child 8(1): 13-17, Fall, 1975.
Outlines the use of a point system with backup reinforcers that utilizes a punch card system.

1631 Currie, Billye Bob McCarver. "The teacher as a variable in the use of operant techniques in the classroom." For a summary see: Diss Abstr Int 31B(4): 2254, October, 1970.

1632 Dinoff, Michael, and Rickard, Henry C. "Learning that privileges entail responsibilities." In: Krumboltz, John D., and Thoresen, Carl E., eds. Behavioral counseling: cases and techniques. New York: Holt, Rinehart & Winston, 1969. 124-29.
Discusses the use of written contracts to promote approved behavior. Examples are given from a camping program and a home situation.

1633 Drabman, Ronald S. "Feedback in behavior modification." Paper presented at the 83rd Annual Meeting of the American Psychological Association, Chicago, August 30-September 2, 1975. 7p. (ED 119 092).
Outlines the methods by which students can be given information about the adequacy of their performance.

1634 Drabman, Ronald S., and Lahey, Benjamin B. "Feedback in classroom behavior modification: effects on the target and her classmates." J Appl Behav Anal 7(4): 591-98, Winter, 1974. (12 References).
Analyzes the effects of feedback applied to a ten-year-old disruptive girl. Indications were that: (1) feedback is an effective procedure; (2) disruptive behaviors of the girl's classmates were also changed although they did not receive direct treatment; (3) the girl's sociometric status was changed; (4) positive comments by classmates to the girl increased; and (5) negative comments from the teacher to the girl were reduced.

1635 Engelmann, Siegfried. "Relating operant techniques to programming and teaching." J Sch Psychol 6(2): 89-96, Winter, 1968. (2 References). (Reprinted in Item No. 26).
Emphasizes the distinction between fixed- and variable-response learning and the importance of this difference in using operant techniques successfully both in the classroom and in the analysis of teaching problems.

1636 Finch, A. J., Jr.; Deardorff, P. A.; Montgomery, L. E. "Individually tailored behavioral rating scales: a possible alternative." J Abnorm Child Psychol 2(3): 209-16, September, 1974. (2 References).
Presents a possible alternative to time sampling or counting each occurrence of a behavior. The system described demonstrated good inter-rater reliability.

1637 George, Paul S. "Better discipline: theory and practice. Classroom applications of behavioral psychology." Res Bull 9(4): 1-78, Summer, 1975.
Discusses general principles of behavior modification, together with specific applications in the classroom. Twenty-three contingency management techniques are presented with lists of potential reinforcers. A question-and-answer session is included.

1638 Gordon, Michael Vinzant Wyatt. "The effect of contingent instrumental music instruction on the language reading behavior and musical performance ability of middle school students." For a summary see: Diss Abstr Int 38A(8): 4646, February, 1978.

1639 Grieger, Russell N., II; Mordock, John B.; Breyer, Norman. "General guidelines for conducting behavior modification in public school settings." J Sch Psychol 8(4): 259-66, 1970. (45 References).
Elaborates on the initial presentation of a behavior modification program to the teaching staff, the relation of teacher personality variables to technique selection, and other aspects of program administration.

1640 Hall, R. Vance; Fox, R.; Willard, D.; et al. "The teacher as observer and experimenter in the modification of disputing and talking-out behaviors." J Appl Behav Anal 4(2): 141-49, Summer, 1971. (13 References).
Presents six case studies that demonstrate the ability of a classroom teacher to act as both observer and experimenter in the classroom setting without the need of an outside observer.

1641 Heimlich, Susan Marilyn. "Time-out from positive reinforcement: a new look at Coventry." For a summary see: Diss Abstr Int 36B(5): 2472, November, 1975.

1642 Keat, Donald B., II. "Survey schedule of rewards for children." Psychol Rep 35(1): 287-93, August, 1974. (4 References).
Discusses possible rewards suitable for children between the ages of five and fifteen years. Individual administration is recommended for the five-to-eight-year-olds and group administration for the nine-to-twelve-year-olds.

1643 Kubany, Edward S., and Sloggett, Barbara B. "Coding procedures for teachers." J Appl Behav Anal 6(2): 339-44, Summer, 1973. (9 References). (Reprinted in Item No. 44).
Presents an observing and recording procedure that can be utilized by the regular classroom teacher without the need to deviate more than momentarily from regular classroom routine. The procedure can also serve as a basic for dispensing token reinforcement.

1644 MacMillan, Donald L.; Forness, Steven R.; Trumball, Barbara M. "The role of punishment in the classroom." Except Child 40(2): 85-96, October, 1973. (60 References).
Recommends that punishment should not be disregarded as an aversive tool, although positive reinforcement should be used whenever possible. The variables that would alter the effectiveness of punishment are examined.

1645 Mash, Eric J., and McElwee, John D. "Manual for coding interactions." In: Mash, Eric J., and Terdal, Leif G., eds. Behavior-therapy assessment: diagnosis, design, and evaluation. New York:

Springer, 1976. 309-33. (Springer Series in Behavior Modification).
Presents a behavior-coding system that provides a sequential description of social interaction across a wide variety of settings.

1646 Mash, Eric J.; Terdal, Leif G.; Anderson, Kathryn. "The response-class matrix: a procedure for recording parent-child interactions." J Consult Clin Psychol 40(1): 163-64, February, 1973. (1 Reference).
Outlines a simple procedure for monitoring dyadic interactions. The procedure provides immediate information about behavior and its context.

1647 Milby, Jesse B., Jr.; Willcutt, Herman C.; Hawk, Jesse W., Jr.; et al. "A system for recording individualized behavioral data in a token program." J Appl Behav Anal 6(2): 333-38, Summer, 1973. (7 References).
Provides the details of a data matrix system which may be used to record and summarize individual behavioral data.

1648 Nay, W. Robert; Schulman, Jeffrey A.; Bailey, Kent G.; et al. "Territory and classroom management: an exploratory case study." Behav Ther 7(2): 240-46, March, 1976. (13 References).
Suggests the use of territory as a reinforcer within the classroom. The study was conducted in a suburban elementary classroom with twenty-four students. The territory around each student's desk was clearly defined. Out-of-seat behavior resulted in a twenty-minute loss of territory and relegation to a desk chair at the side of the classroom.

1649 Persons, W. Scott; Brassell, William R.; Rollins, Howard A. "A practical observation procedure for monitoring four behaviors relevant to classroom management." Psychol Sch 13(1): 64-71, January, 1976. (7 References).
Outlines a simple but reliable procedure for recording classroom behaviors using paraprofessional aides as observers. The four behaviors recorded were student disruption, student attention, and the teacher's use of positive and negative events.

1650 Phillips, Debora; Fischer, Steven C.; Singh, Ratan. "A children's reinforcement survey schedule." J Behav Ther Exp Psychiatry 8(2): 131-34, June, 1977. (6 References).
Traces the development of a children's reinforcement survey schedule and assesses its test-retest reliability. The subjects were forty-four children from a middle-class metropolitan grade school. Possible uses for the schedule are suggested.

1651 Polsgrove, Lewis, and Mosley, William. "Management approaches for inner city classrooms." Paper presented at the 54th Annual International Convention, The Council for Exceptional Children, Chicago, April 4-9, 1976. (47 References). (ED 127 751).
Recommends self-monitoring, goal-setting, self-evaluation, and self-reinforcement. A four-page program is presented to develop these strategies.

1652 Ray, Roberta Shockley. "Naturalistic assessment in educational settings: the classroom behavior observation code." In: Mash, Eric J., and Terdal, Leif G., eds. Behavior-therapy assessment: diagnosis, design, and evaluation. New York: Springer, 1976.

279-85. (11 References). (Springer Series in Behavior Modification).
Presents a behavior coding system by which a nonparticipant observer, utilizing a paper-and-pencil format, can code classroom activity, subjects' and peers' behaviors, and teachers' and students' responses to those behaviors. The process is designed to be used in conjunction with the manual described in Item No. 1628.

1653 Redd, William H. "The effects of adult presence and stated preference on the reinforcement control of children's behavior." Merrill-Palmer Q 22(2): 93-97, April, 1976.
In studies conducted with normal elementary school children, subtle variables were found to influence greater control over the child's behavior than did the contingencies of material reinforcement.

1654 Sanborn, Barbara, and Schuster, William. "Establishing reinforcement techniques in the classroom." In: Krumboltz, John D., and Thoresen, Carl E., eds. Behavioral counseling: cases and techniques. New York: Holt, Rinehart & Winston, 1969. 131-52.
Covers development of a reinforcement program in a school. Several case histories are included, together with guidelines for the implementation of a successful program.

1655 Spence, Janet Taylor. "The distracting effects of material reinforcers in the discrimination learning of lower- and middle-class children." Child Dev 41(1): 103-11, March, 1970. (11 References).
Tests conducted with 100 lower-class and 100 middle-class children from second and third grades indicated that the inferior performance of material reward groups, found in previous studies, may be due to the distracting effects of the reinforcement procedures.

1656 Thompson, Marion; Persons, Scott; Rollins, Howard; et al. Project Success Environment: a behavior modification program for inner city teachers. Atlanta, Georgia: Atlanta Public Schools, 1973, 158p. (36 References). (ED 124 604).
Presents the report of a program that emphasizes preservice and in-service training for teachers. A year-long contingency management program was implemented in the first to eighth grades.

g. Problems in Program Implementation

1657 Babad, Elisha Y., and Weisz, Paula. "Effects of social satiation on efficacy of social and nonsocial reinforcers." J Soc Psychol 100(2): 269-75, December, 1976. (18 References).
A significant satiation effect was found for both social and nonsocial reinforcement in a group of forty second-grade children. While these results conflict with those found in other studies, the reinforcement in previous experiments was dispensed by a machine, and in this case reinforcement was provided by the examiner.

1658 Fine, Marvin J. "Some qualifying notes on the development and implementation of behavior modification programs." J Sch Psychol 8(4): 301-5, 1970. (15 References).
Reviews aspects of program planning, including the manipulation of antecedent and consequent events to the behavior, the inclusion of the child in the planning, and teacher acceptance of the method.

1659 Fine, Marvin J.; Nesbitt, John A.; Tyler, Milton M. "Analysis of a failing attempt at behavior modification." J Learn Disabil 7(2): 70-75, February, 1974. (11 References).
Identifies the variables important for success in a behavior modification program. Variables noted include teacher acceptance, adherence to a systematic program, and the role of the psychologist consultant.

1660 Gallagher, Patricia A. "Behavior-modification? Caution!" Acad Ther 11(3): 357-63, Spring, 1976.
Outlines classroom situations in which behavior modification is contra-indicated or in which it should be used with discrimination. The examples given of such situations include a lack of diagnosis and identification of positive traits, the suitability of a more direct approach, and the fact that a child may not be ready to engage in the target activity.

1661 Goldstein, George S. "Behavior modification: some cultural factors." Psychol Rec 24(1): 89-91, Winter, 1974. (1 Reference).
Cautions that a familiarity with ethnic customs is necessary before embarking on a behavior modification program with a culturally unique population.

1662 Korn, Claire V. "Refusing reinforcement." In: Krumboltz, John D., and Thoresen, Carl E., eds. Behavioral counseling: cases and techniques. New York: Holt, Rinehart & Winston, 1969. 45-48.
Advocates the careful selection of reinforcement especially for those individuals who suspect the use of praise and tangible reinforcers.

1663 MacMillan, A., and Kolvin, I. "Behaviour modification in teaching strategy: some emergent problems and suggested solutions." Educ Res 20(1): 10-21, November, 1977. (58 References).
Discusses three areas that have been found prone to difficulty in program implementation in schools: (1) teacher training; (2) teacher abilities and motivation; and (3) the impact of school organization and administrative structure. Suggestions are made for counteracting these difficulties.

1664 O'Leary, K. Daniel. "Behavior modification in the classroom: a rejoinder to Winett and Winkler." J Appl Behav Anal 5(4): 505-11, Winter, 1972. (36 References).
Criticizes an article by Winett and Winkler (see Item No. 1668) as being too restrictive in the literature reviewed. Studies are cited from journals other than The Journal of Applied Behavior Analysis, indicating that behavior modification has been used in a variety of innovative ways in the classroom. This article is followed by the journal reviewer's comments on both articles.

1665 Phillips, G. Mann. "Implementing behavior modification in the classroom: problems and strategies. Problems of the implementor." Paper presented at the 55th Annual International Convention, The Council for Exceptional Children, Atlanta, Georgia, April 11-15, 1977. 10p. (ED 139 191).
Reviews the problems and strategies in the implementation of a classroom token economy. Among the topics discussed are reinforcement schedules, time out procedures, and the importance of clarifying these issues before commencing a behavior modification program.

1666 Rosenberg, Harry E., and Ehrgott, Richard H. "Performance contracting, programmed learning and behavior modification may inhibit learning of the gifted." Gifted Child Q 17(4): 254-59, Winter, 1973. (12 References).
Advocates a careful assessment of the use of behavioral techniques with the gifted since there is the danger of overlooking the critical internal motivators of the individual.

1667 Varenhorst, Barbara B. "Reinforcement that backfired." In: Krumboltz, John D., and Thoresen, Carl E., eds. Behavioral counseling: cases and techniques. New York: Holt, Rinehart & Winston, 1969. 49-51.
Describes the case of a seventeen-year-old boy in whom praise resulted in a regression in his newly acquired acceptable school behavior.

1668 Winett, Richard A., and Winkler, Robin C. "Current behavior modification in the classroom: be still, be quiet, be docile." J Appl Behav Anal 5(4): 499-504, Winter, 1972. (29 References).
Critical review of the literature in The Journal of Applied Behavior Analysis on the use of behavior modification in the classroom. Attention is drawn to a tendency to perpetuate the status quo by rewarding quietness and docility in the students. The "open classroom" is recommended as the more appropriate setting for behavioral methods, since this form of teaching is already geared to a more individualized approach. For a reply to the criticisms contained in this article see Item No. 1664.

B. SPECIAL EDUCATION SETTINGS

1. Educational Programs for the Mentally Retarded

1669 Anderson, Robert M., and Smith, Robert M., eds. Educating the severely and profoundly retarded. Baltimore, Maryland: University Park Press, 1976. 422p. (Bibliography).
Assembles a collection of fifty-one articles--mostly reprinted from other sources--that cover both educational and training programs, including self-care skills and language development for the severely and profoundly retarded. Supportive services, such as vocational and community programs, are also discussed.

1670 Axelrod, Saul. "Comparison of individual and group contingencies in two special classes." Behav Ther 4(1): 83-90, January, 1973. (10 References).
Response-cost punishment procedures were used in a class of thirty-one educably mentally retarded children. Group and individual contingencies were equally effective in controlling misbehavior. A group-contingency program is recommended as the more convenient system to administer but is one that tends to produce more nontarget behavior incompatible with academic progress.

1671 Ayllon, Teodoro; Layman, Dale; Burke, Sandra. "Disruptive behavior and reinforcement of academic performance." Psychol Rec 22(3): 315-23, Summer, 1972. (13 References).
Reports on a study conducted with four disruptive, educable, mentally retarded children in a special classroom. Tokens exchangeable for privileges and toys were dispensed for academic performance with a resultant decrease in disruptive behavior.

1672 Bijou, Sidney W. "Behavior modification in teaching the retarded child." In: Thoresen, Carl E., ed. Behavior modification in education. National Society for the Study of Education, Yearbook, 72nd, pt. 1. Chicago: University of Chicago Press, 1973. 259-90.
Reviews the theory and applications of behavior modification in teaching the retarded child. Examples of programs are provided and a discussion of problems and issues is included.

1673 Coleman, Richard. "A pilot demonstration of the utility of reinforcement techniques in training programs." Educ Train Ment Retarded 5(2): 68-70, April, 1970. (3 References).
Provides the details of a study conducted with an eight-year-old retarded boy which utilized candy and verbal praise to increase his counting ability.

1674 Deitz, S. M.; Repp, A. C.; Deitz, Diane E. D. "Reducing inappropriate classroom behaviour of retarded students through three procedures of differential reinforcement." J Ment Defic Res 20(3): 155-70, September, 1976. (27 References).
Reports on the successful use of three differential reinforcement procedures (DRL, DRO, and DRI) when used independently of each other and of other procedures. The subjects were twenty-one educable mentally retarded students whose inappropriate classroom behavior was reduced.

1675 Dorow, Laura Gilbert. "Televised music lessons as educational reinforcement for correct mathematical responses with educable mentally retarded." J Music Ther 13(2): 77-86, Summer, 1976. (17 References).
Gains were made in correct mathematical responses and in music listening skills by seventeen educable mentally retarded children.

1676 Edelson, Richard I., and Sprague, Robert L. "Conditioning of activity level in a classroom with institutionalized retarded boys." Am J Ment Defic 78(4): 384-88, January, 1974. (12 References).
Records the attempt to control the hyperactive behavior of sixteen educable mentally retarded boys. A "stabilimetric" cushion was used to document the activity, and money was used as a reinforcer. The results indicated that activity level can be controlled in the classroom by operant conditioning techniques.

1677 Edlund, Calvin V. "Changing classroom behavior of retarded children: using reinforcers in the home environment and parents and teachers as trainers." Ment Retard 9(3): 33-36, June, 1971. (6 References).
Outlines a program conducted with six educable mentally retarded children living at home and attending public school. Academic performance and classroom behavior were improved following the awarding of reinforcers in the home contingent upon school behavior.

1678 Evans, David Francis. "Effects of behavior management training on teachers' attention and the behavior of their retarded pupils." For a summary see: Diss Abstr Int 36B(8): 4152, February, 1976.

1679 Forness, Steven R., and MacMillan, Donald L. "Reinforcement overkill: implications for education of the retarded." J Spec Educ 6(3): 221-30, Fall, 1972. (55 References).

Advocates the systematic use of social reinforcement in preference to tangible reward systems in classrooms for the educably mentally retarded.

1680 Greene, Robert J., and Pratt, Janie J. "A group contingency for individual misbehaviors in the classroom." Ment Retard 10(3): 33-35, June, 1972. (4 References).
A significant decline in misbehavior rate resulted from the use of loss of free time as a contingency in classes for institutionalized retarded adolescents.

1681 Harvey, Eric R., and Christensen, Daniel R. "Programs for retarded children combine behavior modification, training for parents, teachers." Hosp Community Psychiatry 26(7): 421-22, July, 1975.
Describes two complementary programs aimed at providing educational and remedial services to communities so that they can assume greater responsibility for retarded children in the area. Children are admitted to the school for the time necessary to modify their behavior, and written programs are prepared to assist the parents with home management.

1682 Hill, Ada Dana. "The effects of social reinforcers on the task persistence of educable mentally retarded children: an implication for mainstreaming." For a summary see: Diss Abstr Int 37A(5): 2784, November, 1976.

1683 Kazdin, Alan E. "The effect of vicarious reinforcement on attentive behavior in the classroom." J Appl Behav Anal 6(1): 71-78, Spring, 1973. (20 References).
Furnishes details of a study conducted with four moderately retarded children. It was demonstrated that reinforcement of attentive behavior in the target subjects increased attentive behavior in the adjacent peers.

1684 ———. "Vicarious reinforcement and direction of behavior change in the classroom." Behav Ther 8(1): 57-63, January, 1977. (14 References).
Reassesses the effect of vicarious reinforcement on the nontarget subject in a special classroom for the educably retarded. Praising the target subject altered the behavior of both the target and the nontarget subjects. Attentive behavior of the nontarget subject was increased when the target subject was praised independently of the specific behavior praised.

1685 Kazdin, Alan E., and Forsberg, Sara. "Effects of group reinforcement and punishment on classroom behavior." Educ Train Ment Retarded 9(2): 50-55, April, 1974. (19 References).
Both token reinforcement and punishment programs were effective in accelerating appropriate classroom behaviors. The program was conducted with a group of six educably mentally retarded children.

1686 Kazdin, Alan E., and Klock, Joan. "The effect of nonverbal teacher approval on student attentive behavior." J Appl Behav Anal 6(4): 643-54, Winter, 1973. (31 References).
Demonstrates the effective use of contingent nonverbal teacher behavior (smiles and physical contact) in strengthening attentive behavior in twelve moderately retarded elementary school children.

1687 Keilitz, Ingo; Tucker, Dennis J.; Horner, R. Don. "Increasing mentally retarded adolescents' verbalizations about current events." J Appl Behav Anal 6(4): 621-30, Winter, 1973. (24 References).

Provides an example of the effective use of television as a training medium with retarded adolescents. Reinforcement procedures were employed to improve the accuracy of verbal statements emitted by the subjects.

1688 Long, James D., and Williams, Robert L. "The utility of self-management procedures in modifying the classroom behaviors of mentally retarded adolescents." Adolescence 11(41): 29-38, Spring, 1976. (9 References).
Compares self-management using tokens without back-up reinforcement, self-management using graphic feedback, and self-management using free time as back-up reinforcement. The subjects were four twelve-year-old educable mentally retarded children. The highest levels of appropriate behavior were demonstrated during the self-selected free time phases.

1689 Perline, Irvin H., and Levinsky, David. "Controlling maladaptive classroom behavior in the severely retarded." Am J Ment Defic 73(1): 74-78, July, 1968. (9 References).
Reports on a token reinforcement program employed with four severely retarded children in a residential preschool setting. Behaviors were assigned to five operationally defined categories, and decrements were noted in each category. Token presentation and withdrawal were equally effective with or without a time-out procedure. The tokens were exchangeable for edible rewards.

1690 Repp, Alan C.; Deitz, Samuel M.; Deitz, Diane E. D. "Reducing inappropriate behaviors in classrooms and in individual sessions through DRO schedules of reinforcement." Ment Retard 14(1): 11-15, February, 1976. (18 References).
DRO schedules were used in both class and individual sessions to reduce hair twirling, hand biting, and thumb-sucking in three retarded children.

1691 Rosenberg, Harry. "Contingency management for the educable retarded." J Spec Educ Ment Retarded 8(1): 46-50, Fall, 1971.
Briefly describes the organization of a classroom utilizing contingency management. The classroom was divided into two areas: the task area, which was reserved for academic work, and the reinforcement area.

1692 Schrader, Carl. "The effectiveness of intermittent time-out in reducing and maintaining low levels of 'out of seat' behavior in severely retarded children." For a summary see: Diss Abstr Int 36B(12): 6399, June, 1976.

1693 Smith, Donald E. P.; Brethower, Dale; Cabot, Raymond. "Increasing task behavior in a language arts program by providing reinforcement." J Exp Child Psychol 8(1): 45-62, August, 1969.
The work output of retarded readers was increased by reinforcement consisting of teacher praise, a work-break consequence, money, and feedback on quantity of work.

1694 Striefel, Sebastian, and Wetherby, Bruce. "Instruction-following behavior of a retarded child and its controlling stimuli." J Appl Behav Anal 6(4): 663-70, Winter, 1973. (4 References).
Describes the use of positive reinforcement, by means of verbal praise, ice cream, and the fading of physical guidance, to teach a profoundly retarded eleven-year-old boy specific responses to specific verbal instructions.

1695 Sulzbacher, Stephen I., and Houser, Joyce E. "A tactic to eliminate disruptive behaviors in the classroom: group contingent consequences." Am J Ment Defic 73(1): 88-90, July, 1968. (5 References). (Reprinted in Item Nos. 27, 47).
Demonstrates the effectiveness of a simply applied group contingency (loss of recess time) on the disruptive behavior of a class of fourteen educable mentally retarded children.

1696 Teske, June Elizabeth. "An evaluation of behavior modification and reduced class size with disturbed moderately and severely mentally retarded." For a summary see: Diss Abstr Int 36A(6): 3574, December, 1975.

2. Educational Programs for the Autistic Child

1697 Brown, Gerri. Teacher's guide to an educational model for autistic children. Orlando, Florida: Orange County Public Schools, n.d. 193p. (ED 113 921).
Provides descriptive information on the autistic child's behaviors and methods of handling them, together with details on program planning and implementation. Appendices are included with a behavior modification intervention model.

1698 Heskett John, et al. "A post training service concept for teachers of autistic-like children: a project for transferability to public schools." Paper presented at the 54th Annual International Convention, The Council for Exceptional Children, Chicago, April 4-9, 1976. 31p. (ED 122 513).
Offers advice on the best methods of transferring the autistic-like child into the normal school. The aspects of behavior modification that can best be employed by the schools in dealing with such children are mentioned.

1699 Hewett, Frank M. "Teaching reading to an autistic boy through operant conditioning." Read Teach 17(8): 612-18, May, 1964.
Describes the acquisition of rudimentary reading and writing skills in a thirteen-year-old autistic boy by using candy reinforcers.

1700 Hudson, Elizabeth, and DeMyer, Marian K. "Food as a reinforcer in educational therapy of autistic children." Behav Res Ther 6(1): 37-43, February, 1968. (5 References).
Food reinforcers were used, with nine schizophrenic and autistic children, between the ages of three and seven years, in attempts to shape their use of craft and art media. Food was substituted for conventional craft media and used simultaneously as a primary reinforcer. Even though the therapist and the activity itself became reinforcing to all but one child, minimal generalization occurred and none of the children advanced to self-planning or creative activities with the materials.

1701 Koegel, Robert L., and Rincover, Arnold. "Treatment of psychotic children in a classroom environment: I. Learning in a large group." J Appl Behav Anal 7(1): 45-59, Spring, 1974. (30 References). (Reprinted in Item No. 35).
Documents two experiments concerned with the modification of autistic behavior within the classroom setting. In the first study behaviors were successfully modified on a one-to-one basis but were not transferred

consistently to the classroom. In the second study greater success was achieved by a process of "fading-in."

1702 Lovaas, O. Ivar, and Koegel, Robert L. "Behavior therapy with autistic children." In: Thoresen, Carl E., ed. Behavior modification in education. National Society for the Study of Education, Yearbook, 72nd, pt. 1. Chicago: University of Chicago Press, 1973. 230-58. (47 References).
Reviews the contribution made by behavior modification to the education of the autistic child.

1703 Martin, G. L.; England, G.; Kaprowy, E.; et al. "Operant conditioning of kindergarten-class behavior in autistic children." Behav Res Ther 6(3): 281-94, August, 1968. (20 References). (Reprinted in Item No. 21).
Provides a description of the procedures used to condition the classroom behavior of ten autistic children ranging in age from eight to thirteen years. College students, trained in operant conditioning methods, worked with the children daily for a total of sixty sessions over a period of twelve weeks. Tokens, exchangeable for edibles, were used as reinforcers, and progress was made from a one-to-one basis situation to a typical elementary classroom.

3. Educational Programs for the Emotionally Disturbed Child

1704 Allen, K. Eileen; Turner, Keith D.; Everett, Paulette M. "A behavior modification classroom for Head Start children with behavior problems." Except Child 37(2): 119-27, October, 1970. (12 References). (Reprinted in Item Nos. 25, 48).
Presents a report on a demonstration project involving preschool children exhibiting various types of behavioral problems. Two case histories are included of two four-and-one-half-year-old children. One displayed severely disruptive behavior, and the other exhibited immaturity and excessive crying. Behavioral principles and techniques relevant to each of these cases are outlined. Emphasis is placed on the importance of correct teacher-child interaction.

1705 Azrin, N. H., and Powers, M. A. "Eliminating classroom disturbances of emotionally disturbed children by positive practice procedures." Behav Ther 6(4): 525-34, July, 1975. (29 References).
After a disruptive episode a child was required to ask permission to speak out or to leave his seat. Disruptive actions decreased by 95 percent if this contingency was delayed and by 98 percent if it was immediate.

1706 Baer, Ann M.; Rowbury, Trudylee; Baer, Donald M. "The development of instructional control over classroom activities of deviant preschool children." J Appl Behav Anal 6(2): 289-98, Summer, 1973. (8 References).
Demonstrates the effectiveness of a reinforcement system designed to encourage teacher compliance in three negativistic and deviant preschool children. Contingent access to free time and a snack mediated by a token were successfully used as reinforcers.

1707 Behavior modification of emotionally disturbed youth: final report of educational adjustment classes. Great Falls, Montana: Great Falls Public Schools, 1971. 31p. (ED 089 519).

Presents the final report of a three-year program. Planning and the procedures used are described, together with the specific teaching strategies employed. Student selection for the program was based on average or above average intelligence. Guidelines are provided for precision teaching, including the pinpointing of behaviors.

1708 Buckley, Nancy H., and Walker, Hill M. "Free operant teacher attention to deviant child behavior after treatment in a special class." Psychol Sch 8(3): 275-84, July, 1971. (28 References).
Examines various aspects of teacher attention. The subjects were forty-four children identified as exhibitors of deviant behavior in the classroom. It is suggested that a knowledge of behavioral principles and methods increases teacher efficiency in dealing with behavior problems.

1709 Clements, J. Eugene, and Tracy, D. B. "Effects of touch and verbal reinforcement on the classroom behavior of emotionally disturbed boys." Except Child 43(7): 453-54, April, 1977. (7 References).
Attempts to investigate the relative effects of tactile and verbal reinforcement and a combination of both. The subjects were ten emotionally disturbed boys aged nine to eleven years. The target behaviors were attention to task and accuracy of performance in solving arithmetic problems. The results indicate that tactile stimulation is potentially valuable as a reinforcer, especially when combined with verbal praise.

1710 Clements, J. Eugene; Tracy, D. B.; Arensdorf, Janette. "Effect of tactile cueing and praise on undesirable classroom behavior of moderately handicapped institutionalized adolescents." Train Sch Bull 71(3): 149-56, November, 1974. (9 References).
A combination of tactile cueing and praise was the most effective reinforcer of appropriate classroom behavior in thirteen junior high school students.

1711 Coleman, Richard. "An economical model of the engineered classroom." Psychol Rep 28(3): 963-66, June, 1971. (6 References).
Describes the organization and methods used in a class of five disturbed children between the ages of eight and ten years. Specific appropriate behaviors were identified for each child. The goal was to increase those acceptable behaviors so that the child could function on a full-time basis in a regular class.

1712 Dickson, Richard L. "Relationship between attitudes and reinforcers: an investigation with emotionally disturbed children." J Spec Educ 10(4): 365-70, Winter, 1976. (19 References).
Documents the findings of a comparison study conducted with sixty emotionally disturbed children. A comparison was made between the learning of those participating in a pretreatment condition designed to develop positive attitudes toward the examiner and those who did not. No significant differences were noted in learning paired associates between the reinforcement groups.

1713 Drabman, Ronald S. "Child-versus teacher-administered token programs in a psychiatric hospital school." J Abnorm Child Psychol 1(1): 68-87, 1973. (16 References).
This study, conducted with twenty-four children, demonstrated that child-administered programs were just as effective as teacher-administered programs. The average age of the children was 12.5 years.

1714 Drabman, Ronald S., and Spitalnik, Robert. "Social isolation as a punishment procedure: a controlled study." J Exp Child Psychol 16(2): 236-49, October, 1973. (30 References).
Shows the punishing properties of a social isolation contingency for disruptive behavior in a classroom. The study was conducted in the classroom of a state residential psychiatric institution. The methodological limitations of previous studies are outlined, and the alternatives adopted in this study are delineated. A recommendation is made to resolve the terminological confusion in the use of time-out and social isolation.

1715 Durlak, Joseph A. "Description and evaluation of a behaviorally oriented school-based preventive mental health program." J Consult Clin Psychol 45(1): 27-33, February, 1977. (17 References).
Reports on a successful program in which teachers at one elementary school and college student volunteers at another used behavioral reinforcement techniques. The subjects were groups of maladjusted second-grade children. A significant improvement was noted in classroom adjustment. Follow-up data suggest that the improvement was maintained.

1716 Dyer, Venita. "An example: reinforcement principles in a classroom for emotionally disturbed children." Except Child 34(8): 597-99, April, 1968. (2 References).
Describes the behavioral and academic rehabilitation of an emotionally disturbed twelve-and-one-half-year-old girl through the use of reinforcement. The discussion includes the case history and methodology employed in the remedial program.

1717 Frederiksen, Lee W., and Frederiksen, Candace B. "Teacher-determined and self-determined token reinforcement in a special education classroom" Behav Ther 6(3): 310-14, May, 1975. (17 References).
Sets forth the results of a fourteen-week study on the effectiveness of teacher-determined and self-determined token reinforcement. The aims of the program were to control disruptive behavior and to enhance on-task behavior in a junior high school special education classroom. Teacher-determined reinforcement was successful over fourteen weeks. Subsequent self-determined token reinforcement was effective over eleven weeks.

1718 Fry, Lyn, and Thomas, John. "A behaviour modification approach to rehabilitating behaviourally disordered children in an adjustment class." NZ J Educ Stud 11(2): 124-31, November, 1976. (9 References).
Traces the rehabilitation of seven six-year-old children with severe behavior disorders. After special classroom placement, the children were partially, then fully, reintegrated into the regular school classroom.

1719 Gamble, Arlene Libenson. "The effects of dependent and interdependent group contingencies on socially appropriate responses in classes for emotionally handicapped children." For a summary see: Diss Abstr Int 38A(1): 170, July, 1977.

1720 Hamblin, Robert L.; Buckholdt, David; Ferritor, Daniel; et al. The humanization processes: a social, behavioral analysis of children's problems. New York: Wiley-Interscience, 1971. 305p. (Bibliography).

Presents detailed reports on several experimental classrooms in which operant techniques were used to modify behavior. The children involved displayed a wide variety of behavioral and learning problems.

1721 Haring, Norris G.; Hayden, Alice H.; Nolen, Patricia A. "Accelerating appropriate behaviors of children in a Head Start program." Except Child 35(10): 773-84, Summer, 1969. (11 References).
Behavior modification techniques were utilized in a demonstration classroom for children demonstrating severe social, emotional, and/or language deficits. Follow-up reports indicated that the gains were maintained under settings not entirely like those of the demonstration class.

1722 Hewett, Frank M. The emotionally disturbed child in the classroom: a developmental strategy for educating children with maladaptive behavior. Boston: Allyn & Bacon, 1968. 373p. (Bibliography).
Criticizes behavior modification as being a powerful methodology but essentially lacking in special educational goals. The use of a developmental strategy is advocated instead.

1723 Hewett, Frank M.; Taylor, Frank D.; Artuso, Alfred A. "The Santa Monica Project: evaluation of an engineered classroom design with emotionally disturbed children." Except Child 35(7): 523-29, March, 1969. (11 References). (Reprinted in Item No. 25).
Provides the results of a study conducted with fifty-four emotionally disturbed children (ranging in age from 8.10 to 11.11). Behavior modification techniques were used to increase attention to tasks and to enhance reading and arithmetic skills. Improvement in attention-to-task and arithmetic skills were correlated to the experimental condition. Reading skills were not significantly effected.

1724 Kaufman, Kenneth F., and O'Leary, K. Daniel. "Reward, cost, and self-evaluation procedures for disruptive adolescents in a psychiatric hospital school." J Appl Behav Anal 5(3): 293-309, Fall, 1972. (15 References). (Reprinted in Item No. 28).
Consists of the results of a three-part study conducted with sixteen adolescents. Part I investigated the differential effects on academic and social behavior of the application of reward and cost procedures in classroom token programs; Part II evaluated the detrimental side-effects; and Part III utilized a self-evaluation procedure for the students. The program was markedly successful in reducing disruptive behavior and in increasing reading skills.

1725 Kazdin, Alan E. "Role of instructions and reinforcement in behavior changes in token reinforcement programs." J Educ Psychol 64(1): 63-71, February, 1973. (21 References).
Analyzes an investigation conducted over a nine-week period in six elementary school classes. The effects of instructions and reinforcement on behavior problem students were examined. The findings included indications that contingency reinforcement was effective in altering behavior, but that instructions did not augment the efficacy of contingency reinforcement.

1726 Leiberman, Jack Noel. "Effects of a clinical educational and behavior modification program on the classroom behavior of a disturbed adolescent." For a summary see: Diss Abstr Int 31A(6): 2762, December, 1970.

1727 Marholin, David, II; Steinman, Warren M.; McInnis, Elizabeth T.; et al. "The effect of a teacher's presence on the classroom behavior of conduct-problem children." J Abnorm Child Psychol 3(1): 11-25, 1975. (22 References).
Cites the results of a study of six institutionalized conduct-problem children under three reinforcement conditions. The results suggest that reinforcement of academic behavior, rather than of a task or classroom behavior, will improve the latter behaviors and make the teacher's presence less necessary.

1728 Mattos, Robert L.; Mattson, Robert H.; Walker, Hill M.; et al. "Reinforcement and aversive control in the modification of behavior." Acad Ther 5(1): 37-52, Fall, 1969. (6 References).
Reports on the development and testing of a set of specific strategies and measures enabling school personnel to meet educational requirements of behaviorally disturbed children within the regular classroom setting. The study was conducted with fourth-, fifth-, and sixth-grade boys.

1729 Newman, Rebecca. "Behavior management and socialization techniques for severely emotionally disturbed children." Paper presented at the 55th Annual International Convention, The Council for Exceptional Children, Atlanta, Georgia, April 11-15, 1977. 19p. (ED 139 150).
Describes a structured approach to the management of severely disturbed children in primary and secondary classrooms. The approach is reinforced by the use of a play money behavior modification program.

1730 O'Leary, K. Daniel, and Becker, Wesley C. "Behavior modification of an adjustment class: a token reinforcement program." Except Child 33(9): 637-42, May, 1967. (6 References). (Reprinted in Item Nos. 25, 27, 39, 41, 47).
Describes a successful token reinforcement system employed in a class of seventeen emotionally disturbed nine-year-old children. The children received tokens exchangeable for candy and trinkets. Reinforcement was delayed up to four days without a resurgence of the deviant behavior.

1731 Otto, Richard George. "A comparison of positive reinforcement and punishment in two special education classes." For a summary see: Diss Abstr Int 36A(2): 791, August, 1975.

1732 ————. "A comparison of positive reinforcement and punishment in two special education classes." Paper presented at the 54th Annual International Convention, The Council for Exceptional Children, Chicago, April 4-9, 1976. 18p. (32 References). (ED 125 212).
Compares the effects of positive reinforcement and punishment on non-attending behaviors. The subjects were eighteen elementary grade children with social or adjustment problems.

1733 Quay, Herbert C.; Werry, John S.; McQueen, Marjorie; et al. "Remediation of the conduct problem child in the special class setting." Except Child 32(8): 509-15, April, 1966. (17 References).
Offers a conceptualization of the nature of children's behavior disorders and discusses some principles of behavior modification and their implementation in the classroom.

1734 Reinert, Henry R. Children in conflict: educational strategies for the emotionally disturbed and behaviorally disordered. St. Louis, Missouri: Mosby, 1976. 205p. (Bibliography).
This college level text presents a variety of theoretical approaches. Chapter Five deals with the classroom application of learning theory and describes three systems: (1) operant conditioning; (2) contingency management; and (3) behavior modelling. The chapter also contains five vignettes giving practical examples of the methods.

1735 Rickard, Henry C.; Melvin, Kenneth B.; Creel, Joe; et al. "The effects of bonus tokens upon productivity in a remedial classroom for behaviorally disturbed children." Behav Ther 4(3): 378-85, May, 1973. (9 References).
Examines the effects of no tokens, constant tokens, and bonus tokens upon classroom productivity. A dramatic increase in productivity was associated with bonus tokens, and a marked decrease with no tokens.

1736 Rosenberg, Harry. "Modifying teachers' behaviour." Spec Educ: Forward Trends 3(2): 8-9, June, 1976.
Children, who had been in classrooms for the emotionally disturbed, were taught to modify their teacher's behavior toward them when they were reintegrated into the regular classrooms.

1737 Rowbury, Trudylee G.; Baer, Ann M.; Baer, Donald M. "Interactions between teacher guidance and contingent access to play in developing preacademic skills of deviant preschool children." J Appl Behav Anal 9(1): 85-104, Spring, 1976. (42 References).
Token-mediated access to play and snacks, contingent upon completion of academic tasks, produced an increase of completion rates in four deviant children.

1738 Rowe, Wayne; Murphy, Harry B.; DeCsipkes, Robert A. "A behavioral program for problem students." Pers Guid J 52(9): 609-12, May, 1974. (1 Reference).
Presents an overview of a program in which students earned tokens that could be spent in a free play activity room. The study was conducted in an alternative educational program with 164 children ranging in age from twelve to nineteen years. The evaluation indicated: (1) an achievement of a favorable attitude on the part of both the students and their parents; (2) progress in basic academic skills; and (3) a trend toward desired changes in the social behavior of the students.

1739 Sajwag, Thomas; Twardosz, Sandra; Burke, Marianne. "Side effects of extinction procedures in a remedial preschool." J Appl Behav Anal 5(2): 163-75, Summer, 1972. (12 References).
Evaluates the side effects, both desirable and undesirable, of behavior modification techniques used to modify a single behavior. The target behavior was excessive conversation with the teacher on the part of a seven-year-old retarded boy. The data suggest a functional approach to the identification of members of a response class.

1740 Stahl, John Roderick, Jr. "The comparative effects of behavioral contracting, behavioral rehearsal and self-evaluation training on the classroom behavior of problem youth." For a summary see: Diss Abstr Int 36B(7): 3628, January, 1976.

1741 Stoppleworth, Leland J. "Special education and reinforcement theory: are we reinforcing deficient behavior?" Psychol Sch 11(3): 357-59, July, 1974. (5 References).
Advocates careful analysis of reinforcement procedures to ensure that deficient behaviors are not being inadvertently reinforced.

1742 Strain, Phillip S.; Cooke, Thomas P.; Apolloni, Tony. "The role of peers in modifying classmates' social behavior: a review." J Spec Educ 10(4): 351-56, Winter, 1976. (51 References).
Outlines contingency management arrangements which have been used successfully to effect changes in the behavior of problem children. A discussion of the ethical issues is also presented.

1743 ————. Teaching exceptional children: assessing and modifying social behavior. New York: Academic Press, 1976. 152p. (Bibliography). (Educational Psychology).
Provides a history and review of theories and methodologies--including operant learning--of social-emotional education. An amalgam is suggested of the various methodologies to achieve an assessment of the complexities of social behavior and to design effective educational interventions.

1744 Strain, Phillip S., and Wiegerink, Ronald. "The social play of two behaviorally disordered preschool children during four activities. A multiple baseline study." J Abnorm Child Psychol 3(1): 61-69, 1975. (7 References).
Contingent teacher attention produced a dramatic increase in the percentage of time two behaviorally disturbed children engaged in social play. The possible implications of the incorporation of this simple procedure into a daily preschool routine are discussed.

1745 Swift, Marshall S., and Spivack, George. Alternative teaching strategies: helping behaviorally troubled children achieve: a guide for teachers and psychologists. Champaign, Illinois: Research Press, 1975. 217p. (Bibliography).
Provides detailed instructions for teaching methods based on behavioral principles. The emphasis is on dealing with such problems as inattentiveness, irrelevant talk, achievement anxiety, and restlessness.

1746 Weiss, Carol G. "Maintenance of behavior change in a token economy: cognitive correlates of learning." For a summary see: Diss Abstr Int 38B(2): 923, August, 1977.

1747 Woody, Robert H. Behavioral problem children in the schools: recognition, diagnosis, and behavioral modification. New York: Appleton-Century-Crofts, 1969. 264p. (Bibliography).
This volume is divided into two sections. Part I deals with the recognition and diagnosis of behavioral problems in the school age child, and Part II covers the application of behavioral modification techniques in conjunction with other therapeutic strategies. The book is intended for classroom teachers, school counselors, and psychologists treating school children. A basic knowledge of educational psychology is assumed.

1748 Zimmerman, Elaine H., and Zimmerman, J. "The alteration of behavior in a special classroom situation." J Exp Anal Behav 5(1): 59-60, 1962. (Reprinted in Item Nos. 22, 25, 27, 36, 45, 46).

Presents a short report on the elimination of deviant classroom behavior in two emotionally disturbed eleven-year-old boys. Pleasant social consequences were removed contingent upon the behavior, and more acceptable behavior was promoted by the use of social reinforcers.

VII.

Use of Behavior Modification in Special Settings

A. CAMP

1749 Blackmore, Merihelen; Rich, Nancy; Means, Zetta; et al. "Summer therapeutic environment program--STEP: a hospital alternative for children." In: Mash, Eric J.; Handy, Lee C.; Hamerlynck, Leo A., eds. Behavior modification approaches to parenting. Banff International Conference on Behavior Modification, 6th, 1974. New York: Brunner/Mazel, 1976. 75-97. (11 References).
Describes a combination of an eight-week therapeutic summer camp program and a home-based system of reinforcement. The subjects were eight boys between the ages of eight and eleven years who exhibited chronic behavior problems.

1750 Forehand, Rex; Mulhern, Tom; Rickard, Henry C. "Effects of token reinforcement in a therapeutic camp." Psychol Rep 25(2): 349-50, October, 1969. (3 References).
Token reinforcement was employed with two eight-year-old boys in a summer camp program. Crying and aggressive behavior was markedly reduced. The results suggest that token reinforcement is effective in such a setting.

1751 Hanson, Shirley A., and Deysach, Robert E. "Effects of positive reinforcement on physical complaints at a therapeutic summer camp." J Clin Psychol 33(4): 1107-12, October, 1977. (14 References).
Assesses the relationship between somatic complaints and daily interpersonal successes and failures of the camper. It demonstrates that the frequency of complaints can be altered by the amount of social reinforcement administered by the nurse who attends the complaints. The role of the nurse in mental health service delivery networks is discussed.

1752 Hobbs, Tom R., and Radka, Jerome E. "A short-term therapeutic camping program for emotionally disturbed adolescent boys." Adolescence 10(39): 447-55, Fall, 1975. (11 References).
Behavior modification techniques, including a token economy, were used to modify the verbal behavior of emotionally disturbed adolescent boys. The practical problems of program implementation are discussed.

1753 Lyman, Robert D.; Rickard, Henry C.; Elder, Ivan R. "Contingency management of self-report and cleaning behavior." J Abnorm Child Psychol 3(2): 155-62, 1975. (8 References).
Breakfast was used as a reinforcing event for satisfactory cabin-cleaning and self-report behavior in a group of nine male campers.

1754 Rawson, Harve E. "Academic remediation and behavior modification in a summer-school camp." Elem Sch J 74(1): 34-43, October, 1973. (4 References).

A program utilizing behavior modification techniques was used to promote self-confidence and academic achievement and to reduce disruptive behavior in a summer-school camp.

1755 ————. "Residential short-term camping for children with behavior problems: a behavior-modification approach." Child Welfare 52(8): 511-20, October, 1973. (5 References).
Significant gains were noted in children in both behavior and in academic adjustment following their participation in a camping program. The conclusions are drawn that behavior modification is readily adaptable to the camping milieu and that the use of such techniques does not lead to blind acquiescence to authority. The need for follow-up is stressed.

1756 Rickard, Henry C., and Dinoff, Michael. "Behavior modification in a therapeutic summer camp." In: Rickard, Henry C., ed. Behavioral intervention in human problems. New York: Pergamon, 1971. 101-27. (38 References). (Pergamon General Psychology Series, Vol. 10).
Describes a short-term camping program for the emotionally disturbed child in the seven-to-fourteen age range. Two major categories of techniques are discussed: (1) the utilization of overt environmental events to bring about changes in immediate behavioral patterns; and (2) the attainment of greater self-control.

1757 Rickard, Henry C., and Dinoff, Michael, eds. Behavior modification in children: case studies and illustrations from a summer camp. University, Alabama: University of Alabama Press, 1974. 174p. (Bibliography).
Brings together a collection of articles, some of which are reprinted from other sources, dealing with problems that can be successfully handled in a summer camp program. The volume is divided into three sections: (1) case studies; (2) self-control techniques; and (3) studies conducted in the camp classroom.

1758 Rickard, Henry C., and Dinoff, Michael. "Shaping adaptive behavior in a therapeutic summer camp." In: Ullmann, Leonard P., and Krasner, Leonard, eds. Case studies in behavior modification. New York: Holt, Rinehart & Winston, 1965. 325-28. (1 Reference).
Traces the development, by means of systematic social reinforcement, of appropriate adaptive behavior in a thirteen-year-old boy. The boy was demonstrating rebellious behavior and was successfully treated at a summer camp.

1759 Rickard, Henry C., and Saunders, Thomas R. "Control of 'clean-up' behavior in a summer camp." Behav Ther 2(3): 340-44, July, 1971. (9 References).
The cabin-cleaning behavior of eight emotionally disturbed children was brought under control by the use of tokens with back-up prizes.

1760 Rickard, Henry C., and Taylor, Nancy C. "Strategy of multiple-baseline evaluation: illustrations from a summer camp." Percept Mot Skills 39(2): 875-81, October, 1974.
Delineates the advantages of a multiple-baseline design especially in short-term programs. The primary advantage is that it is possible to control two different classes of desirable behavior at the same time. The two behaviors selected for modification in this study were toothbrushing and academic performance in children attending a summer camp for the emotionally disturbed.

1761 Zwaig, Marilyn S. "A successful camp experience for the LD child." Acad Ther 9(6): 445-49, Summer, 1974.
Briefly reports on the use of behavior modification techniques in a one-month camp for the learning disabled, slow learners, and behaviorally maladjusted children.

B. COMMUNITY PROGRAMS

1762 Nietzel, Michael T.; Winett, Richard A.; MacDonald, Marian; et al. Behavioral approaches to community psychology. New York: Pergamon, 1977. 448p. (Pergamon General Psychology Series, Vol. 63).
Reviews and evaluates the extension of behavioral methods to community problems. The chapter on problems in the schools covers the recent research literature and includes a summary of the principles and problems suggested by that literature. The chapter on juvenile delinquency, in addition to reviewing the literature, outlines the historical development of the juvenile justice system and the conceptual basis for the use of behavior modification in juvenile corrections. The book is intended primarily for upper division or graduate students in social work, mental health, and community psychiatry.

1763 Pierce, Charles H., and Risley, Todd R. "Improving job performance of Neighborhood Youth Corps aides in an urban recreation program." J Appl Behav Anal 7(2): 207-15, Summer, 1974. (23 References).
The job performance of Neighborhood Youth Corps members was improved by making the hourly wage more contingent upon job performance. Prior to the institution of this program, only the physical presence of the youth was necessary to ensure payment. The standard of the performance was determined by the use of a simple checklist.

1764 ————. "Recreation as a reinforcer: increasing membership and decreasing disruptions in an urban recreation center." J Appl Behav Anal 7(3): 403-11, Fall, 1974. (21 References).
Membership was increased by awarding extra time in a recreation center to those youths who brought new members. Disruptive behaviors were reduced by closing the center a few minutes earlier for each offense.

1765 Thomas, Edwin J., and Walter, Claude L. "Guidelines for behavioral practice in the open community agency: procedure and evaluation." Behav Res Ther 11(2): 193-205, May, 1973. (4 References).
Focuses on a project involving the use of behavioral assessment and modification in a community agency. The recommended step-by-step procedures are given for the successful implementation of such a project. An illustrative case report is included.

1766 Wahler, Robert G., and Erickson, Marie. "Child behavior therapy: a community program in Appalachia." Behav Res Ther 7(1): 71-78, February, 1969. (13 References). (Reprinted in Item Nos. 21, 44).
Examines a successful community-wide behavior therapy program conducted over a two-year period. The program emphasized the use of nonprofessional volunteer workers trained to function as behavior therapists in home and school settings.

VIII.

Use of Behavior Modification by Professions

A. COUNSELING

1767 Bergan, John R. Behavioral consultation. Columbus, Ohio: Merrill, 1977. 369p. (Bibliography).
This basic text is designed to be used in developing consultation skills in students entering school psychology, school counseling, community psychology, child psychiatry, and social work. It is divided into three sections: Part I covers the basic concepts and techniques of behavioral consultation; Part II elaborates on a problem-solving model with attention to problem identification, analysis and evaluation, and plan implementation; Part III presents applications of behavioral consultation in socialization. Appendices include charts and evaluative forms.

1768 Bowersock, Roger B. "Helping children modify adult behavior." Elem Sch Guid Couns 10(1): 24-30, October, 1975. (5 References).
Advocates a reversal of the usual process by the teaching of some basic behavior modification principles to elementary school students. A case report of a nine-year-old boy is cited. A rapid change in parent-child interactions was accomplished by instructing the boy how to change his parents' yelling behavior.

1769 Castle, Wanda K. "Assuming responsibility for appropriate classroom behavior." In: Krumboltz, John D., and Thoresen, Carl E., eds. Behavioral counseling: cases and techniques. New York: Holt, Rinehart & Winston, 1969. 33-36.
Deals with the modification of the inappropriate behavior of a seventh-grade boy. The school counselor, in cooperation with the boys' teachers, devised a program which consisted of the teachers' giving attention to appropriate behavior and ignoring inappropriate behavior.

1770 Cormier, Louise S., and Cormier, William H. Behavioral counseling: operant procedures, self-management strategies, and recent innovations. Boston: Houghton Mifflin, 1975. 96p. (Bibliography). (Guidance Monograph Series, No. 8: Theories of Counseling and Psychotherapy).
Presents procedures, based on operant learning, that may be employed by the counselor and describes some of the innovative behavioral counseling methods that have emerged within the last decade. The emphasis is on operant and preventive approaches that may be applied to an organization or in an ecological setting as well as with individuals or groups. Included are new developments such as self-management strategies, biofeedback, and systematic training for personal mastery. Possible future trends are also outlined. This is a companion volume to Item No. 1771.

1771 Cormier, William H., and Cormier, Louise S. Behavioral counseling: initial procedures, individual and group strategies. Boston: Houghton Mifflin, 1975. 96p. (Bibliography). (Guidance Monograph Series, No. 8: Theories of Counseling and Psychotherapy).

Introduces the purpose, principles, procedures, and research associated with behavioral methods of counseling. While intended primarily for students and practitioners of guidance and counseling, the volume could also be used by social workers, psychologists, and teachers. It provides a summary of initial procedures in behavioral counseling and some procedures based on social modelling and classical learning. This is a companion volume to Item No. 1770.

1772 Goldstein, Robin Linda. "Effects of reinforcement and female career role models on the vocational attitudes of high school girls." For a summary see: Diss Abstr Int 36A(3): 1304, September, 1975.

1773 Goodwin, Dwight L. "Consulting with the classroom teacher." In: Krumboltz, John D., and Thoresen, Carl E., eds. Behavioral counseling: cases and techniques. New York: Holt, Rinehart & Winston, 1969. 260-64.

Demonstrates the effective use of the school counselor in instructing teachers in the analysis of complex classroom behaviors and the development of treatment plans. A case history of a sixth-grade boy is cited.

1774 Hickey, Delores F. "The attitudes of Colorado high school counselors toward behavior modification as they understand it." For a summary see: Diss Abstr Int 36A(3): 1307, September, 1975.

1775 ————. "School counselors' attitudes toward behavior modification." Pers Guid J 55(8): 477-80, April, 1977.

Furnishes the results of a study conducted with eighty high school counselors. Among other findings, there were indications that behavioral techniques were frequently not understood by counselors, that female counselors were more positive in their attitudes toward it, and that more positive attitudes prevailed among schools in the higher levels of the socioeconomic scales.

1776 Hinds, William C., and Roehlke, Helen J. "A learning theory approach to group counseling with elementary school children." J Couns Psychol 17(1): 49-55, January, 1970. (15 References).

Relates the success of a group counseling program conducted with forty third-, fourth-, and fifth-grade children referred for behavior problems. Techniques included group discussion, role-playing, and videotaping. The children were initially rewarded for appropriate behaviors by a point system which was subsequently replaced by social reinforcement.

1777 Hubbert, Ardelle Kennedy. "Effect of group counseling and behavior modification on attention behavior of first grade students." For a summary see: Diss Abstr Int 30A(9): 3727, March, 1970.

1778 Krumboltz, John D., and Thoresen, Carl E., eds. Behavioral counseling: cases and techniques. New York: Holt, Rinehart & Winston, 1969. 515p. (Bibliography).

This text, which is intended for counselors and psychologists, contains a series of articles dealing with successful behavioral techniques. The articles are grouped by types of technique (e.g., reinforcement, modelling) and a diagnostic table of contents is included. Many of the articles deal with childhood problems.

1779 Lorton, Larry. Operant control of misbehavior: counselor intervention. 6p. (ED 130 176).
Discusses aspects of behavior modification, reviews trends in elementary school counseling, and presents a model around which the counselor can build an effective behavior change program.

1780 Moore, Rosemarie K., and Sanner, Kenneth. "Helping teachers analyze and remedy problems." In: Krumboltz, John D., and Thoresen, Carl E., eds. Behavioral counseling: cases and techniques. New York: Holt, Rinehart & Winston, 1969. 250-59.
Presents two case histories in which guidance counselors assisted teachers in identifying problem behaviors and developing treatment plans. Reinforcement of teacher responses and modelling were two of the techniques used.

1781 Thoresen, Carl E., and Hosford, Ray E. "Behavioral approaches to counseling." In: Thoresen, Carl E., ed. Behavior modification in education. National Society for the Study of Education, Yearbook, 72, pt. 1. Chicago: University of Chicago Press, 1973. 107-53. (137 References).
Discusses the historical developments and the definitions of behavioral counseling. Current techniques are outlined, together with their relevance to contemporary social problems.

1782 Toews, Jay M. "The counselor as contingency manager." Pers Guid J 48(2): 127-33, October, 1969. (10 References).
Cites three case studies that illustrate the role of the counselor as a contingency manager. The counselor can also serve as an advisor to teachers on the application of behavior modification techniques.

1783 Vannote, Vance G. "A practical approach to behavior modification programs." Sch Couns 21(5): 350-54, May, 1974. (16 References).
Outlines a program in which the school counselor assumes responsibility for and the control of a behavior modification project instituted to curb classroom misconduct.

B. DENTISTRY

1784 Albino, Judith E.; Juliano, Daniel B.; Slakter, Malcolm J. "Effects of an instructional-motivational program on plaque and gingivitis in adolescents." J Public Health Dent 37(4): 281-89, Fall, 1977.
Reports on the use of a motivational program for some adolescent students. A group contingency of a movie party was awarded to those students reducing their collective plaque score by the greater amount. An analysis of plaque scores, obtained over a three-year period, indicated significantly better hygiene for the group receiving instructional and motivational activities. The analysis of gingivitis scores did not support these results.

1785 Adelson, Richard, and Goldfried, Marvin R. "Modeling and the fearful child patient." J Dent Child 37(6): 476-89, November-December, 1970. (26 References). (Reprinted in Item No. 1803).

Advocates the use of behavioral modelling to alleviate fears of young children. Advantages of such a procedure include the minimal amount of professional time required and the fact that the process can easily become a part of the office routine. A brief case history is included.

1786 Barenie, James T., and Ripa, Louis W. "The use of behavior modification techniques to successfully manage the child dental patient." J Am Dent Assoc 94(2): 329-34, February, 1977. (17 References).
Proposes a combination of desensitization, modelling, and contingency management in pediatric dentistry. An explanation of each new instrument and procedure is recommended, together with the liberal use of social reinforcers. Rewards should only follow desired behavior.

1787 Chambers, David W. "Behavior management techniques for pediatric dentists: an embarrassment of riches." J Dent Child 44(1): 30-34, January-February, 1977. (28 References).
Behavior modification is included among several methods of handling the young dental patient. A challenge is made to the dental profession to: (1) develop a consensus on standards for appropriate dental behavior in young children; (2) modify the dental curricula to give time and attention to a critical analysis of alternative methodologies; and (3) develop a research literature focused on the need for providing dental care rather than a series of technique demonstrations.

1788 ———. "Managing the anxieties of young dental patients." J Dent Child 37(5): 363-74, September-October, 1970. (27 References). (Reprinted in Item No. 1803).
Briefly reviews the major orientations in the field of psychology with their different views of anxiety. Four specific techniques for handling the anxiety in young children are discussed, including modelling and reinforcement.

1789 Drash, Philip W. "Behavior modification: new tools for use in pediatric dentistry with the handicapped child." Dent Clin North Am 18(3): 617-31, July, 1974.
Summarizes the basic reinforcement techniques and includes an illustrative case history in which a long-standing dental phobia in a twelve-year-old girl was reversed in seven sessions.

1790 Fox, Lawrence A. "The handicapped child: a prelude to care." Dent Clin North Am 18(3): 535-44, July, 1974. (8 References).
Presents a brief overview of various treatment modalities, including behavior modification, in dentistry for the handicapped child.

1791 Gordon, Donald A.; Terdal, Leif; Sterling, Edward. "The use of modeling and desensitization in the treatment of the phobic child patient." J Dent Child 41(2): 102-5, March-April, 1974. (3 References). (Reprinted in Item No. 1803).
Presents a case history demonstrating a management plan for a very fearful parent and child. The technique utilized nine sessions with an average of sixteen minutes per session.

1792 Green, Roy V.; Meilman, Philip; Routh, Donald K.; et al. "Preparing the preschool child for a visit to the dentist." J Dent 5(3): 231-36, September, 1977. (14 References).
Evaluates two commercial films which demonstrate the modelling of appropriate behavior, and compares their effectiveness with a cartoon

(unrelated to dentistry), and with no film, for preparing 145 preschool children for dentistry. The study did not find any significant changes in the behavior of the children as a result of watching the films.

1793 Kohlenberg, Robert; Greenberg, Daniel; Reymore, Larry; et al. "Behavior modification and the management of mentally retarded dental patients." J Dent Child 39(1): 61-67, January-February, 1972. (6 References). (Reprinted in Item No. 1803).
Describes an experiment conducted with seventeen severely retarded subjects (aged eight to twenty years). The program, which included elements of reinforcement, shaping, and fading, was successful in affecting a large decrement in the use of restraints.

1794 Kramer, William S. "Aversion--a method for modifying child behavior." J Nebr Dent Assoc 51(2): 7-13, 17, Winter, 1974. (1 Reference).
The use of aversion--in particular the placing of a hand over a child's nose and mouth--is recommended in order to control tantrum behavior in dental patients.

1795 Machen, J. Bernard, and Johnson, Ronald. "Desensitization, model learning, and the dental behavior of children." J Dent Res 53(1): 83-87, January-February, 1974. (20 References). (Reprinted in Item No. 1803).
Presents the findings of a study conducted with thirty-one preschool children. Desensitization and model learning effectively reduced negative behavior.

1796 Mackenzie, Richard S.; McCollum, Nancy; Nicewonger, Margaret. "Influencing human behavior in the dental clinic." Dent Hyg 42(1): 11-18, 1968. (8 References). (Reprinted in Item No. 1803).
Reports on a study conducted to assess the level of knowledge of behavioral principles on the part of dental hygienists. A number of real clinical situations are presented in which the behavioral principles were employed by the hygienists, thus demonstrating that dental personnel can transfer classroom learning of psychology to the dental clinic.

1797 Melamed, Barbara G.; Hawes, Roland R.; Heiby, Elaine; et al. "Use of filmed modeling to reduce uncooperative behavior of children during dental treatment." J Dent Res 54(4): 797-801, July-August, 1975. (19 References).
Presents the results of a study conducted with fourteen inner-city children, none of whom had had previous dental experience. The effects of a film showing a child undergoing a dental examination were compared with the effects of another film unrelated to dental treatment. The control group's disruptive behavior increased 25.6 percent and the experimental group showed a decrease of 23 percent.

1798 Melamed, Barbara G.; Weinstein, Donald; Hawes, Roland; et al. "Reduction of fear-related dental management problems with use of filmed modeling." J Am Dent Assoc 90(4): 822-26, April, 1975. (18 References).
Presents the results of a study conducted with fourteen inner-city children. A videotape demonstration was used to lessen disruptive behavior in the dental clinic.

1799 Rosenberg, Howard M. "Behavior modification for the child dental patient." J Dent Child 41(2): 111-14, March-April, 1974. (12 References). (Reprinted in Item No. 1803).
Outlines the principles of behavior modification and indicates methods of implementation for the dentist.

1800 Sawtell, Rodney O.; Simon, John F., Jr.; Simeonsson, Rune J. "The effects of five preparatory methods upon child behavior during the first dental visit." J Dent Child 41(5): 367-75, September-October, 1974. (31 References).
Furnishes the data on a comparison study conducted with seventy-three children. The effects of desensitization, behavior modification, and vicarious symbolic modeling on the child's behavior during the first visit to a dental clinic were examined. There was an absence of a significant effect in terms of rate of occurrence of uncooperative behavior. The placebo group manifested the lowest rate, and the control group showed the highest rate. The implications of these findings are analyzed.

1801 Stachnik, Thomas, and Talsma, Eugene. "Oral health practices in children: a behavioral analysis of why brushing and flossing is not their idea of a good time." J Mich Dent Assoc 55(3): 38-41, February, 1973. (3 References). (Reprinted in Item No. 1803).
Analyzes the oral health practices of children and suggests that, if a child is to demonstrate good oral health practice, an immediate positive consequence should be provided. Suggestions are also made for the establishment of simply maintained home programs.

1802 Talsma, E. M. "Contingency management of toothbrushing with an eleven-year-old boy." In: Van Zoost, Brenda, ed. Psychological readings for the dental profession. Chicago: Nelson-Hall, 1975. 169-75. (8 References).
Traces the development of a simply administered home program in which a mother increased the toothbrushing of her eleven-year-old son. The reinforcement used was the addition of coins to the boy's coin collection.

1803 Van Zoost, Brenda, ed. Psychological readings for the dental profession. Chicago: Nelson-Hall, 1975. 176p.
This text is intended for both dental and dental hygiene personnel. It contains a collection of articles, both reprinted and original, most of which have a behavioral orientation. It is divided into three sections which deal with: (1) communication and management of the dental patient; (2) the management of dental anxiety; and (3) the motivation of the dental patient. Each section ends with discussion questions and class exercises.

1804 White, Larry W. "A behavioristic approach to oral hygiene." Am J Orthod 72(4): 406-13, October, 1977. (17 References).
Describes an oral hygiene technique using the principles of modelling reinforcement, and shaping. The modelling consisted of a demonstration and the use of filmstrip. Reinforcement was both positive (a point system) and negative (the use of a bitter-tasting cleanser). Shaping consisted of successive approximations to the desired combinations of appliances and exercises.

1805 White, William C., Jr.; Akers, John; Green, Joseph; et al. "Use of imitation in the treatment of dental phobia in early childhood: preliminary report." J Dent Child 41(2): 106-10, March-April, 1974. (11 References).

Fifteen children between the ages of four and eight years of age participated in a study of the efficacy of modelling as a means of modifying disruptive behavior.

1806 White, W. C., Jr., and Davis, Mary T. "Vicarious extinction of phobic behavior in early childhood." J Abnorm Child Psychol 2(1): 25-32, March, 1974. (11 References).
Results of this examination supported the efficacy of modelling as a means of ameliorating phobic behavior in a dental treatment situation.

1807 Wright, Gerald Z. Behavior management in dentistry for children. Philadelphia: Saunders, 1975. 266p.
Behavior modification is one of the non-pharmacotherapeutic approaches to shaping behavior in the dentist's office. The same principles are also used in the elimination of thumbsucking.

C. NURSING

1808 Amundson, Mary Jane. "Nurses as group leaders of behavior management classes for parents." Nurs Clin North Am 10(2): 319-27, June, 1975. (11 References).
Discusses the reactions of parents to caring for a developmentally disabled child and outlines a program designed to prepare nurses to function as group leaders of parent management groups.

1809 Barnes, Keith E.; Wootton, Margaret; Wood, Sheri. "The public health nurse as an effective therapist-behavior modifier of preschool play behavior." Community Ment Health J 8(1): 3-7, February, 1972. (9 References).
Reports on a study conducted with twenty-four preschool children. Social reinforcement techniques were successfully used by nurses to shape appropriate play behavior.

1810 Berni, Rosemarian; Dressler, Joan; Baxter, Janice C. "Reinforcing behavior." Am J Nurs 71(11): 2180-83, November, 1971. (4 References).
The positive and negative reinforcers for a five-year-old boy were identified and incorporated into his care plan by the nursing staff. The boy slowly progressed from dependent to more independent behavior through the use of positive reinforcement.

1811 Berni, Rosemarian, and Fordyce, Wilbert E. Behavior modification and the nursing process. St. Louis, Missouri: Mosby, 1973. 135p. (Bibliography).
This text for nursing personnel contains chapters that deal with the analysis of behavior, techniques, systems management, ethical issues, and future trends. Each concept is explained and illustrated with examples taken from situations likely to confront the nurse. Examples are included with both child and adult patients. An annotated bibliography of sixty-six items is included. See Item 1812 for a revised edition.

1812 ————. Behavior modification and the nursing process. 2nd ed. St. Louis, Missouri: Mosby, 1977. 160p. (Bibliography).
This revision of Item 1811 restates some points and contains additional examples and case studies. Expanded study examples are included at the end of each chapter.

1813 Carruth, Beatrice F. "Modifying behavior through social learning." Am J Nurs 76(11): 1804-6, November, 1976. (2 References).
Provides an outline of learning theory and its applications in a treatment center for children and in a state hospital for adults.

1814 Closurdo, Janette S. "Behavior modification and the nursing process." Perspect Psychiatr Care 13(1): 25-36, January-March, 1975. (74 References).
Contains a general review of behavior modification concepts, techniques, tools, theoretical models, and ethics. The role of the nurse in directing behavior change programs is also delineated.

1815 Haus, Barbara F., and Thompson, Sharon. "The effect of nursing intervention on a program of behavior modification by parents in the home." J Psychiatr Nurs 14(8): 9-16, August, 1976. (19 References).
Reports on a study conducted with nine neurologically impaired children aged two to four years. Results indicated appreciable behavior change in those children whose families were visited by a nurse on a bi-weekly basis. The nurse provided instruction and encouragement for the continuation of the behavior modification program. No appreciable change was noted in the behavior of children who were not visited by the nurse.

1816 LeBow, Michael D. Approaches to modifying patient behavior. New York: Appleton-Century-Crofts, 1976. 383p. (Bibliography).
This volume is directed to nursing personnel and is divided into two sections. Section I covers the basic principles of behavior modification and is illustrated with examples appropriate to the nursing setting. Section II is a selection of readings dealing with the modification of problems likely to be encountered by the nurse. Several studies dealing with children are included.

1817 ———. Behavior modification: a significant method in nursing practice. Englewood Cliffs, New Jersey: Prentice-Hall, 1973. 271p. (Bibliography). (Scientific Foundations of Nursing Practice Series).
Designed for the practicing or student nurse, this volume covers the basic principles and practice of behavior modification. A chapter is included on those problems likely to be encountered by the nurse. Each chapter concludes with a summary and review questions.

1818 Miron, Nathan. "Behavior shaping and group nursing with severely retarded patients." In: Fisher, Jerome, and Harris, Robert E., eds. Reinforcement theory in psychological treatment: a symposium. Sacramento, California: The State of California Department of Mental Hygiene, 1966. 1-14. (1 Reference). (Research Monograph, No. 8).
Describes the establishment of operant procedures in a ward of severely retarded girls primarily of adolescent age. The concept of "group nursing" (dividing the patients into smaller groups) was utilized, and details of the problems encountered in such an innovation are examined.

1819 O'Neil, Sally M. "Behavior modification: toward a human experience." Nurs Clin North Am 10(2): 373-79, June, 1975. (5 References).
Advocates a careful assessment of the situation before initiating a program of behavior modification procedures. A progression toward self-management is also advised.

1820 Shorkey, Clayton T., and Taylor, John E. "Management of maladaptive behavior of a severely burned child." Child Welfare 52(8): 543-47, October, 1973. (7 References).
Presents a case history of a seventeen-month-old girl who had begun to associate all attention from the nursing staff with painful experiences. The child was conditioned to discriminate between the aversive conditions of the medical treatment and the nonaversive conditions of social interactions.

1821 Stern, Michael R., and Golden, Frederic. "A partial evaluation of an introductory training program in behavior modification for psychiatric nurses." Am J Community Psychol 5(1): 23-32, March, 1977. (13 References).
Provides details on the procedures and evaluation of a four-session introductory training program in behavior modification. The training utilized lecturettes, group discussion, practice in recording behavior seen on videotape, daily practice in observation, and a film. Improvements were not maintained at a four-month follow-up, which indicated the need for subsequent training.

1822 Whitney, Linda. "Operant learning theory: a framework deserving nursing investigation." Nurs Res 15(3): 229-35, Summer, 1966. (40 References).
Sets forth a selective review of the literature with special reference to the training and rehabilitation of the retardate.

1823 Whitney, Linda Rae, and Barnard, Kathryn E. "Implications of operant learning theory for nursing care of the retarded child." Ment Retard 4(3): 26-29, June, 1966. (5 References). (Reprinted in Item No. 1816).
Presents a case history that records the application of the principles of operant learning by a nurse. The patient was a severely retarded fifteen-year-old spastic girl exhibiting undesirable behavior. The program was also used to develop self-feeding skills.

1824 Zangger, Blondina. "Behavior modification in school nurse's office." Ariz Nurse 29(5): 17-20, November-December, 1976.
Encourages school nurses to become familiar with and to use behavior modification techniques in order to promote such desirable behaviors as good grooming and attendance for medication.

D. MEDICINE

1825 Drash, Philip W., and Leibowitz, J. Michael. "Operant conditioning of speech and language in the nonverbal retarded child. Recent advances." Pediatr Clin North Am 20(1): 233-43, February, 1973. (33 References).
This article, intended for the pediatrician, covers recent developments in behavior modification and advocates the early diagnosis of verbal deficiences, together with referral to a behaviorally oriented psychologist.

1826 Harper, Robert G. "Behavior modification in pediatric practice." Clin Pediatr 14(10): 962-67, October, 1975. (5 References).
Provides a general introduction and is intended to aid the pediatrician in counseling parents on simple behavioral problems.

1827 McGuire, Peter F. "Debbie won't stop biting her playmates: behavior modification in family medicine." Maine Med Assoc J 68(8): 267-68, August, 1977. (3 References).
Encourages the use of behavior modification in the family physician's office. The case of a two-year-old girl whose biting behavior was rapidly extinguished is described. The program, which was successful within six weeks, was conducted by the mother following the physician's instructions.

1828 Murray, Michael E. "Behavioral management in pediatrics: applications of operant learning theory to problem behaviors of children." Clin Pediatr 15(5): 465-70, May, 1976. (10 References).
Summarizes basic principles and illustrates their applicability to a number of behavior problems that may be encountered in the pediatrician's practice.

1829 Stedman, Donald J. "The application of learning principles in pediatric practice." Pediatr Clin North Am 17(2): 427-36, May, 1970. (9 References).
Reviews the use of positive reinforcement in dealing with such problems as aggression, excessive crying, negativism, and passivity.

1830 Williams, Redford B., Jr., and Gentry, W. Doyle, eds. Behavioral approaches to medical treatment. Cambridge, Massachusetts: Ballinger, 1977. 268p. (Bibliography).
Provides the practicing physician with an introduction to behavioral treatment approaches for a wide variety of presenting problems. Although most of the problems would be more likely to be encountered in the adult patient, chapters are also included on problems generally occurring in the pediatric population such as enuresis, and fecal incontinence.

E. PROBATION

1831 Burkhart, Barry R.; Behles, Michael W.; Stumphauzer, Jerome S. "Training juvenile probation officers in behavior modification: knowledge, attitude change, or behavioral competence." Behav Ther 7(1): 47-53, January, 1976. (8 References).
Nine juvenile probation officers received six weeks of training in behavior modification while nine others did not. There was no significant difference in their theoretical knowledge, but the trained group did demonstrate that they could do a behavior analysis and construct a behavioral probation plan.

1832 Thorne, Gaylord L.; Tharp, Roland G.; Wetzel, Ralph J. "Behavior modification techniques: new tools for probation officers." Fed Probat 31(2): 21-27, June, 1967. (8 References). (Reprinted in Item No. 22).
Advocates the use of behavior modification techniques in dealing with juvenile delinquents. Four case histories are provided in which rewards were tailored to the subject. Examples of the rewards are: phone and date privileges for a sixteen-year-old girl; a new bicycle for a seventh-grade boy; TV privileges for a fourteen-year-old boy; and use of a car for a sixteen-year-old boy.

F. PSYCHOLOGY

1833 Abidin, Richard R., Jr. "What's wrong with behavior modification." J Sch Psychol 9(1): 38-42, 1971.

Considers some of the parameters, issues, and problems that should be evaluated by the school psychologist recommending a behavior modification program. The necessary preconditions are indicated and common process errors enumerated.

1834 Bergan, John R., and Caldwell, Thomas. "Operant techniques in school psychology." Psychol Sch 4(2): 136-41, April, 1967. (5 References).
Deals with the school psychologist's role as consultant and advocates the use of operant techniques in the classroom as an effective means of developing that role and obtaining satisfactory behavior change.

1835 Breyer, Norman L.; Calchera, David J.; Cann, Christine. "Behavioral consulting from a distance." Psychol Sch 8(2): 172-76, 1971. (6 References).
Demonstrates the feasibility of using behavior modification techniques within an ongoing consultative program. Such techniques can be implemented by minimally experienced personnel under the direction of a supervisor who remains physically remote from the classroom.

1836 Brown, James C.; Montgomery, Richard; Barclay, James R. "An example of psychologist management of teacher reinforcement procedures in the elementary classroom." Psychol Sch 6(4): 336-40, October, 1969. (8 References).
Reports on a demonstration project using behavioral techniques with 225 educationally handicapped and mentally retarded children. A detailed case history of one child is included.

1837 Curry, Dal R. "Case studies in behavior modification." Psychol Sch 7(4): 330-35, 1970.
Presents two case histories, one involving a reading disability and the other disruptive behavior. Emphasis is placed on the school psychologist's role as a consultant to the teacher.

1838 Franks, Cyril M., and Susskind, Dorothy J. "Behavior modification with children: rationale and technique." J Sch Psychol 6(2): 75-88, 1968. (70 References). (Reprinted in Item No. 26).
Reviews the general background of behavior modification and outlines its relevance to the school psychologist. Greater attention is advocated to the evaluation and recognition of limitations. The establishment of training programs for behavior therapists is recommended.

1839 Hops, Hyman. "The school psychologist as a behavior management consultant in a special class setting." J Sch Psychol 9(4): 473-83, Winter, 1971. (38 References).
Investigates the role of the school psychologist in dealing with problems in large special classes. An example is given of the use of a token reinforcement system in the handling of twenty-two boys between the ages of ten and thirteen. In this instance, the psychologist was able to minimize his role as consultant.

1840 McAllister, Loring William. "A demonstration of a consultation program using operant techniques for the secondary school classroom." For a summary see: Diss Abstr Int 29B(6): 2205, December, 1968.

1841 Meacham, Merle L. "Reinforcement theory as a basis for clinical school psychology." Psychol Sch 5(2): 114-17, April, 1968. (25 References).
Reviews the reported uses of behavioral techniques in the schools. The general acceptance of behavioral modification methods by the school psychologist is predicted.

1842 Mordock, John B., and Phillips, Debora R. "The behavior therapist in the schools." Psychotherapy 8(3): 231-35, Fall, 1971. (18 References).
Describes programs in which psychotherapists treat the child within the school environment, in addition to the home and clinic, by behaviorally oriented methods.

1843 Morice, Herbert O. "The school psychologist as a behavioral consultant: a project in behavior modification in a public school setting." Psychol Sch 5(3): 253-61, July, 1968. (39 References).
Reports on a four school project designed to promote the use of behavioral techniques in the classroom. Social psychologists acted as consultants.

1844 Woody, Robert H. "Behavior therapy and school psychology." J Sch Psychol 4(4): 1-14, Summer, 1966. (51 References).
Reviews the basic principles of behavior therapy and their relationship to school psychology. The introduction of these techniques by the school psychologist to both teachers and parents is recommended.

1845 ————. "School psychologist as a behavior therapist: past and future." Psychol Sch 13(3): 266-68, July, 1976. (3 References).
Reviews the role of the school psychologist during the period from 1965 to 1975, with emphasis on the emerging roles of behavior therapist and consultant. Increasing support for behavior modification is predicted and preparatory programs in colleges suggested.

G. SOCIAL WORK

1846 Feldman, Ronald A., and Wodarski, John S. Contemporary approaches to group treatment: traditional, behavior modification, and group-centered methods. San Francisco: Jossey-Bass, 1975. 248p. (Bibliography). (Jossey-Bass Behavioral Science Series).
Describes three group-work methods used in social work. Chapter Five reviews behavior modification concepts and their applicability to group work by the social worker.

1847 Fischer, Joel, and Gochros, Harvey L. Planned behavior change: behavior modification in social work. New York: Free Press, 1975. 525p. (Bibliography).
Provides a thorough introduction to behavior modification as it is applicable to social work. While it deals primarily with adult clients, two chapters are devoted to parent-child and school behavior problems. The types of problems amenable to treatment by behavioral methods are outlined, and examples are given of successful programs.

1848 Frankel, Arthur J., and Glasser, Paul H. "Behavioral approaches to group work." Soc Work 19(2): 163-75, March, 1974. (28 References).
Reviews the literature concerned with techniques of behavior modification and the implementation of such methods in social work groups.

1849 Jehu, Derek; Hardiker, Pauline; Yelloly, Margaret; *et al*. *Behavior modification in social work*. New York: Wiley-Interscience, 1972. 193p. (Bibliography).
Behavior modification is proposed as a method of amending and extending traditional casework methods. Principles, applications, and a discussion of ethics are included, together with many examples of both child and adult cases.

1850 Peterson, C. Leslie. "The consequation exercise: a tool for teaching behavior modification to social work students." *J Educ Soc Work* 13(1): 96-103, Winter, 1977.
Summarizes basic concepts of behavior modification and outlines an exercise designed to give the student practice in carrying out and recording a behavioral intervention.

1851 Sanson-Fisher, Robert, and Stotter, Kim. "Essential steps in designing a successful contract." *Child Welfare* 56(4): 239-48, April, 1977. (21 References).
Outlines the necessary basic steps in drawing up a behavioral contract. The need for adequate monitoring is emphasized, and common reasons for failure are also noted.

IX.

Training in Behavior Modification

A. TRAINING OF TEACHERS

1. Theory; Principles; General Aspects of Training

1852 Andrews, Joseph K. "The results of a pilot program to train teachers in the classroom application of behavior modification techniques." J Sch Psychol 8(1): 37-42, 1970. (18 References). (Reprinted in Item No. 26).

In a study conducted with eleven teachers, the effectiveness of a four-session training program was adequately demonstrated. The teachers were able to affect changes in classroom behavior as a result of participation in the program.

1853 Applegate, Gary Bert. "The development of an educational film demonstrating operant conditioning techniques: a supplement to established teaching methods." For a summary see: Diss Abstr Int 31B(8): 4979, February, 1971.

1854 Awen, Edward Peter. "The effect of a behavior modification mini-course on intern teacher behavior during the initial intern teaching experience." For a summary see: Diss Abstr Int 37A(11): 7083, May, 1976.

1855 Becker, Wesley C.; Engelmann, Siegfried; Thomas, Don R. Teaching: a course in applied psychology. Chicago: Science Research Associates, 1971. 499p.

This text is divided into two parts. Part I is a behavior modification primer for the teacher that focuses on the use of operant techniques to reduce classroom problems. Problems in behavior motivation are stressed. Part II presents the theory and concepts central to the practice of behavior modification. Exercises, reviews of subject matter, and suggested projects are included.

1856 Behavior modification for teachers. College Park, Maryland: Maryland University, College of Education, 1972. 146p. (ED 075 373).

Contains course material on behavior modification and is intended for use with education students. Didactic material and case material are both included.

1857 Bevett, David Leon. "Effects of a behaviorally oriented training program on the frequency of teacher praise and attention in public secondary schools: a comparison study of predominantly black and predominantly white urban schools and achievement levels." For a summary see: Diss Abstr Int 37B(1): 449, July, 1976.

1858 Brown, Diane McGee. "Teacher training in the use of operant principles to reinforce assertive behavior in elementary school children." For a summary see: Diss Abstr Int 37A(8): 4975, February, 1976.

1859 Brownsmith, Keith; Fink, Albert H.; Perky, Christopher Ann. Summative evaluation: behavior management training program. Bloomington, Indiana: Indiana University, Center for Innovation in Teaching the Handicapped, 1976. 68p. (ED 133 985). (Technical Report 31.2).
Reviews the purposes and objectives of a training program for teachers. The training models are described, and reports on the evaluations are included, together with the evaluations of the students who participated in the program. Appendices include sample questionnaires and tests, a list of the behavioral techniques demonstrated, and simulated interview questions.

1860 Cooper, Margaret L.; Thomson, Carolyn L.; Baer, Donald M. "The experimental modification of teacher attending behavior." J Appl Behav Anal 3(2): 153-57, Summer, 1970. (4 References).
Reports an attempt to increase the teacher attention given to desirable child responses on the part of two teachers, neither of whom had received formal training in reinforcement principles. The teachers were provided with factual feedback related to their attending behavior. Following the initiation of feedback, both teachers showed an increase in attending to appropriate responses from the children in their classrooms.

1861 Cotler, Sherwin B.; Applegate, Gary; King, Larry W.; et al. "Establishing a token economy in a state hospital classroom: a lesson in training student and teacher." Behav Ther 3(2): 209-22, April, 1972. (13 References).
Traces the training of a teacher in behavioral techniques and the utilization of those techniques in the teacher's class of fourteen disruptive boys. The mean age of the boys was thirteen years and one month. The results indicated that appropriate study behavior first increased, but then lessened. Problems encountered in the administration of the program are discussed, together with an analysis of the factors contributing to the decrease in work output.

1862 Cramer, Carolyn Ann. "The effects of a cooperating teacher training program in applied behavior analysis on selected teacher behaviors of secondary physical education student teachers." For a summary see: Diss Abstr Int 38A(8): 4655, February, 1978.

1863 Currens, James William. "An applied behavior analysis training model for preservice teachers." For a summary see: Diss Abstr Int 38A(5): 2644, November, 1977.

1864 George, Thomas W. "The reciprocal nature of reinforcement." Education 97(2): 173-76, Winter, 1976.
Reports on the attempt by fourteen elementary school teachers to increase their use of praise over a four-week period. A reciprocal relationship was discerned between the amount of positive reinforcement given and the amount received by the teachers themselves.

1865 Harris, Alice. Problems of quality control in the use of behavior change techniques in public school settings. 1975. 13p. (5 References). (ED 117 893).

Describes a program designed to train student teachers in the use of behavior modification techniques in order to deal with problem children. A set of guidelines is provided, and there is an attempt to anticipate the problems most frequently encountered in the public school setting.

1866 Hosford, Ray E. "Teaching teachers to reinforce student participation." In: Krumboltz, John D., and Thoresen, Carl Ed., eds. Behavioral counseling: cases and techniques. New York: Holt, Rinehart & Winston, 1969. 152-54.
Relates the details of instruction, by a school counselor, of four seventh-grade teachers. The teachers were instructed in operant conditioning techniques. The target behavior was the lack of participation in class discussion of certain students. These students were seen to demonstrate a marked increase in participation following the instruction given their teachers.

1867 Howie, Patricia Anzalone, and Winkleman, Gretchen. Behavior modification: a practical guide for the classroom teacher. West Nyack, New York: Parker, 1977. 214p.
Acquaints the teacher with basic terminology and principles and describes the teacher's role as a "behavior modifier." Programs are described for various classroom settings and for such specific problem children as the disruptive, the quiet, and the defeated. One chapter is devoted to the optimum classroom arrangement.

1868 Kazdin, Alan E., and Moyer, William. "Training teachers to use behavior modification." In: Yen, Sherman, and McIntire, Roger W., eds. Teaching behavior modification. Kalamazoo, Michigan: Behaviordelia, 1976. 170-200. (97 References).
Focuses on the designing of a behavioral training program for teachers. Consideration is given to the definition of goals, data collection, and the evaluation of programs. Instructional methods are discussed, together with the necessity of feedback, and methods of ensuring the maintenance of the programs conducted by the teacher.

1869 Koegel, Robert L.; Russo, Dennis C.; Rincover, Arnold. "Assessing and training teachers in the generalized use of behavior modification with autistic children." J Appl Behav Anal 10(2): 197-205, Summer, 1977. (16 References).
Reports on a study conducted with eleven teachers and twelve autistic children. The results indicated that: (1) it was possible to assess empirically the teachers' proficiency in the use of behavior modification; (2) systematic improvement in the child's behavior could not be expected unless the teacher had received training; and (3) the teachers learned generalized skills that were effective with a variety of children and target behaviors.

1870 Langstaff, Anne L., and Volkmor, Cara B. Contingency management. Columbus, Ohio: Merrill, 1975. 105p. (Bibliography).
Presents a training program designed for preservice and inservice teachers. The total program consists of a book and four sound-filmstrips. Each chapter in the book contains a self-test and tasks to be performed.

1871 McKenzie, Hugh S. "Special education and consulting teachers." In: Clark, F. W.; Evans, D. R.; Hamerlynck, L. A., eds. Implementing behavioral programs for schools and clinics. Banff

International Conference on Behavior Modification, 3rd, 1971. Champaign, Illinois: Research Press, 1972. 103-24. (18 References).
Outlines a program in Vermont that trains and evaluates consulting teachers in the techniques of behavior modification. The consulting teacher is seen as a potential training agent for the regular classroom teacher.

1872 McKenzie, Hugh S.; Egner, Ann N.; Knight, Martha F.; et al. "Training consulting teachers to assist elementary teachers in the management and education of handicapped children." Except Child 37(2): 137-43, October, 1970. (8 References).
Describes a graduate program in the training of consulting teachers. Three case studies are included which illustrate the types of projects conducted by the students.

1873 McKeown, Douglas O'Neal. "Generalization to the classroom of principles of behavior modification taught to groups of teachers." For a summary see: Diss Abstr Int 34B(6): 2943, December, 1973.

1874 McKeown, Douglas, Jr.; Adams, Henry E.; Forehand, Rex. "Generalization to the classroom of principles of behavior modification taught to teachers." Behav Res Ther 13(2/3): 85-92, June, 1975. (20 References).
Evaluates, in terms of knowledge of behavioral principles and change in the frequency of classroom disruptions, the efficacy of various instructional techniques. The subjects were twenty elementary school teachers enrolled in an instructional program.

1875 MacMillan, Donald L. Behavior modification in education. New York: Macmillan, 1973. 238p. (Bibliography).
This text, which is intended for use in preservice or inservice teacher training, covers both the basic principles and the practical application of those principles in the education setting. Chapters are included on schedules of reinforcement, the use of behavior modification in both special and regular classrooms, and token economies. A discussion of controversial issues and a glossary are also included.

1876 Madsen, Charles H., Jr.; Madsen, Clifford K.; Driggs, Dan F. "Freeing teachers to teach." In: Rickard, Henry C., ed. Behavioral intervention in human problems. New York: Pergamon, 1971. 61-75. (35 References).
Provides details of a three-fold program that teaches the use of behavioral techniques to control classroom behavior. By the use of such techniques the teacher is afforded more time to concentrate on the acquisition of new material.

1877 Mira, Mary. "Results of a behavior modification training program for parents and teachers." Behav Res Ther 8(3): 309-11, August, 1970. (5 References).
Traces the techniques that were used over a twenty-one-month period in training parents and teachers in methods of behavior modification. The most commonly used form of training consisted of advising the manager without seeing the child. The parents were found to be as successful as the teachers in the administration of the programs.

1878 Rönneberg, Sten. "A comprehensive training program for behavior therapists." In: Thompson, Travis, and Dockens, William S., III,

eds. Applications of behavior modification. New York: Academic Press, 1975. 451-67. (66 References).
Contains a detailed description of training programs presently existing in Sweden. A comprehensive program for training at various educational levels is outlined.

1879 Rosenfield, Sylvia. "Implementing behavior modification in the classroom: problems of consultants." Paper presented at the 55th Annual International Convention, The Council for Exceptional Children, Atlanta, Georgia, April 11-15, 1977. 16p. (ED 139 192).
Discusses the consultant's role in training teachers in behavior modification techniques. The most effective procedure was found to be a combination of knowledge and guided experience with feedback and support.

1880 Stewart, William A.; Goodman, Gay; Hammond, Brad. "Behavior modification: teacher training and attitudes." Except Child 42(7): 402-3, April, 1976. (1 Reference).
Provides details of a study conducted among the teachers in a moderately large metropolitan school. The prevalence of the use of behavioral techniques was documented. An analysis of 124 responses showed that favorable attitudes toward the methods were positively correlated with the teachers' use of them and with the number of behaviors for which they were used.

1881 Taber, Florence Martha. "Videotapes--an aid in teaching behavior identification and techniques for behavior management." For a summary see: Diss Abstr Int 37A(6): 3555, December, 1976.

1882 Vargas, Julie S. Behavioral psychology for teachers. New York: Harper & Row, 1977. 319p. (Bibliography).
This text, which is intended for the education student, covers the basic principles of behavioral psychology, the methods of measuring behavior, and the techniques, planning, and handling of large numbers of students. Each chapter contains objectives, examples, and problem exercises to be completed.

1883 Winett, Richard A. "Instructing and consulting with teachers in behavior modification and open education." Teach Educ 11(4): 30-34, Spring, 1976. (7 References).
Briefly outlines an instructional course that emphasizes the possible synthesis of behavior modification and open education.

1884 Yen, Sherman, and McIntire, Roger W., eds. Teaching behavior modification. Kalamazoo, Michigan: Behaviordelia, 1976. 264p.
This text aims to provide information on how to introduce behavior modification courses at institutions of higher learning, and how to conduct short-term inservice training programs. The first chapter considers the ethical questions raised by widespread dissemination of such knowledge, and the remaining ten chapters are devoted to the training of different segments of the population, e.g., teachers, parents, paraprofessionals, college students, etc.

2. In-Service Training

1885 Brown, Paul L., and Presbie, Robert J. "The conversion of a public elementary school to a reinforcement-oriented environment with nine hours of in-service training." Paper presented at the 43rd Annual

Meeting of the Eastern Psychological Association, Boston, April, 1972. 6p. (ED 076 477). (7 References).
Describes a training program conducted with twenty-two elementary school teachers. The teachers were able to apply operant techniques successfully after only nine hours of training.

1886 Canter, Lee, and Paulson, Terry. "A college credit model of in-school consultation: a functional behavioral training program." Community Ment Health J 10(3): 268-75, Fall, 1974. (12 References).
Furnishes details of a pilot study combining didactic structure and college credit with the immediacy of an in-school consultation. Teachers were trained in behavior modification methods in their own classrooms and completed an evaluation questionnaire at the end of the course.

1887 Cocreham, Elizabeth Ann. "A study of the effect on attitude, knowledge and evaluation of teachers working with elementary school children after participation in a behavioral modification inservice program." For a summary see: Diss Abstr Int 36A(3): 1386, September, 1975.

1888 Educational development and utilization of a composite approach to teaching the exceptional. Punta Gorda, Florida: Curricula Improvement Center, 1972. 28p. (ED 073 598).
Describes an inservice course for teachers that consists of a teacher handbook and four videotaped model lessons. The target behavior was in-attendance in 400 educably mentally handicapped students. Significant achievements in increased attentiveness were noted following the inservice course.

1889 Feinberg, Theodore Anton. "The effect of in-service training on the ratings of parents, teachers and clinicians regarding behavior problems in elementary school children." For a summary see: Diss Abstr Int 38A(5): 2661, November, 1977.

1890 Gardner, James, and Chavez, Kay. "It isn't all M & M's." Instructor 83(8): 95, April, 1974.
Briefly describes a successful inservice training program on the techniques of behavior modification.

1891 Hall, R. Vance, and Copeland, Rodney E. "The responsive teaching model: a first step in shaping school personnel as behavior modification specialists." In: Clark, F. W.; Evans, D. R.; Hamerlynck, L. A., eds. Implementing behavioral programs for schools and clinics. Banff International Conference on Behavior Modification, 3rd, 1971. Champaign, Illinois: Research Press, 1972. 125-50. (12 References).
Describes a teacher training program that can be a part of inservice training, offered as extension courses, or presented in a workshop format. Appendices contain case histories as well as outlines of course development, format, and examination schedules.

1892 Hall, R. Vance; Panyan, Marion; Rabon, Deloris; et al. "Instructing beginning teachers in reinforcement procedures which improve classroom control." J Appl Behav Anal 1(4): 315-22, Winter, 1968. (11 References). (Reprinted in Item No. 37).

Details studies conducted in the classrooms of three first-year teachers unfamiliar with learning theory who were experiencing difficulties in classroom control. All three were instructed in the use of systematic reinforcement and were able to increase classroom control within a few days.

1893 McNamara, J. Regis, and Diehl, Luther A. "Behavioral consultation with a Head Start program." J Community Psychol 2(4): 352-57, October, 1974. (19 References).
Provides data on an inservice training project conducted as a part of a psychological consultation program in various Head Start centers. Program effectiveness was analyzed on the basis of recording performance, final workshop examination scores, and teacher ratings.

1894 Ringer, V. M. J. "The use of a 'token helper' in the management of classroom behavior problems and in teacher training." J Appl Behav Anal 6(4): 671-77, Winter, 1973. (5 References).
Describes the training, within the classroom, of a fourth-grade teacher. Token and verbal reinforcement were used to reduce disruptive behavior.

1895 Sheekey, Arthur D. "Inservice model for training elementary teachers of individualized learning classrooms to systematically apply contingency management and related behavior modification techniques." For a summary see: Diss Abstr Int 32A(4): 1967, October, 1971.

1896 Sloane, Howard N., Jr., and Allen, John E. "An in-service teacher training program in contingency management." In: Becker, Wesley C., ed. An empirical basis for change in education. Chicago: Science Research Associates, 1971. 375-97.
Outlines an inservice training program that instructs teachers in the techniques of behavior modification by having them follow programs for the correction of specific problem behaviors within their own classrooms.

1897 Ulrich, Roger; Wolfe, Marshall; Bluhm, Marland. Operant conditioning in the public schools. Kalamazoo, Michigan: Behavior Development Corporation, 1968. (Behavior Modification Monographs, 1, No. 1).
Traces the establishment of an inservice training course for teachers in a public school setting.

1898 Wood, W. Scott. The Lincoln Elementary School Project: some results of an in-service training course in behavioral psychology. Kalamazoo, Michigan: Behavior Development Corporation, 1970. (Behavior Modification Monographs, 1, No. 2). (Reprinted in Item No. 22).
Provides data on an inservice training course for elementary teachers. Reports by the teachers on projects carried out within the classrooms are included. The projects dealt with a variety of disruptive behaviors.

3. Teacher Training Manuals

1899 Buckley, Nancy K., and Walker, Hill M. Modifying classroom behavior: a manual of procedure for classroom teachers. Champaign, Illinois: Research Press, 1970. 95p. (Bibliography).
This text is designed for use by teacher trainees and by practicing teachers. It incorporates both prose and programmed items in a format that begins with basic principles and progresses to application of those principles in the classroom.

1900 Canter, Lee. The whys and hows of working with behavior problems in the classroom. San Rafael, California: Academic Therapy, 1974. 63p.
A simply-explained guide for the classroom teacher, this text provides basic background material in the use of positive reinforcement. Examples of worksheets for dealing with the more common classroom behavioral problems are provided.

1901 Carter, Ronald D. Help! These kids are driving me crazy. Champaign, Illinois: Research Press, 1972. 112p.
This short manual on the classroom applications of behavior modification is written in telegraphic style and is illustrated with cartoon-type drawings.

1902 Champagne, David W., and Goldman, Richard M. Teaching parents teaching. New York: Appleton-Century-Crofts, 1972. 268p. (New Century Urban Education Series).
This text is intended for teachers who wish to assist parents in acquiring teaching skills. One section contains step-by-step instructions on teaching reinforcement techniques to parents.

1903 DeRisi, William J., and Butz, George. Writing behavioral contracts: a case simulation practice manual. Champaign, Illinois: Research Press, 1975. 87p. (Bibliography).
This manual is intended for teachers already familiar with behavior modification or learning theory. It sets forth guidelines for the implementation of contingency contracting. Most of the examples are taken from adult and adolescent cases.

1904 Givner, Abraham, and Graubard, Paul S. A handbook of behavior modification for the classroom. New York: Holt, Rinehart & Winston, 1974. 174p. (Bibliography).
This manual, written for the classroom teacher, includes both general principles and specific techniques. Each chapter contains review questions and there is a list of recommended programmed curriculum materials. Appendices include suggested reinforcers and answers to the review questions.

1905 Goodwin, Dwight L., and Coates, Thomas J. Helping students help themselves: how you can put behavior analysis into action in your classroom. Englewood Cliffs, New Jersey: Prentice-Hall, 1976. 205p. (Bibliography). (Prentice-Hall Series in Counseling and Guidance).
This manual is intended for both prospective and experienced classroom teachers. It is divided into three sections: Chapters One and Two introduce the basic concepts and assumptions; Chapters Three through Nine present step-by-step instructions in target selection, assessment, strategy planning, and implementation; Chapters Ten through Thirteen describe alternative and novel methods of application, e.g., group contingencies and the teaching of self-control.

1906 Homme, Lloyd E., et al. How to use contingency contracting in the classroom. Champaign, Illinois: Research Press, 1970. 130p.
This programmed text is intended primarily for elementary or high school teachers. It assumes a familiarity with the basic principles of behavior modification. Self tests conclude each section.

1907 Kozloff, Martin A. Educating children with learning and behavior problems. New York: Wiley-Interscience, 1974. 459p. (Bibliography).
Provides detailed instructions for parents, teachers, and allied health personnel on how to use behavioral methods in order to teach learning readiness skills, large and small motor skills, motor imitation, verbal imitation, and functional speech. Several of the chapters contain written assignments.

1908 Kunzelmann, H. P., ed. Precision teaching: an initial training sequence. Seattle, Washington: Special Child Publications, 1970. 310p. (Bibliography).
This programmed manual is designed for practicing and prospective teachers. Emphasis is placed on continuous evaluation and modification of procedures. Details are included on measurement, charting, planning, and recording.

1909 Mamchak, P. Susan, and Mamchak, Steven R. Personalized behavioral modification: practical techniques for elementary educators. West Nyack, New York: Parker, 1976. 212p.
Presents detailed instructions for the implementation of an individualized program. Numerous examples are included, together with guides for record keeping, and evaluation plans.

1910 Meacham, Merle L., and Wiesen, Allen E. Changing classroom behavior: a manual for precision teaching. 2nd ed. New York: Intext Educational, 1974. 244p. (Bibliography).
This text is divided into two sections: Part One outlines the specific principles that can be employed to enhance learning or eliminate disruption. Part Two covers recent developments in retardation, social deprivation, and severely deviant behavior.

1911 Mink, Oscar G. The behavior change process. New York: Harper & Row, 1970. 209p.
This self-instructional programmed text is intended for classroom teachers and counselors. It provides a combination of constructed response and multiple choice format. Reviews of research, a discussion of principles, illustrative cases, and evaluated data are included.

1912 Morreau, Lanny E., and Daley, Marvin F. Behavioral management in the classroom. New York: Appleton-Century-Crofts, 1972. 149p. (Bibliography). (New Century Urban Education Series).
Presents a student-tested programmed text suitable for practicing and prospective teachers. It would also prove useful for school administrators. The text incorporates a series of laboratory experiments.

1913 Neisworth, John T.; Deno, Stanley L.; Jenkins, Joseph R. Student motivation and classroom management: a behavioristic approach. Lemont, Pennsylvania: Behavior Technics, 1973. 150p. (Bibliography).
This manual presents the basic behavioral principles and illustrates their applications to typical classroom settings. Emphasis is placed on the development and use of token economies. The appendix contains examples of specific objectives for several academic areas.

1914 Poteet, James A. Behavior modification: a practical guide for teachers. Minneapolis, Minnesota: Burgess, 1973. 104p. (Bibliography). (Burgess Educational Psychology Series for the Teacher).

This manual for the practicing teacher provides instruction in the basic techniques of observation, recording, and the modification of classroom behavior. The use of positive reinforcement is emphasized. Materials are included on stimulus control, attitude change, exceptional children, and accountability. A case history is provided.

1915 Walker, Hill M. Walker Problem Behavior Identification Checklist. Los Angeles: Western Psychological Services, 1970.
Provides a fifty-item checklist of behaviors that may be used as an initial screening device.

1916 Walker, Hill M., and Buckley, Nancy K. Token reinforcement techniques: classroom applications for the hard-to-teach child. Eugene, Oregon: E-B Press, 1974. 225p. (Bibliography).
This volume is intended as a college text or as an inservice training manual for teachers. The first half covers basic behavioral principles and their explicit application to token reinforcement systems. The second half summarizes research studies underlying the principles. Test and mastery exercises are included.

1917 Walker, James E., and Shea, Thomas M. Behavior modification: a practical approach for educators. St. Louis, Missouri: Mosby, 1976. 167p. (Bibliography).
This text, which may be used as a self-instructional manual, is designed for use by teachers, teachers in training, and paraprofessionals in the educational setting. Basic principles of behavior modification are covered, and many step-by-step examples of techniques usable in the classroom are provided. Each chapter contains a summary, exercises and projects, and a tear-out work sheet with examples of forms and checklists.

1918 Watson, Luke S., Jr. Child behavior modification: a manual for teachers, nurses, and parents. New York: Pergamon, 1973. 147p. (Bibliography). (Pergamon General Psychology Series, PGPS-24).
This manual, which assumes no background in psychology, is intended for nurses, teachers, and parents dealing with mentally retarded and autistic children in institutions or community settings. The volume can be used as a training text. Each chapter has a summary and true-false, fill-in, and essay-type test materials.

B. TRAINING OF PARENTS

1. Theory; Principles; General Aspects of Training

1919 Berkowitz, Barbara P., and Graziano, Anthony M. "Training parents as behavior therapists: a review." Behav Res Ther 10(4): 297-317, November, 1972. (81 References). (Reprinted in Item No. 35).
Reviews the published literature on the theoretical, empirical, and ethical rationales for the training of parents as behavior therapists for their own children. Areas needing further research are indicated.

1920 Blechman, Elaine A., and Manning, Martha. "A reward-cost analysis of the single-parent family." In: Mash, Eric J.; Hamerlynck, Leo A.; Handy, Lee C., eds. Behavior modification and families. Banff International Conference on Behavior Modification, 6th, 1974. New York: Brunner/Mazel, 1976. 61-90. (110 References).

Proposes that an awareness of the unique nature of the single-parent family should accompany planning for family member behavior change. It is advised that an adjustment of goals and rewards may be necessary. An appendix contains references to seventy-five articles dealing with single-parent families.

1921 Brown, Duane, and Brown Sandra. "Parental consultation: a behavioral approach." Elem Sch Guid Couns 10(2): 95-102, December, 1975. (19 References).
Outlines procedures for instructing parents in behavioral skills. The first session may be broken into six stages: rapport building, structuring, information taking and diagnosis, explaining behavioral principles, reexamining behavior, and goal setting and the selection of techniques. Subsequent sessions deal with the evaluation of progress.

1922 Brown, Joe H.; Gamboa, A. M., Jr.; Birkimer, John; et al. "Some possible effects of parent self-control training on parent-child interactions." In: Mash, Eric J.; Hamerlynck, Leo A.; Handy, Lee C., eds. Behavior modification and families. Banff International Conference on Behavior Modification, 6th, 1974. New York: Brunner/Mazel, 1976. 180-92. (10 References).
Reports on the use of behavioral programming and self-control procedures by twelve mothers whose children were displaying disruptive behaviors within the home. The parents were permitted to select their own treatment programs. A high degree of improvement was reported. Seven short case histories are cited.

1923 Clement, Paul W. "Please, Mother, I'd rather you do it yourself: training parents to treat their own children." J Sch Health 41(2): 65-69, February, 1971. (12 References).
Outlines the advantages and methods of utilizing parents in behavioral correction. A few illustrative case histories are included.

1924 Drabman, Ronald S., and Jarvie, Greg. "Counseling parents of children with behavior problems: the use of extinction and time-out techniques." Pediatrics 59(1): 78-85, January, 1977. (14 References).
Documents the difficulties found in using the ignoring and/or time out procedures in the home setting. Such pitfalls as not taking a baseline, not specifying the target behavior, and reinforcing the undesirable behavior, are described. Remedies are suggested for these difficulties. (For a comment on this article, see Item No. 1946.)

1925 Fodor, Iris E. "The parent as a therapist." Ment Hyg 57(2): 16-19, Spring, 1973.
Briefly reports on a parent training program. The training of parents is advocated as an economical use of the therapist's time.

1926 Fontana, Vincent J., and Robison, Esther. "A multidisciplinary approach to the treatment of child abuse." Pediatrics 57(5): 760-64, May, 1976. (10 References).
Describes a therapeutic approach to the treatment of child abuse. The method includes instruction in behavioral techniques for the abusing mother.

1927 Freeman, B. J., and Ritvo, Edward R. "Parents as paraprofessionals." In: Ritvo, Edward R., ed. Autism: diagnosis, current

research and management. New York: Spectrum, 1976. 277-85. (36 References).
Presents an overview of operant therapy and a rationale for training parents. A list of parent-training manuals is provided.

1928 Gardner, James M. "Training parents as behavior modifiers." In: Yen, Sherman, and McIntire, Roger W., eds. Teaching behavior modification. Kalamazoo, Michigan: Behaviordelia, 1976. 17-53. (81 References).
Summarizes studies of the training of parents in behavior modification. Among the aspects of training considered are the content of the training, practical experience, the use of reinforcement with parents, group versus individual training, and the training of parents from various educational and socioeconomic levels.

1929 Hanson, Teri Rae. "Training parents as reinforcement therapists for their own children." For a summary see: Diss Abstr Int 35B(8): 4174, February, 1975.

1930 Horowitz, Laurence Jerome. "Parental intervention in behavior modification of underachievers." For a summary see: Diss Abstr 27A(12): 4129, June, 1967.

1931 Itani, Mary Helen. "Behavioral cognition as a factor in training parents as therapeutic change agents." For a summary see: Diss Abstr Int 36B(8): 4162, February, 1976.

1932 Johnson, Claudia A., and Katz, Roger C. "Using parents as change agents for their children: a review." J Child Psychol Psychiatry 14(3): 181-200, September, 1973. (77 References).
Reviews procedures and results, types of behavior modified, and methods of parent training. Areas needing further assessment and research are recommended.

1933 Johnson, Sarah Ann. "A comparison of mother versus child groups and traditional versus behavior modification procedures in the 'treatment' of disobedient children." For a summary see: Diss Abstr Int 31B(5): 2989, November, 1970.

1934 Karoly, Paul, and Rosenthal, Mitchell. "Training parents in behavior modification: effects on perceptions of family interaction and deviant child behavior." Behav Ther 8(3): 406-10, June, 1977. (13 References).
Reports on a study which examined the effects of a ten-session parent training group. Aspects examined included the parents' perceptions of the home environment and the problem behaviors of their children. The results indicated that these parents perceived their home environment as more cohesive and as having less conflict following the ten-week sessions.

1935 Lasser, Barbara Ruth. "Teaching mothers of mongoloid children to use behavior modification procedures." For a summary see: Diss Abstr Int 30A(12): 5239, June, 1970.

1936 Lebow, Michael D. "The behavior modification process for parent-child therapy." Fam Coord 22(3): 313-19, July, 1973. (21 References).

Advocates the incorporation of the parents into the treatment process by teaching them behavior modification techniques. Trained parents are more likely to produce long-lasting results and can effectively reduce the amount of professional time needed for each case.

1937 Leigh, Jim. "Behavior modification as an alternative counseling aid." In: Buscaglia, Leo, ed. The disabled and their parents: a counseling challenge. Thorofare, New Jersey: Slack, 1975. 319-26. (16 References).
Briefly introduces the principles of behavior modification and their use by the parents of the disabled child.

1938 Morrey, James G. "Parent training in precise behavior management with mentally retarded children." For a summary see: Diss Abstr Int 31A(7): 3376, January, 1971.

1939 O'Dell, Stan. "Training parents in behavior modification: a review." Psychol Bull 81(7): 418-33, July, 1974. (94 References).
Critically reviews seventy articles on the training of parents. Special emphasis is placed on historical development, applicability of the methods employed, and technological issues.

1940 Perelman, Phyllis F., and Hanley, Edward M. "Training parents in behavior analysis techniques." Paper presented at the 2nd Annual Convention of the Midwestern Association of Behavior Analysis, Chicago, May, 1976. 13p. (ED 136 132).
Discusses state-designed workshops which have provided training in behavior analysis for parents. The four parent workshops implemented successfully demonstrated that participating parents were able to apply behavioral techniques and to change behavior in most children.

1941 Pinkston, Elsie May. "Parents as behavioral therapists for their children." For a summary see: Diss Abstr Int 35B(9): 4660, March, 1975.

1942 Pinsker, Mark Arthur. "A comparison of parent effectiveness training and behavior modification parent training groups on behavior change in target children: self-concept, family intervention and patterns of behavior change." For a summary see: Diss Abstr Int 38A(8): 4694, February, 1978.

1943 Risley, Todd R.; Clark, Hewitt B.; Cataldo, Michael F. "Behavioral technology for the normal middle-class family." In: Mash, Eric J.; Hamerlynck, Leo A.; Handy, Lee C., eds. Behavior modification and families. Banff International Conference on Behavior Modification, 6th, 1974. New York: Brunner/Mazel, 1976. 34-60. (39 References).
Discusses the child-rearing difficulties encountered by the modern family and advocates a comprehensive system of child-rearing assistance for families based on behavioral principles.

1944 Russo, Salvatore. "Adaptations in behavioral therapy with children." Behav Res Ther 2(1): 43-47, February, 1964. (5 References).
Furnishes the results of two experiments designed to teach behavior modification methods to parents. The parents subsequently used the techniques successfully within their home situations.

1945 Salzinger, Kurt; Feldman, Richard S.; Portnoy, Stephanie. "Training parents of brain-injured children in the use of operant conditioning procedures." Behav Ther 1(1): 4-32, March, 1970. (21 References).
Submits the data on a project involving two samples of parents of brain-injured children. All of the parents who carried out the modification programs were effective in changing their children's behavior. Reasons for the failures of other parents are discussed.

1946 Schowalter, John E. "The modification of behavior modification." Pediatrics 59(1): 130-31, January, 1977. (7 References).
Comments on an article by Drabman and Jarvie (Item No. 1924) dealing with the difficulties of implementing behavioral techniques in the home. It is indicated that: (1) there are also intrapsychic and interpersonal aspects to behavior; (2) all children are not alike and may not respond identically; and (3) no one approach is successful with all children.

1947 Tymchuk, Alexander J. "Training parent therapists." Ment Retard 13(5): 19-22, October, 1975.
Outlines a model for working with the parents of the developmentally disabled. The approach combines dynamic and behavioral therapeutic strategies.

1948 Zimmern, Annette Wacks. "Parent Training: its effects upon parents' attitudes, and the behavior of their severely or profoundly retarded children." For a summary see: Diss Abstr Int 37A(6): 3435, December, 1976.

2. Program Development

1949 Benassi, Victor A., and Benassi, Barbara J. "An approach to teaching behavior modification principles to parents." Rehabil Lit 34(5): 134-37, May, 1973. (8 References).
Outlines a seven-week training program for parents that includes a reinforcing environment for the parents themselves.

1950 Bernal, Martha E.; Williams, Donald E.; Miller, William Hansford; et al. "The use of videotape feedback and operant learning principles in training parents in management of deviant children." In: Rubin, Richard D.; Fensterheim, Herbert; Henderson, John D.; et al., eds. Advances in behavior therapy: proceedings of the fourth conference of the Association for Advancement of Behavior Therapy. New York: Academic Press, 1972. 19-31. (7 References).
Reports on a parent training program based in a hospital outpatient department. The program employs videotapes of home parent-child interactions. Reliance is placed on three operant principles: positive reinforcement, punishment, and extinction. Four case histories are included.

1951 Carlaw, Barry Allen. "The development of a behavioral program of instruction for parents of mentally retarded children." For a summary see: Diss Abstr Int 36B(7): 3592, January, 1976.

1952 Christophersen, Edward R.; Barnard, James D.; Ford, Dennis; et al. "The family training program: improving parent-child interaction patterns." In: Mash, Eric J.; Handy, Lee C.; Hamerlynck, Leo A., eds. Behavior modification approaches to parenting. Banff

International Conference on Behavior Modification, 6th, 1974. New York: Brunner/Mazel, 1976. 36-56. (17 References).
Describes an intensive in-home treatment program designed to provide the child with a maximum amount of instructions, feedback, and consequences. Results indicate that the program was more effective than the conventional intervention strategies employed by the traditional child guidance clinic.

1953 Clement, Paul W.; Roberts, Paul V.; Lantz, Cary E. "Mothers and peers as child behavior therapists." Int J Group Psychother 26(3): 335-59, July, 1976. (22 References).
This study, conducted with twenty-eight families, investigated the feasibility of training mothers and children in group behavioral techniques. Positive changes were reported from pre-therapy to post-therapy but not from post-therapy to follup-up. The reasons for such results are discussed.

1954 Evans, J. Gary. "Establishing a reinforcement network to increase consultant's effectiveness in training parental behavioral management." Psychol Rep 41(3, pt. 1): 925-26, December, 1977. (2 References).
Briefly reports on a home-based behavior management project that required only minimal involvement of the consultant. A case history is cited in which, after two planning visits, the mother conducted the program and was herself reinforced for success.

1955 Fredericks, H. D. Bud; Baldwin, Victor L.; McDonnell, John J.; et al. "Parents educate their trainable children." Ment Retard 9(3): 24-26, June, 1971. (6 References).
Describes a program for training parents of retarded children. The parents were taught to utilize behavior modification techniques within the home. The need is emphasized for the daily exchange of data between the teacher and the parent.

1956 Freeman, Stephen W., and Thompson, Charles L. "Parent-child training for the MR." Ment Retard 11(4): 8-10, August, 1973. (11 References).
Eight children and their mothers participated in a study that focused on developing and testing a model parent-child training program for mentally retarded preschoolers.

1957 Goodman, Earl O. "Behavior modification as a therapeutic technique for use with parents of emotionally disturbed children in residential treatment." Child Psychiatry Hum Dev 6(1): 38-46, Fall, 1975. (16 References).
Provides data on a program conducted with twenty-eight parents and their children. The parents were given instruction in behavior modification methods. The focus of the procedures was to foster improved relationships between parents and their children and between spouses. Modelling, prompting, shaping, ignoring, and reinforcement were used with notable success.

1958 Hamm, Phillip M., Jr., and Lyman, David A. Training parents in child management skills with the school as the agent of instruction. Lincoln, Nebraska: Lincoln Public Schools, 1973. 43p. (20 References). (ED 096 572).
Details a program that involved twenty-eight families in training in operant techniques. The results are discussed in terms of the implications for the implementation of future programs.

1959 Kozloff, Martin A. Reaching the autistic child: a parent training program. Champaign, Illinois: Research Press, 1973. 245p. (Bibliography).
Advocates a behavioral approach to the treatment of autism. The research on various methods of training parents is discussed and four case histories of families participating in the research are presented.

1960 Long, Joetta Jean. "The development of a learning package for future parents: a behavioral child management course for high school students." For a summary see: Diss Abstr Int 36B(8): 4137, February, 1976.

1961 Mash, Eric J., and Terdal Leif. "Modification of mother-child interactions: playing with children." Ment Retard 11(5): 44-49, October, 1973. (14 References).
Five groups of mothers were taught to use behavior modification techniques in order to generate effective play behavior between themselves and their mentally retarded children. A change was effected in the cues that the mothers gave as well as the way in which they consequated various child behaviors. Emphasis is placed on evaluating parent-child behavior as a unit.

1962 Morreau, Lanny E. Televised parent training program: reinforcement strategies for mothers of disadvantaged children. Final Report. Minneapolis, Minnesota: Central Midwestern Regional Educational Laboratory, Inc., 1972. 79p. (ED 073 670).
Describes the development and evaluation of a training program that consisted principally of a programmed text and videotape. The program was devised especially for lower socioeconomic parents with limited educational backgrounds.

1963 O'Leary, K. Daniel, and Kent, Ronald N. "A behavioral consultation program for parents and teachers of children with conduct problems." Proc Am Psychopathol Assoc 64: 89-95, 1976. (14 References).
Briefly describes a program conducted for parents and teachers on an outpatient basis. The consultants were graduate students in clinical psychology.

1964 Stein, Theodore J., and Gambrill, Eileen D. "Behavioral techniques in foster care." Soc Work 21(1): 34-39, January, 1976. (11 References).
Furnishes the details of a program in which social workers interact intensively with the foster parents. Contracts are made between the parents and the social workers, and the parents themselves are instructed in behavioral techniques.

1965 Terdal Leif, and Buell, Joan. "Parent education in managing retarded children with behavior deficits and inappropriate behaviors." Ment Retard 7(3): 10-13, June, 1969. (5 References).
In the program described, the parents were involved in all phases of the operation, including data analysis, treatment planning, and implementation. Goals were individualized to fit the problems and needs of each child and family. Through work with their own child the parents were able to observe and practice principles of reinforcement and shaping.

1966 Watson, Luke S., Jr., and Bassinger, Joan F. "Parent training technology: a potential service delivery system." Ment Retard 12(5): 3-10, October, 1974. (27 References).

Describes a fiscally economical training program that provides a vital interaction between home and school. The program has been used effectively with the mildly, the moderately, and the severely retarded, the psychotic, and the emotionally disturbed child. Parents, teachers, peers, and siblings were all involved as change agents and successfully eliminated undesirable behaviors while promoting self-help skills, language development, motor coordination, and social, recreational, and academic skills.

3. Methodologies

1967 Ayllon, Teodoro, and Roberts, Michael D. "Mothers as educateurs for their children." In: Thompson, Travis, and Dockens, William S., III, eds. Applications of behavior modification. New York: Academic Press, 1975. 107-37. (51 References).
Presents a method of training paraprofessionals with low academic qualifications. The program was successful in helping the mothers to teach cognitive skills to disadvantaged preschool children.

1968 Budd, Karen Schlueter. "An analysis of multiple misplaced social contingencies in the mother of a preschool child." For a summary see: Diss Abstr Int 36B(6): 3086, December, 1975.

1969 Corson, John A. "Families as mutual control systems: optimization by systemization of reinforcement." In: Mash, Eric J.; Hamerlynck, Leo A.; Handy, Lee C., eds. Behavior modification and families. Banff International Conference on Behavior Modification, 6th, 1974. New York: Brunner/Mazel, 1976. 317-30. (10 References).
Outlines a strategy of optimizing the children's participation in the planning and implementation of the family mutual control system.

1970 Frey, Carl Eugene. "The effect of a combined cognitive structuring and contingency management procedure utilizing natural and logical consequences of parent-child conflict behavior." For a summary see: Diss Abstr Int 35B(5): 3012, November, 1974.

1971 Gardner, Harold L.; Forehand, Rex; Roberts, Mark. "Time-out with children: effects of an explanation and brief parent training on child and parent behaviors." J Abnorm Child Psychol 4(3): 277-88, 1976. (17 References).
In this study it was determined that although time-out significantly increased compliant behavior, the addition of an explanation did not further alter the effectiveness of the time-out.

1972 Goocher, Buell E., and Grove, David N. "A model for training parents to manage their family systems using multiple data sources as measures of parent effectiveness." In: Mash, Eric J.; Handy, Lee C.; Hamerlynck, Leo A., eds. Behavior modification approaches to parenting. Banff International Conference on Behavior Modification, 6th, 1974. New York: Brunner/Mazel, 1976. 57-74. (4 References).
Focuses on the problem of generalization of new behaviors. Data is provided on a five-part program designed to affect changes in the home environment that will encourage such generalization. The five components of the program are: (1) identification of problem areas; (2) instructional methodologies and strategies; (3) remediation of the problems; (4) maintenance; and (5) evaluation. A case history is cited.

1973 Herbert, Emily W., and Baer, Donald M. "Training parents as behavior modifiers: self-recording of contingent attention." J Appl Behav Anal 5(2): 139-49, Summer, 1972. (15 References).
Demonstrates that required counting, by the mother, of episodes of attention to the desired child behavior was an effective means of modifying both mother and child behavior.

1974 Holland, Cornelius J. "An interview guide for behavioral counseling with parents." Behav Ther 1(1): 70-79, March, 1970. (3 References).
A twenty-one step interview guide is discussed. The guide is intended as an aid for counselors in teaching parents to apply operant techniques in the handling of behavioral problems with their children.

1975 Holstein, Stephen John. "The modification of maladaptive mother-child interaction through modeling and behavior rehearsal." For a summary see: Diss Abstr Int 36B(1): 444, July, 1975.

1976 Kogan, Kate L., and Gordon, Betty N. "A mother-instruction program: documenting change in mother-child interactions." Child Psychiatry Hum Dev 5(3): 189-200, Spring, 1975. (19 References).
Definite changes were demonstrated in mother-child contingency patterns as a result of this program, which was conducted with thirty children and their mothers and utilized a "bug-in-the-ear" technique.

1977 Matefy, Robert E.; Solanch, Larry; Humphrey, Ellen. "Behavior modification in the home with students as co-therapists." Am J Psychother 29(2): 212-23, April, 1975. (9 References).
Focuses on the use of graduate students in a home-centered program which aimed to shape the mother's disciplinary behavior. The program can be divided into six stages: (1) training the co-therapists; (2) observing the family; (3) establishing the basic contingency program; (4) integrating the mother into the program; (5) establishing a token economy; and (6) terminating the therapy.

1978 Patterson, G. R. "Teaching parents to be behavior modifiers in the classroom." In: Krumboltz, John D., and Thoresen, Carl E., eds. Behavioral counseling: cases and techniques. New York: Holt, Rinehart & Winston, 1969. 155-61. (Reprinted in Item No. 27).
Traces the steps involved in teaching parents how to use reinforcement techniques. Cooperation with the teacher in reinforcing classroom work habits is emphasized. Two case histories of first-grade boys are cited.

1979 Peed, Steve; Roberts, Mark; Forehand, Rex. "Evaluation of the effectiveness of a standardized parent training program in altering the interaction of mothers and their noncompliant children." Behav Modif 1(3): 323-50, July, 1977. (30 References).
Assesses the effectiveness of a parent training program in a controlled learning environment. Both parents and children in the treatment group demonstrated multiple behavior changes in the clinic and in the home, whereas the control did not exhibit such changes.

1980 Peed, Steven Franklin. "Generalization to the home of behavior modified in a parent training program for non-compliant children." For a summary see: Diss Abstr Int 36B(9): 4703, March, 1976.

1981 Price, Susan Carol. "The assessment and modification of parental consistency and parents' selections of reinforcement consequences by information feedback." For a summary see: Diss Abstr Int 36B(10): 5276, April, 1976.

1982 Rudestam, Kjell E.; Fisher, Roger H.; Fiester, Alan R. "Differential effectiveness of mother vs stranger in the control of children with behavior problems: an experiment in child swapping." Psychol Rep 35(2): 823-33, October, 1974. (10 References).
An experiment, conducted with three mothers and their children, indicated that the mothers were less effective in modifying the behaviors of their own children than in modifying the behaviors of another mother's child.

1983 Ryback, David, and Staats, Arthur W. "Parents as behavior therapy-technicians in treating reading deficits (dyslexia)." J Behav Ther Exp Psychiatry 1(2): 109-19, June, 1970. (30 References). (Reprinted in Item No. 43).
Provides details on a successful token-reinforced system employed by the parents in the treatment of four dyslexic children. The children ranged in age from eight to thirteen years. Tokens were backed up by monetary reinforcement.

1984 Scarboro, Millard Eugene. "An investigation of the effects of response-contingent ignoring and isolation on the compliance and oppositional behavior of children." For a summary see: Diss Abstr Int 35B(8): 4195, February, 1975.

1985 Wahler, Robert G. "Oppositional children: a quest for parental reinforcement control." J Appl Behav Anal 2(3): 159-70, Fall, 1969. (6 References). (Reprinted in Item Nos. 29, 38).
Demonstrates the effective use of a combined time out and differential attention program in the modification, by the parents, of oppositional behavior in two boys of elementary school age.

4. Group Programs

1986 Cole, Carolyn, and Morrow, William R. "Refractory parent behaviors in behavior modification training groups." Psychotherapy 13(2): 162-69, Summer, 1976. (28 References).
Analyzes the difficulties encountered in a program designed to train small groups of parents. Two refractory patterns of parental behavior that emerged were marital conflicts and excessive authoritarianism. Methods are suggested for dealing with this type of problem.

1987 Fishman, Claire A., and Fishman, Daniel B. "Group training program in behavior modification for mothers of children with birth defects: an exploratory study." Child Psychiatry Hum Dev 6(1): 3-14, Fall, 1975. (21 References).
Results of this study indicate that a fifteen-hour training program can lead to a significant improvement in mother-child interactions. Seventeen mothers of physically handicapped children (aged eight to sixteen years) participated in this study. Statistically significant increases were noted in the areas of communication, self-esteem, enthusiasm, and likability.

1988 Hirsch, Irwin, and Walder, Leopold. "Training mothers in groups as reinforcement therapists for their own children." In:

American Psychological Association, Washington, D.C., 77th, 1969. Proceedings. 561-62. (10 References).
Reports on a sutdy conducted with thirty mothers primarily representing upper middle-class professional families. All the mothers had at least one child that had been diagnosed as severely disturbed. The mothers were provided with systematic instruction in the application of reinforcement techniques. Although the results were generally encouraging, indications were found that a more rigid method of home observation was necessary.

1989 Kyle, Jean R., and Savino, Anne B. "Teaching parents behavior modification." Nurs Outlook 21(11): 717-20, November, 1973. (3 References).
Describes an eight-week parental instruction class conducted by the nursing staff of a neuropsychiatric institute. Group instruction is advocated as a saving of professional time. The importance is stressed of the inclusion in the group of all adult members of the family involved in the care of the child.

1990 Lehrer, Paul M.; Gordon, Steven B.; Leiblum, Sandra. "Parent groups in behavior modification: training or therapy." Paper presented at the American Psychological Association Annual Convention, August 26-31, 1973, Montreal, Canada. 22p. (11 References). (ED 083 513).
Outlines and evaluates a model in which parents were taught to modify their children's behavior. Seventy-seven percent of the group carried out successful programs.

1991 McPherson, Sandra B., and Samuels, Cyrille R. "Teaching behavioral methods to parents." Soc Casework 52(3): 148-53, March, 1971.
Presents a didactic approach that was utilized with a group of parents. The program effectively enabled parents to work with their hyperactive and aggressive children. Analysis of parental responses to evaluative questionnaires indicates that behavioral methods alone were not sufficient to complete treatment. Discussion, play techniques, and counseling were also thought to be necessary.

1992 Mash, Eric J.; Lazere, Richard; Terdal, Leif; et al. Modification of mother-child interactions: a modeling approach for groups." Child Study J 3(3): 131-43, 1973. (4 References).
A group of mothers was taught to respond differentially to selected behaviors of their children. Discussion and demonstration were the two primary modes of instruction. Some evidence for increased compliance in other situations is noted.

1993 Ray, Joel S. "The family training center: an experiment in normalization." Ment Retard 12(1): 12-13, February, 1974. (6 References).
Describes an intensive behavior management program designed to teach families the skills that enable them to maintain a retarded child in the community rather than resorting to institutionalization.

1994 Rose, Sheldon D. "A behavioral approach to the group treatment of parents." Soc Work 14(3): 21-29, July, 1969. (20 References). (Reprinted in Item No. 44).
Details a program of group training of parents in the skills of behavior modification. The parents were primarily from a lower socioeconomic strata. The techniques included programmed instruction, modelling, behavioral rehearsal, and assignments. Results were encouraging.

1995 Schaefer, Jacqueline W.; Palkes, Helen S.; Stewart, Mark A. "Group counseling for parents of hyperactive children." Child Psychiatry Hum Dev 5(2): 89-94, Winter, 1974. (14 References).
Nine sets of parents were taught techniques of behavior shaping and rule enforcement. Surveys indicate that the incidence of hyperactivity is over 5 percent in the elementary school population. The use of behavioral techniques is suggested as an alternative or an adjunct to drug treatment.

1996 Shoemaker, Martin E., and Paulson, Terry L. "Group assertion training for mothers: a family intervention strategy." In: Mash, Eric J.; Handy, Lee C.; Hamerlynck, Leo A., eds. Behavior modification approaches to parenting. Banff International Conference on Behavior Modification, 6th, 1974. New York: Brunner/Mazel, 1976. 167-79. (26 References).
Documents an investigation conducted with sixteen mothers who had experienced difficulty in child and family management. The focus was on increased self-expression in family interaction patterns. Tokens were used for reported improvements. Significant increases were noted in assertive statements.

1997 Tams, Virginia, and Eyberg, Sheila. "A group treatment program for parents." In: Mash, Eric J.; Handy, Lee C.; Hamerlynck, Leo A., eds. Behavior modification approaches to parenting. Banff International Conference on Behavior Modification, 6th, 1974. New York: Brunner/Mazel, 1976. 101-23. (8 References).
A nine-week group treatment program was conducted for parents of children whose age ranged from seven to twelve years. The format included group discussion, use of a manual, and the completion of checklists and inventories. Emphasis was placed on the use of positive, nonaversive procedures in order to facilitate a positive parent-child relationship.

1998 Walder, Leopold O.; Cohen, Shlomo I.; Breiter, Dennis E.; et al. "Teaching behavioral principles to parents of disturbed children." In: Guerney, Bernard G., ed. Psychotherapeutic agents: new roles for nonprofessionals, parents, and teachers. New York: Holt, Rinehart & Winston, 1969. 443-49. (3 References).
Traces a research and development program that included: (1) having educational group meetings with parents; (2) consulting with individual pairs of parents; and (3) structuring a more controlled laboratory-like environment within the home.

1999 Wikler, Lynn; Savino, Anne; Kyle, Jean. Behavior modification parent groups: a training manual for professionals. Thorofare, New Jersey: Slack, 1976. 71p. (Bibliography).
This volume is designed for use by group leaders engaged in training parents in behavioral methods. It contains entry-level tests, suggested procedures, evaluation forms, questionnaires, and a reading list for parents.

2000 Wiltz, Nicholas Anthony, Jr. "Modification of behaviors of deviant boys through parent participation in a group technique." For a summary see: Diss Abstr Int 30A(11): 4786, May, 1970.

2001 Wolf, Montrose M.; Phillips, Elery L.; Fixsen, Dean L. "The Teaching Family: a new model for the treatment of deviant child behavior in the community." In: Bijou, Sidney W., and Ribes-Inesta, Emilio, eds. Behavior modification: issues and extensions. New York: Academic Press, 1972. 51-62. (12 References).

Reports on a model program in which "teaching parents" were given a year's professional training before teaching social, self-care, vocational, and academic skills to deviant youths in a family-styled setting within the community.

5. Case Reports

2002 Advani, Kan. Involving parents in the behavior modification program of their children in home and school. A research project. Kingston, Ontario, Canada: Frontenac County Board of Education, 1973. 38p. (7 References). (ED 084 755).
Six hyperactive and immature kindergarten children were treated in their homes by parents who had been instructed in behavior modification techniques. The children exhibited hyperactive and immature behavior with various emotional, social, and physical problems. All of the six demonstrated improvement over a three-month period.

2003 Arnold, Susan; Sturgis, Ellie; Forehand, Rex. "Training a parent to teach communication skills: a case study." Behav Modif 1(2): 259-76, April, 1977. (17 References).
Provides the details on the training of a mother in methods of teaching communication skills to her retarded adolescent daughter. Modelling, imitation, feedback, and social reinforcement resulted in increases in the use of specific conversational skills. The skills were found to have been maintained at a two-month follow-up.

2004 Barnard, Kathryn E. "Teaching the retarded child is a family affair." Am J Nurs 68(2): 305-11, February, 1968. (3 References).
Documents a study in which the parents of a retarded child were instructed by a nurse in the use of behavioral methods. They were thus able to train their child in walking and self-help skills.

2005 Bernal, Martha E. "Behavioral feedback in the modification of brat behaviors." J Nerv Ment Dis 148(4): 375-85, April, 1969.
Television was used to train mothers in child management. Tailored programs for two male "brats" are presented. Children were qualified as "brats" by virtue of their high frequency of tantrums, assaultive behavior, threats, and defiance. Two essential features that were incorporated into this program were operant learning principles and behavioral feedback.

2006 ————. "Training parents in child management." In: Bradfield, Robert H., ed. Behavioral modification of learning disabilities. San Rafael, California: Academic Therapy Publications, 1971. 41-67. (22 References).
Outlines procedures followed in a program of parent training primarily within the home setting. A detailed case study is included that demonstrates the successful implementation of modification techniques by the parents of an aggressive and hyperactive three-year-old child.

2007 Brockway, Barbara Stephens, and Williams, W. Weston. "Training in child management: a prevention-oriented model." In: Mash, Eric J.; Handy, Lee C.; Hamerlynck, Leo A., eds. Behavior modification approaches to parenting. Banff International Conference on Behavior Modification, 6th, 1974. New York: Brunner/Mazel, 1976. 19-35. (21 References).

Furnishes data on a pilot study conducted with a family demonstrating several behavioral problems. The program was designed to assess the ability of the family to generalize techniques across behavior problems. Results indicated that the mother learned general strategies, but that there was little paternal or sibling involvement.

2008 Budd, Karen S.; Green, Donald R.; Baer, Donald M. "An analysis of multiple misplaced parental social contingencies." J Appl Behav Anal 9(4): 459-70, Winter, 1976. (10 References).
An analysis was made of the interactions between a three-year-old girl and her mother. A remedial program was then devised that corrected the mother's reinforcement of the child's noncompliance and demands for attention.

2009 Christopherson, Edward R., and Arnold, Caroline M. "Behavior modification program for parents of children with behavior problems." In: American Psychological Association, Washington, D.C., 79th, 1971. Proceedings. 665-66. (1 Reference).
Reports on the home treatment of an eleven-year-old boy. The boy had been exhibiting severe behavioral problems and was treated with a token economy system.

2010 Ferber, Harold; Keeley, Stuart M.; Shemberg, Kenneth M. "Training parents in behavior modification: outcome of and problems encountered in a program after Patterson's work." Behav Ther 5(3): 415-19, May, 1974. (8 References).
Reports on the use of behavior modification with seven families of children exhibiting behavioral management problems. The results were evaluated by coded home observation. While three of the families showed positive short-term improvement, only one of the seven families showed substantial long-term improvement. The discrepant results are discussed.

2011 Forehand, Rex, and King, H. Elizabeth. "Noncompliant children: effects of parent training on behavior and attitude change." Behav Modif 1(1): 93-108, January, 1977. (20 References).
Examines the effects of a short-term parent training program on the noncompliant behavior of eleven children. The children ranged in age from three-and-one-half to seven-and-one-half years. The significant changes noted in child behaviors were maintained at a three-month follow-up.

2012 Fry, Lyn, and Barrer, Brigid. "Parents as therapists with a severely atypical child." NZ Med J 79(508): 648-50, February, 1974. (16 References).
Describes the treatment of a seven-year-old boy exhibiting profoundly deviant behavior. The boy was variously diagnosed as psychotic and brain damaged. He was treated with some success by his parents who had received specific instructions in behavior modification methods.

2013 Hawkins, Robert P.; Peterson, Robert F.; Schweid, Edda; et al. "Behavior therapy in the home: amelioration of problem parent-child relations with the parent in a therapeutic role." J Exp Child Psychol 4(1): 99-107, September, 1966. (7 References). (Reprinted in Item Nos. 27, 36, 47).
Presents a case history of a four-year-old boy demonstrating tantrum and destructive behaviors. Behavior modification techniques, including time out for inappropriate behaviors and praise for appropriate behaviors, were instituted by the mother within the home setting. A resultant decrease in objectionable behaviors was noted.

2014 Horne, Arthur M. "Teaching parents a reinforcement program." Elem Sch Guid Couns 9(2): 102-7, December, 1974. (12 References).
Cites the case history of a nine-year-old boy whose parents were taught reinforcement strategies in order to change his soiling behavior. The instructional methods used with the parents included teaching exercises, role playing, and modelling.

2015 Johnson, James M. "Using parents as contingency managers." Psychol Rep 28(3): 703-10, June, 1971. (14 References).
Describes the techniques used by parents to eliminate disturbing mealtime behavior of their two children. The children were never seen by the therapist.

2016 Johnson, Stephen M., and Brown, Richard A. "Producing behavior change in parents of disturbed children." J Child Psychol Psychiatry 10(2): 107-21, October, 1969. (20 References). (Reprinted in Item No. 21).
An outpatient clinic program was effective in producing changes in parental behavior with resultant improvement in parent-child interaction. Two detailed case histories are provided. One involves a preschool child and the other a six-year-old boy, both of whom displayed multiple behavioral deviations. Improvement was noted in both cases.

2017 Koven, Jacqueline Tritt, and Lebow, Michael D. "Teaching parents to remediate the academic problems of their children." J Exp Educ 41(4): 64-73, Summer, 1973. (16 References).
Mothers of three boys (aged seven and eight years) were taught to administer a token reinforcement system. The use of the system resulted in improvement in both reading and spelling. Follow-up at two months revealed that two of the boys had maintained a good proportion of their gains.

2018 Krapfl, Jon E.; Bry, Peter; Nawas, M. Mike. "Uses of the bug-in-the-ear in the modification of parents' behavior." In: Rubin, Richard D., and Franks, Cyril M., eds. Advances in behavior therapy. New York: Academic Press, 1969. 31-35. (2 References).
Presents two case reports that demonstrate the effectiveness of a small, battery-operated hearing-aid-like device to modify parents' responses to their children's behavior. The therapist's prompting is relayed through the device while the parent is involved in a play situation with the child.

2019 Martin, Daun, and McLaughlin, T. F. "Note: contingency contracting at home by parents to increase weight and eating behavior of a child." Psychol Rep 36(2): 622, April, 1975. (1 Reference).
The parents were successfully trained in child management techniques. Although improvement was noted in eating behavior, progress was not confined to this target behavior.

2020 Mathis, Harold I. "Training a 'disturbed' boy using the mother as therapist: a case study." Behav Ther 2(2): 233-39, April, 1971. (8 References).
Structured tasks, games, and operant methods were used to teach reading, communication skills, arithmetic operants, and motor coordination to an eight-year-old boy. Treatment was conducted within the home setting. Follow-up indicated that the boy was reading at an appropriate grade level and making progress in all pertinent social and scholastic areas.

2021 Sajwaj, Thomas. "Difficulties in the use of behavioral techniques by parents in changing child behavior: guides to success." J Nerv Ment Dis 156(6): 395-403, June, 1973. (17 References).
Presents four case histories in which highly cooperative parents encountered serious difficulties in applying behavioral techniques. Suggestions are given for overcoming these types of problems, and a careful analysis and monitoring of the home situation is urged.

2022 Schell, Robert E., and Adams, William P. "Training parents of a young child with profound behavior deficits to be teacher-therapists." J Spec Educ 2(4): 439-54, Summer-Fall, 1968. (24 References).
Reports on an experimental effort to help the parents of an "atypical" boy. The parents were trained to teach their child themselves since they lived in an area where no other facilities were available to them. The parents' effectiveness is discussed, and the evidence for generalization and persistence of change is noted.

2023 Seitz, Sue, and Terdal, Leif. "A modeling approach to changing parent-child interactions." Ment Retard 10(3): 39-43, June, 1972. (4 References).
Documents a case in which the mother of a four-year-old boy was reinforced for observing and modelling her child's therapist. The results indicated a positive change in the previously maladaptive parent-child interaction pattern.

2024 Shah, Saleem A. "Training and utilizing a mother as the therapist for her child." In: Guerney, Bernard G., ed. Psychotherapeutic agents: new roles for nonprofessionals, parents, and teachers. New York: Holt, Rinehart & Winston, 1969. 401-7. (12 References).
A mother of a four-year-old girl was given instruction in behavioral approaches in order to deal with her daughter's disruptive behavior. The methods used by the mother included positive reinforcement and time out. The first improvements were noted within two weeks.

2025 Wagner, Mervyn K. "Parent therapists: an operant conditioning method." Ment Hyg 52(3): 452-55, July, 1968. (8 References). (Reprinted in Item No. 27).
Uses a clinical case history of an eleven-year-old girl to demonstrate the employment of operant conditioning in an outpatient clinic. The child had been referred by a pediatrician for severe home and school problems. A teacher-directed plan was implemented to lengthen her attention span and to deal with her periodic hypomanic behavior, poor peer relations, and masturbation in the classroom. Notable improvements in all these areas were documented within a period of four months. An example of a reinforcement schedule is provided.

2026 Wahler, Robert G.; Winkel, Gary H.; Peterson, Robert F.; et al. "Mothers as behavior therapists for their own children." Behav Res Ther 3(2): 113-24, May, 1965. (6 References). (Reprinted in Item Nos. 23, 28, 36).
Documents an attempt to modify the deviant behavior of three boys by producing specific changes in the reactive behavior of their mothers. The boys were aged between four and six years. The data indicate that the mothers' social behavior was acting as positive reinforcement for their children's deviant behavior. Effective changes in behavior were produced in the clinical setting.

2027 Zeilberger, Jane; Sampen, Sue E.; Sloane, Howard N., Jr. "Modification of a child's problem behaviors in the home with the mother as therapist." J Appl Behav Anal 1(1): 47-53, Spring, 1968. (14 References).
Cites the modification of the undesirable behavior of a four-year-old boy. The boy was treated within the home by his own mother who used time out procedures. Her rewarding attention was focussed on the child's appropriate behaviors rather than on his inappropriate behaviors.

6. Parent Training Manuals

2028 Alvord, Jack R. Home token economy: an incentive program for children and their parents. Champaign, Illinois: Research Press, 1973. 20p. (Bibliography). (ED 117 626).
Contains brief instructions on the implementation of a home token economy. Little explanation is given of the principles involved. A case study and sample contract sheets are provided.

2029 Andrasik, Frank, and Murphy, William D. "Assessing the readability of thirty-nine behavior modification training manuals and primers." J Appl Behav Anal 10(2): 341-44, Summer, 1977. (14 References).
Estimates the reading grade levels of thirty-nine texts and presents them in increasing order of difficulty. The range of reading difficulty varies from the seventh grade to college graduate. It is pointed out that readability should not be the sole criterion for selection, but an attempt should be made to select the text rated at or somewhat below the reading level of the target population.

2030 Baldwin, Victor L.; Fredericks, H. D. Bud; Brodsky, Gerry. Isn't it time he outgrew this? Or: a training program for parents of retarded children. Springfield, Illinois: Thomas, 1973. 209p.
This manual, intended for parents and professionals engaged in parental counseling, covers the use of behavior modification in training the handicapped child. General principles are included, together with specific instructions for teaching self-help and motor skills.

2031 Bannatyne, Alexander, and Bannatyne, Maryl. How your children can learn to live a rewarding life: behavior modification for parents and teachers. Springfield, Illinois: Thomas, 1973. 119p. (Bibliography).
Explanations of terminology and principles are accompanied by details on the techniques of training and teaching. The emphasis is on the development of a positive self-concept in the child. Relevant examples are used to illustrate the nature of behavioral phenomena. An appendix contains a list of suggested reinforcers for home and school use.

2032 Becker, Wesley C. Parents are teachers: a child management program. Champaign, Illinois: Research Press, 1971. 194p.
This programmed text is designed for use with parents, teacher aides, guidance counselors, and similar groups. Many examples and illustrations are included, together with exercises to be carried out with children. An accompanying guide is intended for the use of a group leader.

2033 Becker, Wesley C., and Becker, Janis W. Successful parenthood: how to teach your child values, competence, and responsibility. Chicago: Follett, 1974. 199p. (Bibliography).

This text, intended for parents, provides a straightforward explanation of learning principles using a minimum of technical language. The main points are illustrated with examples taken from situations commonly arising in the home. The emphasis is on the use of positive reinforcement rather than punishment.

2034 Beltz, Stephen. How to make Johnny want to obey. Englewood Cliffs, New Jersey: Prentice-Hall, 1971. 255p.
Deals with the creative use of incentives to increase a child's motivation. The difference is emphasized between a system of bribery and a system of incentives. Both general principles and specific instructions are included. The volume is intended for parents and teachers.

2035 Deibert, Alvin N., and Harmon, Alice J. New tools for changing behavior. Champaign, Illinois: Research Press, 1970. 144p.
This programmed text is directed to parents, physicians, nurses, and teachers. It assumes no previous background in psychology. Both the general rationale and the specific applications of behavioral therapy are covered. Special chapters are devoted to the behaviorally disordered child, the retarded child, and the adolescent.

2036 Gosciewski, F. William. Effective child rearing: the behaviorally aware parent. New York: Human Sciences Press, 1976. 158p. (Bibliography).
This simply-written text is intended primarily for parents who have no background in psychology. The basic principles and techniques of behavioral methods are explained with examples drawn from commonly encountered situations in which such methods might be applied. One chapter is devoted to the concept of parental self-control.

2037 Graubard, Paul S. "How I stopped nagging and started teaching my children to behave." McCalls 104: 90, 93, 95, 96, 209, May, 1977.
Presents an excerpt from the author's book Positive Parenthood (Item No. 2038). Emphasis is placed on the simplicity of, and the positive gains to be made by, the use of behavior modification techniques within the home.

2038 ———. Positive parenthood: solving parent-child conflicts through behavior modification. New York: Bobbs-Merrill, 1977. 192p.
Describes ways in which parents can use behavior modification methods to help children learn self-help skills and to overcome behavioral problems. The areas detailed in particular are eating, sleeping, toilet training, social development, and personal responsibility. Practical examples, with varying age groups, are provided. Many of the examples are taken from the author's experience with his own children.

2039 Hunter, Madeline C., and Carlson, Paul V. Improving your child's behavior. Glendale, California: Bowmar, 1971. 130p.
This programmed text for parents contains an explanation of the principles of reinforcement theory and examples of their practical application. Step-by-step instructions are given for the setting up of a behavior modification program within the family setting.

2040 Krumboltz, John D., and Krumboltz, Helen Brandhorst. Changing children's behavior. Englewood Cliffs, New Jersey: Prentice-Hall,

1972. 268p. (Bibliography). (Prentice-Hall Series in Counseling and Guidance).
This volume is intended for parents with no background in psychology. The behavioral principles are explained with numerous illustrations taken from commonly occurring behavior problems. Cartoons are used to demonstrate the principles.

2041 Larsen, Lawrence A., and Bricker, William A. "A manual for parents and teachers of severely and moderately retarded children." IMRID Papers Rep 5(22): 1-146, 1968.
Presents the principles of behavior modification and describes twenty-three activities. For each activity there is outlined the task definition, a pretest, and a suggested educational program. Appendices include suggested reinforcers, sample forms, a glossary, and the applications of the methods to blind and deaf children.

2042 McIntire, Roger W. For love of children: behavioral psychology for parents. Del Mar, California: CRM Books, 1970. 208p. (Bibliography).
This volume is divided into two parts: "Parenthood by Design" contains six chapters on the use of behavioral principles in raising children. The use of rewards and punishment is covered in this section. "Blueprints for Change" contains details on dealing with specific behavioral problems.

2043 Nielson, Gary E. Helping children behave: a handbook of applied learning principles. Chicago: Nelson-Hall, 1974. 170p. (Bibliography).
Presents an overview of basic principles, and the applications of those principles, for parents, teachers, and other professionals engaged in dealing with children. Six case studies are cited.

2044 Norton, G. Ron. Parenting: a positive approach. Englewood Cliffs, New Jersey: Prentice-Hall, 1977. 198p. (Bibliography). (A Spectrum Book, S-427).
Proposes a method of child management that includes aspects of behavior modification. Each chapter contains examples and concludes with several exercises intended either to allow the parent to evaluate his own interactions with his child or to practice new ways of interacting. Chapters on the use of punishment and rewards are included.

2045 Patterson, Gerald Roy. Families: applications of social learning to family life. Champaign, Illinois: Research Press, 1971. 143p. (Bibliography).
Provides a simply written text for parents that emphasizes the practical applications of behavioral principles in family relations. The book is written in semi-programmed style with many examples taken from typical family situations.

2046 Patterson, Gerald Roy, and Gullion, M. Elizabeth. Living with children: new methods for parents and teachers. Champaign, Illinois: Research Press, 1971. 96p.
This programmed manual is divided into two sections and was used successfully by parents when in manuscript form. Section One presents general principles and methods of behavior modification. Section Two contains methods of changing specific problem behaviors. These behaviors include aggression, negativism, hyperactivity, over-dependency, fearfulness, and withdrawal.

2047 Rettig, Edward B. ABC's (Antecedents-Behaviors-Consequences) for parents: an educational workshop in behavior modification. Session materials and behavior management workbook. Van Nuys, California: Associates for Behavior Change, 1973. 185p. (ED 117 624).
Combines a manual and a workbook to be used together to teach parents the effective use of behavior modification. The workbook contains forms, graph paper for use in charting, and evaluation sheets.

2048 Tymchuk, Alexander J. Behavior modification with children: a clinical training manual. Springfield, Illinois: Thomas, 1974. 133p. (Bibliography).
This manual is intended for use by parents and education and psychology students. It should be accompanied by a text on the theory of operant conditioning. Each chapter contains examples and assignments. Appendices include summaries, review questions, and a glossary.

2049 Valett, Robert E. Modifying children's behavior: a guide for parents and professionals. Belmont, California: Fearon, 1969. 66p.
This manual for parents and teachers emphasizes the use of positive reinforcement. Exercises are provided, together with the answers and examples of recording charts.

2050 Wagner, Rudolph F. Modern child management: behavior modification at school and home: a practical guide for educators and parents. Johnstown, Pennsylvania: Mafex Associates, 1975. 134p. (Bibliography).
Intended for parents and teachers, this manual covers the basic concepts and specific applications of behavioral techniques. A number of case histories are included. Exercises are furnished for simulated practice.

2051 Wahler, Robert G.; House, Alvin E.; Stambaugh, Edward E., II. Ecological assessment of child problem behavior: a clinical package for home, school, and institutional settings. New York: Pergamon, 1976. 81p. (Bibliography). (Pergamon General Psychology Series, No. 58).
This manual describes a measurement device designed to yield an objective picture of the troubled child and his social environment. Included is an interview format, observational procedures, and a standardized category coding system.

2052 Williams, David L., and Jaffa, Elliott B. Ice cream, poker chips, and very goods: a behavior modification manual for parents. College Park, Maryland: The Maryland Book Exchange, 1971. 62p.
Designed for parents and teachers, this manual provides both basic concepts and specific techniques. It is designed to engage the reader in an active manner with the selection and implementation of an actual behavior change program. Professional consultation is recommended.

2053 Zifferblatt, Steven M. Improving study and homework behaviors. Champaign, Illinois: Research Press, 1970. 96p.
This manual is written in nontechnical language and illustrated with many drawings. It is intended for use by parents attempting to improve their children's behavior in the home and has particular reference to homework and studying behaviors.

C. TRAINING OF NONPROFESSIONALS

1. Theory; Principles; General Aspects of Training

2054 Ayllon, Teodoro, and Wright, Patricia. "New roles for the paraprofessional." In: Bijou, Sidney W., and Ribes-Inesta, Emilio, eds. Behavior modification: issues and extensions. New York: Academic Press, 1972. 115-25. (60 References).
Reviews the literature on the use of paraprofessionals with a wide educational and age range. The paraprofessionals are seen to function adequately in the modification of many types of behavior change with a variety of patients.

2055 Gardner, James Michael. "Training nonprofessionals in behavior modification." For a summary see: Diss Abstr Int 33B(11): 5513, May, 1973.

2056 ———. "Training nonprofessionals in behavior modification." In: Thompson, Travis, and Dockens, William S., III, eds. Applications of behavior modification. New York: Academic Press, 1975. 469-84. (34 References).
Summarizes the research in the area of training nonprofessionals in the techniques of behavior modification. The issues investigated by the research include such topics as the selection of the change agent, resistance, personality, training methodology, supervision, and ethics.

2057 Hursh, Daniel Eugene. "Training behavior modifiers: a comparison of written and direct instructional methods." For a summary see: Diss Abstr Int 34B(12, pt. 1): 6241, June, 1974.

2058 Jason, L., and Carter, B. "Paraprofessionals providing behavioural techniques to families of disadvantaged toddlers." Slow Learn Child 22(3): 153-58, November, 1975. (19 References).
Reports on and evaluates the use of trained paraprofessionals in achieving the involvement of family members in a preventive behavioral program for disadvantaged children displaying evidence of developmental lag.

2059 Mayfield, Don, and Bandy, Phyllis. "Behavior modification of a retarded child using a foster grandparent as intervention agent." Behav Ther 5(1): 152-53, January, 1974.
Describes the use of a senior citizen volunteer as an effective contingency manager. The volunteer had had less than a high school education and required only minimal professional supervision.

2060 Talbert, Elizabeth E.; Wildemann, Donald G.; Erickson, Marilyn T. "Teaching nonprofessionals three techniques to modify children's behavior." Psychol Rep 37(3, pt. 2): 1243-52, December, 1975. (11 References).
Compares the effectiveness of video-taped lecturing, video-taped modeling, and a combination of lecturing and modelling in the teaching of behavioral skills to nonprofessionals. While no significant over-all differences were found between the three methods, the subjects trained with both lectures and modelling evinced fewer errors.

2061 Teicher, Joseph D.; Sinay, Ruth D.; Stumphauzer, Jerome S. "Training community-based paraprofessionals as behavior therapists with families of alcohol-abusing adolescents." Am J Psychiatry 133(7): 847-50, July, 1976. (26 References).

Describes the training in behavior therapy techniques of ten paraprofessionals in a large metropolitan area. Preliminary results were encouraging. The model provided a structure for the paraprofessionals to intervene with the families and furnished them with skills applicable to other areas of their work.

2. Training of College Students

2062 Davison, Gerald C. "The training of undergraduates as social reinforcers for autistic children." In: Ullmann, Leonard P., and Krasner, Leonard, eds. Case studies in behavior modification. New York: Holt, Rinehart & Winston, 1965. 146-48. (3 References).
Demonstrates the feasibility of training intelligent, highly motivated students in a very short time. The students were taught to administer a behavior modification program with psychotic children.

2063 Kreitzer, S. F. "College students in a behavior therapy program with hospitalized, emotionally disturbed children." In: Guerney, Bernard G., Jr., ed. Psychotherapeutic agents: new roles for nonprofessionals, parents, and teachers. New York: Holt, Rinehart & Winston, 1969. 226-30. (1 Reference).
Briefly reports on a program in which twenty-one college students were trained in behavioral techniques. They were then utilized to provide an intensive therapy experience for seven seriously disturbed hospitalized children. Target behaviors were selected for each patient and, in general, those behaviors were seen to improve.

2064 Powell, Don R. "Behavior modification: students as paraprofessionals." J Biol Psychol 17(1): 19-25, July, 1975.
Reports on an experimental laboratory situation in which the students were trained to work in a variety of natural settings. They were also taught to design individualized treatment programs. Several case histories are included.

3. Training of Institutional Staff

2065 Bassinger, Joan F.; Ferguson, Raymond L.; Watson, Luke S., Jr., et al. Behavior modification: a programmed text for institutional staff. Libertyville, Illinois: Behavior Modification Technology, 1971. 195p.
This programmed text is intended for use in training people who work in institutions for the retarded. The volume is arranged in a simple-to-follow question-and-answer format and assumes no prior knowledge of behavior modification. A series of photographs is included demonstrating the teaching of dressing skills.

2066 Bettison, S., and Garlington, W. "Behaviour modification with the mentally retarded: a staff training programme." Aust J Ment Retard 3(5): 131-45, March, 1975.
Describes an inservice training program that combines a lecture and discussion with a practical format. Each person being trained is provided with continual feedback. Detailed reports on four projects are furnished and problems encountered in the development of such programs discussed.

2067 Gardner, James M. "Selection of nonprofessionals for behavior modification programs." Am J Ment Defic 76(6): 680-85, May, 1972. (7 References).

Compares results of three studies conducted with groups of nonprofessional trainers implementing behavior modification programs with an institutionalized retarded population. No significant difference was found in the results achieved by new employees and by more experienced attendants. The more successful trainers were found to have higher needs for achievement and affiliation.

2068 Gardner, James M.; Brust, Donna J.; Watson, Luke S., Jr. "A scale to measure skill in applying behavior modification techniques to the mentally retarded." Am J Ment Defic 74(5): 633-36, March, 1970.

Outlines a study conducted with twenty institute attendants enrolled in a behavior modification training program. During the administration of the program a twenty-eight item five-point scale for measuring their skills was developed. Four major components were identified: reinforcing, shaping, communicating, and establishing rapport. Scores correlated highly with a test of the principles of behavior modification and also corresponded to global evaluations of training proficiency.

2069 Martin, Garry L. "Teaching operant conditioning to psychiatric nurses, aides, and attendants." In: Clark, F. W.; Evans, D. R.; Hamerlynck, Leo A., eds. Implementing behavioral programs for schools and clinics. Banff International Conference on Behavior Modification, 3rd, 1971. Champaign, Illinois: Research Press, 1972. 63-79. (22 References).

The training techniques used with the staff of a school for retardates are outlined. Behavioral principles were used to maintain a high level of performance from the staff. Reasons for the failure of previous staff training programs are pinpointed.

2070 Mattos, Robert Lynn. "An investigation of the effects of attendant training in the use of behavior modification techniques on attendant interaction with institutionalized mentally retarded children." For a summary see: Diss Abstr 27A(10): 3318, April, 1967.

2071 Panyan, Marion; Boozer, Howard; Morris, Nancy. "Feedback to attendants as a reinforcer for applying operant techniques." J Appl Behav Anal 3(1): 1-4, Spring, 1970. (10 References).

Investigates the use of a feedback system to maintain the daily use of operant training methods by nonprofessional hall personnel in a state institution for retarded children. The system involved the posting of daily performance records. Results were positive, and the conclusion is drawn that the feedback system is an economical method of sustaining staff performance without daily supervision.

4. Training of School-Age Children

2072 Benassi, Victor A., and Larson, Kathryn M. "Modification of family interaction with the child as the behavior-change agent." In: Mash, Eric J.; Hamerlynck, Leo A.; Handy, Lee C., eds. Behavior modification and families. Banff International Conference on Behavior Modification, 6th, 1974. New York: Brunner/Mazel, 1976. 331-37. (22 References).

Focuses on the child's role in determining parental behavior and summarizes attempts to train children to modify such behavior. It is advocated that all family members be included in programs designed to restructure family interactions.

2073 Crowder, Nettie Jean. "Training elementary school children in the application of principles and techniques of behavior modification." For a summary see: Diss Abstr Int 36B(6): 3029, December, 1975.

2074 Gladstone, Bruce Whyddon. "The development and generalization of behavior modification techniques by high school students working with retarded children." For a summary see: Diss Abstr Int 34B(12, pt. 1): 6237, June, 1974.

2075 Gladstone, Bruce W., and Sherman, James A. "Developing generalized behavior modification skills in high school students working with retarded children." J Appl Behav Anal 8(2): 169-80, Summer, 1975. (19 References).

Training procedures resulted in the development of generalized skills in behavior modification in seven high school trainees. The methods used in training consisted of video-taped modelling, rehearsal, corrective feedback, and praise.

2076 Long, Joetta, and Madsen, Charles H., Jr. "Five-year-olds as behavioral engineers for younger students in a day-care center." In: Ramp, Eugene, and Semb, George, eds. Behavior analysis: areas of research and application. Englewood Cliffs, New Jersey: Prentice-Hall, 1975. 341-56.

Four kindergarten children successfully served as reinforcing agents for four younger children. The social repertoires of the younger children were improved in a relatively short period of time.

2077 McGee, Charles S.; Kauffman, James M.; Nussen, Judith L. "Children as therapeutic change agents: reinforcement intervention paradigms." Rev Educ Res 47(3): 451-77, Summer, 1977. (103 References).

Reviews the research on the generation of therapeutic strategies that may be implemented by children alone or in a group. A section is devoted to methodological considerations. The areas needing further documentation are discussed.

2078 Rouse, Bobbye M., and Farb, Joel. "Training adolescents to use behavior modification with the severely handicapped." Except Child 40(4): 286-88, January, 1974. (6 References).

Reports on a training program conducted with thirteen high school students. The program took place over a four-week period and demonstrated the ability of high school students to work effectively with retarded children. The economical and educational advantages of using such students are discussed.

5. Training of Siblings

2079 Colletti, Gep, and Harris, Sandra L. "Behavior modification in the home: siblings as behavior modifiers, parents as observers." J Abnorm Child Psychol 5(1): 21-30, 1977. (12 References).

Documents two studies in which siblings acted as behavior change agents for their behaviorally disturbed brothers and sisters. In the first experiment, a sibling delivered contingent reinforcement which dramatically increased the bead stringing of an autistic sister. In the second experiment, two siblings worked effectively with a neurologically impaired brother. It was also demonstrated that the parents were effective as observers within their own home.

2080 Lavigueur, Henry. "The use of siblings as an adjunct to the behavioral treatment of children in the home with parents as therapists." For a summary see: Diss Abstr Int 34B(12): 6214, June, 1974.

2081 ————. "The use of siblings as an adjunct to the behavioral treatment of children in the home with parents as therapists." Behav Ther 7(5): 602-13, October, 1976. (15 References).
Investigates the use of a sibling as a therapeutic aid in the home management of disruptive children. Such a procedure is especially advantageous in those families where there is a history of sibling reinforcement of inappropriate behavior. Two case histories are furnished, one concerning a twelve-year-old female target child and the other a nine-year-old male target child.

2082 Miller, Nancy Brown, and Cantwell, Dennis P. "Siblings as therapists: a behavioral approach." Am J Psychiatry 133(4): 447-50, April, 1976. (13 References).
Outlines experiences with two families in which siblings were taught to use simple procedures to encourage desired behaviors in a disturbed brother or sister.

2083 Weinrott, Mark R. "A training program in behavior modification for siblings of the retarded." Am J Orthopsychiatry 44(3): 363-75, April, 1974. (29 References).
Details the training in behavior modification techniques of eighteen siblings of mentally retarded children. The program was conducted during a summer camp. Emphasis was placed on sibling attitudes and interactions. Suggestions are made for further study in this area.

6. Training of Teachers' Aides

2084 Wetzel, Ralph J. "Behavior modification techniques and the training of teacher's aides." Psychol Sch 7(4): 325-30, 1970. (3 References).
Describes a four-week program devoted to the training of teacher aides in the use of behavior modification techniques. Components of the program include the teaching of observing behavior, modelling by the training staff, providing corrective feedback, and discussion.

7. Manuals for Training Nonprofessionals

2085 Bensberg, Gerard J., ed. Teaching the mentally retarded: a handbook for ward personnel. Atlanta, Georgia: Southern Regional Educational Board, 1965. 195p. (Bibliography).
This manual, intended for attendants and others engaged in the care and training of the mentally retarded, is divided into two sections. Section One deals with the various needs of the retarded; Section Two presents general principles and detailed lesson plans for teaching the retarded by positive reinforcement. Two studies are cited in the appendices on the use of behavior modification in a cottage setting, and teaching self-care to the profoundly retarded.

2086 Watson, Luke S., Jr. How to use behavior modification with mentally retarded and autistic children: programs for administrators, teachers, parents, and nurses. Libertyville, Illinois: Behavior Modification Technology, 1972. 237p. (Bibliography).

Contains a section on program design, implementation, and staff training. Detailed examples are given of carefully designed programs for shaping self-help skills, language skills, social-recreational behavior, vocational behavior, and the elimination of undesirable traits. Appendices contain checklists for the evaluation of a child's self-help skills and a trainer's contingency management skills.

X.

Research

A. METHODOLOGIES

2087 Banff International Conference on Behavior Modification, 4th, 1972. Behavior change: methodology, concepts, and practice. Edited by Leo A. Hamerlynck, Lee C. Handy, Eric J. Mash. Champaign, Illinois: Research Press, 1974. 358p.

This volume, which is directed primarily to researchers in the field of behavior modification, consists of conference papers dealing with research issues. The topics range from the collection of data, with its attendant problems of observer effect and bias, through problems of validity, reliability, and experimental design to conceptual issues such as counter-control and stimulus control. Ethical issues and the newer applications of behavioral techniques are also investigated.

2088 Bijou, Sidney W.; Peterson, Robert F.; Ault, Marion H. "A method to integrate descriptive and experimental field studies at the level of data and empirical concepts." J Appl Behav Anal 1(2): 175-91, Summer, 1968. (19 References). (Reprinted in Item No. 38).

Provides details of a methodology for a descriptive field study using frequency-of-occurrence measures. The method offers the possibility of interrelating the data both at the level of the data and at the empirical concept level. An illustrative study uses a preschool boy in a nursery school setting.

2089 Bijou, Sidney W.; Peterson, Robert F.; Harris, Florence R.; et al. "Methodology for experimental studies of young children in natural settings." Psychol Rec 19(2): 177-210, April, 1969. (37 References). (Reprinted in Item No. 44).

Considers procedures for a field-experimental study under the following headings: (1) specifying the field-experimental situation; (2) defining response events; (3) defining stimulus events; (4) evaluating observer reliabilities; (5) collecting data; and (6) analyzing and interpreting data.

2090 Bijou, Sidney W., and Sturges, Persis T. "Positive reinforcers for experimental studies with children--consumables and manipulatables." Child Dev 30(1): 151-70, March, 1959. (37 References).

Analyzes the methods and effectiveness of using consumables (edibles and drinkables) and manipulatables (toys, trinkets, hobby items) in behavior modification research with children. Variables such as the ages of the child and various situational factors are considered.

2091 Browning, Robert M. "A same-subject design for simultaneous comparison of three reinforcement contingencies." Behav Res Ther 5(3): 237-43, August, 1967. (3 References).

Describes a same-subject design that affords comparison among three treatment conditions and an original baseline. The method was used successfully by nonprofessional staff with a nine-year-old boy in a residential cottage.

2092 Gelfand, Donna M., and Hartmann, Donald P. "Behavior therapy with children: a review and evaluation of research methodology." Psychol Bull 69(3): 204-5, March, 1968. (114 References). (Reprinted in Item No. 29).
Reviews the literature covering deceleration of undesirable behavior, promotion of desired behavior, and therapies combining the two approaches. Suggested refinements in research techniques include the provision of adequate baseline measures of the terminal behaviors, systematic variation of reinforcement contingencies, evidence that behavior observations are unbiased, and rigorous follow-up evaluations.

Hamerlynck, Leo A.; Handy, Lee C.; Mash, Eric J., eds.
see Banff International Conference in Behavior Modification, 4th, 1972. Behavior change: methodology, concepts, and practice. (Item No. 2087).

2093 Krasner, Leonard, and Ullmann, Leonard P., eds. Research in behavior modification. New York: Holt, Rinehart & Winston, 1965. 403p. (Bibliography).
Presents a collection of articles dealing with the research that is fundamental to the clinical application of behavior modification techniques. Only a few of the articles deal with children.

2094 MacDonough, Tomi, and Forehand, Rex. "Response-contingent timeout: important parameters in behavior modification with children." J Behav Ther Exp Psychiatry 4(3): 231-36, September, 1973. (33 References).
Discusses eight parameters that need to be considered in the implementation of a time out program. The parameters that hitherto have not been systematically controlled or investigated are verbalized reason, warning, administration, location, duration, time out stimulus, schedule, and release.

2095 MacDonough, Tomi S., and McNamara, J. Regis. "Design-criteria relationships in behavior therapy research with children." J Child Psychol Psychiatry 14(4): 271-82, December, 1973. (76 References).
Reviews research design in the published reports and criticizes the lack of controls on variables. It is noted that the criteria of unbiased observer and follow-up had been controlled in only 46 percent of the studies reviewed. Eighty percent of the studies had incorporated the criteria of control group, baseline, and systematic variation of treatment.

2096 Martin, Sander; Johnson, Stephen M.; Johansson, Sandra; et al. "The comparability of behavioral data in laboratory and natural settings." In: Mash, Eric J.; Hamerlynck, Leo A.; Handy, Lee C., eds. Behavior modification and families. Banff International Conference on Behavior Modification, 6th, 1974. New York: Brunner/Mazel, 1976. 189-203. (24 References).

Reports on a study conducted with thirty-three families that investigated the cross-situational consistency of behavior by comparing data on parental behavior in the home and in a simulated situation in the clinic. There was a lack of significant correlation between the two.

2097 Neuringer, Charles, and Michael, Jack L., eds. Behavior modification in clinical psychology. New York: Appleton-Century-Crofts, 1970. 261p. (Bibliography). (Century Psychology Series).
This volume is a collection of ten papers presented at the Ninth Annual Institute for Research in Clinical Psychology. Emphasis is placed on research and theory, with one chapter devoted to the use of behavior modification techniques to promote socialization in the preschool setting.

2098 Ramp, Eugene, and Semb, George, eds. Behavior analysis: areas of research and application: Papers. Conference on Behavioral Analysis in Education, 4th, University of Kansas, 1973. Englewood Cliffs, New Jersey: Prentice-Hall, 1975. 417p. (Bibliography).
Brings together the papers presented at the Conference on Behavioral Analysis in Education. The topics covered include current trends, programs, and educational research in the field of applied behavior analysis.

2099 Stevenson, Harold W. "Social reinforcement of children's behavior." In: Lipsitt, Lewis P., and Spiker, Charles C., eds. Advances in child development and behavior, Vol. 2. New York: Academic Press, 1965. 97-126. (54 References).
Reviews reported experimental findings prior to 1963 and indicates the complexities of social reinforcement. Questions still to be answered are enumerated.

B. EVALUATION; FOLLOW-UP; COMPARISON STUDIES

2100 Baade, Lyle E. "Mother study groups in behavior modification and Adlerian child rearing practices: an empirical evaluation and comparison of behavior change." For a summary see: Diss Abstr Int 34B(9): 4650, March, 1974.

2101 Bernal, Guillermo; Jacobson, Leonard I.; Lopez, Geraldo N. "Do the effects of behaviour modification programs endure?" Behav Res Ther 13(1): 61-64, February, 1975. (7 References).
Presents the follow-up findings to a study conducted with a microcephalic child with multiple problems (Item No. 1081). Evidence is presented that the conceptual, intellectual, and linguistic gains made by the subject during the initial program had endured for the nine months since the termination of the program and that further acquisition of intellectual skills was possible.

2102 Bidder, R. T.; Bryant, G.; Gray, O. P. "Benefits to Down's Syndrome children through training their mothers." Arch Dis Child 50(5): 383-86, May, 1975. (27 References).
Furnishes the findings of a comparison study involving sixteen mothers of Down's Syndrome children. Eight of the mothers were given instruction and counseling in behavior modification methods, the other eight were not. Results showed gains in both mother and child in the treatment group.

2103 Diament, Charles. "A training program in behavior modification for parents: an evaluation of a group approach." For a summary see: Diss Abstr Int 38B(2): 892, August, 1977.

2104 Doherty, Gillian. "On-going program effectiveness evaluation in a token economy." Can J Behav Sci 7(2): 97-103, April, 1975.
Outlines a simple evaluation system that enables modification of treatment approach and encourages staff-child communication. Components of the system are the maintenance, examination, and discussion among the staff of: (1) target behavior graphs; (2) a histogram showing points gained or lost; and (3) the number of rewards relative to graphs and tables.

2105 Eyberg, Sheila M., and Johnson, Stephen M. "Multiple assessment of behavior modification with families: effects of contingency contracting and order of treated problems." J Consult Clin Psychol 42(4): 594-606, August, 1974. (32 References).
Two treatment components were manipulated in this study, i.e., contingency contracting with parents and the order in which problems of varying difficulty were treated. Those parents involved in contingency contracting achieved better results than did those in the group in which the order of problems was manipulated. A high degree of treatment success was reported by parents but only a modest degree of success was reported by observers. Possible reasons for such discrepancies are discussed.

2106 Gentry, W. Doyle. "Parents as modifiers of somatic disorders." In: Mash, Eric J.; Handy, Lee C.; Hamerlynck, Leo A., eds. Behavior modification approaches to parenting. Banff International Conference on Behavior Modification, 6th, 1974. New York: Brunner/Mazel, 1976. 221-30. (36 References).
Reviews ten studies on two psychological treatment models--operant and respondent--used to effect change in somatic disorders. The emphasis is on the parental role. Seven of the studies deal with asthmatic problems, the other three report on the treatment of headaches, excessive scratching, and spasms associated with cerebral palsy.

2107 Glogower, Fred, and Sloop, E. Wayne. "Two strategies of group training of parents as effective behavior modifiers." Behav Ther 7(2): 177-84, March, 1976. (13 References).
Mothers in one group were taught the principles of behavior modification, followed by emphasis on target behaviors. The other group concentrated immediately on target behaviors. Improvement in the children's behavior was more marked in the first group.

2108 Gordon, Betty N., and Kogan, Kate L. "A mother instruction program: behavior changes with and without therapeutic intervention." Child Psychiatry Hum Dev 6(2): 89-106, Winter, 1975.
Compares mother-child behavior changes during therapeutic intervention and during no-contact periods. The results indicate that more changes occurred in mother-child interactions during instruction than during no-contact periods and that mothers receiving immediate instruction showed greater and more systematic changes.

2109 Green, Donald R.; Budd, Karen; Johnson, Moses; et al. "Training parents to modify problem child behaviors." In: Mash, Eric J.; Handy, Lee C.; Hamerlynck, Leo A., eds. Behavior modification approaches to parenting. Banff International Conference on Behavior Modification, 6th, 1974. New York: Brunner/Mazel, 1976. 3-18. (22 References).

Compares three methods of parent training: (1) written-verbal instructions; (2) instructions and cues; and (3) modelling. All methods were effective, but written-verbal instructions were the most economical of professional time.

2110 Heifetz, Louis James. "Toward freedom and dignity: alternative formats for training parents of retarded children in behavior modification." For a summary see: Diss Abstr Int 35B(8): 4175, February, 1975.

2111 Hendrickson, Jo, and Hester, Peggy. "Implications for training parents: measuring and evaluating parent-child interactions." Paper presented at the 55th Annual International Convention, The Council for Exceptional Children, Atlanta, Georgia, April 11-15, 1977. 20p. (ED 139 133).
Examines the parent training component of an early childhood intervention program with four handicapped children. The children were aged twenty-six to twenty-nine months. An investigation was conducted into antecedent and contingent modelling and their effects on parent-child interactions.

2112 Johnson, Nancy Lee. "Parent training groups in behavior modification techniques: a study of two teaching methods, home program involvement vs no home program involvement." For a summary see: Diss Abstr Int 37B(12): 6331, June, 1977.

2113 Johnson, Stephen M., and Christensen, Andrew. "Multiple criteria follow-up of behavior modification with families." J Abnorm Child Psychol 3(2): 135-54, 1975. (25 References).
Presents termination data for twenty-two families and follow-up data on four families collected at three and eight months after treatment. The results indicate a fairly high level of success at termination in the areas of parent attitude change toward the child and toward the process and outcome of the treatment. Observers noted less improvement than did the parents themselves. These findings are discussed and compared with results obtained in other studies.

2114 Kauffman, James M.; Nussen, Judith L.; McGee, Charles S. "Follow-up in classroom behavior modification: survey and discussion." J Sch Psychol 15(4): 343-48, Winter, 1977. (12 References).
Examines the extent to which attention has been given to the need for longitudinal or follow-up data by those working in the classroom setting. Problems in methodology and research design are also discussed. A greater percentage of studies published prior to 1971 included follow-up data when compared to those studies published since 1971.

2115 Kovitz, Karen E. "Comparing group and individual methods for training parents in child management techniques." In: Mash, Eric J.; Handy, Lee C.; Hamerlynck, Leo A., eds. Behavior modification approaches to parenting. Banff International Conference on Behavior Modification, 6th, 1974. New York: Brunner/Mazel, 1976. 124-38. (21 References).
Furnishes the findings of a comparison study conducted with twenty two-parent families. The results indicate that: (1) a short-term, systematic, educational program could be just as effective as the more traditional methods; (2) group training is as effective as individual training; and (3) such methods are less costly.

2116 Kowalewski, Jerome Francis. "An evaluative study of behavior modification training for parents and parent effectiveness training as methods for affecting parent-child problem resolution and parental attitude change." For a summary see: Diss Abstr Int 37B(12): 6334, June, 1977.

2117 MacMillan, Donald L., and Forness, Steven R. "Behavior modification: limitations and liabilities." Except Child 37(4): 291-97, December, 1970. (38 References). (Reprinted in Item Nos. 25, 37).
Discusses the major limitations of the behavioral approach. The possible disadvantages enumerated include oversimplification, a view of motivation as being completely intrinsic, reliance on arbitrary rather than natural reinforcers, and the potential for misuse.

2118 Marton, Peter Leslie. "A comparison of the effectiveness and efficacy of home based and office based behavior modification with conduct problem children." For a summary see: Diss Abstr Int 38B(4): 1892, October, 1977.

2119 Mash, Eric J., and Terdal, Leif G., eds. Behavior-therapy assessment: diagnosis, design, and evaluation. New York: Springer, 1976. 382p. (Bibliography). (Springer Series in Behavior Modification).
Brings together a collection of papers on the conceptualization of behavior therapy assessment, with the emphasis on problem diagnosis, treatment design, and outcome evaluation. Included are papers on the techniques of assessment and behavioral interviewing, possible self-report measures, an assessment for potential reinforcers, and methods of observational assessment.

2120 Musgrove, Walter J. "A scale to measure attitudes towards behavior modification." Psychol Sch 11(4): 392-402, October, 1974. (1 Reference).
Describes the development of a scale designed to measure the attitudes of teachers toward behavior modification. Data are given from a single application of the scale.

2121 Nay, W. Robert. "A systematic comparison of instructional techniques for parents." Behav Ther 6(1): 14-21, January, 1975. (22 References).
Details the findings of a comparison study conducted with seventy-seven mothers. Four methods of presenting instructions in time out procedures were examined: written presentation, lecture presentation, video-taped modelling, and modelling with role-playing. No significant difference was noted between the methods.

2122 Ney, Philip G. "Combined approaches in the treatment of latency children and their families." Can Psychiatr Assoc J 21(4): 212-16, June, 1976. (15 References).
Advocates the use of behavior modification in combination with other therapeutic techniques in the treatment of children who are delayed in achieving independence. The more consistent, ordered environment results in less anxiety and more cooperation in the children and increased confidence on the part of the parents.

2123 O'Dell, Stanley Lee. "A comparison of parent training techniques in child behavior modification." For a summary see: Diss Abstr Int 36B(8): 4173, February, 1976.

2124 Patterson, G. R. "Multiple evaluations of a parent-training program." In: Thompson, Travis, and Dockens, William S., III, eds. Applications of behavior modification. New York: Academic Press, 1975. 299-322. (56 References).
Investigates the efficacy of a parent training procedure designed to alter the behavior of aggressive children. Data was accumulated over a four-year period and began with observation within the home. The parents were then required to study a programmed text, identify and record data, and construct and execute modification programs within the home.

2125 Rardin, Max W., and Roth, Steven A. "Mothers, we'd rather you do it yourself." Paper presented at the Annual Meeting of the Rocky Mountain Psychological Association, Denver, Colorado, May, 1971. 14p. (ED 130 173).
Reviews case reports of parents acting as therapists for their children and summarizes the results. Emphasis is placed on the frequent error of identifying the child's behavior rather than the parental behavior as the primary target for change. Suggestions are made for improvements in reporting techniques.

2126 Rath, Lisle F. "The effects of two methods of training mothers, behavior modification and child advocacy, on children's low self-concepts and on parental attitudes." For a summary see: Diss Abstr Int 36A(10): 6565, April, 1976.

2127 Redd, William H. "Effects of mixed reinforcement contingencies on adults' control of children's behavior." J Appl Behav Anal 2(4): 249-54, Winter, 1969. (8 References).
Attempts to determine whether an adult who does not follow one particular schedule of reinforcement acquires stimulus control over children's behavior. Results suggest that children react to adults in a manner consistent with how these adults have reinforced them in the past.

2128 Reppucci, N. Dickon, and Saunders, J. Terry. "Social psychology of behavior modification: problems of implementation in natural settings." Am Psychol 29(9): 649-60, September, 1974. (Reprinted in Item No. 35).
Presents a series of eight problems encountered when trying to implement behavior modification techniques in natural settings. The problems included institutional constraints, external pressures, language, two populations, limited resources, labeling, perceived inflexibility, and compromise. Examples are given from relevant research.

2129 Rinn, R. C.; Vernon, J. C.; Wise, M. J. "Training parents of behaviorally-disordered children in groups: a three years' program evaluation." Behav Ther 6(3): 378-87, May, 1975. (11 References).
A long-term evaluation of a parent training program indicated that 88 percent of the parents saw marked improvement in their children. Attention is drawn to the time- and cost-effectiveness of this form of treatment as opposed to out-patient treatment.

2130 Rosenfield, Sylvia, and Houtz, John C. "Evaluation of behavior modification studies using criterion referenced measurement principles." Psychol Rec 26(2): 269-78, Spring, 1976. (26 References).

Calls attention to the fact that few evaluative studies have been undertaken of behavior modification programs in their unique clinical and classroom settings. A model is proposed by which the development and evaluation of a modification program can be undertaken.

2131 Rosenthal, Mitchell. "Effects of parent training groups on behavior change in target children: durability, generalization and patterns of family interaction." For a summary see: Diss Abstr Int 36B(9): 4706, March, 1976.

2132 Schofield, Rodney Gene. "A comparison of two parent education programs: parent effectiveness training and behavior modification and their effects on the child's self-esteem." For a summary see: Diss Abstr Int 36A(4): 2087, October, 1976.

2133 Seipp, Sarah Jane. "A study testing knowledge, value and attitude of parents of elementary-age children participating in a behavioral modification inservice training program." For a summary see: Diss Abstr Int 36A(3): 1402, September, 1975.

2134 Sirridge, Stephen Thomas. "Parent training: assessment of parent attitudes, parent management skills, and child target behavior." For a summary see: Diss Abstr Int 36B(7): 3627, January, 1976.

2135 Stephens, Jane Ann. "Parent training in behavioral approaches to child management: group versus group and individual training." For a summary see: Diss Abstr Int 36B(6): 3076, December, 1975.

2136 Tavormina, Joseph B., Jr. "Relative effectiveness of behavioral and reflective group counseling with parents on mentally retarded children." For a summary see: Diss Abstr Int 35B(1): 527, July, 1974.

2137 ————. "Relative effectiveness of behavioral and reflective group counseling with parents of mentally retarded children." J Consult Clin Psychol 43(1): 22-31, February, 1975. (29 References).

Documents a study conducted with fifty-one mothers of mentally retarded children. The superiority of behavioral over reflective counseling is demonstrated. The behavioral groups were taught operant techniques; the reflective groups focused on the principles of reflecting feelings, setting appropriate limits, and providing alternative activities.

2138 Vogel, Margaret Dean. "Maternal attitude change toward self and child as a result of training in behavior modification." For a summary see: Diss Abstr Int 36B(6): 3079, December, 1975.

2139 Vogler, Roger E. "Awareness and the operant conditioning of a cooperative response." J Psychol 69(1): 117-27, May, 1968. (18 References).

Describes a study conducted with ten pairs of children to investigate the mediational role of awareness in conditioning. The children ranged in age from six to eight years. Only those children who verbalized an awareness of the response-reinforcement contingency during the experiment were conditioned to cooperate.

2140 Watson, Luke S., Jr. "The relative effectiveness of academic and practicum training on developing behavior modification skills in parents." Paper presented at the 82nd Annual Meeting of the American Psychological Association, New Orleans, Louisiana, August 30-September 3, 1974. 20p. (18 References). (ED 099 117).
This study, conducted with three parents, indicates that academic training influenced academic performance but had little influence on practicum performance. Practicum training was the primary factor influencing practicum performance.

2141 Wiltz, N. A., and Patterson, G. R. "An evaluation of parent-training procedures designed to alter inappropriate aggressive behavior of boys." Behav Ther 5(2): 215-21, March, 1974. (15 References).
Reports on a model group parent-training program that sought to reduce aggressive behavior in the sons. A programmed text and group discussion were used, and a marked improvement in the targeted behaviors was noted within five weeks.

2142 Wood, William Scott, ed. Issues in evaluating behavior modification: Proceedings of the Drake Conference on Professional Issues in Behavior Analysis, 1st, Drake University, 1974. Champaign, Illinois: Research Press, 1975. 264p. (Bibliography).
Provides a report on a conference concerned with: (1) the certification and competency evaluation of behavior modifiers; (2) quality control in the training of behavior modifiers and in treatment programs; and (3) the need for accountability and ethical responsibility.

C. INTELLIGENCE TESTING

2143 Ayllon, Teodoro, and Kelly, Kathy. "Effects of reinforcement on standardized test performance." J Appl Behav Anal 5(4): 477-84, Winter, 1972. (10 References).
Presents the findings of a comparison study that examined the effects of reinforcement (using edibles and privileges) and nonreinforcement upon the standardized test performance of two student populations. The groups were composed of trainable retardates and normal fourth graders. In both groups test performance was enhanced by reinforcement.

2144 Busch, John Christian, and Osborne, William Larry. "Significant vs meaningful differences in the effects of tangible reinforcement on intelligence test achievement and reliability of TMR subjects." Psychol Sch 13(2): 219-25, April, 1976. (28 References).
Concludes that the use of tangible reinforcement does not appreciably increase the accuracy of measurement, but that the children performed significantly better when reinforcement was used.

2145 Clingman, Joy Moore; Auerbach, Stephen M.; Bowman, Philip C.; et al. "Differential effects of candy, social, and token rewards on the IQ scores of children of above average intelligence." Psychol Sch 14(1): 95-98, January, 1977.
Results of this study, conducted with thirty children aged between ten and twelve-and-one-half years and with an IQ range of 101-146, indicate that IQ scores increased considerably as a function of token rewards but with only minor or no changes for social or candy reinforcement. It is concluded that the scores of children of above average intelligence can be raised if appropriate rewards are provided.

2146 Edlund, Calvin V. "The effect on the behavior of children, as reflected in the IQ scores, when reinforced after each correct response." J Appl Behav Anal 5(3): 317-19, Fall, 1972. (7 References).
Demonstrates an appreciable, statistically significant improvement in IQ scores when correct responses were reinforced with candy. The subjects were seventy-nine children aged between five and seven years.

2147 Higgins, Martin J., and Archer, N. Sidney. "Interaction effect of extrinsic rewards and socioeconomic strata." Pers Guid J 47(4): 318-23, December, 1968. (3 References).
Examines two conflicting theories--the early damage theory and the alienation theory--in an attempt to account for the poor test performance of lower socioeconomic status (SES) children. In a study conducted with 250 upper- and lower-SES children, it was found that the test performance of lower-SES children can be improved when extrinsic rewards are available.

2148 Larman, Darryl Sander. "The effects of social reinforcement on children's verbal IQ." For a summary see: Diss Abstr Int 38A(8): 4732, February, 1978.

2149 Miller, Robert Allen. "Social milieu and the effects of reinforcement on IQ tests." For a summary see: Diss Abstr Int 35B(1): 517, July, 1974.

2150 Witmer, J. Melvin; Bornstein, Alan V.; Dunham, Richard M. "The effects of verbal approval and disapproval upon the performance of third and fourth grade children on four subtests of the Wechsler Intelligence Scale for Children." J Sch Psychol 9(3): 347-56, 1971. (26 References).
Indicates that test performance can be significantly influenced by the verbal behavior of the examiner. Those children receiving verbal approval tend to do better than those receiving verbal disapproval.

D. GENERALIZATION OF TREATMENT EFFECTS

2151 Andersen, Barbara L., et al. "Programming generalization through stimulus fading in remedial and special education settings." Paper presented at the Society for Research in Child Development Convention, New Orleans, Louisiana, March 17-20, 1977. 11p. (ED 140 567).
Examines two studies dealing with the transfer of newly acquired skills from a structured, one-to-one setting to an unstructured setting. Generalization training resulted in a marked improvement in transfer.

2152 Blanchard, Edward B., and Johnson, Roger A. "Generalization of operant classroom control procedures." Behav Ther 4(2): 219-29, March, 1973. (16 References). (Reprinted in Item No. 35).
Reports on an attempt to determine the degree of generalization of operant classroom procedures, such as ignoring inappropriate behavior and praising appropriate behavior. In this study, conducted with ten seventh grade students, it is noted that generalization to a second class was more evident when tangible rewards were used.

2153 Combs, Melinda Louise. "Sequential use of self-instructional and operant training procedures with social deficits of young children: stringent measures of generalized effect." For a summary see: Diss Abstr Int 38B(8): 3870, February, 1978.

2154 Conway, John B., and Bucher, Bradley D. "Transfer and maintenance of behavior change in children: a review and suggestions." In: Mash, Eric J.; Hamerlynck, Leo A.; Handy, Lee C., eds. Behavior modification and families. Banff International Conference on Behavior Modification, 6th, 1974. New York: Brunner/Mazel, 1976. 119-59. (138 References).
Reviews the literature dealing with the generalization of treatment effects across settings and behaviors and maintenance, across time, of behavior change in children.

2155 Craighead, W. Edward; O'Leary, K. Daniel; Allen, Jon S. "Teaching and generalization of instruction-following in an 'autistic' child." J Behav Ther Exp Psychiatry 4(2): 171-76, June, 1973. (3 References).
Outlines a program that utilizes operant reinforcement procedures. The program was successfully demonstrated with a four-year-old boy who had been diagnosed as autistic. The procedures were used to increase instruction-following, and the behavior was seen to generalize across people and situations when the primary treatment interaction was withdrawn.

2156 Holman, Jacqueline. "Facilitating generalization of on-task behavior through self-monitoring of academic tasks." For a summary see: Diss Abstr Int 38A(7): 4047, January, 1978.

2157 Johnson, Stephen M.; Bolstad, Orin D.; Lobitz, Gretchen K. "Generalization and contrast phenomena in behavior modification with children." In Mash, Eric J.; Hamerlynck, Leo A.; Handy, Lee C., eds. Behavior modification and families. Banff International Conference on Behavior Modification, 6th, 1974. New York: Brunner/Mazel, 1976. 160-88. (55 References).
Examines the generalization of behavior problems and treatment effects in thirty-five children. The mean age of the children was 7.9 years and their behavior problems had been displayed either in the home or in the school setting. Also discussed is the "contrast effect" in which improvement in one setting is accompanied by regression in another. The conclusion is drawn that if children have difficulty in both home and school, they should probably receive simultaneous treatment in both settings.

2158 Lovaas, O. Ivar; Koegel, Robert; Simmons, James Q.; et al. "Some generalization and follow-up measures on autistic children in behavior therapy." J Appl Behav Anal 6(1): 131-66, Spring, 1973. (33 References).
Provides follow-up data on twenty autistic children who were treated by behavioral methods over a period of seven years. In addition to case studies and documented results, a theoretical discussion is included on the broader implications of the study.

2159 Rincover, Arnold, and Koegel, Robert L. "Setting generality and stimulus control in autistic children." J Appl Behav Anal 8(3): 235-46, Fall, 1975. (19 References).
Assesses the transfer of treatment gains across settings. The study was conducted with ten autistic children, six of whom showed some transfer across settings.

2160 Walker, Hill M., and Buckley, Nancy K. "Programming generalization and maintenance of treatment effects across time and across settings." J Appl Behav Anal 5(3): 209-24, Fall, 1972. (16 References).

Investigates the effects of three experimental and one control strategy in facilitating generalization and maintenance of treatment effects after two months of treatment in a token economy. The subjects were forty-eight children in grades three, four, five, and six, who were referred because of academic and behavioral problems. The results suggest that peer programming strategy is a powerful technique. An appendix contains definitions of behavior categories and agent responses.

2161 Walker, Hill M.; Hops, Hyman; Johnson, Stephen M. "Generalization and maintenance of classroom treatment." Behav Ther 6(2): 188-200, March, 1975. (22 References).
Reports on two experiments involving elementary school children with behavior problems. The first experiment investigated the maintenance of appropriate classroom behavior following treatment in an experimental classroom. The second experiment investigated the cross-situational consistency and generalization of treatment effects. The effects of the combined treatment generalized to a greater degree in the subsequent academic year than did the treatment effects to those students involved in only the experimental classroom procedures.

2162 Wehman, Paul; Abramson, Marty; Norman, Charles. "Transfer of training in behavior modification programs: an evaluative review." J Spec Educ 11(2): 217-31, Summer, 1977. (43 References).
Focuses on the evaluation of the effectiveness of generalization as reported in the literature. The most influential factors were found to be varying stimulus conditions, parent training, and peer programming. Emphasis is placed on the importance of programming for generalization.

2163 Wildman, Robert W., II, and Wildman, Robert W. "Generalization of behavior modification procedures: a review--with special emphasis on classroom applications." Psychol Sch 12(4): 432-48, October, 1975. (89 References).
Presents a selected review of the literature relevant to the generalization of the effects of behavior modification procedures. Fifteen suggestions are made for ways in which programming for generalization may be accomplished.

2164 Wulbert, Margaret; Barach, Roland; Perry, Martha; et al. "The generalization of newly acquired behaviors by parents and child across three different settings: a study of an autistic child." J Abnorm Child Psychol 2(2): 87-98, June, 1974. (19 References).
Although contingency management techniques were taught to the parents of an autistic child, generalization did not occur until the contingencies and stimulus cues were specifically designed to promote a change in behavior in each setting.

XI.

Addendum

2165 Agras, S., and Werne, J. "Behavior therapy in anorexia nervosa: a data-based approach to the question." In: Brady, John Paul, and Brodie, H. Keith, eds. Controversy in psychiatry. Philadelphia: Saunders, 1978. 655-73.

2166 Akamatsu, T. J., and Farudi, P. A. "Effects of model status and juvenile offender type on the imitation of self-reward criteria." J Consult Clin Psychol 46(1): 187-88, February, 1978.

2167 Alexander, H. L. "The use of applied behavioral analysis techniques in reducing retarded mannerisms in trainable retarded children and young adults." For a summary see: Diss Abstr Int 38A(12, pt. 1): 7265, June, 1978.

2168 Andrews, K. W. "Family training in contingency management: preparation of the work furloughee for family re-entry." For a summary see: Diss Abstr Int 38B(9): 4436, March, 1978.

2169 Baer, R.; Ascione, F.; Casto, G. "Relative efficacy of two token economy procedures for decreasing the disruptive classroom behavior of retarded children." J Abnorm Child Psychol 5(2): 135-45, 1977.

2170 Barber, R. M., and Kagey, J. R. "Modification of school attendance for an elementary population." J Appl Behav Anal 10(1): 41-48, Spring, 1977.

2171 Barker, P.; Docherty, P.; Hird, J.; et al. "Living and learning: a nurse administered token economy programme involving mentally handicapped schoolboys." Int J Nurs Stud 15(2): 91-102, 1978.

2172 Barkey, P. "Behavior modification in special education in the Federal Republic of Germany." Exceptional Child 24(1): 44-49, 1977.

2173 Barnard, J. D.; Christophersen, E. R.; Wolf, M. M. "Parent mediated treatment of children's self-injurious behavior using overcorrection." J Pediatr Psychol 1(3): 56-61, Summer, 1976.

2174 Bates, P., and Wehman, P. "Behavior management with the mentally retarded: an empirical analysis of the research." Ment Retard 15(6): 9-12, December, 1977.

2175 Baumeister, A. A., and Baumeister, A. A. "Suppression of repetitive self-injurious behavior by contingent inhalation of aromatic ammonia." J Autism Child Schizo 8(1): 71-77, March, 1978.

2176 Biberdorf, J. R., and Pear, J. J. "Two-to-one versus one-to-one student-teacher ratios in the operant verbal training of retarded children." J Appl Behav Anal 10(3): 506, Fall, 1977.

2177 Bijou, S. W. "Behavioral modification and optimal learning." Pediatr Ann 7(5): 339-47, May, 1978.

2178 Billingsley, F. F. "Effects of self- and externally-imposed schedules of reinforcement on oral reading performance." J Learn Disabil 10(9): 549-59, November, 1977.

2179 Bloomfield, B. L., and Goodman, G. "Good newsletters: weekend reinforcement." Acad Ther 13(3): 351-54, January, 1978.

2180 Brown, B. S. "Behavior modification: perspective on a current issue." Conn Med 41(5): 289-92, May, 1977.

2181 Brownell, K. D., and Stunkard, A. J. "Behavioral treatment of obesity in children." Am J Dis Child 132(4): 403-12, April, 1978.

2182 Bugental, D. B.; Collins, S.; Collins, L.; et al. "Attributional and behavioral changes following two behavior management interventions with hyperactive boys: follow-up study." Child Dev 49(1): 247-50, March, 1978.

2183 Bull, M., and LaVecchio, F. "Behavior therapy for a child with Lesch-Nyhan syndrome." Dev Med Child Neurol 20(3): 368-75, June, 1978.

2184 Burch, H. "Dangers of behavior modification in treatment of anorexia nervosa." In: Brady, John Paul, and Brodie, H. Keith, eds. Controversy in psychiatry. Philadelphia: Saunders, 1978. 645-54.

2185 "Child abuse: intervention--a behavioural approach." Nurs Times 74(6, suppl.): 42-44, February 9, 1978.

2186 Cone, J. D., and Hawkins, R. P. Behavioral assessment: new directions in clinical psychology. New York: Brunner/Mazel, 1977. 400p.

2187 Darch, C. B., and Thorpe, H. W. "The principal game: a group consequence procedure to increase classroom on-task behavior." Psychol Sch 14(3): 341-47, July, 1977.

2188 Dews, P. B., ed. Festschrift for B. F. Skinner. New York: Irvington, 1977. 413p. (Bibliography). (Century Psychology Series).

2189 Dougherty, E. H., and Dougherty, A. "The daily report card: a simplified and flexible package for classroom behavior management." Psychol Sch 14(2): 191-95, April, 1977.

2190 Dubey, D. R., and Kaufman, K. F. "Home management of hyperkinetic children." J Pediatr 93(1): 141-46, July, 1976.

2191 Edwards, C. H. "Relation of productivity in elementary school science to token reinforcement involving liked and unliked peers." J Res Sci Teach 14(5): 449-54, September, 1977.

2192 Elardo, R. "Behavior modification in an elementary school: problems and issues." Phi Delta Kappan 59(5): 334-38, January, 1978.

2193 Ellington, C. "A point system of rewards." Pointer 20(3): 27-29, Spring, 1976.

2194 Emery, R. E., and Marholin, D., II. "An applied behavior analysis of delinquency. The irrelevancy of relevant behavior." Am Psychol 32(10): 860-73, October, 1977.

2195 Epstein, J. H. "Modeling, instructions, and reinforcement: a training program to develop social eating skills in trainable mentally retarded adolescents." For a summary see: Diss Abstr Int 38A(12, pt. 1): 7225, June, 1978.

2196 Fagen, S. A., and Hill, J. M. Behavior management: a competency-based manual for in-service training. Rockville, Maryland: Montgomery County Public Schools, 1977. 299p.

2197 Fagot, B. I. "Reinforcing contingencies for sex-role behaviors: effect of experience with children." Child Dev 49(1): 30-36, March, 1978.

2198 ————. "Teachers' reinforcement of sex-preferred behaviors in Dutch preschools." Psychol Rep 41(3, pt. 2): 1249-50, December, 1977.

2199 Favell, J. E.; McGimsey, J. F.; Jones, M. L. "The use of physical restraint in the treatment of self-injury and as positive reinforcement." J Appl Behav Anal 11(2): 225-41, Summer, 1978.

2200 Finley, W. W.; Wansley, R. A.; Blenkarn, M. M. "Conditioning treatment of enuresis using a 70% intermittent reinforcement schedule." Behav Res Ther 15(5): 419-27, 1977.

2201 Foxx, R. M. "Attention training: the use of overcorrection avoidance to increase the eye contact of autistic and retarded children." J Appl Behav Anal 10(3): 489-99, Fall, 1977.

2202 Foxx, R. M., and Shapiro, S. T. "The timeout ribbon: a nonexclusionary timeout procedure." J Appl Behav Anal 11(1): 125-36, Spring, 1978.

2203 Franzini, L. R.; Litrownik, A. J.; Magy, M. A. "Immediate and delayed reward preferences of TMR adolescents." Am J Ment Defic 82(4): 406-9, January, 1978.

2204 Freeman, B. J. "Evaluating autistic children." J Pediatr Psychol 1(3): 18-21, Summer, 1976.

2205 Gast, D. L., and Nelson, C. M. "Time out in the classroom: implications for special education." Except Child 43(7): 461-64, April, 1977.

2206 George, T. W.; Coleman, J.; Williams, P. "The systematic use of positive and negative consequences in managing classroom encopresis." J Sch Psychol 15(3): 250-54, 1977.

2207 Gerhard, M. The behavioral outcomes handbook: a practical guide for teachers and administrators. West Nyack, New Jersey: Parker, 1977. 216p. (Bibliography).

2208 Glasgow, R. E., and Rosen, G. M. "Behavioral bibliotherapy: a review of self-help behavior therapy manuals." Psychol Bull 85(1): 1-23, January, 1978.

2209 Goralsky, J. "Tangible and nontangible reinforcement as an adjunct to the treatment of emotionally disturbed adolescent students in a day school program." For a summary see: Diss Abstr Int 39B(1): 380, July, 1978.

2210 Greenberg, J. S. "Study of behavior modification applied to dental health." J Sch Health 47(10): 594-96, December, 1977.

2211 Gundel, R. C. "Three behavioral procedures by locus of control in emotionally disturbed boys." For a summary see: Diss Abstr Int 38A(11): 6618, May, 1978.

2212 Gupta, P., and Bhargava, P. "Sharing behaviour in children as a function of model generosity and vicarious reinforcement." Psychologia 20(4): 221-25, December, 1977.

2213 Harris, A., and Kapche, R. "Behavior modification in schools: ethical issues and suggested guidelines." J Sch Psychol 16(1): 25-33, Spring, 1978.

2214 Haskett, J., and Hollar, W. D. "Sensory reinforcement and contingency awareness of profoundly retarded children." Am J Ment Defic 83(1): 60-68, July, 1978.

2215 Hayes, C. S., and Weinhouse, E. "Application of behavior modification to blind children." J Vis Impair Blindness 72(4): 139-46, April, 1978.

2216 Heifetz, L. J. "Behavioral training for parents of retarded children: alternative formats based on instructional manuals." Am J Ment Defic 82(2): 194-203, September, 1977.

2217 Hersen, M., and Bellack, A. S., eds. Behavior therapy in the psychiatric setting. Baltimore, Maryland: Williams & Wilkins, 1978. 404p.

2218 Hill, A. D., and Strain, P. S. "The effects of teacher-delivered social reinforcement on the task persistent behavior of educable mentally retarded children." Psychol Sch 14(2): 207-12, April, 1977.

2219 Hill, M. M. "A film study demonstrating the effect of positive reinforcement for teaching social behavior to inner-city prekindergarten children." For a summary see: Diss Abstr Int 38A(10): 5910, April, 1978.

2220 Holland, C. J. "A token economy system for home-based behavior modification." Can Ment Health 25(4): 17-19, December, 1977.

2221 Huber, H., and Lynch, F. "Teaching behavioral skills to parents: a preventive role for mental health." Child Today 7(1): 8-10, January-February, 1978.

2222 Hughes, H. M. "Behavior change in children at a therapeutic summer camp as a function of feedback plus individual and group contingencies." For a summary see: Diss Abstr Int 38B(12, pt. 1): 6156, June, 1978.

2223 Karraker, R. J. "Self versus teacher selected reinforcers in a token economy." Except Child 43(7): 454-55, April, 1977.

2224 Kaur, R.; Rao, U.; Murthy, S. "Modification of specific undesirable behavior in a psychotic child." Child Psychiatry Q 10(2): 18-23, 1977.

2225 Keefe, F. J.; Kopel, S. A.; Gordon, S. B. A practical guide to behavioral assessment. New York: Springer, 1978. 212p. (Bibliography). (Springer Series in Behavior Modification, Vol. 4).

2226 Kellerman, J. "Anorexia nervosa: the efficacy of behavior therapy." J Behav Ther Exp Psychiatry 8(4): 387-90, December, 1977.

2227 Klein, J. "Can a child be self-reinforced?" Psychology 15(1): 45-47, February, 1978.

2228 Klein, R. H., and Ciottone, R. A. "The effects of response contingent parental reinforcement upon schizophrenics' learning." J Psychiatr Res 13(3): 143-53, 1977.

2229 Kotses, H.; Glaus, K. D.; Bricel, S. K.; et al. "Operant muscular relaxation and peak expiratory flow rate in asthmatic children." J Psychosom Res 22(1): 17-23, 1978.

2230 Kramer, W. S. "Aversion: a method for modifying child behavior." Tex Dent J 93(7): 22-26, July, 1975.

2231 Krumrine, H. W., and Thomas, M. "Behavior shaping." Pointer 21(1): 50-53, 1976.

2232 Lazar, A. L., and Lazar, P. E. "A reading club serves as a reinforcer." Pointer 20(3): 48-49, Spring, 1976.

2233 Liberman, R. P. "Behavior therapy in psychiatry: new learning principles for old problems." In: Brady, John Paul, and Brodie, H. Keith, eds. Controversy in psychiatry. Philadelphia: Saunders, 1978. 429-67.

2234 Linscheid, T. R., and Cunningham, C. E. "A controlled demonstration of the effectiveness of electric shock in the elimination of chronic infant rumination." J Appl Behav Anal 10(3): 500, Fall, 1977.

2235 Litrownik, A. J.; Freitas, J. L.; Franzini, L. R. "Self-regulation in mentally retarded children: assessment and training of self-monitoring skills." Am J Ment Defic 82(5): 499-506, March, 1978.

2236 Lovitt, T. C. "New applications and new techniques in behavior modification." J Spec Educ 12(1): 89-93, Spring, 1978.

2237 Luiselli, J. K. "Case report: an attendant-administered contingency management programme for the treatment of a toileting phobia." J Ment Defic Res 21(4): 283-88, December, 1977.

2238 Luiselli, J. K.; Helfen, C. S.; Colozzi, G.; et al. "Controlling self-inflicted biting of a retarded child by differential reinforcement of other behavior." Psychol Rep 42(2): 435-38, April, 1978.

2239 McDonald, J. E. "Don't scold: praise." Lutheran Educ 113(3): 135-40, 1978.

2240 ————. "Parent training in positive reinforcement and extinction to effect a decrease in noncompliant child behavior." J Assoc Stud Percept 12(2): 16-21, Fall, 1977.

2241 ————. "Pharmacologic treatment and behavior therapy: allies in management of hyperactive children." Psychol Sch 15(2): 270-74, April, 1978.

2242 McKirdy, L. S., and Rovee, C. K. "The efficacy of auditory and visual conjugate reinforcers in infant conditioning." J Exp Child Psychol 25(1): 80-89, February, 1978.

2243 McNamara, J. R. "Socioethical considerations in behavior therapy research and practice." Behav Modif 2(1): 3-24, January, 1978.

2244 Magrab, P. R., and Papadopoulou, Z. L. "The effect of a token economy on dietary compliance for children on hemodialysis." J Appl Behav Anal 10(4): 573-78, Winter, 1977.

2245 Marholin, D., II. Child behavior therapy. New York: Gardner, 1978. 476p.

2246 Marholin, D., II, Steinman, W. M. "Stimulus control in the classroom as a function of the behavior reinforced." J Appl Behav Anal 10(3): 465-78, Fall, 1977.

2247 Marholin, D., II; Taylor, R. L.; Warren, S. A. "Learning to apply psychology: didactic training, experience and opinions about behavior modification." Teach Psychol 5(1): 23-26, February, 1978.

2248 Marlowe, R. H.; Madsen, C. H., Jr.; Bowen, C. E.; et al. "Severe classroom behavior problems: teachers or counsellors." J Appl Behav Anal 11(1): 53-66, Spring, 1978.

2249 Martin, J. A. "Behavior modification and cerebral palsy." J Pediatr Psychol 1(3): 48-50, Summer, 1976.

2250 Mash, E. J., and Terdal, L. G. "After the dance is over: some issues and suggestions for follow-up assessment in behavior therapy." Psychol Rep 41(3, pt. 2): 1287-1308, December, 1977.

2251 Meichenbaum, D. H. Cognitive-behavior modification: an integrative approach. New York: Plenum, 1977. 305p. (Bibliography). (Plenum Behavior Therapy Series).

2252 Mistur, R. J. "Behavioral group counseling with elementary school children: a model." For a summary see: Diss Abstr Int 38A(12, pt. 1): 7156, June, 1978.

2253 Moracco, J. C., and Fasheh, V. "Effects of contingency management of academic achievement and conduct of mentally retarded Arab students." Am J Ment Defic 82(5): 487-93, March, 1978.

2254 Moreland, K. L. "Stimulus control of hyperactivity." Percept Mot Skills 45(3, pt. 1): 916, December, 1977.

2255 Morris, S., and Messer, S. B. "The effect of locus of control and locus of reinforcement on academic task persistence." J Genet Psychol 132(1): 3-9, March, 1978.

2256 Mulac, A., and Tomlinson, C. N. "Generalization of an operant remediation program for syntax with language delayed children." J Commun Disord 10(3): 231-43, September, 1977.

2257 Murphy, R. J., and Doughty, N. R. "Establishment of controlled arm movements in profoundly retarded students using response contingent vibratory stimulation." Am J Ment Defic 82(2): 212-16, September, 1977.

2258 Nicholas, A. M. "Models of treatment for the autistic child: an evaluation of intervention efficacy." Except Child 24(1): 3-11, 1977.

2259 Nilsson, D. E. "Treatment of encopresis: a token economy." J Pediatr Psychol 1(1): 42-45, Winter, 1976.

2260 Odell, S.; Flynn, J.; Benlolo, L. "A comparison of parent training techniques in child behavior modification." J Behav Ther Exp Psychiatry 8(3): 261-68, September, 1977.

2261 O'Leary, K. D., and O'Leary, S. G. Classroom management: the successful use of behavior modification. 2nd ed. New York: Pergamon, 1977. 444p. (Bibliography). (Pergamon General Psychology Series, Vol. 27).

2262 O'Leary, S. G., and O'Leary, K. D. "Ethical issues of behavior modification research in schools." Psychol Sch 14(3): 299-307, July, 1977.

2263 O'Leary, S. G., and Pelham, W. E. "Behavior therapy and withdrawal of stimulant medication in hyperactive children." Pediatrics 61(2): 211-17, February, 1978.

2264 Page, D. P., and Edwards, R. P. "Behavior change strategies for reducing disruptive classroom behavior." Psychol Sch 15(3): 413-18, July, 1978.

2265 Parsons, J., and Davey, G. C. L. "Imitation training with a four-year-old retarded person: the relative efficiency of time-out and extinction in conjunction with positive reinforcement." Ment Retard 16(3): 241-45, June, 1978.

2266 Penn, J. V. "A model for training foster parents in behavior modification techniques." Child Welfare 57(3): 175-80, March, 1978.

2267 Peters, A. D. "The effect of positive reinforcement on fluency: two case studies." Lang Speech Hear Serv Sch 8(1): 15-22, January, 1977.

2268 Polirstok, S. R., and Greer, R. D. "Remediation of mutually aversive interactions between a problem student and four teachers by training the student in reinforcement techniques." J Appl Behav Anal 10(4): 707-16, Winter, 1977.

2269 Prout, H. T. "Behavioral intervention with hyperactive children: a review." J Learn Disabil 10(3): 141-16, March, 1977.

2270 Ross, N. A. "A training program with multiply handicapped adolescents." Aust J Ment Retard 4(7): 21-23, 1977.

2271 Saigh, P. A. "The effect of type of reinforcer and reinforcement schedule on the level and reliability of performances of EMR students on selected subtests of the Wechsler Intelligence Scale for Children--revised." For a summary see: Diss Abstr Int 38A(11): 6666, May, 1978.

2272 Sanders, R. W. "Systematic desensitization in the treatment of child abuse." Am J Psychiatry 135(4): 383-84, April, 1978.

2273 Schaefer, Charles E., and Millman, Howard L. Therapies for children: a handbook of effective treatments for problem behaviors. San Francisco: Jossey-Bass, 1977. 501p. (Bibliography). (The Jossey-Bass Behavioral Science Series).

2274 Schulman, J. L.; Stevens, T. M.; Suran, B. G.; et al. "Modification of activity level through biofeedback and operant conditioning." J Appl Behav Anal 11(1): 145-52, Spring, 1978.

2275 Schwartz, G. J. "College students as contingency managers for adolescents in a program to develop reading skills." J Appl Behav Anal 10(4): 645-55, Winter, 1977.

2276 Seipel, R. M. "A study of the effects of behavior modification, using a program of positive reinforcement on the attendance rate of selected junior high school students." For a summary see: Diss Abstr Int 38A(12, pt. 1): 7240, June, 1978.

2277 Serbin, L. A.; Geller, M. I.; Geller, S. E. "Effects of social reinforcement for visual attention on classroom learning by disadvantaged preschoolers." Percept Mot Skills 45(3, pt. 2): 1339-46, December, 1977.

2278 Shelton, J. L., and Meyer, E. M. "Catch them being good: training parents as behavioral engineers." Sch Couns 25(2): 110-15, November, 1977.

2279 Singh, N. N. "Reprogramming the social environment of an autistic child." NZ Med J 87(606): 135-38, February 22, 1978.

2280 Sirbu, W. I. "Behavioral parent training in groups: an evaluation." For a summary see: Diss Abstr Int 38B(12, pt. 1): 6175, June, 1978.

2281 Solnick, J. V.; Rincover, A.; Peterson, C. R. "Some determinants of the reinforcing and punishing effects of timeout." J Appl Behav Anal 10(3): 415-24, Fall, 1977.

2282 Stafford, K. P. "The effects of reinforcement differences on normal and under achieving children." For a summary see: Diss Abstr Int 38B(9): 4483, March, 1978.

2283 Stokes, T. F.; Fowler, S. A.; Baer, D. M. "Training preschool children to recruit natural communities of reinforcement." J Appl Behav Anal 11(2): 285-303, Summer, 1978.

2284 Stolz, S. B. Ethical issues in behavior modification: report of the American Psychological Association Commission. San Francisco: Jossey-Bass, 1978. 200p. (Bibliography). (Jossey-Bass Social and Behavioral Science Series).

2285 Strain, P. S., and Pierce, J. E. "Direct and vicarious effects of social praise on mentally retarded preschool children's attentive behavior." Psychol Sch 14(3): 348-53, July, 1977.

2286 Stumphauzer, J. S. Behavior modification principles: an introduction. Kalamazoo, Michigan: Behaviordelia, 1977. 176p.

2287 Thompson, R. J., Jr.; Palmer, S.; Linscheid, T. R. "Single-subject design and interaction analysis in the behavioral treatment of a child with a feeding problem." Child Psychiatry Hum Dev 8(1): 43-53, Fall, 1977.

2288 Thompson, T. I., and Grabowski, J. Behavior modification of the mentally retarded. 2nd ed. New York: Oxford University Press, 1977. 570p. (Bibliography).

2289 Twentyman, C. T., and Martin, B. "Modification of problem interaction in mother-child dyads by modeling and behavior rehearsal." J Clin Psychol 34(1): 138-43, January, 1978.

2290 Upper, D., ed. Perspectives in behavior therapy. Kalamazoo, Michigan: Behaviordelia, 1977. 294p. (Behavioral Psychology Series).

2291 Valenti, R. J. "Ethical issues in applied behavior modification and implications for use in public school settings." South J Educ Res 11(3): 159-67, Summer, 1977.

2292 Walen, S. R.; Hauserman, N. W.; Lavin, P. J. Clinical guide to behavior therapy. Baltimore, Maryland: Williams & Wilkins, 1977. 572p. (Bibliography).

2293 Warner, S. P.; Miller, F. D.; Cohen, M. W. "Relative effectiveness of teacher attention and the "Good Behavior Game" in modifying disruptive classroom behavior." J Appl Behav Anal 10(4): 737, Winter, 1977.

2294 Wasserman, T. H. "Negative reinforcement to alter disruptive behavior of an adolescent in a day treatment setting." J Behav Ther Exp Psychiatry 8(3): 315-17, September, 1977.

2295 ———. "The utilization of a clock-light cueing device to signal group progress towards reinforcement in a classroom setting." Psychol Sch 14(4): 471-79, October, 1977.

2296 Watkins, S. L. "Tad appeared helpless--yet he was controlling us." Nursing 8(6): 63-64, June, 1978.

2297 Wehman, P. "The use of positive practice training in work adjustment with two profoundly retarded adolescents." Vocat Eval Work Adjust Bull 10(3): 14-22, September, 1977.

2298 Wehman, P.; Abramson, M.; Norman, C. "Transfer of training in behavior modification programs: an evaluative review." J Spec Educ 11(22): 217-31, Summer, 1977.

2299 Wehman, P., and Marchant, J. "Reducing multiple problem behaviours in a profoundly retarded child." Br J Soc Clin Psychol 17(2): 149-52, June, 1978.

2300 Weir, K., and Ford, D. "Modification of behaviours of delinquent youths in a token economy: Lentara Project." Aust NZ J Criminol 10(3): 153-64, September, 1977.

2301 Wells, K. C.; Forehand, R.; Hickey, K. "Effects of a verbal warning and overcorrection on stereotyped and appropriate behaviors." J Abnorm Child Psychol 5(4): 387-403, December, 1977.

2302 Wildman, R. W., II, and Simon, S. J. "An indirect method for increasing the rate of social interaction in an autistic child." J Clin Psychol 34(1): 114-49, January, 1978.

2303 Williams, C. "An introduction to behavioural principles in teaching the profoundly handicapped." Child Care Health Dev 4(1): 21-27, January-February, 1978.

2304 Wilson, B. J. "Component analysis of a home-based token reinforcement program for remedial reading." For a summary see: Diss Abstr Int 38B(9): 4492, March, 1978.

2305 Wolpe, J. "The human value of behavior therapy." Psychother Psychosom 29(1-4): 58-64, 1978.

2306 Wolraich, M.; Drummond, T.; Salomon, M. K.; et al. "Effects of methylphenidate alone and in combination with behavior modification procedures on the behavior and academic performance of hyperactive children." J Abnorm Child Psychol 6(1): 149-61, March, 1978.

2307 Woody, R. H. "State departments of education and behavior modification." J Sch Psychol 16(1): 79-83, Spring, 1978.

2308 Workman, E. A. "The effect of a covert behavioral self-control procedure on the on-task behavior of elementary school children: a time series analysis." For a summary see: Diss Abstr Int 38B(9): 4495, March, 1978.

2309 Wright, L., and Walker, C. E. "Behavioral treatment of encopresis." J Pediatr Psychol 1(1): 35-37, Winter, 1976.

Appendix A:

Basic Bibliographical Tools

1. Bibliographic Index
2. Birth Defects: Abstracts of Selected Articles
3. Books in Print
4. British Education Index
5. British Medicine
6. Child Development Abstracts
7. Cumulative Book Index
8. Cumulative Index to Nursing and Allied Health Literature
9. Current Citations on Communication Disorders
10. Current Contents
11. Current Index to Journals in Education
12. Developmental Disabilities and Mental Retardation Abstracts
13. Dissertation Abstracts International
14. Education Index
15. Exceptional Child Education Abstracts
16. Excerpta Medica
17. Hospital Literature Index
18. Index Medicus
19. Index to Dental Literature
20. International Nursing Index
21. Monthly Catalog of U.S. Government Publications
22. National Library of Medicine Audiovisual Catalog

23. National Library of Medicine Current Catalog

24. National Union Catalog

25. Popular Periodicals Index

26. Psychological Abstracts

27. Psychopharmacology Abstracts

28. Public Affairs Information Service

29. Readers' Guide to Periodical Literature

30. Recurring Bibliography: Education in the Allied Health Professions

31. Rehabilitation Literature

32. Research Relating to Children

33. Resources in Education (ERIC)

34. Science Citation Index

35. Social Sciences Index

36. Sociological Abstracts

37. Subject Guide to Books in Print

38. Vision Index

Appendix B:

Audiovisual Materials

The ABC's of Behavioral Education [Motion Picture]. Baltimore, Maryland: Hallmark Films, 1972, 20 min., col., 16 mm.

Achievement Place [Motion Picture]. Lawrence, Kansas: University of Kansas, 1970, 30 min., b&w., 16 mm.

Applied Behavior Analysis Research Designs [Motion Picture]. Lawrence, Kansas: University of Kansas, 1973, 40 min., col., 16 mm.

Ask Just for Little Things [Motion Picture]. Baltimore, Maryland: Hallmark Films, n.d., 20 min., 16 mm. (Film Number 2 in The Step Behind Series).

Behavior Guidance in Dental Treatment [Motion Picture]. Cleveland, Ohio: Case Western University School of Dentistry, n.d., 15 min., col., 16 mm. Intended audience: dental, medical, and health students.

Behavior Modification in the Classroom [Motion Picture]. Washington, D.C.: U. S. Office of Education, 1970, 24 min., col.

Behavior Modification in the Classroom: Excessive Talking [Videorecording]. Kalamazoo, Michigan: Behaviordelia, 1974, 132 slides and audiotape cassette, 23 min., col.

Behavior Modification in the Classroom: Underachievement [Videorecording]. Kalamazoo, Michigan: Behaviordelia, 1974, 140 slides and audiotape cassette, 23 min., col.

Behavior Modification Strategies for Child Psychotherapists [12 Audiotape Cassettes]. Leonia, New Jersey: Sigma Information, 1972.

Behavior Modification: Teaching Language to Psychotic Children [Motion Picture]. New York: Appleton-Century-Crofts, 1970, 42 min., col., 16 mm. Intended audience: undergraduate and graduate students in speech pathology and medicine.

Behavior Modification: Treatment or Coercion? [Videorecording]. Los Angeles: University of California Extension Media Center, 1975, 1 cassette, 60 min., b&w.

Behavior Theory in Practice [Motion Picture]. New York: Appleton-Century-Crofts, 1965, 70 min., col., 16 mm.

Behavior Therapy Techniques for the Psychiatrist [Sound Recording]. Glendale, California: Audio-Digest Foundation, 1976, 3 cassettes, 180 min.

Behavior Therapy with an Autistic Child [Motion Picture]. Atlanta, Georgia: National Medical Audiovisual Center, 1965, 42 min., b&w., 16 mm.

A Behavioral Approach to Nursing Care [Motion Picture]. Lincoln, Nebraska: Nebraska Television Council for Nursing Education, n.d., 30 min., b&w. Intended audience: nurses and nursing students.

Behavioral Objectives [Motion Picture]. Detroit, Michigan: Directions for Education in Nursing Via Technology, n.d., 27 min., b&w. Intended audience: nurses and nursing students.

B. F. Skinner and Behavior Change: Research, Practice and Promise: The Nature and Uses of Modern Behaviorism [Motion Picture]. Solana Beach, California: Media Guild, n.d., 45 min., col. Intended audience: high school and college students, adults.

Childhood Aggression: A Social Learning Approach to Family Therapy [Motion Picture]. Solana Beach, California: Media Guild, n.d., 31 min., col. Intended audience: college students.

A Conversation with B. F. Skinner [Motion Picture]. New York: McGraw-Hill, 1972, 23 min., col. Intended audience: senior high school students, college students, and adults.

Development of Perceptual Motor Skills in a Profoundly Retarded Child [Motion Picture]. Lawrence, Kansas: University of Kansas, 1971, 10 min., col. Intended audience: undergraduate, graduate, and continuing education in the medical, nursing, and allied health fields.

Discipline [Videorecording]. Atlanta, Georgia: Calhoun Medical Library, 1974, 22 min., b&w.

Genesis [Motion Picture]. Baltimore, Maryland: Hallmark Films, n.d., 25 min., col., 16 mm. (Film Number 1 in The Step Behind Series).

Hearing Assessment for the Young and Difficult to Test [Motion Picture]. Lawrence, Kansas: University of Kansas, 1975, 12 min., col., 16 mm.

Help for Mark [Motion Picture]. Englewood Cliffs, New Jersey: Prentice Hall Film Library, 1970, 17 min., col., 16 mm.

Horizon of Hope [Motion Picture]. Berkeley, California: University of California Extension Media Center, n.d., 15 min., col.

I'll Promise You a Tomorrow [Motion Picture]. Baltimore, Maryland: Hallmark Films, n.d., 20 min., col., 16 mm. (Film Number 3 in The Step Behind Series).

An Individual Behavior Modification Program [Motion Picture]. Camarillo, California: Camarillo State Hospital, n.d., 14 min., col., 16 mm.

Jamie: A Behavioral Approach to Family Intervention [Motion Picture]. Solana Beach, California: Media Guild, 1976, 15 min., col., 16 mm. Intended audience: undergraduate, graduate, and continuing education in medical, nursing, and allied health fields.

One Step at a Time: An Introduction to Behavior Modification [Motion Picture]. New York: McGraw-Hill, 1973, 32 min., col. Intended audience: senior high school, college, and adult.

Operant Audiometry with Severely Retarded Children [Motion Picture]. Lawrence, Kansas: University of Kansas, 1968, 15 min., col., 16 mm. Intended audience: undergraduate, graduate students in medicine, allied health, speech and hearing, and psychology.

Operation Behavior Modification: A Demonstration Program for Intensive Training of Institutionalized Mentally Retarded Girls [Motion Picture]. Lawrence, Kansas: University of Kansas, 1966, 40 min., b&w., 16 mm. Intended audience: undergraduate and graduate students in allied health and nursing.

Out of the Shadows [Motion Picture]. Lawrence, Kansas: University of Kansas, n.d., 17 min., col., 16 mm.

Peer-Conducted Behavior Modification [Motion Picture]. Solana Beach, California: Media Guild, 1976, 24 min., col., 16 mm. Intended audience: undergraduate and graduate students in allied health, psychology, counseling, special education.

Pinpoint, Record and Consequate [Motion Picture]. Kansas City, Kansas: Film Fund, n.d., 14 min., col., 16 mm.

The Present and Future of Behavior Therapy [Sound Recording]. Leonia, New Jersey: Sigma Information, 1972, 1 cassette, 60 min. Intended audience: undergraduate, graduate, and continuing education students in allied health, medicine, nursing, and psychology.

Randy [Motion Picture]. Boston: Harvard Medical School, 1970, 27 min., b&w., 16 mm. Intended audience: graduate and continuing education students.

Reinforcement Therapy: Studies in Applying Learning Theory to Treating the Mentally Ill and to Teaching the Mentally Retarded [Motion Picture]. Atlanta, Georgia: National Medical Audiovisual Center, 1966, 45 min., b&w., 16 mm. Intended audience: undergraduate, graduate, and continuing education students.

Reward Procedures for Behavior Management [Motion Picture]. Lemont, Pennsylvania: Behavior Technics, 1971, 25 min., b&w., 16 mm.

Rewards and Reinforcements in Learning [Motion Picture]. Scottsdale, Arizona: Behavior Modification Productions, 1969, 26 min., b&w., 16 mm.

The Santa Monica Project [Motion Picture]. Washington, D.C.: George Washington University, n.d., 20 min., col., 16 mm.

The Self-Management of Behavior [Motion Picture]. Solana Beach, California: Media Guild, 1976, 33 min., col., 16 mm. Intended audience: undergraduate, graduate, and continuing education students.

Shift of Stimulus Control: A Clinical Procedure in Articulation Therapy [Motion Picture]. Lawrence, Kansas: University of Kansas, 1970, 37 min., col., 16 mm. Intended audience: graduate and continuing education students.

Siblings as Behavior Modifiers [Motion Picture]. Solana Beach, California: Media Guild, 1976, 25 min., col., 16 mm. Intended audience: undergraduate students.

The Skinner Revolution: Close-Up on a Great Thinker and His Influential Ideas [Motion Picture]. Solana Beach, California: Media Guild, n.d., 22 min., col. Intended audience: high school, college students, and adults.

Teaching Language Skills to Children with Behavioral Disorders [Motion Picture]. Libertyville, Illinois: Behavior Modification Technology, 1972, 40 min., b&w., 16 mm.

Teaching Self-Help Skills to Children with Behavioral Disorders [Motion Picture]. Libertyville, Illinois: Behavior Modification Technology, 1972, 40 min., b&w., 16 mm.

Teaching Social Recreational Skills to Children with Behavioral Disorders [Motion Picture]. Libertyville, Illinois: Behavior Modification Technology, 1972, 40 min., b&w., 16 mm.

Teaching the Mentally Retarded: A Positive Approach [Motion Picture]. Atlanta, Georgia: National Medical Audiovisual Center, 1967, 21 min., b&w., 16 mm.

Timeout: A Way to Help Children Behave Better [Motion Picture]. Lemont, Pennsylvania: Behavior Technics, n.d., b&w., 16 mm.

Token Economy: Behaviorism Applied [Motion Picture]. New York: McGraw-Hill, 1972, 23 min., col. Intended audience: senior high school and college students, adults.

Who Did What to Whom? [Motion Picture]. Solana Beach, California: Media Guild., n.d., 17 min., col., 16 mm.

AUDIOVISUAL DISTRIBUTORS

Appleton-Century-Crofts
Educational Division
Meredith Corporation
440 Park Avenue South
New York, New York 10016

Audio-Digest Foundation
1250 South Glendale Avenue
Glendale, California 91205

Behavior Modification Productions
Box 3217
Scottsdale, Arizona 85257

Behavior Modification Technology
P. O. Box 597
Libertyville, Illinois 60048

Behavior Technics, Inc.
Box 116
Lemont, Pennsylvania 16851

Behaviordelia, Inc.
P. O. Box 1044
Kalamazoo, Michigan 49005

(A.W.) Calhoun Medical Library
Emory University School of Medicine
69 Butler Street, S.E.
Atlanta, Georgia 30303

Camarillo State Hospital
Camarillo, California 93010

Case Western Reserve University
Health Sciences Communications Center
Room WA-6400
University Circle
Cleveland, Ohio 44106

Directions for Education in Nursing Via Technology
College for Lifelong Learning
Wayne State University
5557 Cass Avenue
Detroit, Michigan 48202

Film Fund
Box 3026
Kansas City, Kansas 66103

George Washington University
Washington, D.C. 20006

Hallmark Films and Recordings, Inc.
Educational Division
1511 East North Avenue
Baltimore, Maryland 21213

Harvard Medical School
Mental Health Training Films
33 Fenwood Road
Boston, Massachusetts 02115

McGraw-Hill Book Co.
Text Film Division
1221 Avenue of the Americas
New York, New York 10020

Media Guild
118 South Acacia
Solana Beach, California 92175

National Medical Audiovisual Center
Station K
Atlanta, Georgia 30324

Nebraska Television Council for Nursing Education, Inc.
P. O. Box 8311
Lincoln, Nebraska

Prentice-Hall Film Library
P. O. Box 500
Englewood Cliffs, New Jersey 07632

Sigma Information
240 Grand Avenue
Leonia, New Jersey 07601

United States Office of Education
200 Independence Avenue, S.W.
Washington, D.C. 20207

University of California
Extension Media Center
Berkeley, California 94720

University of Kansas
Bureau of Visual Instruction
6 Bailey Hall
Lawrence, Kansas 66044

Appendix C:

Glossary

ACCELERATION

An increase in the rate of responding or in the number of responses.

ADAPTIVE BEHAVIOR

Behavior that is regarded as appropriate within a given context, e.g., within the classroom.

AVERSIVE STIMULUS

Any stimulus that the individual will, if given a choice, terminate or avoid.

AVOIDANCE BEHAVIOR

Behavior that either postpones or avoids an aversive stimulus.

BACK-UP REINFORCER

A reinforcer that is purchased with earned tokens.

BASELINE

The frequency that the target behavior is performed as determined during the pretreatment period.

BEHAVIOR RATING SCALE

An instrument that allows the observer to record the estimated magnitude of a behavior.

BEHAVIOR REHEARSAL

A technique in which the desired behavior is practiced until it can be performed without difficulty.

CHAINING

The development of a series of behavioral responses. A performance of one element of the series produces the conditions that make the next element possible. See also: FORWARD CHAINING, REVERSE CHAINING.

CONDITIONING (CLASSICAL CONDITIONING)

The pairing of a neutral stimulus with an unconditioned stimulus that produces a reflex response. By repeated pairing the neutral stimulus will gain the power to elicit the response without being paired.

CONTINGENCY

The conditions under which a response is followed by a positive or a negative reinforcing stimulus or the removal of the stimulus; an explicit dependency of one condition upon another.

CONTINGENCY CONTRACT

A negotiated agreement between someone who wishes a behavior to change and the person whose behavior is to be changed. The agreement specifies the consequences of the performance of a particular behavior.

CONTINGENCY MANAGEMENT

The change of a behavior by the control of the consequences of that behavior.

CONTINGENT REINFORCEMENT

A reinforcement that is delivered as a consequence of the performance of a specific behavior.

CONTINUOUS REINFORCEMENT

A schedule of reinforcement in which a response is reinforced every time it is performed.

CONTRACT (SEE CONTINGENCY CONTRACT)

DESENSITIZATION

A sequence of procedures designed to reduce or eliminate phobic reactions to specific stimuli. Following training in deep muscle relaxation, a graded list of stimuli is presented and mentally reproduced by the subject. Presentation of higher level stimuli is made contingent upon complete relaxation in the presence of lower level stimuli. The real stimuli may be used in place of imaginary ones.

DIFFERENTIAL REINFORCEMENT

The reinforcement of specified responses and the nonreinforcement of other responses.

DIFFERENTIAL REINFORCEMENT OF HIGH RATES OF RESPONDING (DRH)

A reinforcement schedule in which reinforcement is delivered for rates of responding that exceed some minimal level.

DIFFERENTIAL REINFORCEMENT OF LOW RATES OF RESPONDING (DRL)

A reinforcement schedule in which a response is reinforced only after a specified time has elapsed since the immediately preceding response.

DIFFERENTIAL REINFORCEMENT OF OTHER BEHAVIOR (DRO)

The reinforcement of any response except the target response. This has the effect of decreasing the frequency of the target behavior.

DISCRIMINATIVE STIMULUS

A cue that signals that reinforcement will follow a certain response.

ESCAPE BEHAVIOR

A response that is reinforced by the termination of an aversive stimulus.

EXTINCTION

The reduction of a conditioned response to its preconditioned level by a discontinuation of reinforcement for that response.

FADING

The gradual removal of discriminative stimuli, prompts, or reinforcement.

FEEDBACK

Information presented to the subject on his performance.

FIXED INTERVAL SCHEDULE (FI)

The schedule of reinforcement in which the first response occurring after a specified time interval is reinforced. The time interval begins from the moment when the last response was reinforced.

FIXED RATIO REINFORCEMENT (FR)

A schedule of reinforcement in which the reinforcement is made contingent upon the completion of a fixed number of responses.

FLOODING

A technique employed in the treatment of phobias in which aversive stimuli are presented in intense forms, either in imagination or in reality. The emotional reaction to the stimuli either lessens or ceases to occur entirely.

FORWARD CHAINING

A technique in which the first component in a chain of responses is established first, then the next is added, then the next until the chain is completed.

GENERALIZATION

The transfer of treatment effects to other stimulus conditions or situations.

GROUP CONTINGENCY

A contingency that is shared by the whole group and is determined either by an individual's behavior or by the behavior of the group.

IMPLOSION (IMPLOSIVE THERAPY)

An anxiety reduction technique in which the patient is presented repeatedly with vivid accounts of hazards produced by the feared object.

INTERMITTENT REINFORCEMENT

A schedule of reinforcement in which not every response is reinforced.

JOB ANALYSIS

The breaking down of a job into its component parts. This is usually followed by a breaking down of those parts into the necessary stimulus-response components. (See Task Analysis)

LOCUS OF CONTROL

The degree to which the individual perceives that a reward follows from or is contingent upon his own behavior.

MODELLING

A procedure in which the individual observes a model's performance and then imitates that performance.

MOLDING

A technique in which the trainer provides physical guidance of the trainee.

NATURAL REINFORCER

A reinforcer that is available as part of the environmental setting, e.g., praise, attention.

NEGATIVE REINFORCEMENT

A process in which the omission or termination of an aversive stimulus increases the frequency of the preceding behavior.

NONCONTINGENT REINFORCEMENT

Reinforcement that is given without reference to the preceding behavior.

OPERANT BEHAVIOR

Voluntary behavior, involving primarily the skeletal musculature, that may be controlled by a manipulation of its consequences.

OPERANT CONDITIONING

Learning in which behaviors are altered by regulating the consequences that follow them.

OVERCORRECTION

A punishment procedure that consists of correcting the consequences of the undesirable behavior and thoroughly practicing the desired behavior.

POSITIVE REINFORCEMENT

The process in which the presentation of a stimulus increases the frequency of the behavior it follows.

PREMACK PRINCIPLE

A principle that states that if behavior A is more probable than behavior B, then behavior B can be strengthened by making behavior A contingent upon behavior B.

PRIMARY REINFORCER

A reinforcer that satisfies the physiological needs of the subject (e.g., water, food) and, therefore, does not rely upon prior learning to achieve effectiveness.

PUNISHMENT

A process by which a behavior is weakened either by the presentation of an aversive stimulus or by the withholding of a positive reinforcer.

RECIPROCAL INHIBITION

A technique in which the elicitation of one response brings about a decrease in the strength of a simultaneous response.

REINFORCEMENT

A process that increases the strength of a behavior by the delivery of a particular consequence for that behavior. The consequence may be either a positive reinforcer or a negative reinforcer.

REINFORCER

Any stimulus that is used to strengthen the behavior that precedes it.

RESISTANCE TO EXTINCTION

The degree to which a behavior is maintained when its reinforcement is removed.

RESPONSE COST

The punishment procedure in which a positive reinforcer is removed or a contingent penalty is imposed.

REVERSE CHAINING

A technique in which the last element of a chain is taught first, then the second to last element is taught, using the discriminative stimulus for the last element as the reinforcer. This process is continued until the chain is complete.

SATIATION

The provision of an excessive amount of reinforcement or the continuation of a reinforcer, resulting in a loss of effectiveness for that reinforcer.

SCHEDULE OF REINFORCEMENT

The program that specifies which response will be reinforced and how often.

SELF-ADMINISTERED REINFORCEMENT (SELF-REINFORCEMENT)

The subject delivers reinforcement to himself.

SELF-CONTROL (SELF-MANAGEMENT)

The undertaking, by the subject, of certain behaviors in order to achieve self-selected goals.

SELF-MONITORING (SELF-OBSERVATION)

The recording, by the subject, of his own behavior.

SHAPING

The development of a new behavior by the reinforcement of successive approximations to the desired behavior.

SOCIAL REINFORCEMENT

A reinforcement resulting from interpersonal interaction such as attention, praise, smiling, physical contact.

STIMULUS

Any event or condition that may have an effect on the subject's behavior.

SUCCESSIVE APPROXIMATIONS

Responses that increasingly approach the desired behavior.

SYMPTOM SUBSTITUTION

The belief that, if a maladaptive behavior is treated without any attention being given to the underlying cause, another maladaptive behavior will take the place of the original one.

TARGET BEHAVIOR

The behavior that the experimenter or therapist wishes to establish, strengthen, decrease, or eliminate.

TASK ANALYSIS

The breaking down of a job analysis into its stimulus-response components. Stimulus and appropriate responses are identified for each component.

TIME OUT

A punishment procedure in which access to positive reinforcement is denied. The subject is usually removed from the setting in which the reinforcement is provided.

TOKEN

A tangible reinforcer, such as poker chips, stars, tickets, etc., that may be exchanged for back-up reinforcers.

TOKEN ECONOMY

A reinforcement system in which tokens are earned by specific behaviors. The tokens are exchangeable for a variety of back-up reinforcers.

VICARIOUS REINFORCEMENT

The effect of reinforcement on individuals who observe others being reinforced but are not themselves directly reinforced.

Author Index

In the list below, the numbers after each name

refer to item numbers in the Bibliography

C

XYZ

Selective Key Word Subject Index

In the list below, the numbers after each word refer to item numbers in the <u>Bibliography</u>

A

E

XYZ

List of Journal Abbreviations

Abbreviation	Title
A	A
Acad Ther	Academic Therapy
Adolescence	Adolescence
Adv Behav Ther	Advances in Behavior Therapy
Adv Child Dev Behav	Advances in Child Development and Behavior
Am Ann Deaf	American Annals of the Deaf
Am Assoc Educ Sev Profoundly Handicap Rev	American Association for the Education of the Severely/ Profoundly Handicapped Review
Am Correct Ther J	American Corrective Therapy Journal
Am Educ	American Education
Am J Clin Hypn	American Journal of Clinical Hypnosis
Am J Community Psychol	American Journal of Community Psychology
Am J Dis Child	American Journal of Diseases of Children
Am J Ment Defic	American Journal of Mental Deficiency
Am J Nurs	American Journal of Nursing
Am J Occup Ther	American Journal of Occupational Therapy
Am J Optom	American Journal of Optometry
Am J Optom Physiol Opt	American Journal of Optometry and Physiological Optics
Am J Orthod	American Journal of Orthodontics
Am J Orthopsychiatry	American Journal of Orthopsychiatry
Am J Psychiatry	American Journal of Psychiatry
Am J Psychother	American Journal of Psychotherapy
Am Orthopt J	American Orthoptic Journal
Am Psychol	American Psychologist
Ann NY Acad Sci	Annals of the New York Academy of Sciences
Arch Dis Child	Archives of Disease in Childhood
Arch Gen Psychiatry	Archives of General Psychiatry
Ariz Nurse	Arizona Nurse
ASHA Monogr	ASHA Monographs
Audiology	Audiology
Aust J Ment Retard	Australian Journal of Mental Retardation

Abbreviation	Title
Aust NZ J Criminol	Australian and New Zealand Journal of Criminology
Aust NZ J Psychiatry	Australian and New Zealand Journal of Psychiatry
Aust Paediatr J	Australian Paediatric Journal
B	B
Behav Modif	Behavior Modification
Behav Modif Monogr	Behavior Modification Monographs
Behav Res Ther	Behaviour Research and Therapy
Behav Sci	Behavioral Science
Behav Ther	Behavior Therapy
Biomed Sci Instrum	Biomedical Sciences Instrumentation
Br J Audiol	British Journal of Audiology
Br J Educ Psychol	British Journal of Educational Psychology
Br J Psychiatry	British Journal of Psychiatry
Br J Soc Clin Psychol	British Journal of Social and Clinical Psychology
Br Med J	British Medical Journal
Bull Br Psychol Soc	Bulletin of the British Psychological Society
C	C
Can J Behav Sci	Canadian Journal of Behavioural Science
Can Med Assoc J	Canadian Medical Association Journal
Can Ment Health	Canada's Mental Health
Can Psychiatr Assoc J	Canadian Psychiatric Association Journal
Child Care Health Dev	Child: Care, Health and Development
Child Care Q	Child Care Quarterly
Child Dev	Child Development
Child Psychiatry Hum Dev	Child Psychiatry and Human Development
Child Psychiatry Q	Child Psychiatry Quarterly
Child Study J	Child Study Journal
Child Today	Children Today
Child Welfare	Child Welfare
Clearing House	Clearing House
Clin Pediatr	Clinical Pediatrics
Community Ment Health J	Community Mental Health Journal
Conn Med	Connecticut Medicine
Contemp Educ	Contemporary Education
Contemp Educ Psychol	Contemporary Educational Psychology
Correct Psychiatry J Soc Ther	Corrective Psychiatry and Journal of Social Therapy
Correct Soc Psychiatry J Appl Behav Ther	Corrective and Social Psychiatry and Journal of Applied Behavior Therapy

Abbreviation	Title
Correct Soc Psychiatry J Behav Technol	Corrective and Social Psychiatry Journal of Behavioral Technology, Methods, and Therapy
Crim Justice Behav	Criminal Justice and Behavior
Curr Concepts Nutr	Current Concepts in Nutrition
Curr Psychiatr Ther	Current Psychiatric Therapies
D	D
Day Care Early Educ	Day Care and Early Education
Dent Clin North Am	Dental Clinics of North America
Dev Med Child Neurol	Developmental Medicine and Child Neurology
Dev Psychol	Developmental Psychology
E	E
Educ Res Q	Educational Research Quarterly
Educ Technol	Educational Technology
Educ Train Ment Retarded	Education and Training of the Mentally Retarded
Educ Vis Handicap	Education of the Visually Handicapped
Education	Education
Elem Sch Guid Couns	Elementary School Guidance and Counseling
Elem Sch J	Elementary School Journal
Except Child	Exceptional Children
Exceptional Child	Exceptional Child
F	F
Fam Coord	Family Coordinator
Fam Process	Family Process
Fed Probat	Federal Probation
Focus Except Child	Focus on Exceptional Children
G	G
Gifted Child Q	Gifted Child Quarterly
H	H
Health Serv Rep	Health Services Reports
High Sch J	High School Journal
Hosp Community Psychiatry	Hospital and Community Psychiatry
Howard J Penology Crim Prev	Howard Journal of Penology and Crime Prevention
I	I
Ill Sch Res	Illinois School Research
IMRID Papers Rep	IMRID (Institute on Mental Retardation and Intellectual Development) Papers and Reports

Abbreviation	Title
Indian J Pediatr	Indian Journal of Pediatrics
Instructor	Instructor
Int J Addict	International Journal of the Addictions
Int J Clin Exp Hypn	International Journal of Clinical and Experimental Hypnosis
Int J Educ Blind	International Journal for the Education of the Blind
Int J Group Psychother	International Journal of Group Psychotherapy
Int J Nurs Stud	International Journal of Nursing Studies
Int Psychiatry Clin	International Psychiatry Clinics
J	J
J Abnorm Child Psychol	Journal of Abnormal Child Psychology
J Abnorm Psychol	Journal of Abnormal Psychology
J Abnorm Psychol Suppl	Journal of Abnormal Psychology and Supplement
J Abnorm Soc Psychiatry	Journal of Abnormal and Social Psychiatry
J Allergy Clin Immunol	Journal of Allergy and Clinical Immunology
J Am Acad Child Psychiatry	Journal of the American Academy of Child Psychiatry
J Am Dent Assoc	Journal of the American Dental Association
J Appl Behav Anal	Journal of Applied Behavior Analysis
J Assoc Stud Percept	Journal of the Association for the Study of Perception
J Asthma Res	Journal of Asthma Research
J Autism Child Schizo	Journal of Autism and Childhood Schizophrenia
J Behav Ther Exp Psychiatry	Journal of Behavior Therapy and Experimental Psychiatry
J Biol Psychol	Journal of Biological Psychology
J Child Psychol Psychiatry	Journal of Child Psychology and Psychiatry
J Chronic Dis	Journal of Chronic Diseases
J Clin Child Psychol	Journal of Clinical Child Psychology
J Clin Psychol	Journal of Clinical Psychology
J Commun Disord	Journal of Communication Disorders
J Community Psychol	Journal of Community Psychology
J Comp Physiol Psychol	Journal of Comparative and Physiological Psychology
J Consult Clin Psychol	Journal of Consulting and Clinical Psychology
J Consult Psychol	Journal of Consulting Psychology
J Couns Psychol	Journal of Counseling Psychology
J Dent	Journal of Dentistry
J Dent Child	Journal of Dentistry for Children

Abbreviation	Title
J Dent Res	Journal of Dental Research
J Educ	Journal of Education
J Educ Psychol	Journal of Educational Psychology
J Educ Res	Journal of Educational Research
J Educ Soc Work	Journal of Education for Social Work
J Exp Anal Behav	Journal of the Experimental Analysis of Behavior
J Exp Child Psychol	Journal of Experimental Child Psychology
J Exp Educ	Journal of Experimental Education
J Exp Psychol	Journal of Experimental Psychology
J Exp Res Pers	Journal of Experimental Research in Personality
J Fam Couns	Journal of Family Counseling
J Fam Pract	Journal of Family Practice
J Genet Psychol	Journal of Genetic Psychology
J Hist Behav Sci	Journal of the History of the Behavioral Sciences
J Humanistic Psychol	Journal of Humanistic Psychology
J Learn Disabil	Journal of Learning Disabilities
J Ment Defic Res	Journal of Mental Deficiency Research
J Ment Sci	Journal of Mental Science
J Music Ther	Journal of Music Therapy
J Nerv Ment Dis	Journal of Nervous and Mental Disease
J Nutr Educ	Journal of Nutrition Education
J Okla State Med Assoc	Journal of the Oklahoma State Medical Association
J Pediatr Psychol	Journal of Pediatric Psychology
J Pers	Journal of Personality
J Pers Soc Psychol	Journal of Personality and Social Psychology
J Psychiatr Nurs	Journal of Psychiatric Nursing and Mental Health Services (formerly Journal of Psychiatric Nursing)
J Psychiatr Res	Journal of Psychiatric Research
J Psychol	Journal of Psychology
J Psychol Theol	Journal of Psychology and Theology
J Psychol Ther	Journal of Psychological Therapy
J Psychosom Res	Journal of Psychosomatic Research
J Public Health Dent	Journal of Public Health Dentistry
J Res Music Educ	Journal of Research in Music Education
J Res Sci Teach	Journal of Research in Science Teaching
J Sch Health	Journal of School Health
J Sch Psychol	Journal of School Psychology
J Soc Psychol	Journal of Social Psychology
J Spec Educ	Journal of Special Education
J Spec Educ Ment Retarded	Journal for Special Educators of the Mentally Retarded

Abbreviation	Title
J Speech Hear Disord	Journal of Speech and Hearing Disorders
J Speech Hear Res	Journal of Speech and Hearing Research
J Teach Educ	Journal of Teacher Education
J Vis Impair Blindness	Journal of Visual Impairment and Blindness
JAMA	Journal of the American Medical Association
K	K
Kans Stud Educ	Kansas Studies in Education
L	L
Ladies Home J	Ladies Home Journal
Lang Speech Hear Serv Sch	Language, Speech, and Hearing Services in Schools
Learning	Learning
Libr J	Library Journal
Lutheran Educ	Lutheran Education
M	M
McCalls	McCall's
Maine Med Assoc J	Maine Medical Association Journal
Med Clin North Am	Medical Clinics of North America
Med J Aust	Medical Journal of Australia
Med Proc (South Africa)	Medical Proceedings. Mediese Bydraes. (South Africa)
Ment Hyg	Mental Hygiene
Ment Retard	Mental Retardation
Merrill-Palmer Q	Merrill-Palmer Quarterly
Mind Matter	Mind Over Matter
Music Educ J	Music Educator's Journal
N	N
Neurology	Neurology
New Outlook Blind	New Outlook for the Blind
Nurs Clin North Am	Nursing Clinics of North America
Nurs Forum	Nursing Forum
Nurs Mirror	Nursing Mirror
Nurs Outlook	Nursing Outlook
Nurs Res	Nursing Research
Nurs Times	Nursing Times
Nursing	Nursing (Jenkintown)
NZ J Educ Stud	New Zealand Journal of Educational Studies
NZ J Nurs	New Zealand Journal of Nursing
NZ Med J	New Zealand Medical Journal
NZ Nurs J	New Zealand Nursing Journal

Abbreviation	Title
P	P
Parents Mag	Parents' Magazine
Pedagog Semin	Pedagogical Seminary
Pediatr Ann	Pediatric Annals
Pediatr Clin North Am	Pediatric Clinics of North America
Pediatr Res	Pediatric Research
Pediatrics	Pediatrics
Percept Mot Skills	Perceptual and Motor Skills
Pers Guid J	Personnel and Guidance Journal
Perspect Psychiatr Care	Perspectives in Psychiatric Care
Phi Delta Kappan	Phi Delta Kappan
Phys Ther	Physical Therapy
Plast Reconstr Surg	Plastic and Reconstructive Surgery
Pointer	Pointer
Practitioner	Practitioner
Proc Am Psychopathol Assoc	Proceedings of the American Psychopathological Association
Proc R Soc Med	Proceedings of the Royal Society of Medicine
Prof Psychol	Professional Psychology
Prog Behav Modif	Progress in Behavior Modification
Prog Behav Ther	Progress in Behavior Therapy
Psychiatry	Psychiatry
Psychol Aspects Disabil	Psychological Aspects of Disability
Psychol Bull	Psychological Bulletin
Psychol Rec	Psychological Record
Psychol Rep	Psychological Reports
Psychol Sch	Psychology in the Schools
Psychol Today	Psychology Today
Psychologia	Psychologia
Psychology	Psychology: A Journal of Human Behavior
Psychon Sci	Psychonomic Science
Psychopharmacol Bull	Psychopharmacology Bulletin
Psychother Psychosom	Psychotherapy and Psychosomatics
Psychotherapy	Psychotherapy: Theory, Research, and Practice
R	R
Read Improv	Reading Improvement
Rehabil Lit	Rehabilitation Literature
Res Bull	Research Bulletin
Rev Child Dev Res	Review of Child Development Research
Rev Educ Res	Review of Educational Research
S	S
S Afr Med J	South African Medical Journal
SALT: Sch Appl Learn Theory	SALT: School Applications of Learning Theory
Sch Couns	School Counselor

Abbreviation	Title
Sch Psychol Dig	School Psychology Digest
Sci Am	Scientific American
Science	Science
Semin Psychiatry	Seminars in Psychiatry
Slow Learn Child	Slow Learning Child
Small Group Behav	Small Group Behavior
Soc Casework	Social Casework
Soc Work	Social Work
South J Educ Res	Southern Journal of Educational Research
South Med J	Southern Medical Journal
Spec Educ	Special Education
Spec Educ Can	Special Education in Canada
Spec Educ: Forward Trends	Special Education:Forward Trends
T	T
Teach Coll Rec	Teachers College Record
Teach Educ	Teacher Educator
Teach Except Child	Teaching Exceptional Children
Teach Psychol	Teaching of Psychology
Teach Psychol Newsl	Teaching of Psychology Newsletter
Tex Dent J	Texas Dental Journal
Theory Pract	Theory in Practice
Todays Educ	Today's Education
Train Sch Bull	Training School Bulletin
Trans Anal J	Transactional Analysis Journal
V	V
Vocat Eval Work Adjust Bull	Vocational Evaluation and Work Adjustment Bulletin
Volta Rev	Volta Review
Y	Y
Young Child	Young Children

ABOUT THE AUTHOR

Hazel B. Benson is a Licentiate of the College of Speech Therapists, London, England, and has practiced speech pathology in Canada and in the United States. She received her masters degree in library science from the University of Oregon and is currently Assistant Professor of Library Administration and Head, Public Services, Health Sciences Library, The Ohio State University. She is the co-compiler of *Recurring Bibliography on Education in the Allied Health Professions.*